Learned Lives in England
1900–1950

Learned Lives in England

1900–1950

Institutions, Ideas and Intellectual Experience

William C. Lubenow

THE BOYDELL PRESS

First published 2020
The Boydell Press, Woodbridge

ISBN 978 1 78327 550 2

The Boydell Press is an imprint of Boydell & Brewer Ltd
PO Box 9, Woodbridge, Suffolk IP12 3DF, UK
and of Boydell & Brewer Inc.
668 Mount Hope Ave, Rochester, NY 14620–2731, USA
website: www.boydellandbrewer.com

A catalogue record for this book is available
from the British Library

The publisher has no responsibility for the continued existence or accuracy of
URLs for external or third-party internet websites referred to in this book, and
does not guarantee that any content on such websites is, or will remain, accurate or
appropriate

This publication is printed on acid-free paper

For Professor Sir David Williams, Dr Gordon Johnson,
Professor Sir Richard Evans and Professor Jane Clarke
the Presidents of Wolfson College, Cambridge
and for the Fellows and Staff of Wolfson College

Contents

Acknowledgements

This sort of project, any sort of research, is never an individual effort and the author has to take responsibility, but can never claim the credit, for the results of it. I have strong feelings of gratitude for the individuals and the institutions who have thrown their shoulders behind the wheel in this process. Naturally, I owe much to Stockton University, its president, its provost, and especially to Dean Lisa Honecker of the Arts and Humanities for their support. I also owe thanks to my colleagues in the History Faculty for their advice, tolerance and patience. However, great thanks are due to the president and fellows of Wolfson College, Cambridge for electing me as a visiting fellow and having welcomed me to live among them on the many visits to their college in order to pursue the research that has led to this book. I am grateful to the archivists and librarians who have led me to the materials I have used in this research, especially those at Trinity and King's College, Cambridge, the Manuscripts Department and the Rare Books Department of the Cambridge University Library and the archivists at the Royal Society. Ms Karen Syrett, at the British Academy, has been especially welcoming and helpful in providing materials from the archives there for use in these researches. There are many personal debts to recognise: Professor Hugh Bevan, Dr Edward Owen and Jo Owen, Dr Gordon Johnson and Mrs Faith Johnson, Professor Sir Richard Evans, Dr Christine Corton, Ieuen Jones, Lady Sally Williams and Richard Castle. Professor John Naughton, his merry band of press fellows, and Professor Laura Zucconi have added constant inspiration and encouragement at breakfast over many mornings. Discussions with Professor Jonathan Parry, Professor Eugenio Biagini, Professor Martin Daunton, Mr James Stourton and Dr John Gibbins have pointed me in directions I ought to go. Professor Sir David Cannadine has over the years stimulated and inspired this and the many other projects we have discussed. Dr Donald Adamson, for twenty-five years, has provided intellectual guidance, corrections and friendship. I am grateful to Dr Michael Middeke, Dr Megan Milan and Dr Elizabeth Howard and the editorial staff at Boydell Press who have been extremely accommodating and helpful in advancing this project. Anne Lubenow, Stephen Philpott, William Philpott and Cole Philpott – and the various family and other cousins who gather in Wisconsin in July to celebrate Holland Day with bratwurst, beer and rhubarb pie – make all of this worthwhile.

WCL
Wolfson College, Cambridge
18 July 2019

Abbreviations

AVHL	A. V. Hill Papers
BAA	British Academy Archive
BL	British Library
CH	Companion of Honour
CKFT	Cockcroft Papers
CUL	Cambridge University Library
DNB	Dictionary of National Biography
FBA	Fellow, British Academy
FRS	Fellow, Royal Society
GOEV	Goodeve Papers
GWP	Prothero Papers
JMK	John Maynard Keynes Papers
KC	King's Counsel
KEYN	Richard Keynes Papers
MP	Member of Parliament
NGA	Noel Annan Papers
NIH	National Institutes of Health
OM	Order of Merit
PBA	President of the British Academy
PC	Privy Council
PRS	President of the Royal Society
QC	Queen's Counsel
WIA	Warburg Institute Archives (General Correspondence)

Introduction

It is the glory of God to conceal a thing, but the honour of
kings to search matters out.   Proverbs 25: 2

[A]s for knowledge, it will come to an end. For we know only
part ... but when the complete comes, the partial will come to
an end.   1 Corinthians 13: 8–10

Detailed investigations, however valuable and interesting, are
after all but materials to be merged into generalizations, and
generalizations proceed mainly from armchairs.
Alfred Cort Haddon[1]

Robust intellectual institutions in Britain from 1900 to 1950 – universities, the Royal Society, the British Academy – stabilised, legitimised and
authorised knowledge. Less formal coteries in the nooks, crannies, niches on
the margins of robust institutions – such as Bloomsbury, the Tots and Quots,
the Theoretical Biology Club – served as charismatic sites for stimulating
curiosity, imagination and originality. Both, in a certain sense, were necessary;
both functions were useful, but they were in tension with each other. Both
were productive in different ways, but their relations were unsettled. Robust
social units concerned with the protection of conventional, commensurable,
conceptions do not stir with creative impulses. Cognitive social units outside
those defensive circles entertain incommensurable conceptions that provoke
creative impulses.

Were that the Whig Interpretation of History was true.[2] If the Whig
interpretation was applied to the history of cognition, knowledge in the first
half of the twentieth century – in contrast to the nineteenth century – would
have been disciplined, coordinated, bureaucratic and integrated. The diffuse
map of knowledge of the nineteenth century would have been replaced by
the clear, bright disciplinary lines in the twentieth century. The universities,

---

[1]   Alfred Cort Haddon, *History of Anthropology* (London: 1934), p.vi.
[2]   Herbert Butterfield, *The Whig Interpretation of History* (Cambridge: 1931).

the Royal Society and the British Academy would have corralled learning, with hedgehog-like robustness, into recognisable mental spaces. On the other hand, small, eccentric clubs and societies, with their fox-like deviousness and insidiousness, would have fallen into disuse and would have passed out of existence. To be sure, the universities, the Royal Society and the British Academy hardened epistemological edges and restrained intellectual adventurism, defensively fending off charlatans, cranks and crackpots. However, at the same time, charismatic individuals, at the epistemological edges, formed ephemeral societies that became sites and niches for curiosity, originality and the formation of different forms of knowledge. So, there was no comforting trajectory, as the Whig Interpretation of History would have had it, from the clumsy, awkward knowledge forms of the nineteenth century to clear, bright, disciplinary intellectual forms of the twentieth century. The Whig Interpretation of History cannot contain or explain, in a satisfactory way, the emergence of the complicated, complex and internally riven knowledge map of the twentieth century.

Thomas Kuhn laid waste to the Whig Interpretation of History.[3] Kuhn's essential insight was to reject the Whig interpretation's linearity, its implication of progress, its implicit positivism, and its insistence on the cumulative accession of knowledge. (Examples of which are the purported statements of Newton that 'he stood on the shoulders of giants' and 'hypotheses non fingo.'[4]) Where the Whig interpretation saw essential continuities, Kuhn saw discontinuities and disruptions in which communities of the learned were plunged into periods of turmoil and out of which different conceptual schemes emerged. He famously called these 'paradigm shifts.' The concept of the 'paradigm,' which Kuhn made famous and which has become ever present even in ordinary discourse, is no simple concept. Scholars have pointed out how even Kuhn used the concept in multiple ways. Guided by neither doctrine nor dogma, a paradigm is an intellectual coalition or cluster containing theories, evidence, bodies of scholarly writing and a series of agreed-upon practices. As a concept it has sloping frontiers rather than sharp borders; it is epistemologically vital

3   Thomas Kuhn, *The Structure of Scientific Revolutions* (Chicago: 1962), *passim*. See John Naughton, 'Thomas Kuhn: The Man Who Changed the Way the World Looked at Science,' *Observer* (13 August 2012). Joel Isaac, *Working Knowledge: Making the Human Sciences from Parsons to Kuhn* (Cambridge, Mass./London: 2012), pp.227–233. See also K. Brad Wray, 'Kuhn's Social Epistemology and the Sociology of Science,' in William J. Devlin and Alisa Bekuvich (eds), *Kuhn's Structure of Scientific Revolutions Fifty Years On* (Cham: 2015).
4   Sarah Dry, *The Newton Papers: The Strange and True Odyssey of Isaac Newton's Manuscripts* (Oxford: 2014). Keynes famously called Newton the 'last of the magicians' rather than the first scientist. John Maynard Keynes, 'Newton the Man,' in Donald Moggridge and Elizabeth Johnson (eds) *The Collected Works of John Maynard Keynes*, vol. 10 (Cambridge: 1972), pp.363–374. See also Jed Z. Buchwald and Mordechai Feingold, *Newton and the Origin of Civilization* (Princeton/Oxford: 2013).

but is ontologically unstable. Prior to a 'paradigm shift', according to Kuhn, in 'normal' times, scholars engage in 'puzzle solving', reconciling whatever anomalies they find in the existing order of things. Far from aiming at novelty, they correct the status quo and discover, if 'discover' is the correct word, what they expect to discover. They accommodate the exceptions they were dealing with by elementary incrementalism or by accounting for them as experimental or observational blunders.

Eventually, however, as Kuhn argues, the number of anomalies overwhelm the existing conceptual schemes and then crisis occurs. Then some find it necessary to try almost anything, even philosophy, and turn aside from mere experimentalism and positivism to reconsider their working conceptual schemes *au fond*. This is what Kuhn considers a 'revolution', out of which a different conceptual scheme emerges. This different conceptual scheme, one must recognise, is different; it is not necessarily an improvement or an advance. As Mary Hesse pointed out, a paradigm shift 'is not cumulative in the sense of a progress of toward truth about nature'.[5] If it is an advance it is because, as a matter of practice, it works better than other conceptual schemes. It is different because, as Kuhn argues, it is not commensurable with other conceptual schemes. Its terms and conditions cannot be compared with or squared with other conceptual schemes. As John Naughton points out, there is no way of assessing the respective merits of these different conceptual schemes. Kuhn, as he himself made pains to point out, was no relativist, nor did he yield to subjectivism. However, he stuck a large stick in the ever-rolling wheel of positivism.[6]

An important yet hidden assumption within the Whig Interpretation of History is that people think they know what they know without realising or appreciating that they do not know what they do not know. This breeds a sense of confidence, conviction and certainty. Yet this is a blinding illusion and, like all illusions, it is comfortable and comforting. A hidden assumption in Kuhn's dishing of the Whig interpretation is that some people realise that they know what they do not know, which it itself a kind of knowledge. This breeds possibilities for speculation, curiosity and originality. Kuhn stressed the importance of competing intellectual communities, tribes as it were, which have to be investigated anthropologically. Each hover about advancing and defending the conceptual schemes that carry sacred weight for them

---

5   Mary Hesse, 'Review of the *Structure of Scientific Revolutions*,' *Isis*, 54 (1963): 286.
6   Kuhn, of course, has his critics, among whom are practising bench scientists who resented Kuhn's view that they are 'merely' engaged in 'puzzle-solving': Steven Weinberg, *To Explain the World: The Discovery of Modern Science* (New York: 2015), pp.14, 28–29 and also 'Eye on the Present – The Whig History of Science,' *New York Review of Books* (17 December 2015): 82–84. Among others are scholars in the philosophy and history of science, disciplines Kuhn's research did so much to spawn and renovate: Imre Lakatos, *Mathematics, Science, Epistemology*, ed. John Worrell and Gregory Currie (Cambridge: 1980).

because these conceptual schemes constitute their very identities. In these communities learned people lived, moved and had their being.

The present study takes up the subject of learned communities in England between 1900 and 1950. It would be well to make clear that this is not a study of institutions in themselves. An institutional history of those communities might be good and valuable to have, but it would exceed the scope and scale to which the present study is necessarily limited. To gain the greatest possible sharpness and coherence to the subjects of this study it is necessary to call attention to some issues and to exclude others. Choices of this kind are predicated on assumptions that bring the greatest clarity possible to my central contention: that English learned societies in the early twentieth century incubated research by mediating the impulses that pushed towards those formal structures that encouraged loyalty, authority, intellectual sovereignty and the impulses guiding those less formal, interstitial, societies that encouraged curiosity, originality and charisma. Still, the subject is a sprawling one and in order to gain focus it is well to confine it to the Oxford–Cambridge–London axes, that is, to 'England' rather than 'Britain.' Therefore, the chapters that follow serve as prisms to illuminate larger intellectual issues and problems rather than more scattered and detailed subjects.

So, bearing this limitation in mind, this study is a study of the relations between concepts, the people who held them and the communities to which they belonged. The subject of relations is a difficult one to study because relations cannot be observed directly and a purely empirical approach fails. Clifford Geertz's hermeneutic anthropology spoke to these issues in interesting ways. In his aphoristic manner, Geertz examined the cultural problems with which he sought to deal as more than patterns of behaviour papering over with reassuring ideals – as something more mysteriously obscure, something like dark matter, fluid and riven with contradictions and ironies that affect a variety of mental actions.[7] Geertz contrasted the 'chaos of incident,' the 'cluster of schemes and surprises,' with the 'cosmos of sentiment,' the patterns of thought and feeling that 'compose a culture.'[8] The learned communities, the people who lurked within them, and the concepts they held, I wish to argue, filled the gap between 'incident' and 'sentiment.'

Neither 'incident' nor 'sentiment' are homogeneous, unitary, hermetically sealed or integrated concepts. Rather, both are mental coalitions of ideas, values, theories and feelings. 'Incident' refers to the observable public world. 'Cosmos' refers to the charismatic world of imagination and speculation. Previously I have argued that the concept of liberalism played a mediating

---

[7] Jeffrey Alexander, Philip Smith and Matthew Norton (eds), *Interpreting Clifford Geertz: Cultural Investigation in the Social Sciences* (London/New York: 2011), p.2.
[8] Clifford Geertz, *The Interpretation of Cultures: Selected Essays* (New York: 1973), p.331.

role in negotiating the space between 'incident' and 'cosmos.'[9] What follows shows how the mental habits associated with liberalism persisted deep into the twentieth century and explains why there was 'no strange death of liberal England.'[10] Knowledge communities were the agents that assisted in the transmission of these clusters of values, theories and feelings. An analogy from thermal physics may assist in understanding how these processes worked. As Harold Morowitz argued, 'the flow of energy through a system acts to organize the system.'[11] In these communities of the learned, the cooperation, competition, social friction and sociability of their members provided the flow of mental energy that acted to organise the systems that formed, organised, transmitted and dissolved knowledge.

For those who remember their reading of Max Weber, this may come as a surprise. One might have expected these less formal learning societies to have become 'disenchanted' and sucked into Weber's iron cage of modernity. However, as Weber himself observed, the 'most sublime values' have been taken into the 'transcendental realm of mystic life or into the brotherliness of direct and personal human relations.'[12] Far from becoming ossified in bureaucratic structures, these learned communities, whether within universities and grand intellectual societies or outside them, found the breath of new life. As Maynard Keynes, in his usually aggressive way, remarked, '[w]e have to invent new wisdom for a new age. And in the meantime we must, if we are to do any good, appear unorthodox, troublesome, dangerous, disobedient to them that begat us.'[13]

In an earlier study I used E. M. Forster's famous phrase 'Only Connect' as a way to describe the patterns of social association in the nineteenth-century's map of learning.[14] 'Only Connect' is a phrase that should not be disregarded in describing twentieth-century learning niches. However, in the twentieth century, and this is rather a cardinal point, those connections were different. They differed from their predecessors in that some were more robust and sought greater mental integrity, but others remained only loosely associated. Nineteenth-century connections gained confidence in the certainties produced by positivism and its observation–verification orthodoxy. In the twentieth

---

9   William C. Lubenow, 'Mediating the "Chaos of Incident" and the "Cosmos of Sentiment": Liberalism in Britain, 1815–1914,' *Journal of British Studies*, 47 (3) (July 2008): 492–504.

10   George Dangerfield, *The Strange Death of Liberal England* (London: 1935); E. H. H. Green and D. M. Tanner (eds), *The Strange Survival of Liberal England* (Cambridge: 2007).

11   Harold J. Morowitz, *Energy Flow in Biology: Biological Organization as a Problem in Thermal Physics* (New York/London: 1968), p.2.

12   Max Weber, 'Science as a Vocation,' in H. H. Gerth and C. Wright Mills (eds), *From Max Weber: Essays in Sociology* (New York/London: 1946), p.155.

13   Keynes, *Complete Works, Volume 9*, quoted in Richard Davenport Hines, *Universal Man: The Seven Lives of John Maynard Keynes* (London: 2015), p.139.

14   William C. Lubenow, *'Only Connect': Learned Societies in Nineteenth-Century Britain* (Woodbridge, Suffolk: 2015).

century, learned communities consisted of diverse and densely extended social and mental networks of great complexity. Some network connections were denotative and proceeded though procedures that were computational and definitive and achieved detailed and specific results. Other network connections were connotative and proceeded through procedures that were metaphorical, paradoxical and ironic – and achieved general results. These approaches were not necessarily oppositional binaries. That is, they did not occupy positions on extreme ends of the same cognitive and emotional dimension. Rather, they might be best visualised as realisations of different but complementary dimensions of mental activity.

The notion of networks has become almost ubiquitous. Networks appear almost everywhere in scholarly literature in the same way that Kuhn's concept of the paradigm has done. For some, everything is a network. Others are more austere.[15] Bruno Latour and others have set forward Actor-Network Theory as an argument to show the ways non-human entities exercise agency.[16] Some have criticised the assignment of purpose and will to non-human entities as the 'heresy of hylozoism.'[17] While this controversy rages on, let it be sufficient to say here that networks are composed of human beings and that their behaviour is not irrelevant in networks' actions. Yet, networks have consequence for human behaviour. 'Aggregate spillover effects' take place because of membership in networks.[18] These have been called network effects. Connections within and across networks have consequences because networks are not confined to three dimensions: verticality, horizontality and depth. Embeddedness within them also has knock-on consequences because networks also have density, intensity and contain emotional commitments. Loose connections rather than tight connections might produce greater social and mental strength.[19] Friendship or love might be more powerful in shaping connections than strict rules.

[15] Anne-Marie Slaughter, *The Chess-Board and the Web: Strategies of Connection in a Networked World* (New Haven/London: 2017).

[16] See, in general, Bruno Latour, *We Have Never Been Modern*, trans. C. Porter (Cambridge, MA.: 1993); idem., *Pandora's Hope: Essays on the Reality of Science Studies* (Cambridge, MA.: 1999) esp. pp.174–215. See also Bonnie H. Erickson. 'Social Networks and History,' *Historical Methods* 30 (3) (Summer, 1997) and Robert Micael Morrissey, 'Archives of Connection: "Whole Network" Analysis and History,' *Historical Methods*, 48 (2) (April/June 2015): 6779.

[17] Simon Schaffer, 'The Eighteenth Brumaire of Bruno Latour,' *Studies in the History and Philosophy of Science Part A*, 22 (1) (1991): 174–192. For a general assessment of these matters see Edwin Sayes, 'Actor-Network Theory and Methodology: Just What Does it Mean to Say that Nonhumans have Agency?' *Social Studies of Science*, 44 (1) (February 2014): 134–149.

[18] For one attempt to describe this behaviour, see Peter Dolton, 'Identifying Social Network Effects,' *Economic Record*, 93 (Special Issue) (June 2017): 1–15.

[19] Mark S. Granovetter, 'The Strength of Weak Ties,' *American Journal of Sociology*, 78 (6) (May 1973): 1360–1380.

Let one example, the career of Edgar Adrian, illustrate the complexity, the density and the looseness of these connections in twentieth-century learned life. Adrian came up from Westminster School to Trinity College as an undergraduate, and Cambridge was one centre of his life's career. He rose to command his own laboratory and held his own professorship. He became Master of Trinity, Vice-Chancellor of the university and then its Chancellor. However, in addition, he was a member of the Eranus Society, an intellectual club devoted to the discussion of new research interests among members of different colleges in the university. When Adrian became President of the Royal Society his new duties, he felt, compelled him to resign from the society. The other members, however, felt he was so important to them that they allowed him to relinquish his obligations to them only temporarily so that he could return as an ordinary member when his presidency ended. He also read papers to the Hardy Club, and he was a member of the Family, perhaps the oldest of the Cambridge dining societies. He received a Nobel Prize, became a fellow of the Royal Society and later became its president. He was a member of THE CLUB. He was appointed to the Order of Merit and raised to the peerage, taking as his motto on entering the House of Lords a phrase from Epicharmus of Kos: 'Never Forget to Disbelieve.' These complexly diverse social and mental associations were part of an intellectual world of multiple loyalties. Each of these associations bred different social and mental relations, some of which complemented each other, and others of which conflicted with each other. How far it is possible to generalise from this one case to intellectual life in twentieth-century Britain is a matter of conjecture, but, at the very least, it is a highly suggestive illustration and gives pause to anyone who wishes to contemplate the nature of learned behaviour in the modern world.

Having said all of this as a kind of prolegomena, the thesis of the present study is as follows: robust intellectual institutions between 1900 and 1950 in Britain stabilised, legitimised and authorised learning through a sustained insistence on Huxleyite positivism; charismatic, informal societies and clubs on the margins of intellectual life – in their nooks, crannies and niches – blunted regnant positivism by fostering curiosity, imagination and originality. This study attacks this thesis archivally, biographically and conceptually.

This project is archival. It is based to no inconsiderable extent on the unpublished correspondence and manuscripts of members of British learned societies. It recognises that unpublished correspondence and manuscripts are highly subjective. Those who composed them were preoccupied with their own dispositions and understandings, which were different from ours. Whether they intended that their unpublished manuscripts should be preserved and used by people with very different intellectual interests is a matter for our conjecturing. These materials, consequently, are highly resistant to anyone who probes them, because they are based on assumptions that those who investigate them do not share. Moreover, unpublished correspondence and manuscripts, insofar as they have been classified or organised at all, are at the mercy of time, of the descendants of those who composed them, and of the sometimes unsympathetic treatment of archivists and librarians who have their own professional standards and their own ideas about what is important to save and how to preserve them. Those who use these materials have to find ways to breach these barriers.

This project is biographical. Ecological and compositional fallacies always lurk. One cannot find the large in the small; neither can one find the small in the large. It is difficult to generalise from the particular to the general or from the general to the particular. Yet one cannot understand groups without understanding the characteristics of people who belonged to those groups. Nor can one understand individuals without understanding the groups to which they belonged. Seeking to grasp the best of all possible worlds, this study is a study in collective biography: by studying the composition of various social groups one hopes to understand the behaviour of their members. Sir Ronald Syme in his study of the ancient world (*The Roman Revolution*,1939) and Sir Lewis Namier in his study of eighteenth-century politics (*The Structure of Politics at the Accession of George III*, 1929) were the great pioneers using such an approach. Because of the materials they used, they focused rather too narrowly on the functioning of kinship networks. The present study, however, uses a richer body of material about those who figure in this study. These include parents' occupations (when known), the educations of members of these societies, their fields of study, their intellectual aspirations, their careers, the symbols of recognition they received, their marriages and their political affiliations. Some might argue that the individuals in this study were 'certainly clever and learned but in the end, they didn't matter all that much.'[20] So, while as individuals they may interest some people but not others, what is important is that the issues and questions with which they wrestled are of great interest to us. Whatever its weaknesses, this method has the advantage of defying anachronism and rescues the members of these societies from the condescension of the present.

This project is conceptual. Concepts are those tools one uses to hack through the jungles of archival materials and the insights of scholars who have studied those materials. They are the weapons of investigation and study. Concepts, such as 'science', 'letters', 'curiosity', 'originality' and 'research' have their ironies and paradoxes. As Harold Bloom pointed out (and has given warning), all statements and representations are subject to the Rashomon effect; all are open to multiple readings.[21] Concepts, thick or thin, dense or porous, are bundles of theories, techniques, information, interpretations, values and

---

[20] Ian Sharpe, '"Secular Intellectuals," review of William C. Lubenow, *Liberal Intellectuals and Public Culture in Modern Britain, 1815–1914: Making Words Flesh*' (Woodbridge: 2010), in *Journal of Liberal History*, 73 (Winter, 2011–2012): 50.
[21] Harold Bloom, *The Anxiety of Influence: A Theory of Poetry* (New York: 1973), *passim*.

aspirations. As they are applied to archival and biographical materials, concepts themselves have to be scrutinised and criticised. Ultimately, like the leaves of the field, acts of research and investigation all wither and decay. The tools for research, like the objects and subjects against which they are deployed, are affected by the intellectual practices for which they are used. Such is the nature of knowledge in the twentieth century. Knowledge, we learn, is not some sort of stable entity; it is a series of processes and procedures. Therefore, while honouring the traditions of accuracy and criticism, this project is also hermeneutic and interpretative. The facts never speak for themselves; intuition and imagination are necessary to tease out intellectual significance and to form explanatory theories.

These, then, are its cardinal contentions about British learned societies in the period from 1900 to 1950, which arise from these methods and procedures:

First, the great universities, and new ones such as the London School of Economics, came to appreciate the demands of research only slowly and research impulses were felt in clubs and societies at the margins of university life. *Second*, the great institutions of learning – the Royal Society and the British Academy – recognised and accepted different forms of learning through complicated institutional renovations. *Third*, curiosity, imagination and originality were expressed most powerfully at the margins and peripheries of learned life in less formal and less rigid social formations. *Fourth*, the demographic and conceptual bases of British intellectual life shifted when the Society for the Protection of Science and Learning facilitated the great diaspora of continental scholars from Central Europe during the political crisis of the 1930s. The transportation of the Warburg Library and Institute from Hamburg to London was a cardinal event in this process. *Fifth*, some of the leaders of learning from the Victorian and Edwardian periods lived on deep into the twentieth century, merging and mingling with new recruits to intellectual life. Families, deeply associated with the traditions of British learning, modified and reorganised themselves between 1900 and 1950. In these processes British people of learning reconsidered and renovated their intellectual and social identities. *Sixth*, processes of mental change were associated with processes of intellectual and political change in such a way as to produce tangled loyalties and intricate reorganisations of personal and institutional associations.

British intellectual life in the nineteenth century had been preoccupied with the quest for objectivity and certainty; the learned in the twentieth century found ways to sustain objectivity at the same time that they recognised uncertainty. The acculturating systems of Victorian and Edwardian times may have persisted deep into the twentieth century, but wars and intellectual entanglements after 1900 initiated a period of intellectual fragmentation in which people of the mind increasingly realised the tacit nature of knowledge and sought different avenues for mental change.[22] British learned societies incubated curiosity, originality and research by mediating the impulses between formal structures and charismatic behaviour. Because of Niels Bohr's concept of complementarity and Werner Heisenberg's uncertainty principle, people like Arthur Eddington (FRS, OM, member of THE CLUB, Plumian Professor of Astronomy) could conclude that the atom is porous, that physical science is concerned with a world of shadows, and that therefore the concept of causality is dead, leaving behind no clear distinction between the natural, the supernatural, the material and the mental.[23]

[22] Peter Mandler and Susan Pedersen (eds), *After the Victorians: Private Conscience and Public Duty in Modern Britain* (London/New York: 1994), p.19.
[23] Arthur Eddington, *The Nature of the Natural World* (Cambridge: 1929), pp.xvii, 309.

Chapter 1

Research in the Universities

Oxford and Cambridge have been homes of learning, frequently
of the highest learning, for seven hundred years, yet much of
the best and most creative work even in the region of English
learning has been done outside their walls or the walls of any
university.   Sir Maurice Powicke[1]

Conceptual leaps have a cultural value that is worthwhile in
itself.   Martin Rees[2]

INSPIRED by Wilhelm von Humboldt in the fever of the revolutionary
period, the spirit of research first appeared in Prussia.[3] The combined
inspiration of *Wissenschaft* and *Bildung*, technical and detailed studies and
the quest for self-fulfilment, spurred and drove what has been called the
'research imperative.'[4] Research thrived in the German states for much of

[1] Sir Maurice Powicke, 'Universities and Scholarship,' in Ernest Barker (ed.), *The
Character of England* (Westport, Connecticut: 1947), p.234. Powicke, Frederick Maurice
(1879–1963): father, a congregational minister and historian of seventeenth-century
Puritanism; ed. Stockport Grammar School and Owens College, Manchester (where he
came under the influence of T. F. Tout) and Balliol College, Oxford where he read classics
with only modest success – he took a second class in *literae humaniores* (1902); Langton
research fellow at Manchester University (1902–1905); assistant lecturer at Liverpool
(1905–1906); assistant lecturer at Manchester (1906–1908); prize fellow at Merton
College, Oxford (1908); professor of modern history at Queen's University, Belfast
(1909–1919); professor of medieval history at Manchester (1919–1928); regius professor
of modern history at Oxford (1928–1947); at Manchester he laid more emphasis on
teaching students the procedures of research than had been possible before and as Regius
Professor he attempted to carry to Oxford what he had done in Manchester; he had
insufficient support to carry this programme forward; used his presidency of the Royal
Historical Society (1935–1937) to promote cooperative projects between historians; FBA
(1927); knighted (1946).
[2] Martin Rees, 'Anniversary Address, 30 November 2009,' *Notes and Records of the Royal
Society*, 64 (2010): 166.
[3] For the background see R. Steven Turner, 'The Prussian Universities and the Concept
of Research,' *Internaltionales Archiv für sozialgeschichte de deutschen Lituratur*, 6 (1)
(January 1980): 68–93.
[4] For the undifferentiated nature of these studies see Lorraine Daston and Glenn W.

the nineteenth century, encouraged but also shackled by state control until, undermined by the poison of nationalism and militarism, its mandarins committed their own treason of the clerks.[5] If Oxford and Cambridge were not shackled by the state, they were shackled by the successes of what has been famously called 'the revolution of the dons' whereby college fellows and lecturers snatched back undergraduate teaching from coaches in the towns.[6] Highly successful in educating young men for positions in the Church, the state and the professions, the Tripos at Cambridge and the Honours Schools at Oxford were delinquent in educating them for research.

The Royal Commissions on the universities in the nineteenth and twentieth centuries did much good by provoking reforms in university and college governance, in the increasing and broadening subjects of study and in attention to university finance, but their attention to the question of research and the actual advancement of learning was only minor. The Asquith Commission urged Oxford to become a greater centre for research and postgraduate education but gave few suggestions as to the way these objectives might be achieved.[7] The great change was the result of the admission of graduates to the university. Not buildings and financial resources alone, or even new approaches, research was propelled and 'marked more by the change in men.'[8] At Cambridge, for example, the change in university statutes in 1895 allowed the admission of graduates from other universities with their different outlooks, knowledge and techniques. Observation and reasoning, the established features of the Cavendish tradition, were now added to by new impulses of imagination and resourcefulness. The new members of the university, if after two years' residence and the presentation of an acceptable thesis based on their research, were entitled to a University Master of Arts degree. Presently, the university replaced this provision with a Doctor of Philosophy degree. Rutherford, in 1918, regarded this departure as the greatest revolution in modern times. Oxford granted 159 PhDs between 1920 and 1930; Cambridge granted 318. British universities granted 1,824 PhDs between 1920 and 1939.[9]

The examination system was made of stern stuff and persisted. Even university reformers did not quell it. Herbert Butterfield, whose capacity for research was great and growing, conceived of the purpose of university

---

Most, 'History of Science and History of Philologies,' *Isis*, 106 (2) (June 2015): 378–390.
[5] Fritz Ringer, *The Decline of the German Mandarins: The German Academic Community, 1890–1933* (Cambridge, Mass.: 1969).
[6] Sheldon Rothblatt, *The Revolution of the Dons: Cambridge and Society in Victorian England* (Cambridge: [1968] 1981).
[7] A. H. Halsey, 'Oxford and the British Universities,' in Brian Harrison, *The History of the University of Oxford, volume 8, The Twentieth Century* (Oxford: 1994): 613.
[8] J. G. Crowther, *The Cavendish Laboratory* (London: 1974), p.159.
[9] Renate Simpson, *How the PhD Came to Britain: A Century of Struggle for Postgraduate Education* (Guildford: 1983), pp.164–165.

teaching of history to be a preparation for public life. 'As far as I am concerned,' he said to Ved Mehta, 'the point of teaching history to under-graduates is to turn them into future public servants and statesmen.' He much admired Sir Lewis Namier for his 'all embracing and flawless' research. But Butterfield regarded Namier's influence on university teaching as 'perni-cious.' 'In some colleges people have burrowed themselves like moles into smaller and smaller holes – a little biographical hole here, a little diplomatic hole there – and their minds have ceased to develop.'[10] As late as 1973, in his survey of the Historical Tripos, Kitson Clark pointed out that it did not exist to produce professional historians. The teaching of history, he went on, 'is as honourable, as useful, as arduous a task as historical research and the writing of history books.'[11] Further, the university and its examination system, like all complex institutions, suffered bureaucratic sclerosis. Senior members of the university and the Rockefeller Foundation rejected plans put forward by Joseph Needham, Dorothy Wrinch and other members of the Theoretical Biology Club in the 1930s for an institute of 'mathematico-phys-ico-chemical morphology.' The reasons for the rejection of this scheme were never made quite clear but their trampling of disciplinary boundaries, the lateral rather than hierarchical organisation of the proposed institute, and the unorthodox political views of Needham, Waddington, Dorothy Crowfoot (later Hodgkin) and Bernal could not have much appeal to the university bureaucrats and those in the Rockefeller Foundation who spoke the language of management rather than the language of learning.[12]

At Cambridge, Rutherford, from New Zealand, was among the first of the research students to come to the Cavendish, and even in the early days these graduates came from all over the world: Edwin Plimpton Adams and John Mead Adams came from Harvard; D. M. Bose from Calcutta; G. A. Bodsky from Kiev; Harriet Brooks and Fanny Cook Gate from Montreal; Clement Child from Cornell University; Gordon Ferrie Hull from Dartmouth; George Jaffé from Munich; Max Levin from Göttingen; Vladimir Novák from Prague.[13] Going beyond the Cavendish and considering graduates in all fields one can gather a more general picture of this transformation in Cambridge University. In 1928 and 1929 there were 18 studying biochemistry, 12 studying organic chemistry, 24 studying physical chemistry and 39 studying physics. These graduates ranged into arts subjects as well: 21 in history, 22 in English and 5 in

10   Ved Mehta in *Fly and the Fly-Bottle* (London: 1963), pp.195–196.
11   George Kitson Clark, 'A Hundred Years of the Teaching of History at Cambridge, 1873–1973,' *Historical Journal*, 26 (3) (1973): 551–552.
12   Pnina G. Abir-Am, 'The Biotheoretical Gathering, Trans-Disciplinary Authority and the Incipient Legitimation of Molecular Biology in the 1930s: New Perspective on the Historical Sociology of Science,' *History of Science*, 25 (1) (March 1987): 18–23. This is a subject to which I shall return in Chapter 3.
13   *A History of the Cavendish Laboratory, 1871–1910* (London: 1910), pp.324–334.

economics.[14] On the eve of the Second World War there were 53 studying chemistry, 19 studying biochemistry and 42 studying physics. In arts subjects: 28 in history, 25 in English and 14 in economics.[15] In 1952 there were 767 research students in residence in Cambridge (10 in theoretical chemistry, 23 in colloid science, 40 in biochemistry, 43 in physical chemistry, 107 in physics) and 245 in arts subjects (24 in classics, 84 in history, 43 in economics and 58 in English).[16]

They came to Cambridge from other British universities, of course, but also from the Empire, the Continent and from North America, creating what one scholar has called an 'empire of scholars.' Coming to Britain to acquire intellectual procedures and processes unavailable to them in the colonies they could return home to find academic jobs and brighten the mental landscape in the settler universities there.[17] In 1928 there were 7 such research students at Cambridge from continental Europe, 6 from New Zealand, 20 from Australia, 15 from Canada and 31 from the United States.[18] Of the 411 research students in 1938 and 1939, 24 were from continental Europe, 24 from India, 20 from Canada, 21 from Australia and 37 from the United States.[19] In 1952 there were 47 from Canada, 27 from India, 8 from Pakistan, 64 from Australia, 32 from New Zealand and 68 from the United States.[20] While these reckonings are for Cambridge alone, the figures for Oxford cannot vary from them to any marked degree – and Oxford had the advantage of the influx of Rhodes scholars from the world over.[21]

Research at Oxford

The peculiarities of Oxford and Cambridge as collegiate universities and their scattering thither of laboratories and institutes had disadvantages. Decentralised systems, if there were systems, lacked the capacity to provide institutional conviction, direction, control and institutional legitimacy to support research. On the other hand, loose networks of intellectual connections left room for charismatic authority to find cognitive niches for creative activity. Novelty opens opportunities for disruption and robust agencies can accommodate change.

[14] 'Research Students, 1928–1929,' *Cambridge University Reporter*, 59 (23 February 1928), p.203.
[15] 'Research Students, 1938–1939,' *Cambridge University Reporter*, 69 (21 February 1939), p.652.
[16] 'Reseach Students, 1952–1953,' *Cambridge University Reporter*, 83 (13 March 1953), pp.926–927.
[17] Tamson Pietsch, *Empire of Scholars: Universities, Networks and the British Academic World 1850–1939* (Manchester/New York: 2013).
[18] 'Research Students, 1928–1929,' *Cambridge University Reporter*, 59 (23 February 1928), p.203.
[19] 'Research Students, 1938–1939,' *Cambridge University Reporter*, 69 (21 February 1939), p.62.
[20] 'Research Students, 1952–1953,' *Cambridge University Reporter*, 83 (13 March 1953) pp. 926–927.
[21] Thomas J. Schaeper and Kathless Schaeper, *Rhodes Scholars, Oxford and the Creation of an American Elite* (New York/Oxford: 1998).

Archibald Sayce, the orientalist and comparative philologist, condemned the examination system. Fit for boys, he said, but not for men. Examinations were unmanly; they infantilised. They were 'destructive of originality and independence of thought.' Thomas Henry Huxley, Darwin's bulldog, had been successful before the examiners, but he was 'ashamed to think how very little knowledge underlay the torrent of stuff which I was able to pour out on paper.'[22] Even after the Natural Sciences Tripos displaced the weight and fame of the Mathematical Tripos the hold of the examination system held, and undergraduate teaching was dominated by application and experiment rather than theory, much less research.[23] It was what has been called 'the workshop world,' where students were taught to conceptualise the world as physical models, manipulating instruments, reading scales and dials blowing and sealing glass apparatuses.[24] Oxford and Cambridge students colonised the new universities. As late as 1914 half of those holding chairs of physics in England and Scotland had been trained in Cambridge's Mathematical Tripos where, rather than having a theoretical basis for their science, were trained, and correspondingly trained their students, to jump through the technical hoops of solving problems in mechanics, hydrostatics, hydrodynamics, optics and electromagnetism.[25] Certain prejudices within this experimental tradition served to block impulses towards research. Desmond Bernal, the 'Sage,' feared the atmosphere at the Cavendish was 'opposed to any idea of speculation [because it was] not sound science.' Ernest Rutherford, the director of the Cavendish Laboratory, declared: 'Don't let me catch anyone talking about the Universe in my laboratory.'[26] Rutherford, who rarely attended the V²V Club (for which more below), scoffed at the theorists who 'play with their symbols [while] we at the Cavendish turn out the real facts of nature.'[27]

22 Sayce and Huxley are quoted in Lubenow, 'Only Connect': Learned Societies in Nineteenth-Century Britain, pp.31–32.

23 Roy MacLeod and Russell Moseley, 'The "Naturals" and Victorian Cambridge: Reflections on the Anatomy of an Elite, 1851–1914,' Oxford Review of Education, 6 (2) (1980): 177–195.

24 Andrew Warwick, 'The Worlds of Cambridge Physics,' in Richard Staley (ed.), The Physics of Empire (Cambridge: c.1994): p.85; see also Warwick's Masters of Theory: Cambridge and the Rise of Mathematical Physics (Chicago: 2003).

25 P. Bockstaele, 'The Mathematical and Exact Sciences,' in Walter Rüegg (ed.), A History of the University in Europe, Volume III: Universities in the Nineteenth and Early Twentieth Centuries (1800–1945) (Cambridge: 2004): 515.

26 J. D. Bernal, The Origin of Life (London: 1967), p.x. Rutherford, Ernest (1871–1937): born in New Zealand; father, flour and saw-miller; ed. Nelson College (New Zealand), Trinity College, BA (1897), MA (1919), Hon. ScD (1926); Macdonald Professor of Physics McGill University, Montreal (1898–1907); Langworthy Professor, University of Manchester (1907–1919); Cavendish Professor, Cambridge University (1919–1937); FRS (1903); President of the Royal Society (1925–1930); President of the British Association for the Advancement of Science (1931); knighted (1914); raised to the peerage (1931); Nobel Prize (1908); Order of Merit (1925).

27 Quoted in Graham Farmelo, The Strangest Man: The Hidden Life of Paul Dirac, Mystic

Percy Gardner, the Lincoln and Merton Professor of Archaeology from 1887 to 1925, among others, noted Oxford's marked deficiencies.[28] Gardner, deeply touched by an internationalist spirit of scholarship, was less than patient with Oxford's reluctance to take on research and learning as the primary business of the university. His own approach to his subject was situated in historical, literary and linguistic knowledge rather than aesthetics, and he sometimes worried that his students' preoccupation with artistic style might lead them to forget the spirit and content of things Greek. He laid out his criticism of Oxford in *Oxford at the Crossroads* (1903). The worse side of study at Oxford, he stressed, was not 'its encouragement of superficiality nor its one-sidedness, but its exclusion of personal research' and 'its discouragement of all advanced study.' From all leaders, he noted, 'one hears a general chorus that England in the competition of nations is falling behind, that we are too lethargic, that our rivals are moving faster than we are, that we shall lose our place among the nations unless we bestir ourselves, and alter our ways.' Oxford had more funds than other universities and these could be disposed towards research. 'The great foundation of All Souls' seems made for the endowment of research; but instead of being thus used, its Fellowships are held by rising young barristers, or even members of the Indian Civil Service.' To be sure 'some brilliant pieces' of research have been done by such Oxford men as Arthur Evans, 'but if it be inquired what part of the funds required for the researches of these scholars is provided by the University, the answer is anything but satisfactory':

> In fact, in the acquisition of knowledge as much as in the production of works of art, ideal purpose is necessary to raise the worker to a higher level, and to give dignity to his life. Knowledge in itself will not necessarily make a man than will skill in painting, or fine scholarship, or delicate taste. But I venture to say that even from an ethical point of view research has high claims on the universities. As a mental and moral tonic nothing can be more effective than the search for fact: the more deeply the fact is hidden, the longer and severer the search, the more stimulating it grows. And the qualities which it inculcates – patience, distrust of mere theories, delight in what will bear the test – are of great value in life. By degrees, as one learns how to proceed, one finds keys which will unlock door after door until the whole world of history ceases to be an irregular and arbitrary collection of events, and become a scene of law and order, though not of law so fixed and definite as that in the world of nature.

---

of the Atom (New York: 2009), p.66.

[28]   Gardner, Percy (1846–1937): father, of the Stock Exchange; ed. City of London School, Christ's College, Cambridge, BA (1860) with first classes in the Classical Tripos and the Moral Sciences Tripos; Fellow of Christ's College (1872); assistant in the Department of Coins and Medals in the British Museum (1871); Disney Professor of Archaeology at Cambridge (1880–1887); Lincoln and Merton Professor of Archaeology at Oxford (1887–1925); FBA (1903).

Foreign advanced students, Gardner warned, would come to exploit the 'wealth of the Bodleian.' They would use the tools of research to contribute to learned journals 'while English students go stolidly on their way.' This was a future to which they could not look forward with equanimity. 'Truly it is time to consider our ways.'[29]

Lord Curzon, as Oxford's Chancellor (1907–1925) was prepared to consider those ways.[30] Lewis Farnell, the rector of Exeter College, a member of a dining society known simply as The Club – a society to advance the claims of Oxford professors over those of the college tutors – as Vice-Chancellor attempted to prosecute the objectives of The Club rather aggressively.[31] Other Heads of Houses appealed to Curzon seeking to prevent Farnell from taking the customary second term of office. Curzon supported Farnell.[32] Curzon was aware of the most familiar criticism of the university: 'it provides insufficiently for advanced study and research.' Curzon identified three sorts of problems. First, there was the lack of 'the true scientific spirit' at Oxford. Second, the university failed to provide encouragement for research in the form of fellow-ships, scholarships and 'other pecuniary endowments.' Third, there was no formal procedures under which the promising student could, 'under the eye of his master, acquire the methods of higher study.' Oxford, Curzon argued, 'should train its scholars not merely to acquire knowledge, but [should] increase it.' As Curzon concluded, 'the amount of original work as yet turned out from Oxford is inconsiderable.' Further, the question of the 'attitude toward Research' had never been considered by the university as a whole. But then he offered only tepid suggestions for improvement. The university and the colleges should coordinate their resources and work out a plan whereby 'each member of the federation should contribute, according to his means and inclination,

29 Percy Gardner, *Oxford at the Crossroads: A Criticism of the Course of Litterae Humaniores in the University* (London: 1903), pp.18, 47, 54–55, 59–60, 61.
30 Curzon, George Nathaniel (1859–1925): father, 4th Baron Scarsdale, Rector of Kedleston; ed. Wixenford School, Eton (where he was a member of Pop and favourite of Oscar Browning); Balliol College, Oxford where he failed to achieve a first-class degree in Greats but won the Lothian and Arnold prizes and was president of the union; Prize Fellow of All Soul's (1883); MP for Southport, Lancashire (1886), Assistant Private Secretary to Lord Salisbury; Under-Secretary of State for India (1891); Under-Secretary for Foreign Affairs (1895); Viceroy of India (1899–1905); Foreign Secretary (1919–1924); on his appointment to India he was created Baron Curzon in the Irish peerage; in 1911 he was created Earl Curzon of Kedleston; on his father's death he became 5th Baron Scarsdale (1916); in 1921 he was created Marquess of Curzon of Kedleston and Earl of Kedleston.
31 Farnell, Lewis Richard (1856–1934); father, a draper who became manager of a brewery; ed. City of London School under E. A. Abbott, Exeter College, Oxford, first class in classical moderations (1875) and *literae humaniores* (1878); fellow of his college (1880), appointed classical lecturer (1883), senior tutor (1893–1913); rector (1913–1928), vice-chancellor (1920–1923); university lecturer in classical archaeology (1908–1911); first Wilde lecturer in natural and comparative religion; Hibbert lecturer (1911); Gifford lecturer at St Andrew's University (1920–1921, 1924–1925); DLitt (1901); FBA (1916).
32 Lewis Farnell, *An Oxonian Looks Back* (London: 1934).

to the common end.' The colleges should set apart 'for Research purposes a certain number of Fellowships, with a rotation of subjects prescribed by the University.' Provision should be made for professorial libraries and rooms to make the teaching of research techniques 'more influential and productive.' This, he said, 'was the most pressing of the material needs of the University, and ought to be taken in hand without delay.' But, the real need at Oxford was not for more advanced instruction and instructors, but for more advanced students. The university, 'by the encouragement that it gives and the rewards that it offers,' should do more to attract such advanced students.[33]

When Arthur Evans returned to Oxford to take charge of the Ashmolean after a life of adventure he found collections there in disarray.[34] Evans came from a distinguished intellectual family. His father, Sir John Evans, a distinguished geologist, antiquary and collector, became a fellow of the Royal Society in 1864 and its treasurer in 1878. So Arthur Evans was of the fourth generation of his family to become FRS. His brother Lewis was also a distinguished collector. His half-sister, his junior by forty years, Dame Joan Evans the art historian, was the first woman to become President of the Society of Antiquaries (1959). Sir John was a member of the group of scholars – Sir John Lubbock, Edward Tylor, Francis Galton, Augustus Pitt-Rivers – who installed anthropology and prehistorical archaeology on what they considered 'a scientific basis' in Britain.[35] Young Arthur, on leaving Oxford and passing a year's study at Göttingen, travelled with his brother, Lewis, to Herzegovina, Finland and Lapland. A fervent Liberal, Evans at his home, the Casa San Lazzaro at Ragusa, devoted himself to the history, antiquity and politics of the southern Slav peoples until his association with the Crivoscian insurrectionaries led the Austrian authorities to arrest him and condemn him to death (though they issued a reprieve and expelled him).

The Ashmolean Museum owed its origins and its name to Sir Elias Ashmole (1617–1692), the son of a Midlands saddler who settled into Oxford and established the museum to house his 'curiosities' when the court of Charles II resided there. Ancient in origins, when Evans came to it the Ashmolean, if ever it had had some institutional coherence, had fallen into further neglect and he was determined to resuscitate it. It was cramped for space because the

---

[33] Lord Curzon of Kedleston, *Principles and Methods of University Reform: Being a Letter Addressed to the University of Oxford* (Oxford: 1909), pp.179–187.

[34] Evans, Arthur John (1851–1941): father, member of the firm of John Dickerson and Co. paper makers (and much else); ed. Harrow and Brasnose College, Oxford where he was placed in the first class in modern history (1874); Keeper of the Ashmolean Museum (1884–1908); FRS (1901); FBA (founding Fellow); knighted (1911); President of the Society of Antiquaries (1914–1919); President of the British Association for the Advancement of Science (1916–1919); excavator of Knossos.

[35] J. J. Myres, 'Arthur John Evans, 1851–1941,' *Obituary Notices of Fellows of the Royal Society*, 3 (1851–1941): 941.

Randolph Galley in Beaumont Street – under the control of W. M. Ramsay, the first Lincoln and Merton professor of classical archaeology and art[36] – with its collections of classical sculpture and vases, competed for institutional space and resources. The Ashmolean's collections of coins and manuscripts had been stripped away and sent to the Bodleian. Its natural history collections went to the new University Museum. Evans had the Ashmolean collections moved to a new building behind the Randolph but this was always overflowing and had to be constantly enlarged. However, enclosed by other buildings, it was unable to expand. Evans was determined to transform the institution he had inherited. Finding a patron in Charles Drury Edward Fortnum, an entomologist as well as an enthusiast of art, he was able to extend the building in Beaumont Street and incorporate into it Fortnum's collection of classical and Renaissance art. In doing so Evans was able to cajole the university into integrating together the Ashmolean and the University Galleries.[37]

The new institution, the Ashmolean Museum of Art and Archaeology, consisted of two independent departments: the Department of Antiquities and the Department of Fine Art. There was no single director for overall management of the Ashmolean until 1973. Though divided in these ways the Ashmolean, perhaps because divided in these ways, provided certain real intellectual opportunities. Kenneth Clark,[38] when he came to it as Keeper of Fine Art, recognised it as a 'real scholar's post' where he would find friends 'who really know what scholarship is & value a man who gives his time to it.' There, he would be free of London connoisseurs, those whom Clark called 'the Burlington-Bond St. Gang' who 'had little pull there.' Living some distance from Oxford and with work he found 'necessarily light,' Clark could pursue his

[36] Ramsay, William Mitchell (1851–1939): father, lawyer (his grandfather and great-grand-father had also been Scottish advocates; ed. the Gymnasium, Old Aberdeen, University of Aberdeen, St John's College, Oxford where he got a first class in classical moderations (1874) and in *literae humaniores* (1876), Göttingen where he studied Sanskrit with Theodor Benfey, getting insight into some of the methods of modern literary scholarship; research fellow, Exeter College, Oxford (1982); Lincoln and Merton Professor of Classical Archaeology and Art and a fellow of Lincoln College (1885–1886); Regius Professor of Humanity at Aberdeen (1886–1911); FBA (founding fellow but resigned in 1924); Gold Medal of Pope Leo XIII (1893); knighted (1906).

[37] L. W. B. Brockliss, *The University of Oxford: A History* (Oxford: 2016), pp.488–489.

[38] Clark, Kenneth (1903–1983): father, a wealthy Scot, lucre came from his family's connection with the textile trade; ed. Wexford School, Winchester, St John's College, Oxford where he studied the history of art; Keeper of Fine Arts at the Ashmolean (1933); Director of the National Gallery (1938) where he supervised the relocation of its collections to protect them during the Blitz; Keeper of the King's Pictures (1934); Slade Professor of Fine Art, Oxford (1950); KCB (1938), CH (1959), OM (1976), FBA (1949), raised to the peerage (1969); lectured worldwide (considered the art galleries in Australia the worst in the world but their collections of pornography the best); received into the Roman Catholic Church on his deathbed.

own intellectual interests and not become involved in university society, 'that grave of so many valuable abilities.'[39]

As in the case of research in the art and literary world of Oxford, research in the natural sciences also took place in a dishevelled environment. When Max Perutz[40] first visited Dorothy Hodgkin[41] in her work rooms in Oxford's University Museum (what he called 'Ruskin's Cathedral of Science') he had to walk past 'skeletons of extinct species and then 'descending the stone steps to Dorothy's crypt office':

> Her tables were piled high with structure-factor and Fourier calculations; there were viewing boxes for looking at X-ray pictures. Her X-ray and dark rooms were adjoining. The gothic window was high above as in a monk's cell, and beneath it there was a gallery, reachable only by a ladder, on which stood a table with Dorothy's polarizing microscope. To mount one of her precious crystals of penicillin, Dorothy would climb up there, clutching her treasure with one hand while holding on the to the ladder with the other. I don't think she ever lost a crystal.

But, Perutz concluded, '[f]or all its gloomy setting, Dorothy's lab was a jolly place.' There 'she labored on the structure of life in a place that was, but for her vitality, quite dead.'[42]

[39] Kenneth Clark to Bernard Berenson, 22 June 1931, printed in *My Dear BB: The Letters of Bernard Berenson and Kenneth Clark, 1925–1959* ed. and annotated by Robert Cumming (New Haven/London: 2015), p.104.

[40] Perutz, Max Ferdinand (1914–2002): born in Vienna; father, textile manufacturer; ed. University of Vienna where he took his undergraduate degree (1936); Cambridge University where he became a research student under J. D. Bernal and took his PhD under William Lawrence Bragg; rejected in the King's and St John's fellowship elections, but elected by Peterhouse (because he said it had the best food); an alpinist (his first research was on glaciers) he had a knowledge of crystals; interned briefly in Newfoundland during the Second World War; with the support of Bragg and a grant from the Medical Research Council he turned to research on the molecular structure of biological systems; founder and chairman (1962–1979) of the Medical Research Council Laboratory of Molecular Biology, Cambridge; FRS (1954), CBE, CH (1975), OM (1988); Nobel Prize (1962); born Jewish, baptised Roman Catholic, an atheist but opposed those (such as Richard Hawkins) who abused others for their religious views.

[41] Hodgkin, Dorothy Crowfoot (1910–1994): born in Cairo; both parents were archaeologists, her father was Education Officer in Khartoum; Sir John Leman Grammar School, Beccles; Somerville College, Oxford where she studied with Cyril Hinshelwood and took a first-class honours degree, only the third woman to achieve this accomplishment (1932); studied for the PhD at Cambridge where she was supervised by J. D. Bernal with whom she also had a personal relationship; research fellow at Somerville College (1934); fellow and tutor at Somerville (1936–1977) where one of her students was Margaret Roberts (who achieved fame for other abilities and under another name); Royal Society Wolfson Research Professor (1960–1970); FRS (1947); Royal Medal of the Royal Society (1956); Nobel Prize (1964); Copley Medal of the Royal Society (1976); Lomonosov Gold Medal (1982); Lenin Peace Prize (1987); OM (1965); president of the Pugwash Conference on Science and World Affairs (1976–1988); banned from entering the United States because of her husband's association with communism and her own pronounced political proclivities.

[42] Max Perutz, 'Forty Year's Friendship with Dorothy,' in G. G. Dodson, J. P. Glusker, S. Rameshan and K. Venkasesan (eds), *The Collected Works of Dorothy Crowfoot Hodgkin,*

Such conditions in which Hodgkin worked may be accounted for by the incremental manner in which Oxford's laboratories emerged in the nineteenth century as people became awakened to the importance of studies in natural philosophy and as new courses of study entered the honours examinations. Magdalen built the first college laboratory in 1848. Charles Giles Brindle Daubeny, a polymath and praelector in the teaching of chemistry from 1820 to 1867, frustrated by the gloomy buildings in which he worked, got Magdalen's agreement to build a block for teaching in the Physic Garden. Balliol, under the influence of Jowett, in 1855, followed by building a chemical laboratory in the cellars of the Slavin building, which, according to Harold Harley, continued 'the subterranean tradition of chemistry in Oxford for ninety years.' Christ Church constructed its laboratory, after Vernon Harcourt's election to the Lee's Readership in 1859, by converting a school of anatomy on the south side of the dining hall for the teaching of chemistry and elementary physics. Queens built a laboratory in 1900 and Jesus the Leoline Jenkins Laboratory in 1907. Nevil Sidgwick (the nephew of Henry and Arthur and the son of William Sidgwick) recognised the need for more space and greater organisation when he returned to Oxford from Tübingen to teach at Magdalen and Lincon in 1901. To create some sort of order in this mélange of institutional arrangements, T. H. Baker, who succeeded Harcourt in 1903, proposed that each college laboratory should assume responsibility for a distinct aspect of work and, accordingly, Balliol and Trinity, later supplemented by Jesus, took up physical chemistry, Christ Church took organic chemistry and Magdalen quantitative analysis.[43] In general, research in the college laboratories eclipsed research done in the University Museum, the central system insofar as there was one at Oxford. The college laboratories excelled in inductive rather than deductive procedures and designed simple experiments that expressed the basic principles of their subjects. Consequently, despite what has been recognised as their 'unattractive and poorly equipped laboratories,' these conditions worked no crippling damages upon them. Yet, on the other hand, these circumstances were not calculated to produce startling intellectual innovations. Still, when the University Laboratory of Physical Chemistry, built with a benefaction from Lord Nuffield, was finally opened in 1941 it displayed the coats of arms of Trinity and Balliol to reflect the role of these colleges in the early history of physical chemistry in Oxford.[44]

Volume III: General Crystallography and Essays (Bangalore: 1994), p.xiii. *Idem. I Wish I Had Made You Angry Earlier: Essays on Science and Scientists* (Oxford: 1998), pp.210–212.

[43] For all of the above see Sir Harold Hartley, 'The Contribution of College Laboratories,' *Chemistry in Britain*, 1 (1965): 521–524.

[44] Keith L. Laidler, 'Chemical Kinetics and the Oxford College Laboratories,' *Archive for the History of the Exact Sciences*, 38 (3) (1988): 281–292.

When G. H. Hardy came over to Oxford from Cambridge in 1920 to take up the Savilian chair in geometry and a fellowship at New College he set about to give some order to research in mathematics.[45] He proposed to establish a 'school of advanced study and research,' a Mathematical Institute. He rejected Cambridge's example, where he had been a staunch critic of its Mathematical Tripos. Cambridge had, he said, 'the most difficult, the most notorious, the best advertised examination in the world,' but, if in this regard Oxford lagged behind Cambridge, Cambridge lagged behind continental centres of mathematical learning. It is not possible, Hardy argued, 'to found a school of learning on any examination.' Oxford suffered a deficiency of mathematical fellows. At Cambridge, Trinity had four mathematical lecturers, St John's had three, and every other college had at least one. At Oxford, the colleges of Exeter, Lincoln, Magdalen, Oriel, Pembroke, Trinity, University, Wadham and Worcester had not one mathematician among them. At Cambridge there was no one who had any hope of understanding Hilbert or Russell, Einstein or Schrödinger.

It was a question in the first instance of 'primarily buying men.' Mathematicians, Hardy argued, are inexpensive. They needed no laboratory and no professor should have 'to grovel before a College Bursar when he wants a room and a decent blackboard.' Beyond that, however:

> We can raise the prestige of Oxford mathematics in Oxford only by raising it first outside, and it is plain that we can do this only by making our school primarily a school of advanced study and research. There is no word which excites such bitter feeling in a 'teaching university' as the word 'research,' and I do not wish to suggest that the advancement of knowledge is the only worthy outlet for a don's activities. The fact remains that it is quite impossible to erect a school of any science on any other foundation. The world, when asked to admire the Oxford School, will inquire 'what has it done,' and will be quite uninterested unless it can show that it has done something substantial. It is already practically impossible for a mathematician who has not 'added to knowledge' even to start an academical career.

The Clarendon Press had wrested a mathematical journal, the *Quarterly Journal*, from the Cambridge University Press, but why, Hardy asked, 'should Oxford

[45] Hardy, Godfrey Harold (1877–1947): father, a schoolmaster; ed. Winchester and Trinity College, Cambridge where he was fourth wrangler (1898) and elected to a prize fellowship at Trinity (1900), an Apostle; fell under the influence of A. E. H. Love who introduced him to Jordan's *Cours d'Analyse de l'École Politechnique*, which he claimed marked his entrance into his career as a real mathematician; collaborated with J. E. Littlewood and Srinivasa Ramanujan; elected Savilian Professor of Geometry at Oxford and a fellowship at New College (1920); elected to the Sadleirian chair of pure mathematics and a fellowship at Trinity College, Cambridge (1931); an entertaining conversationalist on many subjects; played several games well, especially real tennis, but cricket was his passion; violently anti-clerical, he had many clerical friends; a fellow of the Royal Astronomical Society, which he joined in order to hear Eddington and Jeans discuss relativity theory.

almost alone among great Universities have no centre of any kind for its mathematical work?' 'We now have a journal,' he said, 'and we demand a home.'[46]

The Trustees of Henry Hyde, 1st Earl of Clarendon, laid out £10,000 to build the Clarendon Laboratory, the first building specifically built for the doing of physics, which was completed in 1872. Its first director, R. B. Clifton, came from Owens College (later the University of Manchester). (The electors had wished to elect Hermann von Helmholz (1821–1894), professor of physiology at Heidelberg, but Max Müller, professor of modern languages at Oxford, told them that von Helmholz would not come at the salary they proposed to offer.) Clifford, apparently, had done promising work as a young man,[47] but he had published but one paper in physics and he actually discouraged research at the Clarendon. So while the Cavendish, under Clerk Maxwell, Lord Rayleigh and J. J. Thomson at Cambridge flourished, the Clarendon languished for fifty years. When Frederick Alexander Lindemann was elected Dr Lee's professor of experimental philosophy and head of the Clarendon in 1919 he inherited no research staff, no mains electricity and only packing cases of unused optical gadgets.[48]

Lindemann's last original paper was published in 1924 but his great skill was his ability to assemble small groups of physicists and encourage them in their research by providing the resources at his command. So from his contacts at Berlin he brought scholars whose work, in terms of quality and quantity, made their and the laboratory's mark. Most gained their fellowships in the Royal Society. But funds were always short and Lindemann's physicists worked in overcrowded attics and cellars. The university's grant for annual operating costs was but £2,000 and several of his recruits, like Lindemann himself, had private means that enabled them to supply equipment and technical assistance. Lindemann, early on, anticipated the dangers of Nazism, and was especially aggressive in recruiting and assisting, with funds from the colleges and from industry, scholars who had been purged in Germany and Austria after 1933.

Prickly and aggressive, his remarks on behalf of his science were often hostile and sarcastic. With his independent wealth, inherited from his father

---

46   G. H. Hardy, 'Mathematics,' *Oxford Magazine* (5 June 1930): 819–821.
47   G. Gooday, 'Precision Measurement and the Genesis of Teaching Laboratories in Victorian Britain' (Kent: PhD dissertation, 1986), Chapter 6, cited by Brockliss, *The University of Oxford*, p.505.
48   Lindemann, Frederick Alexander (1886–1957): born in Baden Baden (a fact he resented all his life); father, a wealthy man but also an astronomer of distinction; ed. at Blair Lodge, Polmont, Scotland, the Real Gymnasium and then at Hochschule in Darmstradt, and got his PhD at the Physikalishch-Chemisches Institut, Berlin (1910); was playing tennis in Germany before the war broke out but left in haste to avoid being interned; joined the Royal Aircraft Factory at Farnborough (1915); Lee's Professor of Experimental of Philosophy and fellow of Wadham College (1919); scientific adviser to Churchill; FRS (1920); raised to the peerage (1941); PC (1943); CH (1953); created Viscount Cherwell (1956).

in 1927, he moved in different social circles than those of his colleagues. He much preferred the houses of dukes to the villas of North Oxford. Mad about tennis, he had competed as a young man at Wimbledon. Tennis and an introduction by J. C. Masterman brought him into Lord Birkenhead's circle. The Duke of Westminster introduced him to Winston Churchill. Though a fellow of Wadham, Lindemann was elected to a studentship without being on the governing body at Christ Church and there he lived from 1921 for the rest of his life. In spite of all this, perhaps because of all of this, he coaxed and bullied the university in 1937 to provide small sums for a new building to replace the Victorian Gothic structure in which they had been trying to do their science.[49]

Research in Cambridge

While worthy scholars – Henry Sidgwick, Keynes – made important intellectual contributions within Cambridge, the research environment on the Cam was as haphazard as it was on the Isis. When Frederick Gowland Hopkins[50] came to Cambridge as a lecturer in chemical physiology – at the invitation of Sir Michael Foster[51] – in 1898, he was an alien to university life, having gained medical certification at Guy's Hospital. His subject was in disrepair but so were his personal situation and the conditions under which he was expected to work. His stipend was meagre. Heavy tutorial work at Emmanuel College, which was financially necessary for him, robbed him of time for research and brought him to a nervous breakdown. Finally, a Trinity praelectorship, with

[49] For the above see B. Bleaney, A. H. Cooke, N. Kurti and K. W. H. Stevens, 'F. A. Lindemann, Viscount Cherwell (1886–1957)', *Physics Bulletin*, 37 (6) (1986): 261–263.

[50] Hopkins, Frederick Gowland (1861–1947): father, engaged in the bookselling and jewellery trades; ed. at a dame's school in Eastbourne, City of London School; after six months in an insurance office he was articled to a consulting analyst in the City; took a course in chemistry under Sir Edward Franklin; studied at University College, London for an associateship of the Institute of Chemistry; began to read for the BSc (London), graduated in 1890 having entered Guy's Hospital as a medical student; gained his medical qualification (1894); an assistant in the Department of Physiology at Guy's; lecturer in chemical physiology at Cambridge (1898); raised to a reader (1902); praelector at Trinity (1910); professor of biochemistry (1914), alas an unpaid chair; FRS (1905); knighted (1925); Nobel Prize (1929); PRS (1930–1935); President of the British Association for the Advancement of Science (1933); OM (1935).

[51] Foster, Michael (1836–1907): father, a Baptist surgeon; ed Huntington Grammar School, University College School, London, University of London, BA (1854), MB (1858), MD (1859); studied in Paris; joined his father's practice; teacher in practical physiology, University College, London (1867); succeeded Huxley as Fullerian Professor of Physiology at the Royal Institution; on Huxley's recommendation he was appointed to the new post of praelector in physiology at Trinity College, Cambridge (1870); Professor of Physiology at Cambridge (1883); FRS (1872); succeeded Huxley as biological secretary of the Royal Society (1881), a position he held for twenty-two years; created KCB (1899); Liberal Unionist MP for the University of London (1900); his confidence in the value of the direct observation of natural life was accompanied by confidence in the value of research that he passed on to his students.

no obligations other than the pursuit of his own researches, rescued him personally. Yet he had only dire conditions in which to work. He had but a small and ill-fitted laboratory room, 'incredibly restricted and unsuitable,' among the physiologists, where even menial assistance was only at a minimum and his experimental rats, which required specialised care and attention, were lodged in a cellar.[52]

Yet, fruitful interpersonal relationships within Hopkins's laboratory created opportunities for intellectual advances. Hopkins gave his colleagues the choice of their own research subjects and several were able to engage in important collaborative projects.[53] Hopkins, diminutive but marked by inspiration and a kind of wisdom, presided over this community. He found these conditions congenial for his own research and he both gave and gained from the stimulation of daily contact with his associates. Known universally as 'Hoppy,' cheerful and friendly, he 'basked in the flow of the admiring comradeship with which they surrounded him.'[54] Hopkins's lack of a managerial manner and bureaucratic temperament did not please all and he had his critics both within Cambridge and without. Hopkins bridled against administrative and political controls. After the end of the Great War he sensed there was a 'rebellion against all *officials* of the old type':

> Things have been muddled by the official class, and among the young men at any rate, there is impatience and intended rebellion. Who, afterall [sic] are these people who have taken our destinies into inefficient hands? A producer of privilege, a narrow type of education, and a rotten examination system: A la lanterine! Voila![55]

Despite all the disadvantages of university incumberousness, Hopkins and his colleagues – J. B. S. Haldane as well as several women (including Kathleen Lonsdale and Dorothy Moyle Needham) – achieved intellectual distinction.[56]

Forster's physiology brought Hopkins to Cambridge, but there he was trapped, epistemologically and cognitively, by Foster's physiology. Institutional conventions and the lack of resources prevented Hopkins from enlarging the scope of biochemical research. He wished to liberate biochemistry and create it as an independent discipline equal in intellectual significance to physiology. His was a subject that he wished to attach to biology rather than medicine. Joseph Needham, who became the Dunn Reader in Biochemistry, described

---

52 Henry Dale, 'Frederick Gowland Hopkins, 1861–1947,' *Obituary Notices of the Fellows of the Royal Society*, 6 (1918–1949): 134.

53 Harmke Kamminga, 'Hopkins and Biochemistry,' in Joseph Needham and Ernest Baldwin (eds), *Cambridge Scientific Minds* (Cambridge: 2002): p.178.

54 Dale, 'Frederick Gowland Hopkins, 1861–1947,': 135–136.

55 Frederick Gowland Hopkins to Walter Fletcher, 3 April 1918, Medical Research Council Archives, PF 106, quoted in Robert Kohler, 'Walter Fletcher, F. G. Hopkins and the Dunn Institute of Biochemistry: A Case Study in the Patronage of Science,' *Isis*, 69 (3) (September 1978): 377.

56 Kamminga, 'Hopkins and Biochemistry,': 178–179.

Hopkins's vision.[57] Hopkins was 'not a man of cold intellectual calculation.' He knew about the living cell 'not only ratiocinatively but intuitively':

> The cell, he felt, was the theatre of an orderly sequence of chemical events controlled by a special organization of proteins, lipids, carbohydrates and other constituent substances in the interests of normal growth, differentiation and adult function … How many times did we hear him descant upon the 'geography of cell.' Indeed, long before the days of the electron-microscope pictures which today reveal so much of the internal matrix and framework of chemical events, his imagination had led him decisively into the realms of ultra-structure.[58]

Such a vision was only realised through the patronage of the Medical Research Council of which Hopkins's friend, Walter Morley Fletcher, was secretary.[59] Fletcher and the Medical Research Council gained the patronage of the trustees of the Sir William Dunn estate who provided £200,000 for a new building, equipment, and endowment for a research programme with Hopkins as the first chair and J. B. S. Haldane as the first reader. Forty researchers, working in temporary quarters, moved into the new laboratories and between the wars they contributed 40 per cent of the papers to the *Biomedical Journal.* Arthur Balfour, then Chancellor of the university, opened the Dunn Biochemistry Laboratory on 9 May 1924, and called it the official recognition of a new scientific discipline.[60]

As the Dunn bequest illustrates, the most powerful thrusts towards research came from sources somewhat independent of the university itself. The case of William Cavendish, 7th Duke of Devonshire (1808–1891) who presented the Cavendish Laboratory and the professorship of experimental physics to the university, was the most munificent and influential of such bequests. Cavendish had been educated at Eton and Trinity College where he took the BA in 1829 as second Wrangler, eighth classic and first Smith's Prizeman. He was chairman of the Royal Commission on Scientific Instruction and the Advancement of Science and succeeded the Prince Consort as Chancellor

---

[57] Needham, Noel Joseph Terence Montgomery (1900–1995): father, physician; ed. Oundle School, Gonville and Caius College, Cambridge, Fellow of Gonville and Caius, Master (1966–1976); Sir William Dunn Reader in Biochemistry, Cambridge; FRS (1941); FBA (1971); Fukuoka Asian Culture Prize (1990); CH (1992).

[58] Joseph Needham, 'Sir Frederick Gowland Hopkins, OM, FRS (1861–1947),' *Notes and Records of the Royal Society of London,* 17 (2 December 1962): 119, 156.

[59] Fletcher, Walter Morley (1873–1933): father, an independently minded Congregationalist and chief inspector of the local government board in London; ed. University College School, London, Trinity College Cambridge, first class in part I of the Natural Sciences Tripos (1894), first class in part II (1895), BA (1894), MA (1898), MB (1900), MD (1908); fellow and tutor of Trinity (1897); athletics 'Blue' (1892); senior demonstrator in physiology (1903); proctor (1904); FRS (1915); member of the Royal Commission on Oxford and Cambridge (1919–1922);Secretary of the Medical Research Council (1914); KBE (1918), CB (1929).

[60] Kohler, 'Walter Fletcher, F. G. Hopkins and the Dunn Institute of Biochemistry,': 331–355.

of the university. James Clerk Maxwell was the first Cavendish Professor, succeeded by Lord Rayleigh, J. J. Thomson and Ernest Rutherford.

Thomson's election as the third professor of experimental physics and Director of the Cavendish was something of a surprise because his reputation was as a mathematician rather than as an experimentalist.[61] He was second Wrangler in the Tripos and second Smith's Prizeman. He himself did not feel wholly competent to succeed Rayleigh. 'I felt like a fisherman who with light tackle had casually cast a line in an unlikely spot and hooked a fish too heavy for him to land.'[62] Earlier, however, Clerk Maxwell had seen his potential: 'Thomson will never know the difference between things that are hard and things that are easy for they all come alike to him.'[63] But upon his election Thomson won his spurs quickly: *Applications of Dynamics to Physics and Chemistry* (1880), *Notes on Recent Researches in Electricity and Magnetism* (1893), *Elements of the Mathematical Theory of Electricity and Magnetism* (1895). All these reflect Thomson's change in intellectual interests and his growing self-confidence.[64] Thomson's charismatic leadership was bolstered at the Cavendish Laboratory by the work of the Lucasian professors in Thomson's time – Sir George Stokes, Sir Joseph Lamor and, later, P. A. M. Dirac – who contributed to the strengthening of mathematical physics.[65] Moreover, Thomson took full advantage of the rush of new talent in the Cavendish as a result of the admission of university graduates to do research there.[66]

At the Great War's ending the Cavendish was a comparatively large and well-established research institution and had the foundations for future fundamental research. Thomson's main research was completed and he had been deeply involved in public affairs during the war. Therefore, when the venerable Henry Montagu Butler died and the Trinity mastership fell open Lloyd George looked to Thomson as his successor. When asked about his choice Lloyd George responded: 'his super-eminence as a scientist was known, even to a barbarian like myself who never had the advantage of

---

[61]   Thomson, Joseph John (1856–1940): father, publisher and bookseller; ed. Owens College, Manchester, Trinity College, Cambridge, BA second Wrangler (1880). MA (1883), Hon. Sc.D (1920); fellow (1880–1917); master (1917–1940); Cavendish Professor of Experimental Physics (1884–1918); FRS (1884): Nobel Prize (1906); President of the Royal Society (1916–1920); knighted (1908); OM (1912); member of The Family.

[62]   J. J. Thomson, *Recollections and Reflections* (New York: 1937), p.98.

[63]   Cambridge University Library/MSS, Add. 7655, II (d) 6, 41 and Add. 8385, 10, 9. Quoted in Dong-Won Kim, 'J. J. Thomson and the Emergence of the Cavendish School, 1885–1990,' *The British Journal for the History of Science*, 28 (2) (June 1995): 194.

[64]   Kim, 'J. J. Thomson and the Emergence of the Cavendish School,': 195.

[65]   Arthur Eddington, *The Cavendish Laboratory* (Cambridge: 1935), p.4.

[66]   Kim, 'J. J. Thomson and the Emergence of the Cavendish School,': 214–216. For more, see below and Lubenow, *'Only Connect': Learned Societies in Nineteenth-Century Britain*, pp.231–232.

any university training.'[67] Thomson presided in the master's lodge, perhaps not with the thorough dignity (and pomposity) of Montagu Butler, but with vigorous eccentricity. On the occasion of the Fellowship Admission dinner he sometimes revealed his personal thoughts. When Anthony Blunt was elected Thomson observed how it was the first time they had elected a fellow in art history 'and I very much hope it was to be the last.' Of Victor Rothschild's election he was compelled to say that 'we looked only for intellectual merit and paid no attention to race, creed, social position or great wealth.'[68]

Thomson's removal to Trinity's master's lodge was eased because Butler was dead. But Thomson's relinquishing of the chair of experimental physics and the directorship of the Cavendish Laboratory was freighted with difficulty. As is the case of many people who have had the exercise of power, it was not easy for him to give way and he made it clear he still wished to keep control over the Cavendish. Rutherford was his natural successor, and Lamore, one of the electors, wrote to Thomson pointing out the advantages to the university of bringing Rutherford back to Cambridge. Rutherford, for his part, was unwilling to come from Manchester to share authority with his teacher. Fully aware of these personal difficulties, Rutherford wrote to Thomson:

> I feel that no advantages of the post could compensate for any further disturbance of our long continued friendship or any possible friction, whether open or latent, that might possibly arise if we did not have a clear mutual understanding with regard to the laboratory and research arrangements.[69]

In the end Thomson resigned and was appointed (without salary) to a special professorship in physics with his own laboratory. As Thomson's son remarked delicately, 'this arrangement, though not as well defined as it might have been worked relatively well.' Seven Nobel Prizes came to those who had worked under him and a great majority of chairs in British universities and large numbers of chairs in English-speaking countries came to be held by those who had done research in the Cavendish. 'In this way his ideas, and even more his habits of research, were perpetuated long after he had ceased to be active.'[70]

However, it was Rutherford who led the Cavendish into a new age of discovery as it turned from the study of large-scale matter and forces to the study of the fundamental particles of which matter consists. According to William Lawrence Bragg, Thomson may have opened the door to the new

---

[67] Quoted in J. G. Crowther, *The Cavendish Laboratory* (London: 1974), p.172.

[68] Alan Hodgkin, *Chance and Design: Reminiscences of Science in War and Peace* (Cambridge: 1992), pp.73–74.

[69] Quoted in Crowther, *The Cavendish Laboratory*, pp.172–175.

[70] George Paget Thomson, *J. J. Thomson and the Cavendish Laboratory of his Day* (London: 1964), pp.152, 173.

physics but did not go through it himself. It was Rutherford who went through the door into the house of the new physics.[71] Arthur Eddington[72] called the Cavendish the 'Mecca of physics for the Empire.' There, in the twelve-month period of 1932–1933, Cavendish physicists discovered the artificial transmission of the elements, the neutron, the positron and heavy hydrogen.[73]

However, resistance from the university itself, established social customs and less than adequate funding hindered the thrust into large scale physics. Despite the injection of Cavendish cash in the foundation of the laboratory, more was needed as research proceeded from Ernest Rutherford's use of 'string and sealing wax' (as Rutherford was proud to say) to larger-scale experimental devices. In 1893 the university's annual grant to the Cavendish was but £266, £214 of which was given over to pay assistants' wages. Students' fees and outside sources funded research, apparatus and building extensions. University funding remained meagre for more than thirty years. Exceptionally, the university proposed to offer £445 from the Common University Fund for new buildings. The university agreed to pay £22 to repair the drains at the Cavendish. In the building of instruments the Cavendish, from early days, had clever experimentalists who had an interest in constructing the needful gadgets.[74] Rayleigh had devoted part of his Nobel Prize money to additional buildings in the laboratory. But research at the Cavendish was carried out under extremely difficult conditions. Kapitza, when he came from the Soviet Union, had to erect his dynamo in a shed of the department of physical chemistry. Cockcroft assembled his accelerator, using glass cylinders of the sort used in gasoline pumps, in a corner of the chemistry store room. In these cramped spaces experimenters' competition for apparatuses and space among growing numbers of those engaged in research produced conflicts requiring Rutherford's diplomatic skills to hold them together. So long as their research rested on precise experimentalism and keen eyes for significant phenomena, the string-and-sealing-wax approach that Rutherford preferred was sufficient. However, growing demands for more extensive theoretical knowledge to interpret the phenomena of the new physics outstripped the university's and other resources at the Cavendish's disposal.[75] As Eddington pointed out in 1935, it was always necessary to reach out further 'to the friends of science and Cambridge' to meet the demands of future research. Some have

---

71   Crowther, *The Cavendish Laboratory*, p.183.
72   Eddington (Sir) Arthur Stanley (1882–1944): father, headmaster of a Friends School; ed. Owens College, Manchester; BSc (1902); Trinity College, Cambridge, BA, senior Wrangler (1904); Plumian Professor of Astronomy, Cambridge (1913); FRS (1914); knighted (1930); appointed to the Order of Merit (1938); member of THE CLUB.
73   Eddington, *The Cavendish Laboratory*, pp.3, 11.
74   Kim, 'J. J. Thomson and the Emergence of the Cavendish School,': 205, 218–220.
75   Crowther, *The Cavendish Laboratory*, p.217.

attributed the vitality of the Cavendish to its financial independence from the university. To be sure, such independence freed it from the strictures of Boards of Studies and other bureaucratic hindrances. Such independence, however, points to its lack of its prestige in the university and its lesser institutional legitimacy.[76] But this meant also its intellectual power and influence gave it wider prestige in the larger intellectual community.

Research at the London School of Economics

All who speak of the London School of Economics (LSE) address its special charm and uniqueness. This has to do with more than its physical ambience. By engaging in 'the quest for the Science of Society,' the LSE, as its most recent historian has said, 'resolves one of the great dilemmas of the life of the mind, the dilemma of the ascetic and the worldly, detachment and the world of involvement.'[77] Unlike Oxford and Cambridge the LSE was always more of a *Gesellschaft* than a *Gemeinschaft*.[78] How far this dilemma of which Dahrendorf spoke was actually resolved remains to be seen. Certainly, however the dilemma was expressed, the LSE opened a different research domain: the social sciences. A swift survey of the intellectual interests of the directors of the 'School' (as they all call it) illustrates the variousness of their variety as opposed to the heads of Oxford's and Cambridge's colleges and even their difference as over against the presidents of the Royal Society and the British Academy. William Albert Samuel Hewins was an economist and a Conservative politician; Halford Mackinder, a geographer; William Pember Reeves, a New Zealand politician, a historian and a poet; William Beveridge, born in Rangpur, an economist and social reformer; Alexander Carr-Saunders, a biologist and sociologist; Sydney Caine, an economist; Walter Adams, a historian; Ralf Dahrendorf, a British-German politician (he maintained houses in both London and Germany), sociologist, philosopher and political scientist. While members of the school each had their own specialisation, they maintained the fiction of intellectual unity and enjoyed the notion of belonging to a single school. The Common Room was small, they had no departmental structure or deans. The Appointments Committee took responsibility for the entire school.[79]

The LSE's social and physical ambience made a difference too. Dahrendorf called it a 'lively and lonely place' characterised by a 'curious intimacy and

[76] Romualdas Sviedrys and Arnold Thackray, 'The Rise of Physical Science at Victorian Cambridge with Commentary and with Reply,' *Historical Studies in the Physical Sciences*, 2 (1970): 143–144, 151; Romualdas Sviedrys, 'The Rise of Physics Laboratories in Britain,' *Historical Studies in the Physical Sciences*, 7 (1976): 435.

[77] Quoting Ralf Dahrendorf: Ernest Gellner, 'No School for Scandal: Dahrendorf's LSE and the Quest for the Science of Society,' *Times Literary Supplement* (26 May 1995): 3.

[78] Ralf Dahrendorf, *LSE: A History of the London School of Economics* (Oxford: 1995), p.360.

[79] Dahrendorf, *LSE*, p.209.

indeed exclusiveness.' Located in the Strand, it had none of the Arcadian atmosphere of Oxford and Cambridge (though it retreated to Peterhouse during the Second World War), yet it created its own kind of Eden. Some considered it a movement rather than a university. But it was never the locus or focus of a political party. But its members felt their fancies could flourish in the midst of a sometimes shabby setting. It was a setting for the active as well as the contemplative life. As Darhendorf puts it, the LSE's 'mixture of intimacy and tension' held 'people of most diverse origins and opinions together.'[80]

Rerum cognoscere causas (To know the Causes of Things): the social sciences and the history of the LSE are virtually coterminous. But what sort of 'science' are the 'social' sciences? This question was bitterly contested, especially during the directorship of Beveridge, and, inevitably, it goes on.[81] This is not the place to settle such a maddening question, but perhaps it may be possible to use the LSE as an illustration of what the question is exactly.

Beveridge regarded himself as a scientist *manqué*. He resented the teaching he received at Charterhouse, which shunted him aside from natural philosophy and into classics and mathematics. At Balliol he turned aside from the metaphysical speculations of the master, Edward Caird, and towards the positivist studies of Huxley. Beveridge, following Huxley, thought the study of society by 'observation and experiment, comparison and classification' would create a 'truly scientific science of society.'[82] In his inaugural lecture on his coming to the LSE, 'Economics as a Liberal Education' on 4 October 1920, Beveridge began by discussing economics in its widest sense. It was, he said, all those subjects that 'come within the scope of the Faculty of Economics in the University of London,' including commerce and industry. Then he turned to T. H. Huxley's lecture 'The Value of the Natural History Sciences' (1854). Huxley had laid out what he considered the methods of all

---

[80] Dahrendorf, *LSE*, pp.128–129.
[81] See the collection of essays edited by Paul Rabinow and William M. Sullivan, *Interpretive Social Science* (Berkeley/London: 1979); Charles Taylor, *Philosophy and the Human Sciences: Philosophical Papers*, 2 (Cambridge: 1985), esp. pp.15–57; Steve Fuller, 'Disciplinary Boundaries and the Rhetoric of the Social Sciences,' in Ellen Messer-Davidow et al., *Knowledges: Historical and Critical Studies in Disciplinarity* (Charlotteville/London: 1993): pp.125–149; George Steinmetz (ed.), *The Politics of Method in the Human Sciences: Positivism and its Epistemological Others* (Durham/London: 2005). So, scholars have meditated on the problem. One, quoting John Dewey, has written: 'The history of the social sciences confirms John Dewey's observation: "[i]ntellectual progress usually occurs through sheer abandonment of questions together with both of the alternatives they assume – an abandonment that results from their decreasing vitality and change of interest. We do not solve them; we get over them."' Dorothy Ross, 'Getting Over It? From the Social to the Human Sciences,' *Modern Intellectual History*, 11 (1) (2014): 191. The quotation from Dewey can be found in 'The Influence of Darwin on Philosophy (1909),' in Jo Ann Boydston (ed.), *John Dewey, the Middle Works*, 15 vols (Carbondale: 1976), 4: p.14.
[82] Jose Harris, *William Beveridge: A Biography* (Oxford: 1997), pp.77–78, 277–278.

sciences: observation, comparison, deduction, and verification of deduction by further observations. Beveridge then went on to argue that '[m]ere accumulation of facts is not a science. Mere deduction from one or two narrow premises is not a science':

> [The] practical distinction between the sciences arises from their relative age and maturity. The biological sciences ... are more in the inductive stage than the mathematical and physico-chemical ones. The economic sciences must for the present be more inductive still. There was a time when the natural sciences had to be freed from the purely deductive method. The chief discredit of political economy in the past has been due to premature deduction on too narrow a basis of fact and induction.

The subjects of inquiry should lead to the training of the mind and the understanding of the environment. 'The dominating element in man's environment to-day is not nature but his fellow-men.' So to find explanations for the environment one must look to economics, history, political science and sociology.[83]

To root his science of society in the natural sciences, Beveridge, with the encouragement of Rockefeller Fund money, established a chair of social biology. Lancelot Hogben was its first and only occupant.[84] H. G. Wells, who welcomed him to the chair, said he 'had come here this afternoon, as a learner and witness, while Professor Hogben drives his first furrow across this new, vast, almost virgin and most promising field, that has been given him to cultivate.'[85] Beveridge agreed to give Hogben the use of a small building opposite the main block of the LSE on Houghton Street to use as a laboratory with such funds as he could scrape together from the Medical Research Council. As Hogben observed, '[i]t was somewhat like a dilapidated nineteenth-century Baptist Chapel but had a basement suitable for keeping tiers of rabbits and tanks of *Xenopus* for my

---

[83]   William Beveridge, 'Economics as a Liberal Education,' *Economica*, 1 (January 1921): 2, 4, 7, 8, 15.

[84]   Hogben, Lancelot Thomas (1895–1975); born in Portsmouth to Plymouth Brethren parents; ed. Tottenham County School, London; Trinity College, Cambridge where as a medical student he studied physiology, BA (1915) with an Ordinary Degree; a pacifist and imprisoned in Wormwood Scrubs during the Great War; after recovering his health he took lecturing positions in London universities; University of Edinburgh in the Animal Breeding Department (1922); McGill University; took a chair in zoology at the University of Cape Town (1927); took the chair of social biology at the London School of Economics (1930); FRS (1936); Regius Professor of Natural History, University of Abedeen (1937); a founder of the Society for Experimental Biology (1923); a member of the Theoretical Biology Club (see below); during the Second World War he had responsibility for the British army's medical statistics; Mason Professor of Zoology (1941–1947) and Professor of Medical Statistics (1947–1961) at University of Birmingham; a socialist and atheist (in a small boat during a storm at sea he and a fellow research student prayed to Darwin, Marx and Bernard Shaw but he soon gave up on Marx because, he said, having rejected religious dogmatism he would not exchange one fanatical system for another.

[85]   *Economica*, 31 (February 1931): 4.

unfinished work on reproductive physiology.'[86] His subject, Hogben said in his inaugural lecture, could no longer be confined to an older intellectual tradition. In every branch of humanities 'investigation is turning from the discussion of why things should happen to how things do happen.' Evolutional biology brought to the study of society neither 'a philosophy of social reform nor a philosophy of social reaction, but a philosophy of social discovery.' Hogben did not underestimate the difficulties his studies posed:

> The factors which determine man's social behaviour are so obscure and elusive that neither historical experience nor the study of other living creatures at present enable us with assurance to disentangle the genetic and environmental agencies which are significant.

In drawing attention to these difficulties Hogben warned against haste. 'Every experimental biologist recognizes the disastrous consequences of constructing evolutionary hypotheses on the testimony of the pigeon fancier and the stock breeder.' He called for the necessity of devising new methods of investigation. He reminded his listeners of Nietzsche's aphorism: 'The most valuable knowledge is the knowledge of methods, and the knowledge of methods comes last.' He encouraged them to take the long view. Human life, he estimated, has existed for five hundred thousand years; civilization for five thousand; modern science for five hundred. In judging the role of biology in the science of society he asked them to take an astronomical view of time. If they regarded 'his new departure with suspicion,' he asked them 'to cherish it tenderly while it is sending forth its first green shoots.' His own optimism, he trusted, would be tolerated 'in a school with an unique tradition of free inquiry.'[87]

Beveridge's lecture on his leaving of the School[88] was, he said, a bishop's *Nunc Dimittis* in comparison to his inaugural address, which he regarded as something of a curate's first sermon. His was, however, an unrepentant *Nunc Dimittis*.

> To me the Social Sciences are sciences – the youngest members of that great family of studies which, in 400 years of revolutionary growth have given mankind to-day understanding of their environment and powers over nature, undreamt of by earlier generations.

There had been, in the time since his inaugural lecture, growing appreciation for those studies for 'solving the riddles of economic and political and social organization.' Yet, 'the field of our studies is still a wilderness for pioneers, not an

86   Adrian and Anne Hogben (eds), *Lancelot Hogben, Scientific Humanist: An Unauthorised Autobiography* (Woodbridge: 1998), p.121.
87   Lancelot Hogben, 'The Foundation of Social Biology,' *Economica*, 31 (February 1931): 5, 12, 19, 23–24.
88   For what follows in this paragraph and the next see William Beveridge, 'The Place of the Social Sciences in Human Knowledge,' *Politica*, 2 (9) (September 1937): 459–460, 461–462, 463–464, 467–468.

ordered realm of knowledge.' 'We cannot claim to be scientists,' Beveridge said, 'unless our methods are scientific.' Not one to take on mental midgets, he took as his target for criticism John Maynard Keynes who had considered taking up the directorship himself and whose *The General Theory of Employment, Interest and Money* had been published the previous year. Economics, Keynes felt strongly, was a moral rather than a natural science. Economics 'employs introspection and judgment of value' and it 'deals with motives, expectations [and] psychological uncertainties.' Therefore, '[o]ne has to be constantly on guard against treating the material as constant and homogeneous.'[89]

Beveridge granted to Keynes keen intellectual abilities. He was 'a man whose intellectual gifts every one of us would like to possess, a man of wide sympathies and understanding of many forms of study. He would have been a leader in any field of learning to which he had turned.' Beveridge chose not to challenge the findings of Keynes's *General Theory*, but Beveridge found Keynes's methods wanting. Keynes, driven by his deductivism, had failed to advance the social sciences:

> Mr. Keynes neither starts from facts nor returns to them. Mr. Keynes starts, not from any fact, but from a definition of a concept, of what he (Mr. Keynes) means when he says 'involuntary unemployment.' He proceeds to a fresh series of concepts and definitions. In a large proposition of these definitions, words are used in senses different from those of most other economists and of Mr. Keynes himself six years ago. Mr. Keynes does not return to facts for verification. There is no page throughout his work on which a generalisation is set against marshaled facts for testing.

Keynes's position was more complex than Beveridge would allow. As Keynes had remarked in the *Treatise on Money* (1930):

> These conclusions are, of course, obvious, and may serve to remind us all that these equations are purely formal; they are mere identities; truisms which tell us nothing in themselves. In this respect they resemble all other versions of the quality theory of money. Their only point is to analyse and arrange our material in what will turn out to be a useful way of tracing cause and effect, when we have vitalised them by the introduction of extraneous facts from the actual world.[90]

In this way Keynes, always the sceptic, sought to deal with the tensions between empiricism and speculation.

Beveridge realised, in speaking thus about Keynes, that he would make enemies because he was challenging 'a hundred years of political economy in which facts have been treated, not as controls on theory, but as illustrations.' He

[89] John Maynard Keynes to Roy Harrod, 4 July 1938 and 16 June 1939, printed in Donald Moggeridge (ed.), *The Collected Writings of John Maynard Keynes, Volume 14: The General Theory and After, Defense and Development* (London: 1973), pp.297, 300.
[90] John Maynard Keynes, *A Treatise on Money* in Moggeridge (ed.) *The Collected Writings of John Maynard Keynes, Volume 5* (London: 1971), p.125.

went on to criticise a large part of writing on economics of his day as derived 'from the positions of philosophers' such as Ricardo, Marx and Marshall. However, Beveridge admitted that the LSE made Bachelors of Science in Economics, 'but the title of the degree is the only connection with Science that we have. In all practical affairs we are joined, not with the other Sciences, but with the Faculty of Arts.' When the British Academy elected Beveridge to its fellowship he accepted it only reluctantly because he wished to be associated with the life of science rather than the life of letters. The character of social science for Beveridge was a personal matter.

Beveridge also waged war on another front at the LSE: the frontier between free inquiry and political action.[91] Early in his directorship he approved of a connection between the life of learning and public affairs. He strongly defended the social and political views of R. H. Tawny and Harold Laski as irrelevant to their intellectual commitments. Later, though, Beveridge's pronounced empiricism, the growth of the LSE – depriving it of its earlier intimacy – and the politics of the 1920s and 1930s moved him otherwise. Even then, however, Beveridge entertained the possibility of acquiring the library and some of the staff of the Frankfurt Institut für Sozial Forschung as part of his activities to assist refugee German scholars after 1933. Throughout, Beveridge thought, social scientists had an obligation not only to advance knowledge on their subject but also to give 'expert advice, not only on theoretical but on practical issues.' However, they could not appear to 'partisan without lessening confidence in [themselves] and [their] science.' 'The business of a social scientist,' he held, 'was to study and compare the properties of economic and political and social institutions, as the biologist studies living individuals and species or as the chemist studies matter.' The work of the social scientist and the politician differed and could not 'be combined without harm to one or the other.' Science abhorred haste and compromise; politics required both. 'It is the duty of the scientist not to speak until he is sure; he should speak seldom.'[92] Beveridge's views on the nature of knowledge and action were at one with his empiricism. His views, perhaps, were reinforced by those of his long-time assistant, secretary of the LSE in his time there, and later his wife, Jessy Mair. After meeting with A. V. Hill and Professor Watson in the search for someone to fill the chair in social biology she wrote to Beveridge on 26 November 1929:

What joy they had in their work. What dears they are, how pure, pure science is. How free from worldliness, how perfect a brotherhood. Can you wonder why I have always wanted that spirit in this place. How I can by nature by training sheer off from the mind which is bent on this or that propaganda this or that social reform, this or that religion. The cool detachment of the dogged search

91 Harris, *William Beveridge*, pp.283–295.
92 Beveridge, 'The Place of the Social Sciences in Human Knowledge': 473–474.

after what is true: that is where the soul reaches its completion, believe me. That is the real university spirit and only that.[93]

Disputes over the relationship between knowledge and politics raged in the school in the 1930s, stoked by the growth of the LSE, increased anonymity, a decreased sense of comradeship, the economic crisis of the time, and Beveridge's (and Mrs Mair's) firm (and sometimes heavy-handed) administration of the school.[94]

As in the case of Oxford and Cambridge, the research of the LSE required financing from without. The LSE had been founded, after all, with the bequest of Henry Hunt Hutchinson, one of whose executors was Sidney Webb. Hutchinson, a Fabian, stipulated that £20,000 should be applied to the purposes of the Fabian Society. Webb, inspired by the work of the École Libre des Sciences Politiques in Paris, the Massachusetts Institute of Technology, and the German Technische Hochschulen, pressed for the creation of an association where scholars could do original work. So, from its foundation and throughout its history, the fortunes of the LSE were tied to the fortunes of various funding authorities. In Beveridge's time 40 per cent of the LSE's funding came from government grants. After the Second World War, the public funding, 75 per cent of the LSE's resources, came from the University Grants Committee and 15 per cent from student fees. Still it relied on substantial contributions from the Rockefeller Endowment, the Cassel Trust, the Ford Foundation, the Leverhulme Trust and the Nuffield Foundation. Between 1923 and 1937, 25 per cent of LSE expenditure for buildings and library holdings came from Rockefeller grants.[95] Yet such support was always uncertain. When the hard times of the 1930s came, and when they became dissatisfied with Hogben's line of research, the Rockefeller Foundation withdrew its support from the social biology project.[96]

At the Liminalities

One might have thought that after the eagerness for research had begun to penetrate the universities the workings of more informal societies would be less needful and would pass into desuetude. One would be wrong. Such informal societies throve. Some were relics of the past and persisted: the Eranus Society, the Moral Sciences Club, the Family at Cambridge, the Club at Oxford, for example.[97] With the emergence and success of the Natural Sciences Tripos at Cambridge the Ray Club's weekly meetings

---

93 Quoted in Dahrendorf, *LSE*, 254.
94 Harris, *William Beveridge*, p.288.
95 Dahrendorf, *LSE*, p.315–316.
96 Dahrendorf, *LSE*, p.318 and *passim*.
97 Lubenow, *'Only Connect': Learned Societies in Nineteenth-Century Britain*, pp.29 ff.

were suspended and had to be resuscitated in the 1950s.[98] And, of course, there were many student clubs such as the Quintic Club at Peterhouse and the Adams Society at St John's College, Cambridge.[99] At Oxford the Junior Scientific Club had been founded to rectify unsatisfactory teaching in 1882. However, as undergraduate teaching improved and as specialisation took a firmer hold, separate disciplinary clubs such as the Chemical Club (later the Alembic Club), the Biological Club, the Morphology Club and the Junior Physiological Club assumed its activities.[100] These societies stimulated and promoted an active interest in research more than the universities themselves did. The liminalities are transitional places, spaces of mystery where intellectual power arises from ambiguity and disorientation. There, fractures and discontinuities blur distinctions to open the way from what was to what might be. These are not neutral spaces, neither are they settled enclaves; those who inhabit them are mental nomads moving about bemused and sometimes tinged with suspicion as they seek and sometimes fail to find different ways to communicate with each other.

Even the LSE, new and different from the other universities, was incubated in the sociality of a dining club. In its infant years the first three directors of the school were members of the Coefficients Club. The LSE and the Coefficients Club were both agents of Fabian permeation. Sidney and Beatrice Webb both believed, according to Lancelot Hogben, that 'a *marriage de convenance* between economic theory and factual social studies, if solemnised with a sufficient dowry to the latter, would advance the Fabian cause on a wide front.'[101] Beatrice Webb suggested the idea of a dining club to discuss the concept of efficiency. Sidney Webb gave it its name, calling it out over his shoulder as he led Halford Mackinder and Beatrice Webb on a bicycle ride during a holiday at their summer retreat in Gloucestershire. H. G. Wells, who became one of its members, gave a thinly disguised description of the club in his *New Machiavelli*. Members were of all parties and experiences. They dined monthly at the Ship Tavern on Whitehall though they moved later to St Ermin's Hotel. Dinner was given over to general conversation. Then, after the waiters had cleared away the dinner rubble, one member would deliver himself of his views on a specific question. Then all members, in turn, would express their views, after which the conversation would become general again. '[I]t is odd,' Wells remarked, 'how warm and good the social atmosphere of that little gathering became as time went on.' Wells claimed to

98 D. G. Hughes and K. Lund to C. P. Snow, 23 April [1961] and 10 June 1962, Harry Ransom Center, C. P. Snow MSS 70/13.
99 See the John Lennard-Jones Papers, Churchill College, Cambridge. LEJO/38.
100 P. J. Rowland, 'Student Participation in Science Teaching: The Early Years of the Oxford University Junior Scientific Club,' *Oxford Review of Education*, 9 (3) (1983): 133–136.
101 Adrian and Anne Hogben (eds), *Lancelot Hogben*, p.120.

have learned much at those dinners but what was of special importance, he thought, was that he became 'familiarized with the habits of mind of the other diners.'[102]

Its membership was diverse. It included Sidney Webb himself, William Pember Reeves, H. G. Wells, Halford Mackinder, William Hewins, Leopold Amery (who had been the *Times* correspondent in South Africa), Carlyon Bellairs (a naval expert), Clinton Dawkins (a man of finance), Sir Edward Grey (then at the Foreign Office), L. J. Maxe (a journalist), Alfred Milner, Richard Burton Haldane (a Liberal, lawyer and philosopher), Henry Newbolt (a poet), J. L. Garvin (another journalist), Henry Birchenought (a businessman and civil servant) and Bertrand Russell. Each was reputed to be an 'expert' in their particular field.[103] Russell described a week's reading party he had spent at Grantchester (where he read the *Bacchae* to the party). It was a visit he regarded as 'most profitable' to himself and others. Then he returned to London:

> I returned to the dinner of the Coefficients at Haldane's, where we discussed the mechanism for political unity in the empire. People's intellects impressed me as good; Sir E Grey was very interesting; but I had no sympathy with any of them except Reeves and Wells.[104]

Russell found Mackinder interesting because 'he had climbed Kilimanjaro with a native guide who walked barefoot except in villages, where he wore dancing pumps.' He regarded Bellairs as a 'breezy naval officer who was engaged in a perpetual ding-dong for the Parliamentary representation of King's Lynn.' Mackinder's brush with politics – as a Liberal Unionist and as an associate with Chamberlain – convinced him of the shallowness of politicians' narrow horizons and his first paper to the club was on education. Hewins confided to Russell that he had been brought up a Roman Catholic but had replaced his faith in the Church with a faith in the empire.[105] The club, divided between Liberal Imperialists and Little Englanders, was the end of a political movement rather than the beginning of one.[106] But its influence generated a new impetus toward the sciences of society. According to Dahendorf, if the LSE needed a Board of Directors these members of the Coefficients Club likely would have been its members.[107]

---

[102] H. G. Wells, *The New Machiavelli* (London: 1926 [2015]), pp.285–286.
[103] G. R. Searle, *The Quest for National Efficiency: A Study in British Politics and Political Throught* (Berkeley/Los Angeles: 1971), pp.150–151.
[104] Bertrand Russell, 'Journal [1902–1905],' in Richard A. Rempel, Andrew Brink and Margaret Moran (eds), *Collected Paper of Bertrand Russell, Volume 12: Contemplation and Action, 1902–1914* (London: 1985), p.15.
[105] Bertrand Russell, *Portraits from Memory and Other Essays* (London: 1956), pp.76–77.
[106] Searle, *The Quest for National Efficiency*, p.151.
[107] Dahrendorf, *LSE*, p.76.

The new research students coming into the universities at the end of the nineteenth and in the twentieth century, with their different experiences and backgrounds, required new social procedures to draw them into British intellectual life. From the outset J. J. Thomson recognised the need for greater social and comradely gatherings and in 1893 he established the Cavendish Physical Society, which assisted in the creation of a 'Cavendish-type of personality.'[108] Meeting fortnightly during term time they held discussions on research problems led by Thomson. Mrs Thomson served tea. Within five years their growing numbers justified a dinner at the end of each Michaelmas Term. Their rousing songs composed by themselves to verses concocted from Clark Maxwell's equations sometimes excited the suspicions of the university proctors until it was explained that these were merely the outbursts of youthful research scholars.[109]

P. L. Kapitza recognised the need for new social forms when he arrived at the Cavendish Laboratory in 1921. He duly formed the Kapitza Club. Kapitza arrived in Cambridge in a state of depression. Four members of his family had died within months of each other. One of his new colleagues thought he looked 'like a tragic Russian prince.' Never losing his affection for his homeland, he took his holidays in the Caucasus, but found research in Britain highly satisfactory. He once asked a friend of C. P. Snow whether a foreigner like himself could become a peer.[110] Chatting merrily in a high-pitched voice, he spoke what one writer has called 'Kapitzarene': a mixture of Russian, English and French, all at the same time.[111] After rejecting him initially, Rutherford took him into the Cavendish where Kapitza, knowing how flattery could be useful, became one of Rutherford's favourites. Rutherford, at best non-political and at worst a Conservative, warned Kapitza against talk of Soviet propaganda in the Cavendish. Kapitza was never a member of the Communist Party and he spoke quietly at the scientists' bench but in private he never made secret his approval of Lenin's policies and the liquidation of the Russian aristocracy during the revolution.[112] C. P. Snow regarded him as 'one of the most brilliant ornaments of the golden age of physics.' Snow, and others who knew him, thought his ambition, never directly expressed, would have been firmly established at the same time in the Soviet Academy of Sciences and as Rutherford's successor in the House of Lords.[113]

108 Crowther, *The Cavendish Laboratory, 1874–1974*, p.121.
109 Lubenow, *'Only Connect': Learned Societies in Nineteenth-Century Britain*, pp.231–232.
110 C. P. Snow, *Variety of Men* (New York: 1966), p.17.
111 Farmelo, *The Strangest Man: The Hidden Life of Paul Dirac, Mystic of the Atom* (New York: 2009), p.64.
112 Farmelo, *The Strangest Man*, p.65.
113 See Snow's comments on Kapitza's *Experiment, Theory, Practice* (Drodrecht: 1977 [1980])

Kapitza deployed his considerable gifts in the Kapitza Club. As Kapitza wrote from Moscow to his wife, still in England, when he had been forbidden by the authorities to return to England:

> Even in Cambridge I left my mark. Take the club which it is the custom to connect with my name, of which, like old Pickwick, I was a permanent president. I think it will stay a long time.[114]

J. G. Crowther called the club (he first heard of James Chadwick's discovery of the neutron there) a unique social invention. Kapitza, he said, 'created in Cambridge a new standard of general discussion of physics and engendered a freer exercise of the scientific intellect.'[115] Kapitza, though he found the British universities superior to those on the Continent, thought British intellectual habits were too rigid and formalised. Young men were treated more like schoolboys than adults. He founded the club to reduce their inhibitions and to allow them to express their ideas. When these young men first came to the club they behaved in a conventional manner and said nothing, fearing they might expose their ignorance, until asked and then being non-committal. Kapitza broke down these inhibitions by opening the discussions with ludicrous assertions so obvious that even the most inexperienced researcher was unafraid of correcting him. The club met on Tuesday evenings in Kapitza's rooms in Trinity College. He stressed informality, though there were a few rules: members were allowed to miss only a few consecutive meetings; one was a permanent member only after he had given a paper of his own.

Kapitza encouraged interruptions. At one meeting an American visitor gave a paper on Clerk Maxwell's theorem that currents in a network adjust themselves, making the energy production a maximum. Kapitza interjected by asking 'Don't you mean a minimum?' When some agreed with him and others sided with the speaker Kapitza leapt to his feet and hauled Clerk Maxwell's treatise, which he treated as almost a scriptural text, from his bookshelves. Kaptiza said: 'Ah yes, it says minimum in Book II (chapter 7).' At which someone quipped 'Verse 12,' which led members of the club to burst into laughter.[116] C. P. Snow described his own experience as a member of the Kapitza Club:

> I myself enjoyed the one tiny scientific triumph of my life there. At the time Kapitza barely tolerated me, since I did spectroscopy, a subject he thought fit for only bank clerks: in fact I had never discovered why he let me join. One night I offered to give a paper outside my own subject, on nuclear spin, in which I had been getting interested: I didn't know much about it, but I reckoned that most

in University of Texas, Ransome Center, C. P. Snow MSS 126/21; Snow, *Variety of Men*, p.17.
[114] Kapitza to his wife, 23 February 1935, printed in Lawrence Badash, *Kapitza, Rutherford, and the Kremlin* (New Haven: 1985), p.65.
[115] J. G. Crowther, *Fifty Years with Science* (London: 1970), pp.94–95.
[116] J. W. Boag, P. E. Rubinin and D. Shoenberg (eds), *Kapitza in Cambridge and Moscow: Life and Letters of a Russian Physicist* (Amsterdam/Oxford: 1990), p.42.

of the Cavendish knew less. The offer was unenthusiastically accepted. I duly gave the paper. Kapitza looked at me with his large blue eyes, with a somewhat unflattering astonishment, as at a person of low intelligence who had contrived inadvertently to say something interesting. He turned to Chadwick, and said incredulously, 'Jimmy, I believe there *is* something in this.'[117]

These affairs were largely non-alcoholic. Members drank large cups of coffee with milk. However, at a celebratory meeting in 1966 at Caius College, when Kapitza was finally allowed to return to Cambridge after years of enforced stay in Moscow, which Shoenberg, Cockcroft and Dirac attended, they drank dessert wines.[118] On that occasion Kapitza and Dirac discussed the effect they had discovered in 1933 – that it was possible for light to diffract electrons.[119]

The Kapitza Club drew not only the younger into its precincts, but also the great and the good from the world of physics. Patrick Blackett discussed 'The evolution of the solar system' on 3 March 1924 and 'Angular Momentum and Electron Impact' on 5 August 1924.[120] Dirac discussed 'Bose's and de Broglie's deductions of Planck's Law' on 4 August 1925.[121] J. D. Bernal presented papers on 'Pauling rules for crystal structure' on 25 November 1929 and on 'Methods of X-ray Crystal Structures' on 20 October 1931.[122] In the minutes for 27 January 1925 one wag made the following entry:

> In discussion our chief, P Kapitza
> Goes off suddenly like a howitzer
> He's been known to say: 'No!'
> It's not at all so
> It is thus, as you are bound to admit, Sir[123]

Nils Bohr came to the club on 16 May 1925 where he expressed his view that current atomic theory was only provisional and one with better intellectual foundations would have to be found.[124] He also addressed the club on 'Quantum Problems' on 2 November 1927 and on 'The Problem of Measurement and Consistency in Atomic Theory' on 26 July 1933.[125] Robert Millikan came from the United States to talk about 'Cosmic Ray Possibilities' on 23 November 1931.[126] Schrödinger visited the club to discuss 'Physical Meaning of Quantum

117 Snow, *Varieties of Men*, p.18.
118 Minutes of the Kapitza Club, Churchill College, Cambridge, Cockcroft Papers [hereinafter CKFT] 7/3/30.
119 Farmelo, *The Strangest Man*, pp.381, 341–432.
120 Minutes of the Kapitza Club, Church College, Cambridge, CKFT 7/2/7, 9.
121 Minutes of the Kapitza Club, Churchill College, Cambridge. CKFT 7/2/15.
122 Minutes of the Kapitza Club, Churchill College, Cambridge, CKFT 7/2/ 34v, 40.
123 Minutes of the Kapitza Club, Churchill College, Cambridge, CKFT 7/2/12.
124 Farmelo, *The Strangest Man*, p.81.
125 Minutes of the Kapitza Club, Churchill College, Cambridge, CKFT 7/2/27, 46.
126 Minutes of the Kapitza Club, Churchill College, Cambridge, CKFT 7/2/41.

Mechanics' on 10 March 1928.[127] Heisenberg came. It was there that Robert Oppenheimer met Niels Bohr and where Max Born converted him from experimental physics, at which he was manually inept anyway, to theoretical physics.

There was also at Cambridge an exclusive biophysics association called the Hardy Club. It was named for William Bate Hardy,[128] a physiologist and fellow of Caius College:

He never wavered in his conviction that no solution of a practical problem was worthwhile unless it was based on an adequate knowledge of the fundamental science that lay behind it, and therefore that it is a man with a sound training in academic research who is best fitted to unravel the practical problems and reach that solution.[129]

It was he who 'pitchforked' the young Joseph Needham into chemistry. Needham had wanted to do nothing but biological studies but Hardy said:

No, my boy, that's not the way to the future at all. Atoms and molecules, atoms and molecules my boy, that is what you should study. You'll never do anything in biology if you don't have that chemical and physical basis.[130]

Utterances like this show why the founders of the club named it after Hardy. Membership was by invitation alone. A society of the young, its founders rose only to prominence when they were recognised and fellows of the Royal Society and Nobel laureates. Some had known each other in the war, for example as members of the Ratio Club, to which Alan Turing had belonged, and where they attempted to revive the 'ghost' of 'creative anarchy' and the spirt of 'democratic association of young scientists which had characterized the war years.'[131]

In 1949 Richard Keynes (Maynard Keynes had been his uncle) wrote to Alan Hodgkin, Andrew Huxley, Victor Rothschild, Francis Crick, J. C. Kendrew and others proposing the formation of 'a small club' for reading

[127] Minutes of the Kapitza Club, Churchill College, Cambridge, CKFT/7/2/27.
[128] Hardy, William Bate (1864–1933): ed. Framlingham College and Gonville and Caius College, Cambridge, first class in the Natural Sciences Tripos (zoology) (1888); elected a fellow of his college (1892), tutor (1900–1918); university lecturer in physiology (1913); Royal Medalist, Croonian Lecturer and Bakerian Lecturer of the Royal Society; President of the British Association for the Advancement of Science at the time of his death; knighted (1925); one of the finest yachtsmen of his time. A. V. Hill, who wrote Hardy's entry for the DNB, said in his memoirs that '[a]ll his life Hardy was a gay adventurer in new fields,' a phrase that was slightly modified for the DNB entry. A. V. Hill papers [hereinafter AVHL], Churchill College, Cambridge, 1/3/33.
[129] Obituary Notices of the Fellows of the Royal Society, I (1932–1935): 331.
[130] Quoted by Christopher Brooke, A History of Gonville and Caius College (Woodbridge, 1985), p.208.
[131] Soraya de Chadarevian, Designs for Life: Molecular Biology after World War II (Cambridge: 2002), p.91, n. 91. Some members of the Ratio Club had worked in the Telecommunications Research Establishment during the war where they held what they called 'Sunday Soviets.' Andrew Hodges, Alan Turing: The Enigma (New York: 1983), pp.411–412.

papers 'discussing problems in the general field of biophysics.'[132] It was to have 'a minimum of organization' (no formal rules or a chairman) and 'a maximum of speculation.' Keynes became the secretary but 'his only duties being to send out reminders to the members before each meeting.'[133] Like many such societies it declined after a decade or so. On 21 November 1958 Keynes observed how 'the membership of the club has become rather vague during the last few years,'[134] but he urged Sydney Brenner to revive the club in the 1960s.

They excluded their seniors. In the 1950s it had but one FRS (Hodgkin) and but one peer (Rothschild) They drew themselves from laboratories across the university, a sign that their fundamental loyalties were not to their colleges (though they all held college fellowships) or even their departments. The need for the Hardy Club demonstrates the fragmentation of knowledge and the need for some sort of coordination in the formation of new ideas. Perutz, Kendrew, Hugh Huxley and Aaron Krug were from the Medical Research Council Medical Biology Laboratory. V. P. Whittaker and R. Hill were from Biochemistry. Alan Hodgkin and Richard Adrian were from Physiology. T. Weiss-Fogh was from Zoology. Richard Keynes was from the Agricultural Research Council Institute of Animal Physiology.[135] James Watson joined the Hardy Club when he was in Cambridge and on 1 May 1953 read a paper called 'Some Remarks on Desoxyribonucleic Acid.'[136] Crick, his collaborator in the great struggle to determine the structure of DNA, was not only a member of the Hardy Club; he was also a member of the Kapitza Club and the V²V Club.[137]

---

132 Keynes, Richard Darwin (1919–2010): the son of Geoffrey Keynes and Margaret Darwin; ed. Oudle and Trinity College, Cambridge (where he was the student of Alan Hodgkin though he claimed that his only recollection of the first-year course in physiology was a lecture by Edgar Adrian (later Lord Adrian, OM, PRS and Chancellor of Cambridge University) who demonstrated muscle action potentials by plunging a hypodermic electrode into his own arm); before going up to Cambridge Keynes spent three summer months with M. Paul Desjardins at the thirteenth-century Cistercian Abbaye de Pontigny called L'amitié enseignante de l'antibabel, drinking the local Chablis to such an extent that the nightingales kept him awake at night; lecturer in physiology, Cambridge; fellow of Peterhouse; FRS (q959); fellow of Churchill College, Cambridge; Deputy Director (later Director) of the Agricultural Research Council's Institute of Animal Physiology at Babraham; Professor of Physiology, Cambridge (1973).
133 Hardy Club Minute Book, Churchill College, Cambridge, Richard Keynes Papers [hereinafter KEYN] 24/1–3.
134 Richard Keynes, 21 November 1958, Hardy Club Minute Book, Churchill College, Cambridge KEYN 24/47.
135 Richard Keynes to Sydney Brenner, 27 September 1965; Sydney Brenner to Richard Keynes, 19 November 1965 with various lists of members of the Hardy Club, Cold Springs Harbor Archives Laboratory, Brenner Papers.
136 Hardy Club Minute Book, 1 May 1953, Churchill College, Cambridge, KEYN 24/22.
137 V²V: A common symbol in mathematical physics. 'This club – the nearest the theoreticians came to having a seminar programme – was attended by dons as well as students so its proceedings were more in keeping with the stiff ambiance of the mathematics department.' Farmelo, The Strangest Man, p.66. According to the 'Rules of the V²V Club' its purpose was to discuss questions in mathematical physics. It was to meet twice a term and

The Hardy Club met one or two times a term. To keep the club small they met in the college rooms of one of the members, often in Hodgkin's rooms R5 Great Court Trinity, or in the Panelled Combination Room of Caius, or Kendrew's room in 4 The Hostel, Peterhouse. However, they sometimes ventured slightly further afield. When they met for a meeting on 3 March 1950 at 60 Grange Road, Keynes's invitation card read 'You are requested to walk straight into the house; the bell doesn't work.'[138] On 9 February 1951 they met at Merton Hall, Rothschild's home, where as host he read a paper on 'Fertilisation.' The host at each meeting was expected to provide refreshments. At the meeting on 15 February 1961 where Aaron Klug and Hugh Huxley talked about the 'Structure of some Nucleic Proteins' the cost came to £1 10s 0d for sandwiches and £1 4s 6d for beer.[139] Sometimes the cost for speakers coming from outside the university became more than the secretary could take. Keynes wrote to the membership on 21 November 1958:

> It has been the custom for members of the club to provide refreshments when they have been addressing the club themselves, and for me to pay for the refreshments when the speaker has been a visitor to the university. The total cost for 14 such occasions has been £33.17.2. A subscription levied in December 1955 raised £9-10-0, and another in June 1954 had produced £8-0-0. As I am somewhat out of pocket, I am afraid I must ask for further contributions of £1.[140]

For the fiftieth meeting of the club they decided to have a celebratory dinner in the Combination Room at Peterhouse. Eighteen attended. They drank two bottles of sherry, two bottles of vodka, four bottles of Nachenheimer, six bottles of Burgundy and two bottles of port. The menu included Sturgeon Nucleoprotein, Nutrient Broth, Filet de Sole Keynes, Psoas Muscle Huxley-Huxley, Bombe Hardy and Barquetts de Gruyère.[141]

The most recurring subjects in their discussions were nerves, muscles, membranes and proteins. Babel, that is the search for a common language, brought them together in an effort to find common problems to explore. On 3 February 1950 Kendrew read on 'Polypeptide Chains.'[142] On 26 May 1950 Alan Hodgkin read on 'Ionic Exchange and Nervous Activity.'[143] On 9

---

have twenty ordinary members. The membership fee was five shillings. A member had to hold the BA degree or be a research student and would cease to be a member of the club if absent for four consecutive meetings. The length of the part of the minutes describing a paper that has been read to the club should not exceed two hundred words. 'Rules of the V²V Club,' Churchill College, Cambridge WLTN 1/11.

[138] Hardy Club Minute Book, 3 March 1950, Churchill College, Cambridge, KEYN 24/7.

[139] Hardy Club Minute Book, 15 February 1961, Churchill College, Cambridge, KEYN 24/58.

[140] Hardy Club Minute Book, 21 November 1958, Churchill College, Cambridge, KEYN 24/47.

[141] Hardy Club Minute Book, 29 April 1961, Churchill College Cambridge, KEYN 24/61.

[142] Hardy Club Minute Book, 3 February 1950, Churchill College, Cambridge KEYN 24/6.

[143] Hardy Club Minute Book, 26 May 1950, Churchill College, Cambridge, KEYN 24/8.

November 1951 Crick read on 'X-Rays, Proteins, and the Pauling Helix.'[144] Crick read again on 4 December 1956. His subject was 'Molecular Genetics.'[145] He returned to the club, meeting in the parlour at Peterhouse on 31 January 1962, to speak on 'The Genetic Code.'[146] Lord Adrian read a paper on 'Smell' on 6 March 1956.[147] J. D. Bernal came to the club on 13 December 1957 and read a paper on what was to become his book *The Origin of Life*.[148] Richard Keynes read a paper on 'The Utilization of Phosphate-Bond Energy for Sodium Transport in Giant Axons?' on 14 May 1958.[149] Just as the Babel of new intellectual problems brought them together to seek solutions to those problems, ultimately the movement of the Hardy Club's members into different careers outside Cambridge and the Babel of disciplinary specialisation led them to speak different intellectual languages. The last recorded meeting of the club, its sixty-first, was on 16 April 1968.

Whether or not the group from the Cavendish Laboratory – who took lunch at the Eagle pub or afternoon tea at the Bun Shop – could even be considered 'societies,' or even 'associations,' may be a moot point, but the beer and tea they drank were probably indispensable lubrications for the invention of the model of DNA. Meetings over lunch and tea were certainly more important to those who gathered there than their colleges.[150] When a new laboratory was built to accommodate those working in molecular biology Max Perutz insisted that it had to have a canteen on the top floor. Francis Crick, realising that more complex organisational forms made it difficult to know and understand what others were doing, regarded the canteen as one of the more important contributions to research. 'This mixed people,' Crick said, 'in an informal way and was invaluable.'[151]

George Gamow's RNA Tie Club was only slightly more organised.[152] James Watson gave an account of the club's origins and purposes:

[144] Hardy Club Minute Book, 9 November 1951,Churchill College, Cambridge, KEYN 24/14.
[145] Hardy Club Minute Book, 4 December 1956, Churchill College, Cambridge, KEYN 24/34.
[146] Hardy Club Minute Book, 31 January 1962, Churchill College, Cambridge, KEYN 24/64.
[147] Hardy Club Minute Book, 6 March 1957, Churchill College, Cambridge, KEYN 24/35.
[148] Hardy Club Minute Book, 13 December 1957, Churchill College, Cambridge, KEYN 24/39.
[149] Hardy Club Minute Book, 14 May 1958, Churchill College, Cambridge, KEYN, 24/44.
[150] Soraya de Chadarevian, *Design for Life*, p.92.
[151] Francis Crick, 'Ruthless Research in a Cupboard,' *New Scientist* (21 May 1987): 67–68; de Chadareian, *Design for Life*, pp.265–266.
[152] Gamow, George (1904–1968): ed. Novorossiga University, Odessa and the University of Leningrad, studied at Göttingen, the Cavendish Laboratory, at the University of Copenhagen; elected a corresponding member of the Academy of Sciences of the USSR at the age of twenty-eight; defected to the West at the Solvey Conference at Brussels in 1933; taught at George Washington University (1934–1954), the University of Colorado (1956–1959); father of the 'Big Bang' theory; founded the RNA Tie Club with James Watson (1954).

> To avoid boring frustration, Leslie Orgel and I, on a trip to Berkeley, suggested to the theoretical physicist George Gamow the idea of the RNATIECLUB with members who would pool diverse talents toward understanding how the RNA sequences were translated into precise amino acid sequences of polypeptides.[153]

According to Crick they never met, but Watson claims that they met once in the summer of 1954 at Woods Hole.[154]

The RNA Tie Club had notepaper and a tie, the pin for which had etched on it the name of an amino acid, one for each of its twenty members. Gamow chose Alanine, so his pin was marked ALA. Watson chose Proline, so his was marked PRO. The tie itself was manufactured by a haberdasher in Los Angles. When Watson wore his tie to dinner at the Athenaeum Club (the one in Pasadena) he hoped it would demonstrate the 'thinking man's response to academic dullness.'[155] The club's notepaper listed the officers and the club's motto: 'Do or Die, or Don't Try.' As officers of the club Gamow was the 'Synthesizer' and Watson was the 'Optimist.' Crick was the 'Pessimist.' Richard Feynman and Edward Teller were other members. The club existed as an instrument for the circulation of speculative papers to the few people who might be interested. Francis Crick regarded his unpublished paper 'On Degenerate Templates and the Adaptor Hypothesis' as his most influential work. Its conclusions were so sufficiently pessimistic that Crick put towards the end of it a quotation from an obscure eighteenth-century poet: 'Is there anyone so utterly lost as he seeks a way when there is no way.' Crick concluded his paper by writing '[i]n the comparative isolation of Cambridge, I must confess that there are times when I have no stomach for the coding problem.'[156]

Oxford, Cambridge and the LSE, according to Noel Annan, spawned the denizens of what he called with some self-satisfaction 'Our Age' because those were the three places where 'ideas fermented.'[157] It is hard to gainsay such an authority. Still, as this chapter has shown, the fermentation of these ideas sometimes had little to do with encouraging curiosity and originality. There was a tension within these institutions about the nature and the place of research in them. Attention from Royal Commissions had worked to rectify the universities' governance, finances and courses of study but institutional sclerosis and bureaucratic rigidity often inhibited the taking of those mental risks that are necessary for fundamental intellectual change – and often the spur to research occurred in clubs and societies at the margins of

---

[153] James Watson, 'Minds that Live for Science,' *New Scientist* (21 May 1987): 64–65.

[154] Francis Crick, *What Mad Pursuit: A Personal View of Scientific Discovery* (New York: 1988), p.95; Watson, 'Minds that Live for Science': 65.

[155] James Watson, *Genes, Girls and Gamow: After the Double Helix* (New York: 2002), p.111.

[156] Crick, *What Mad Pursuit*, pp.95–96.

[157] Noel Annan, *Our Age: Portrait of a Generation* (London: 1990), p.3.

the universities. So it would be until at least the end of the Second World War before the research imperative would seize a firm grip on the universities. Therefore, it is important to look outside the universities and explore there the possibilities for intellectual differentiation.

Chapter 2

The Great and the Good in the Scholarly World: The Royal Society and the British Academy

History is not pure science, it is not exact science, but it is science nonetheless. For science can be nothing but ordered knowledge, and whenever truth is sought by the method appropriate to the case, a scientific investigation is in progress, even if the results be indefinite.   Percy Gardner[1]

[Francis Haverfield] knew so much that he could acknowledge uncertainty and the doubt that arises from insufficient evidence, without attempting to fill the gaps by dogmatism. But in one respect the best was the enemy of the good. It is, I think, to his unwillingness to put down on paper anything of which he was not certain that we must attribute the paucity of his published work.
                                                                                    F. G. Kenyon[2]

A good deal of my research work in physics has consisted in not setting out to solve some particular problem, but simply examining mathematical quantities of a kind that physicists use and trying to fit them together in an interesting way regardless of any application that the work may have. It is simply a search for pretty mathematics.
                                                                                    P. A. M. Dirac[3]

The world around us teems with mysteries. There is scarcely one section of it that does not lead to bewilderment which an attempt is made to probe it to its depths. But there is one clue given to us which enables us to thread the maze. However multitudinous, however varied, however confusing in their interaction the laws of Nature may be, we have the firm belief

---

[1]   Percy Gardner, *Oxford at the Crossroads: A Criticism of the Course of Litterae Humaniores in the University* (London: 1903), p.81.
[2]   Frederic Kenyon, 'Presidential Address' delivered at the Annual General Meeting, 21 June 1919, *Proceedings of the British Academy, 1919–1920*: 21.
[3]   P. A. M. Dirac, 'Pretty Mathematics,' *International Journal of Theoretical Physics*, 21 (8/9) (1982): 603–605.

that they are immutable. On this single base rests the whole of Science. The answer that is wrung from Nature by experiment to-day holds good for all time.

The Right Hon. Lord Moulton, KBC, FRS[4]

I long for all academic institutions – colleges, academies, universities – to put up a large notice upon which might be inscribed in bold letters Hinshelwood's words 'There is no quicker way of making a first-class institution third-class than by appointing second-class men.'

Isaiah Berlin[5]

THE Royal Society and the British Academy sought to capture scholarship and research in the twentieth century. Yet, as the prescripts that introduce this chapter show, such capturing was never clear, certain or coherent. The Royal Society and the British Academy existed to establish their intellectual boundaries but scholarship and research remained indeterminate. Gardner's remark about history being neither pure nor exact but a science nonetheless illustrates scholarship's methodological elasticity. Frederick George Kenyon's notice of Francis Haverfield, the great scholar of ancient Rome, contains themes that run through the history of scholarship in the twentieth century: the insistence on evidence; the refusal to slink into dogmatism; and the realisation that positivism can be the enemy of scholarship.[6] Paul Dirac's remark about 'pretty mathematics' recognised the importance of aesthetics in research. Fletcher Moulton's confidence in the certainty of knowledge obtained by

4   The Right Hon. Lord Moulton, 'Introduction,' A. C. Seward, *Science and the Nation: Essays by Cambridge Graduates* (Freeport, New York: 1917 [1967]), pp.xii–xiii. Moulton, John Fletcher (1844–1921): father, a Wesleyan clergyman; ed. Kingswood School, Bath, London University, St John's College, Cambridge; senior wrangler with the highest marks in the Mathematical Tripos until that time, BA (1866); fellow of St John's College and mathematical lecturer; barrister, QC, MP, PC, judge; created Baron Moulton of Bank (1912).
5   Isaiah Berlin to Hugh Trevor-Roper, 3 January 1984 in Isaiah Berlin, *Affirming: Letters, 1975–1997*, ed. Henry Hardy and Mark Pottle with the assistance of Nicholas Hall (London: 2015), p.227. Hinshelwood, Cyril Norman (1897–1967): father, chartered accountant; ed. Westminster City School, Balliol College, Oxford where he took his degree with distinction and was elected a fellow; lecturer in chemistry at Trinity College (1921–1936); Dr Lee's Professor of Chemistry (1937–1964); FRS (1929); PRS (1955–1960); knighted (1948); Nobel Prize (1956); OM (1960).
6   Kenyon, Frederick George (1868–1952: father, fellow of All Souls and Vinerian Professor of Law; mother, daughter of Edward Hawkins, FRS, Keeper of Antiquities at the British Museum; ed. Winchester, New College, Oxford; first class in both classical moderations (1883) and *literæ humaniores* (1886); fellow of Magdalen (1888); entered the department of manuscripts as assistant (1889) where he worked on the collection of Greek papyri; promoted to Assistant Keeper (1898); Director of the British Museum (1909–1930); FBA (1903), PBA (1917–1921), Secretary (1930–1949); entered the Territorial Army, received his commission in 1906, promoted to captain in 1912 and lieutenant colonel in 1917; served in France in 1914 but recalled at the request of the Trustees of the British Museum; appointed CB (1911), KCB (1921), GBE (1918) and usher of the purple rod.

experimental investigation is accompanied by his recognition of the teeming mysteries of the natural world. Isaiah Berlin's demand for the appointment of only the first-class to learned societies is a reminder of the importance to all of them of competence in the struggle for truth.

These themes mark the histories of the Royal Society and the British Academy. The presidents and the council members as well as the regular fellows of these learned societies had captured intellectual and public respectability. They were marked by public school educations, university degrees, college fellowships, university professorships, some peerages (James Bryce and Edgar Adrian), honorary degrees, and appointments to the Order of Merit. Some fellows of the Royal Society were Nobel Prize recipients. Their membership and official positions in these learned societies certified not only the personal accomplishments but also their corporate committments. These were the 'New Men' about which C. P. Snow (for he was one of them) wrote in 1954 and will be discussed in detail in Chapter 5. For all their attainments, these societies were marked by anxiety: Who should belong to these societies? How many should belong to them? What species of learning should they represent? These questions are taken up here. These scholarly societies represented no one thing; they were not unified institutional entities.

The Royal Society of London, perhaps the most distinguished of the seventeenth-century academies, established a tradition that, at least historiographically speaking and in its own mythology, seems like the Whig interpretation of history translated into the history of science. The Royal Society, according to this view, was preoccupied from its early days with the 'curiosities' of a coffee-house culture – and gradually, increasingly and inevitably narrowed its membership to those who practised empirical experimentalism only.[7] This is a generous position and, naturally, like most generous positions it can be exaggerated. Even at the dawn of the history of such academies and societies, members of Federico Cesi's Accademia dei Lincei, in Galileo's time, each had their disparate intellectual interests. So the twentieth-century Royal Society's history displayed increasing specialisation with a fragmenting effect, which cannot always be expressed as part of a trajectory leading to, and ending with, Rutherford's string-and-sealing-wax empiricism. The character of the work of the presidents of the Royal Society in the twentieth century reveals an ever widening and differentiating diffusion of intellectual interests that fail to conform to a neat teleological pattern. William Crookes (1913–1915) was a chemist and physicist. J. J. Thomson (1915–1920) was a physicist. Charles Scott Sherrington (1920–1925) was a neurophysiologist, histologist, bacteriologist and pathologist. Rutherford (1925–1930) was a physicist and chemist.

---

7   Marie Boas Hall, *All Scientists Now: The Royal Society in Nineteenth Century* (Cambridge: 1984), *passim*.

Frederick Gowland Hopkins (1930–1935) was a biophysicist. William Henry Bragg (1935–1940) was a physicist, chemist and mathematician. Henry Hallett Dale (1940–1945) was a pharmacologist and physiologist. Robert Robinson (1945–1950) was an organic chemist. Edgar Adrian (1950–1955) was an electro-physiologist. Cyril Hinshelwood (1955–1960) was a physical chemist. Howard Florey (1960–1965) was a pharmacologist and pathologist. Patrick Blackett (1965–1970) was a physicist. Alan Hodgkin (1970–1975) was a physiologist and biophysicist. Scientists they were all, but hardly the same kind of scientist. The pattern of interests they represent is one of inclusion and exclusion at the same time, revealing a broadening rather than a narrowing of intellectual interests.

Such broadening expressed itself in the careers of some ordinary fellows of the Royal Society. John Scott Haldane, it was said, regarded biology as an independent science with modes of interpretation different from those of physics and chemistry but this did not mean, for him, that physics and chemistry had no place in researches into the study of the processes of life.[8] He was one whose work had implications that extended beyond his immediate field of inquiry. From the physiological point of view, he said, the phenomena of life 'express the maintenance of a coordinated whole which included within itself relations to the environment as well as the mutual relationships of details of internal structure and activity.'[9] Such a view reflected, at the same time, both intellectual differentiation as well as its organising principle.

A different sort of broadening can be observed in the career of Alfred Cort Haddon who bridged zoology (he was elected a fellow of the Royal Society (FRS) in 1899) and anthropology.[10] In 1888–1889 Haddon went to the Torres Straits to study marine biology. He returned with many specimens but also with the determination to record the details of the lives of people before the contact with Europeans destroyed their

[8]   Haldane; John Scott (1860–1936): father, Robert Haldane, writer to the signet, of Cloan; ed. Edinburgh Academy; University of Jena; graduated in medicine at Edinburgh (1884); demonstrator in physiology at University College, Dundee; joined his uncle John Burdon-Sanderson, Wynflete Professor of Physiology at Oxford as his demonstator (1887); elected a fellow of New College, Oxford (1901); reader in physiology at Oxford (1907–1913)' FRS (1897); Royal Medalist (1916); Copley Medalist (1934); CH (1928) for his work on industrial disease; brother of Viscount Richard Haldane; father of John Burdon Sanderson Haldane (FRS) and Naomi Mitchison.

[9]   Quoted in G. C. Douglas, 'John Scott Haldane, 1860–1936,' *Obituary Notices of Fellow of the Royal Society*, 2 (1936–1939): 116.

[10]   Haddon, Alfred Cort (1855–1940): father, a Baptist and head of a firm of type-founders and printers with business interests in Africa and the South Seas; ed. King's College, London; Christ's College, Cambridge where he was close to F. M. Balfour and Michael Foster and took a first class in the Natural Sciences Tripos (comparative anatomy); awarded a university grant to spend six months at the *Stazione Zoologica* at Naples (1879); curator of the Zoological Museum at Cambridge and demonstrator in zoology; professor of zoology at the Royal College of Science and assistant naturalist at the Science and Art Museum in Dublin; lecturer in physical anthropology at Cambridge (1894–1898); university lecturer in ethnology and fellow of Christ's College, Cambridge (1901).

native customs. Thenceforth he became preoccupied with preserving information about native peoples. He was essentially a field worker who stressed first-hand observation and direct contact with the subjects of his researches.[11] He had taken from his former work in zoology a recognition of the necessity of 'a combination of the observational with the comparative method.'[12] Haddon's later return to the Torres Straits, New Guinea and Sarawak marked the beginning of serious anthropological research, and Haddon, with his wit and capacity for comradeship, collected about himself a group of students and colleagues bound together by affection and respect. What brought anthropology within the scope of the Royal Society was Haddon's previous experience as a zoologist but also the processes of sociality characteristic of his work with his colleagues and students.

Haddon's work brought him into contact with J. G. Frazer who got the grant for Haddon that took him to the Torres Straits. Frazer himself became a fellow of the Royal Society under the statute conferring election because of 'conspicuous service to the cause of science.'[13] Frazer's claim to the Royal Society fellowship could not have been based on his being any kind of a methodological experimentalist. Frederic Kenyon, however, called him 'the most learned and industrious writer alive on mythological and folklore subjects.'[14] H. J. Fleure regarded him as having a 'poetic vision' and as one who 'cultivated the field of documentary evidence':

> Frazer was the patient searcher into endless documents, scrupulously careful, methodical to a fault, indeed he was wont to describe himself unaffectedly, if adequately as dull. He went his own way, disregarding abuse, and disdained the attacks of prejudice; he could follow the advice of Marcus Aurelius and retire into his own soul and be at rest and free from all business.

Frazer's work, according to Fleure, was 'the scientific study of man's work and ways.' His intellectual achievements had 'the deepest scientific influence on

[11]   H. J. Fleure, 'Alfred Cort Haddon, 1855–1940,' *Obituary Notices of Fellows of the Royal Society*, 3 (1939–1941): 450.

[12]   A. C. Haddon, 'Presidential Address of Section H of the British Association for the Advancement of Science,' *Reports of the British Association for the Advancement of Science*, 75 (1905): 512 quoted in Henrika Kuklick, *The Savage Within: The Social History of British Anthropology, 1885–1945* (Cambridge: 1991), p.137.

[13]   Frazer, James George (1854–1941): father, partner in a firm of chemists; ed. Larchfield Academy, Trinity College, Cambridge, second in the first class of the Classical Tripos (1878); fellow of Trinity College (1878); read law and called to the Bar at the Middle Temple; chair in social anthropology at the University of Liverpool (1907–1922) but resided for but one session because of his life-long preference for his study at Trinity; founding fellow of the British Academy (1902); FRS (1920); knighted (1914); OM (1925).

[14]   Frederic Kenyon to Lord Stanfordham, 19 November 1924, Royal Archives, PS/GV/1978/13 quoted in Stanley Martin, *The Order of Merit: One Hundred Years of Matchless Honour* (London: 2007), p.301.

religious thought since Darwin's.'[15] Such was the claim Frazer could make to a fellowship in the Royal Society.

The Royal Society also took on board as fellows some whose connection with experimental research was so obscure as to be non-existent. They accepted Edgar Vincent, Viscount D'Abernon, who had been President of the Council of the Ottoman Public Debt and Ambassador to the German Republic after 1920.[16] He became the chairman of the Central Control Board (Liquor Traffic) in 1915, which was his first and perhaps his only contact with experimental research. (He advised heavy taxation on all forms of alcoholic drink because of its effects on human health.) A connoisseur, a Soul, and, with his wife, he was a great social personage. He lived not long enough to play any kind of role in the Royal Society but Henry Dale thought that had D'Abernon lived in an earlier age 'he might have recalled the traditions of the Society's earlier days, when great men of his type were more frequent among its fellow than in more recent years.'[17]

There were limits to the kinds of scholarship the Royal Society would accept. They shunned scholars of literary learning, as the case of their relationship with the British Academy shows.[18] They would refuse, except for anthropology (such as Haddon) and archaeology (such as Arthur Evans), scholars of the sciences of humanity. Even their tolerance for anthropology and anthropologists was limited. In 1883 only 2 per cent of the ordinary fellows of the Royal Anthropology Institute were FRS, a proportion that rose to only 6 per cent in 1900 and then declined to 4 per cent in 1920 and to 2 per cent in in 1930.[19] From time to time in the twentieth century they were urged to accept what has come to be called the social sciences.

---

[15] H. J. Fleure, 'James George Frazer, 1854–1941,' *Obituary Notices of Fellows of the Royal Society*, 3 (1939–1941): 899–901.

[16] Vincent, Edgar (1857–1941): father, the Rev. Sir Frederick Vincent, Bt., rector of Slinford and canon of Chichester; ed. Eton; qualified as a student Dragoman at Constantinople but instead chose a military career; moved to a diplomatic career after serving as assistant to HM commissioner for the evacuation of the territory ceded to Greece by Turkey; financial adviser to the government of Egypt; governor of the Imperial Ottoman Bank; elected as Tory MP for Exeter (1899–1906); stood as a Liberal for Colchester in 1910 but was defeated; his capacity for seeing all sides of an argument did not suit him for politics; claimed to belong to no party except Balfour's; ambassador to the German Republic.

[17] Sir Henry Dale, 'Edgar Vincent, Viscount D'Aubernon, 1857–1942,' *Obituary Notices of Fellows of the Royal Society*, 4 (11) (November 1943): 83–86.

[18] Lubenow, *'Only Connect': Learned Societies in Nineteenth-Century Britain*, pp.89–93 and in this chapter, below.

[19] Kuklick, *The Savage Within*, p.299. The small proportions, and then declining proportions of fellows of the Royal Anthropology Institute who were FRS, might be explained by the fact that the Royal Anthropology Institute welcomed all comers into its membership but the Association of Social Anthropologists (founded in 1946) took on board only those who held the PhD in anthropology and therefore syphoned off those who might claim expert knowledge and meet the prejudices of the Royal Society.

In 1941 Archibald Vivian Hill responded to a letter in *The Times* by Dr George Catlin calling for the Royal Society to help in establishing 'a representative body of the highest body of the highest academic standing, able to command the respect in the field of the social sciences.'[20] Hill objected to this proposal, thinking that 'the task must be undertaken by the social scientists themselves.' He favoured the applications of scientific findings to questions of human welfare, 'but the social or political convenience of a fact or theory is no part of the evidence' for Catlin's proposal. Achievements in the natural sciences, he said, had been produced by the method of controlled experiment. He regretted the confusion that had been caused 'by supposing that this method, with its proved effectiveness in its own field, is commonly – or even generally – applicable to political, social, or economic studies.' He urged a special place and responsibility for students of the natural world:

> The virtues to be cultivated by the scientific man are courage, integrity, friendliness, and humility; courage to insist on the value both of ascertainable fact and of its logical consequence; integrity in experiment, argument, and in criticism; friendliness to ensure that research, so far as possible, is of concern to every reasonable man anywhere; humility to provide a consciousness that one might conceivably be wrong and the other man right.

It does one good to work 'for a while' on research recognised for its national or international value to humanity. It does good to have researchers exchange experience in their special fields and experience in industry or government. But the desire for social improvement, he held, should not shape conclusions or scientific judgements: 'The sole object of science is to arrive at the facts, that no consideration of religion, morals, or politics should be allowed to deflect it by one hair's breadth from its integrity.' What is important, he argued, is for institutions such as the Royal Society to remain independent. The great advantage of the Royal Society, he said, was, 'as yet,' its independence from the 'Establishment.' He would regard it as a sad day if and when the officers of the Royal Society came to be considered officials of a government department and were expected to take orders from ministers: 'The price of freedom is perpetual watchfulness.'

Again, as recently as 1961, Charles Frederick Goodeve, Director of the British Iron and Steel Research Association, FRS and member of the Royal Society Club, brought the question of the place of the social sciences in the

---

20 Hill, Archibald Vivian (1886–1977): ed. Blunders School, Trinity College, Cambridge (where he was third wrangler); Stirling Professor of Physiology, University College, London (1923); a founder and vice-president of the Academic Assistance Council; a founder of research into biophysics and operations research; FRS (1918), Royal Medal (1928), Copley Medal (1948); Nobel Prize (1922); OBE, CH; MP for Cambridge University (1940–1945); married Margaret Keynes and, therefore, Maynard Keynes and Geoffrey Keynes were his brothers-in-law and Richard Keynes was his nephew. Hill records this incident in his *Memories and Reflections*, Churchill College, Cambridge, A. V. Hill Mss [hereinafter AVHL] /5/4/271, 313-314, 344, 496–407.

Royal Society before its Club.[21] He, of course, contacted Royal Society officers such as Howard Florey, the then president, D. C. Martin, the society's assistant secretary, and Henry Dale, a former president. It is curiously important that Goodeve should raise the question in the Royal Society Club; it is a reminder of the ways that intellectual decisions should require an atmosphere of sociality and civility rather than an atmosphere of bureaucracy and formality. In the autumn of 1960 Goodeve wrote to Martin asking him if he had seen a summer issue of the *Economist* that had raised the question of a place of economists in the Royal Society. The writer had asked:

> [W]ould the Royal Society elect economists? Probably not; apart from the fact that some of its Fellows would regard economic science as barely emerging from the stage of alchemy, the elaborate revision of the Royal Society Statutes in 1847, which originated in the very careful process that leads any candidate to the coveted letters FRS today, sets the bounds rather firmly around the physical and biological sciences.[22]

Goodeve asked Martin whether these statements were correct and whether or not the Royal Society had of recent years taken any interest in the social sciences. Goodeve thought the matter of some importance because of late some fellows had taken interest in broader subjects, including the study of society. Yet, he also noted, those studies 'are not quite compatible with the methods [used by] us in the physical and biological sciences.' The gap seemed great and was bridged only by statisticians and others engaged in precise studies. Goodeve wondered whether some members of the society might be interested in 'discussing the possibilities of something being done to bridge the gap.'[23]

For Martin much depends on what one means by a social science. On one side there were such as the experimental psychologist Sir Frederick Bartlett who had been a fellow for twenty-eight years, had given two lectures to the Royal Society and had been awarded its Royal Medal. On the other hand there were those whose studies 'tend to come within the purview of the British Academy rather than the Royal Society.' Martin thought the matter had been raised before and always had been resolved by reaffirming that the fellowship should be limited by the 'Society's Charter with its emphasis on experiment.'[24] Goodeve promised

---

[21] Goodeve, Charles Frederick (1904–1980): born in Manitoba; ed. Kelvin High School, Winnipeg, Manitoba, University College, London; assistant lecturer, Manitoba University (1925–1927), assistant lecturer (1928–1930), lecturer (1930–1938), reader (1938–1945) in physical chemistry, University College, London; Director, British Iron and Steel Research Association (1946–1969), Member, Lord President's Advisory Committee on Scientific Policy (1953–1956); OBE (1941), knighted (1946). For the Royal Society Club see Lubenow, *'Only Connect': Learned Societies in Nineteenth-Century Britain*, pp.211–216.
[22] [anon.], 'The Elect of Science,' *The Economist* (16 June 1960): 293–294, at 293.
[23] Charles Goodeve to D. C. Martin, 12 October 1960, Churchill College, Cambridge. Goodeve Mss [hereinafter GOEV] /7/7
[24] Martin to Goodeve, 14 October 1960, Churchill College Cambridge, GOEV/7/7.

to review the charter when next he was in Burlington House but pointed out how the argument hinged on what one meant by 'experiment.' The concept of an 'experiment,' he pointed out, includes the notion of 'careful observation of phenomena which cannot be influenced by the "experimentor [sic]."' Once one accepts the concept of 'observation' it becomes difficult to make sharp distinctions. 'Much of the field of social science and economics involves first-class observations and analysis and someday we may accept this as inside the "scientific method" so closely guarded by the Royal Society.'[25]

Taking matters into his own hands, Goodeve had lunch with Howard Florey, the then president of the Royal Society, at the Athenaeum to lay out plans for such a discussion. He contacted the senior treasurer of the Royal Society Club, Professor A. R. J. P. Ubbelohde, about the use of the club for a discussion of the place of the social sciences in the Royal Society. Ubbelohde and he agreed to invite some social scientists to the dinner to open a discussion on the question and to encourage the chair of the evening to make a point of keeping the members focused on the subject of the social sciences. Goodeve proposed to invite Dr Henry Durand, 'the leading scientist in this country concerned with attitude and behaviour survey,' to the dinner, and to invite to a later dinner Professor David Glass of the LSE who had been engaged in sociological demography, which 'many people would class as highly scientific.'[26]

Receptive to the idea of such a discussion at the dinner of the Royal Society Club, which might assist the social sciences, Florey still regarded them as 'rather a vague field.' 'One of the difficulties,' he said, was 'to know what social science is most like the experimental and other sciences that the Royal Society is principally interested in.'[27] In response, Goodeve confessed modestly that he was 'far from being knowledgeable about the subject' and proposed another lunch at the Athenaeum where he might lay out his conception of the sorts of subjects that might preoccupy the kinds of social sciences in which the Royal Society might be interested. Paramount of these, he said, were attitude and behaviour studies, 'basic to the whole of the social sciences.' Demography also was '"fairly scientific" in that precise measurements can be made and the results can be analysed.' He also included social anthropology though he admitted to not knowing much about it. Goodeve also wished to include industrial psychology, which ranged from applied psychology 'to vague things such as management relations.' 'It claims to have high scientific content,' he said, 'but I am not very sure.' Goodeve included social economics, 'economics in a very broad sense of the word,' in his list of subjects he thought might interest the Royal Society. However, he

25 Goodeve to Martin, nd, Churchill College Cambridge, GOEV/7/7.
26 Goodeve to Florey, 27 January 1961, Churchill College, Cambridge, GEOV/7/7.
27 Florey to Goodeve, 1 February 1961, Churcill College, Cambridge, GEOV/7/7.

thought this was a field in which 'unfortunately the gap between the methods of thought of the economist and the natural scientist is also the greatest.'[28] Such hesitancy as Goodeve presented could hardly have reassured the more sceptical fellows of the Royal Society. Yet, he invited various members of the Royal Society Club to dine. These included: Vivian Hill, Solly Zuckerman, J. Z. Young, Cyril Hinchelwood, Peter Medawar, Patrick Blackett, Henry Dale, John Cockcroft and George P. Thomson (the son of J. J. Thomson).[29]

Henry Dale's response was, in part, bureaucratic because he was a past president of the Royal Society. He feared the secretaries of the society would be swamped if the society included those pursuing the human sciences. Beyond that, though, he referred rather sneeringly to the 'not very clearly defined group of the so-called social sciences.' He was aware of the existence, 'outside the limits of such essentially scientific studies, of a wide fringe of speculative and argumentative theses claiming to deal with matters of the "social sciences."' The Royal Society catered, he said, to the 'more clearly recognized ranges of the experimental, mathematical and directly observational sciences.' He 'trembled,' he said, of what would happen if the society would 'open its doors more widely to anything calling itself science in the range of studies of "human attitudes and behaviours."' He was prepared to have Goodeve scorn him as 'an old fuddy-duddy; but there it is.'[30] Modern society, Goodeve responded politely, faced grave problems to which 'very good brains are attracted to social problems which are becoming more and more urgent.' Many scientific bodies and fellows of the Royal Society, he argued, are taking an interest in the social sciences out of a sense of duty and not because they were the fashion or because 'there was a band-wagon on which to jump.'[31]

Goodeve's tightly framed proposal was limited to a conception of the sciences of society as subjects that can be measured and classified. He doubtless put it forward in a defensive sort of way to make them most appealing to fellows of the Royal Society. In fact this defensiveness mirrored defensiveness expressed by students of society themselves. William Beveridge restricted his own work, modelled after the ideas of T. H. Huxley and by his own travails at the LSE in seeking to mediate the activist efforts of such as Harold Laski, to 'observation, experiment, comparison, and classification.'[32] Both the study of society[33] and the study of the natural world were, at their outset and in their working out,

[28] Goodeve to Florey, 8 February 1961, Churchill College, Cambridge, GOEV/7/7.
[29] Goodeve to various members of the Club, 4 February 1961, Churchill College, Cambridge, GOEV/7/7.
[30] Henry Dale to Goodeve, 14 February 1961, Churchill College, Cambridge GOEV/7/7.
[31] Goodeve to Dale, 21 February 1961, Churchill College, Cambridge, GOEV/7/7.
[32] Harris, *William Beveridge*, pp.277 ff. For Huxley see 'On the Value of the Natural History Sciences,' *Lay Sermons, Addresses and Reviews* (London: 1872).
[33] See Stefan Collini, Donald Winch and John Burrow, *That Noble Science of Politics: A Study in Nineteenth-Century Intellectual History* (Cambridge: 1983), p.3.

expressed aspirationality and multiplicity. Both the study of nature and the study of society were aspirational and therefore incomplete; they were multiple and therefore not unified projects. Aspirationality is a kind of freedom, a kind of hope, because it is open, but, because it is open and its goal is unknown and incomplete, it produces anxiety. These were reasons for making their claims austere. As wags have put it, the sciences of society have not achieved intellectual security by finding a Newton for themselves. As the history of science in the twentieth century shows, even Newton was inadequate for those examining the small world of the atom.

The question of the relationship of the sciences of society to the Royal Society and to 'science itself' rests on the difficulty of coming to grips with the concept of empiricism. The Royal Society's motto from the beginning – *Nullius in verba* (trust no one's *word*) – haunted this difficulty. From its beginning *Wissenschaft* was a complicated construction and contained both 'accuracy' and 'interpretation'. It contained both the search for positive knowledge and *Verstehen*. Von Ranke spoke of the capturing 'pure' fact. 'The external appearance,' he went on to say, 'is not the final thing which we have to discover.' This 'pure' fact has a 'spiritual content' that can only be discovered by intuition and acts of imagination. 'The spirit from which things come, and the knower will be one. In this theory of knowledge the most subjective is at the same time the most general truth.'[34] If one examines the practices of the early philologists and natural philosophers in the nineteenth century one cannot help but observe the entangledness of their procedures and problems. Both preoccupied themselves with the same kinds of intellectual anxieties.[35]

Because the conception of *Bildung*, the cultivation of self-awareness, was incorporated in the concept of *Wissenschaft* it is impossible to escape Heisenberg's uncertainty principle. The very act of investigation distorts the object of investigation. As Bernard Bosanquet argued in the early twentieth century, one can only make sense of a 'fact' by taking into account the whole of human experience.[36] Without that, he said, a fact 'is a dead psychical mass':

34   Leopold von Ranke, *The Secret of World History: Selected Wrtings on the Art and Science of History*, ed. Roger Wines (New York, 1981, p.1). The phrases here found are quoted in Peter Novick, *The Noble Dream: The 'Objectivity Question' and the American Historical Profession* (Cambridge: 1988), p.28.
35   Lorraine Daston and Glenn W. Most, 'History of Science and History of Philologies,' *Isis*, 106 (2) (2015): 378–390. See also Denise Phillips, 'Francis Bacon and the Germans: Stories from when "Science" Meant "Wissenschaft,"' *History of Science*, 53 (4) (2015): 378–394.
36   Bosanquet, Bernard (1848–1923): father, a clergyman; ed. Harrow, Balliol College, Oxford; first class in classical moderations (1868) and *literae humaniores* (1870); fellow of University College, Oxford (1870) but resigned and in 1881 moved to London to engage in philosophical writing; member of the Aristotelian Society (1886) of which he was president (1894–1898); held the chair of moral philosophy at St Andrew's University (1903–1908) but resigned when he thought original work and lecturing were incompatible; Gifford Lecturer at Edinburgh (1911–1912); he put down his interest in philosophy first to the practical

As every student of social matters knows by his own experience, it is impossible to touch a physical fact, or a statistical datum, or a legal enactment, in reference to its social bearing, without at once, so to speak, coming alive in his hands, and attaching itself to an underlying relation of mind as the only unity which will make it intelligible, and correlate it with other experiences, by themselves no less fragmentary.[37]

To try to trap science as well as social science into the narrow confines of observation, experimentation and classification would serve neither well.

Disciplines emerge from the gallimaufry of intellectual studies but their structures and limits are not inherent in the subjects of study themselves. These structures and limits are creatures of the government and management of knowledge, chiefly, but not entirely in the universities. Such structures and limits can become reductionist essentialisations, which in turn can provoke intellectual hostility, anxiety and disciplinary jealousy, giving rise to the thought that there might actually be 'two cultures.' They can become narcissism of minor difference written into the history of mental life. An appreciation of the role hermeneutics can play in blunting the effects of an observation–verification orthodoxy can come to the rescue. Interpretation, as Charles Taylor has pointed out, is central to the spirt of investigation because it is an attempt 'to make clear, to make sense of, an object of study.' It 'aims to bring to light an underlying coherence or sense.'[38] An interpretation, in its explanatory function, by rendering the fragmentary coherent and by rendering clear what seems confusing, creates an elision between the object of a study and its expression by breathing life into a desiccated entity.

Both 'science' and 'social science' are bedevilled and at once blessed by the incorporation of *Bildung* into *Wissenschaft*. This incorporation makes it seem that what is personal, the anarchy of the charismatic self, may threaten objectivity and Truth[39] – the studies of society the more so because they are concerned with subjects more immediately associated with the welfare and the improvement of social conditions. But what is welfare and what is improvement are highly debatable and subject to partisan charges and counter charges. Yet the sciences of society have been associated with ideas of modernity since the eighteenth century. Gaining a great reputation before and during the Second World War, having faced the challenges of fascism

---

workings of the family estate that his father himself farmed, and, second, to the importance he felt for aesthetic experience.

[37] Bernard Bosanquet, *The Meaning of Extremes in Contemporary Philosophy* (London: 1921), p.197, quoted in Sandra M. den Otter, *British Idealism and Social Action: A Study in Late Victorian Thought* (Oxford: 1996), p.75.

[38] Charles Taylor, *Philosophy in the Human Sciences: Philosophical Papers, 2* (Cambridge: 1985), p.15.

[39] Lorraine Daston and Peter Galison, *Objectivity* (New York: 2010), *passim* and esp. pp.372–375.

and communism, they fell to their knees in the 1960s with the failure of modernisation theory, rational choice theory, and the implications of the Vietnam War.[40] Some have always suspected them of having physics envy. It may be the case that the social sciences sullied themselves by making excessive positivistic claims so that their efforts to become scientific made them scientistic. When the National Science Foundation was established the sciences of society, though not formally excluded, were isolated as 'other sciences' in such a way as to limit their expectations for support.[41] Such bracketing should not obscure the great reputation and authority they achieved in the twentieth century. For Dorothy Ross, one of the most forceful and important historians of the social sciences, '[t]he liberal Enlightenment vision of a progressive modern society guided by science gained energy and urgency from the defeat of fascism, the disintegration of colonial empires, and the threat of communism.'[42] There is, of course, a vast literature on the history of the social sciences.[43]

The even more austere claims of the Royal Society itself have masked the way in which their procedures were more relaxed and elastic than they would want to admit, and therefore it is a nonsense to try to speak of something like 'science itself.' The Royal Society's project consisted of a series of elisions separating some subjects of study while connecting others. The intellectual jealousies of the Royal Society efforts to protect its precincts should not obscure its internal intellectual rivalries. If the Royal Society's fellowship was divided by the fragmentation and specialised differentiation, it was also divided by epistemological and procedural impulses: deductivism and inductivism. These intellectual rivalries and epistemology differences also sowed the seeds of its own destruction as a unified activity. As Lorraine Daston has pointed out, the third scientific revolution in the twentieth century, relativity theory and quantum mechanics, 'overturned the achievements of Galileo and Newton [and] also challenged our deepest intuitions about space, time and causation.'[44]

40   Nils Gilman, *Mandarins of the Future: Modernization Theory in Cold War America* (Baltimore: 2005).
41   Roger E. Backhouse and Philippe Fontaine, 'Introduction' to *A Historiography of the Modern Social Sciences*, ed. Roger E. Backhouse and Philippe Fontaine (Cambridge: 2014), p.3.
42   Dorothy Ross, 'Changing Contours of the Social Science Disciplines,' in T. M. Porter and Dorothy Ross (eds), *The Cambridge History of Science, volume 7: The Social Sciences* (Cambridge: 2003), p.229.
43   Mary Furner, *Advocacy and Objectivity: A Crisis in the Professionalization of American Social Science, 1865–1905* (Lexington: 1975); Thomas L. Haskell, *The Emergence of Professional Social Science: The American Social Science Association and the Nineteenth-Century Crisis of Authority* (Urbana: 1977); Dorothy Ross, *The Origins of American Social Science* (Cambridge: 1991); Reba Soffer, *Ethics and Society in England: The Revolution in the Social Sciences, 1870–1914* (Berkeley: 1978).
44   Lorraine Daston, 'When Science Went Modern,' *Hedgehog Review*, 18 (3) (Fall 2016).

At its foundation, the Royal Society cherished innovation but not renovation. Newton, after all, claimed he stood on the shoulders of giants and *hypotheses non fingo*, two statements that have been wildly misunderstood. But even more than a century later Ernst Mach instructed his colleagues in a policy of mental restraint. They should attend to what can be observed and not allow themselves to be unleashed into speculations about the unseen, the unobservable world of molecules and atoms.[45] And so into the twentieth century. Patrick Blackett recalled how Ernst Rutherford thought continental physicists 'do not seem the least interested to form a physical idea as a basis of Planck's theory.' They are, Rutherford said, 'quite contented to explain everything on a certain assumption, and not to worry their heads about the real cause of things. I must, I think say that the English point of view is much more physical and much to be preferred.' Blackett also quoted Einstein's view of the difference between his and Rutherford's approach to things. Einstein said: 'I concentrated on speculative theories, whereas Rutherford managed to reach profound conclusions on the basis of almost primitive reflection combined with relatively simple experiments.'[46]

Once optimistic, the very successes of positivism and the delights of observation encouraged for some a sense of morbidity. Even Max Weber, who cherished science as a vocation, echoed Tolstoy by thinking that modern science was meaningless because it led neither to God nor nature. '[C]ivilized man,' Weber wrote, 'placed in the midst of the continuous enrichment of culture by ideas, knowledge and problems, may become "tired of life."' '[B]ecause death is meaningless, civilized life as such is meaningless; by its very "progressiveness" it gives death the imprint of meaninglessness.'[47] Yet Weber's morbidity was not necessarily hopeless. As Karl Jaspers said of Weber, his research 'produced work that remained fragmented ... because of his boundless knowledge, because it is the purport of knowledge to flounder at the boundaries in order to set free the expanse for deeper truth in action and existence.'[48]

Niels Bohr, the founder of the Institute of Theoretical Physics at Copenhagen, called attention to the problem of empiricism and inter-pretation and, in the end, rejected the idea of a conflict between them. Bohr had a number of contacts with colleagues in Britain. Bohr knew J. J. Thomson when he was at the Cavendish Laboratory. He addressed

---

[45] Ernst Mach, *Die Principien der Wärmelehre: Historisch-kritisch entwickeit* (Leipzig: 1896), p.115, quoted by Daston, 'When Science Went Modern.'

[46] The quotations of Rutherford and Einstein can be found in Lord Blackett, 'Rutherford,' *Notes and Records of the Royal Society of London*, 24 (1) (August 1972): 58.

[47] Max Weber, 'Science as a Vocation,' in H. H. Gerth and C. Wright Mills (eds), *From Max Weber: Essays in Sociology* (New York: 1946), p.140.

[48] Quoted in John Patrick Diggins, *Max Weber: Politics and the Spirit of Tragedy* (New York: 1996), p.275.

the Warburg Institute in London soon after its transfer from Hamburg. He was a foreign fellow of the Royal Society. After addressing the International Congress of Anthropological and Ethnological Sciences,[49] he sent a copy of his address to A. V. Hill saying how much pleasure he felt in talking to Hill about the 'problems of life and science which units [sic] us.' He went on to hope that in his discussion with Hill of the relationship between human cultures he would learn whether Hill 'after reading it with some forbearance will find that it is [not] quite as unscientific as you thought first when I told you about it.'[50] In his lecture to the International Congress Bohr described anthropology and ethnography as 'sciences' of which he confessed to have no first-hand knowledge. Yet, he held, it may be of interest if he drew 'direct attention to the epistemological aspect of the latest development of natural philosophy and its general bearing on human problems.' It was difficult, he said, 'to distinguish sharply between natural philosophy and human culture':

> The physical sciences are, in fact an integral part of our civilization, not only because our ever increasing mastery of the forces of Nature has so completely changed the material conditions of life, but also because the study of these sciences has contributed so much to clarify the background of our existence.

Bohr compared the penetration of the atom to the exploration of the earth since the fifteenth century and the exploration of astronomers into outer space. The art, he called it, of physical experimentation has 'removed the last traces of the old belief that the coarseness of our senses would ever prevent us from obtaining direct information about individual atoms.' It has revealed that atoms themselves consist of 'still smaller corpuscles' that can be isolated and separately studied. Causation itself, 'so far considered the foundation for all interpretation of natural phenomena,' has fallen to the ground. Causation 'has proved too narrow a frame to embrace the peculiar regularities governing individual atomic processes.' There was an analogy, Bohr argued, between 'the analysis of atomic phenomena' and 'the characteristic features of the problem of observation in human psychology.' It was impossible to distinguish between the phenomena themselves and the perception of them. 'We all know the old saying that, if we try to analyse our own emotions, we scarcely possess them any longer.' He extended Heisenberg's

---

49   Bohr, Niels (1885–1962): father, Professor of Psychology, University of Copenhagen, a member of a wealthy Danish/Jewish family with strong banking and parliamentary connections; ed. Grammelholm Latin School, Copenhagen University and Cambridge University where he met J. J. Thomson at the Cavendish Laboratory; founded the Institute for Theoretical Physics at Copenhagen; Nobel Prize (1922); president of the Royal Danish Academy of the Arts and Sciences; foreign member of the Royal Society (1926); Order of the Elephant (1947); a postage stamp (1963) depicted Bohr, the hydrogen atom and the formula for the energy difference between any two hydrogen energy levels: $hv = e_2 - e_1$.
50   Niels Bohr to A. V. Hill, 4 July 1939, Churchill College, Cambridge, AVHL/II/410.

uncertainty principle to ethnography: physicists and ethnologists both distort the cultures they study by contact with them but also their own attitudes are changed by their contacts with what they study.[51]

In these ways Bohr laid waste to the concept of 'two cultures' and any crude distinction between empiricism and interpretation, as if there was somehow a conflict between accuracy and hermeneutics. All observation, he and others came to think, is theory-laden. All this, in the present, has given rise to a substantial literature about the anxieties of twentieth-century science. George Ellis and Joe Silk have written about defending 'the integrity of physics.' Ellis has written about the question of multiverses. Natalie Wolchover has written about the 'Fight for the Soul of Science.'[52] Some have called for the social sciences to abandon their pretensions of having positivistic knowledge.[53]

Peter Medawar launched several interventions against the naive, positivistic inductivism of the Royal Society's foundational myth.[54] These were intellectual disruptions suggesting the very unsteadiness of science itself. The first was Medawar's promotion of Karl Popper as a fellow of the Royal Society.[55] When Popper's *Logik der Forchung* (1934) was first published in English as the *Logic of Scientific Discovery* (1959) many, perhaps most, of the British scientific community greeted it, at best, with indifference, while Medawar, on the other hand, regarded Popper as the most prominent philosopher to speak on scientific questions. There were a number of features of Popper's life and career that made Medawar's proposal of him as a fellow of the Royal Society unattractive to the society's fellows. Born an Austrian Jew and educated in Vienna, he and his way of thinking could be dismissed as unBritish. Popper had difficulties gaining positions in the philosophical establishment because, according to Gilbert Ryle,

[51] Niels Bohr, 'Natural Philosophy and Human Cultures,' *Nature*, 143 (18 February 1939): 1–4, 6, 10–11. The copy I examined is in Churchill College AVHL/II/4/10.
[52] George Ellis and Joe Silk, 'Defend the Integrity of Physics,' *Nature*, 516 (18) (25 December 2015); George F. R. Ellis, 'Does the Multiverse Really Exist?' *Scientific American*, 392 (2) (August 2011); Natalie Wolchover, 'A Fight for the Soul of Science,' *Quanta Magazine* (2016).
[53] Michael Lind, 'Let's Abolish Social Science: A Proposal for the New University,' *The Smart Set* (August 2015).
[54] Medawar, Peter (1915–1987): father, a Brazilian businessman of Lebanese extraction; ed. Marlborough and Magdalen College, Oxford, first-class honours in zoology (1936); DSc (1947); senior-demi at Magdalen; senior research fellow, St John's College, Oxford; fellow by special election of Magdalen; Mason Professor of Zoology, Birmingham University (1951–1962); Jodrell Professor of Zoology and Comparative Anatomy, University College, London; Director, National Institute for Medical Research, Mill Hill (1962–1971); worked in the Medical Research Council Clinical Research Centre, Harrow (1971–1986); FRS (1949); CBE (1958); knighted (1965); CH (1972); OM (1981); Nobel Prize (1960); member, Theoretical Biology Club; President of the British Association for the Advancement of Science (during which he suffered a stroke while reading the lesson at the Association's service in Exeter Cathedral).
[55] See Neil Calver, 'Sir Peter Medawar: Science, Creativity and the Popularization of Karl Popper,' *Notes and Records of the Royal Society*, 67 (2013): 301–314.

he 'had a reputation for being rather intolerant and overbearing with his students and resentful if their opinions differed radically from his own.' Popper visited with Medawar at Birmingham to discuss the problems of Popper's personality. Medawar reassured him and shortly thereafter the London School of Economics appointed him to its Chair of Logic and Scientific Method.[56]

Popper was as far from being a bench scientist as it was possible to be. But especially Popper's intellectual disposition – the hypothetical-deductive system – was at odds with the Royal Society's orthodox inductivism. According to Medawar, who took up and clarified these views, Popper understood how imagination and critical reasoning were essential components of scientific methodology. As Medawar put it:

> All advances of scientific understanding, at every level, begin with a speculative adventure, an imaginative preconception *of what be true* – a preconception which always, and necessarily, goes a little way (sometimes a long way) beyond anything which we have logical or factual authority to believe in. It is the invention of a possible world, or of a tiny fraction of that world. The conjecture is then exposed to criticism to find out whether or not that imagined world is anything like the real one. Scientific reasoning is therefore at all levels an interaction between two episodes of thought – a dialogue between two voices, the one imaginative and the other critical; a dialogue, if you like, between the possible and the actual, between proposal and disposal, conjecture and criticism, between might be true and what is in fact the case.[57]

Such were the views Medawar promoted and articulated to defend Popper's conceptions of the nature of science and its workings to promote Popper's candidacy as a fellow of the Royal Society.[58] These defences worked in two complementary directions. They broke the strictures of Huxleyian inductionism to liberate the study of the natural world from its narrowness. Medawar wrote: 'Isolation is over; we all depend upon and sustain each other':

> As to scientists' becoming ever narrower and more specialized: the opposite is the case. One of the distinguishing marks of modern science is the disappearance of sectarian loyalties. Newly graduated biologists have wider sympathies today than they had in my day, just as ours were wider than our predecessors. At the turn of the century an embryologist could still peer down a microscope into a little world of his own. Today he cannot hope to make head or tail of

---

[56] Peter Medawar, *Memoirs of a Thinking Radish: An Autobiography* (Oxford/New York:1988), p.114.

[57] Peter Medawar, 'Science and Literature: Perspectives in Biology and Medicine,' the Romanes Lecture given at the Sheldonian Theatre, Oxford, published in *Encounter* (January 1969): 532–533.

[58] Peter Medawar, 'Hypothesis and Imagination,' *Times Literary Supplement* (25 October 1963); 'Two Conceptions of Science,' the Henry Tizard Memorial Lecture, *Encounter* (143) (August 1965) [these last two lectures are reprinted in Peter Medawar, *The Strange Case of the Spotted Mice and Other Classic Essays on Science* (Oxford/New York: 1996), pp.12–32, 59–71]; *Induction and Intuition in Scientific Thought* (London: 1969).

development unless he draw evidence from bacteriology, protozoology, and microbiology generally; he must know the gist of modern theories of protein synthesis and be pretty well up in genetics.[59]

At the same time Medawar's articulation of Popperian hypothetico-deductivism created new intellectual space for what he regarded as a firmer foundation for the work of the Royal Society.

At the same time he was promoting Popper's claim for fellowship in the Royal Society, Medawar deployed the same intellectual preconceptions against what he regarded as Lord Rothschild's 'injudicious advocacy', his 'Think Tank' to reconstruct the funding of the Research Councils into a customer's–contractor's guide to direct research.[60] Rothschild, polished and urbane – a scientist himself, FRS and a member of the Hardy Society at Cambridge – was a friend of Medawar's who recuperated in Rothschild's house in Bermuda, fortified by martinis and games of backgammon. But Rothschild had spent many years in business and was convinced of the power of market forces, a view to which some members of the Royal Society might be receptive if they felt utility added to the legitimacy of their science. Medawar, because of his stroke, was prevented from taking up the post of President of the Royal Society. His place was taken by Alan Hodgkin, who advanced the Royal Society's resistance to Rothschild's policy on the grounds of its being rushed though without adequate consultation.[61] Medawar's objection to the Rothschild report was intellectually deeper and rested on Popper's epistemological principles. Popper and Medawar were convinced of the unity of science and, therefore, deplored Rothschild's distinction between pure and applied science as an anachronism harking back to earlier times and out of keeping with recent intellectual (that is to say, Popper's) developments. As Medawar put it to Alan Hodgkin:

> The hard and fast distinction between pure and applied science is a quaint relic of the days when it was widely and authoritatively believed that axioms and generative ideas of some privileged sciences (the 'Pure' Sciences strictly so called) were known with certainty by intuition or revelation, while the Applied Sciences grew out of merely empirical observations concerning 'matters of fact

---

[59] Printed in Medawar, *The Strange Case of the Spotted Mice*, p.61.

[60] Medawar, *Memoirs of a Thinking Radish*, p.160; for a full discussion of this incident see Neil Calver and Miles Parker, 'The Logic of Scientific Unity?: Peter Medawar, the Royal Society and the Rothschild Controversy', *Notes and Records of the Royal Society*, 70 (1) (20 March 2016): 83–100; Tessa Blackstone and William Plowden, *Inside the Think Tank: Advising the Cabinet, 1971–1983* (London: 1988); Kenneth Rose, *Elusive Rothschild: The Life of Victor, Third Baron* (London: 2003), pp.173–194, esp. 182–184.

[61] In retrospect Hodgkin came to feel its haste was not altogether a bad thing because haste prevented 'a prolonged debate [that] would have inhibited many normal scientific activities at the Royal Society and elsewhere': Hodgkin, *Chance and Design*, pp.383–386.

or existence.' The distinction between pure and applied science persisted in Victorian and Edwardian times as the basis of a class distinction between activities which did or did not become a gentleman.[62]

Medawar opposed Rothschild's imposition on twentieth-century science of what some might regard as a class-based characterisation of the past in the form of a customer–contractor spur to research. This, in his view, would damage science itself, and indeed all intellectual work, because it refused to accept the way in which imagination and criticism were both, and at the same time, the shaping force of all research.

Quantum mechanics, relativity theory, now string theory, by necessarily abandoning the search for explanations in what is merely observable, measurable and classifiable, opened the way to ponder deeper and denser mental spheres. Bence Nanay, Professor of Philosophy at the Centre for Philosophical Psychology at the University of Antwerp and Senior Research Associate at Peterhouse, has been granted €2 million by the European Research Council to study 'things you don't see.' Roger Penrose has spent no little time studying non-mathematical algorithms to unlock the mysteries of consciousness. Arthur Eddington recognised that since knowledge of the natural world was elastic the study of it, therefore, must be plastic as well. In his lecture at Swarthmore in the United States in 1929 (where as a Quaker speaking to other Quakers) he posed the subject, as his title suggested, 'Science and the Unseen World.' He said '[m]ind is the first and most direct thing in our experience; all else is remote inference.' The most massive change in his time, Eddington said, 'is that we are no longer tempted to condemn the spiritual aspect of our nature as illusory.' The remote inferences of which he spoke could only be expressed by symbols. With the methods of physics, he said, 'we reach only a symbolic description.' Physics no longer identifies reality with concreteness. 'Materialism in its literal sense is long since dead,' he observed. The mental and spiritual nature of human beings makes it possible to transcend physics:

> The environment of space and time and matter, of light and colour and concrete things, which seem so vividly real to us is probed deeply by every device of physical science and at the bottom we reach symbols. Its substance has melted into shadow. None the less it remains a real world if there is a background to the symbols – an unknown quantity which the mathematical x stands for.

The 'stirring of consciousness' gives meaning to the symbols. 'Symbolically it is at the end, but looking behind the symbolism it is the beginning.'[63] A. D. Ritchie, who gave the first Eddington Memorial Lecture in 1947, pointed to some of the difficulties Eddington raised. The statement $2 \times 3 = 6$ is certainly

---

[62] Medawar to Hodgkin, 31 December 1971, Royal Society/ARF/879 quoted in Calver and Parker, 'The Logic of Scientific Unity?': 94.
[63] Arthur Eddington, *Science and the Unseen World* (London: 1920), pp.21–22, 23–25, 31–32.

true. But it is true to the extent that it describes the relations between two and three. We still know nothing about what '2,' '3,' much less what 'x' or '=' mean.[64] They are symbols that can be used to represent certain entities but what those symbols represent, in themselves, remains a mystery.

Cyril Hinshelwood, who became president of the Royal Society, gave the Eddington Memorial Lecture in 1961, and echoed Eddington's conception of the physical world as a world of shadows expressed symbolically:

> The behaviouristic description in terms of information and response does not however do justice to the richness of the visual world as experienced in their consciousness by men. This world exists in its own right, and though conditioned by external reality is not identical with it. It differs probably in some degrees from one individual to another, as may be inferred by elaborate cross-checking of their several descriptions of it.[65]

Unsurprisingly, since he was a painter himself,[66] Hinshelwood drew on his knowledge of art and artists in his discussion of those external and internal worlds. Art and studies of the natural world had, in his view, similar origins. Nature might smile on both but 'she has not given herself entire.' Both art and science were gripped by 'the instinct to inquire "why" and "how" when confronted by the phenomena of nature.' Great theories about the natural world, while they lend themselves to quantitative statements, always contain qualitative values. Language cannot present the external world; it can only symbolise it. The same, Hinshelwood held, was true of mathematical formulae. He denied some sort of complete distinction between subjectivity and objectivity:

> Science and poetry are each in fact both subjective and objective. The construction of an image of reality in terms, say, of the so-called wave functions familiar to physicists is at least as subjective in the highly important sense that it only conveys satisfaction to certain kinds of mind, while to others, even to some capable of the technical operations of mathematics, it means nothing. It certainly is a convention, a schematic ordering of the world no more inherently real than a poetic simile.

The separation of studies of the natural world from studies of humane letters is, he felt, 'the falsest of false dichotomies.' To ignore any aspect of the whole is

[64] A. D. Ritchie, *Reflections on the Philosophy of Sir Arthur Eddington* (Cambridge: Cambridge University Press, 1948), pp.18–19.

[65] Cyril Hinshelwood, *The Vision of Nature* (Cambridge: 1961), pp.9–10.

[66] Hinshelwood's entire career was spent at Oxford but on his retirement he removed himself to the small house in Chelsea he had shared with his mother until her death. There he rather happily painted the streets and parks of London and enjoyed his recordings of Wagner's music and his collection of Chinese porcelain and Eastern rugs.

to impoverish it: without poetry it loses colour, [and] without science it loses structure and coherence.'[67]

In sum, then, the Royal Society in the twentieth century protected its mental frontiers by shunting off the social sciences except in their more austere forms and, to that extent, preserved its observation–verification orthodoxy. Yet, as the writings of Medawar, Eddington and Hinschelwood show, they increasingly questioned the narrowness of Huxleyian experimentalism – observation, classification, measurement – and opened their studies to wider methodological and mental possibilities. Further, the fissiparousness of natural knowledge did not drive them into disciplinary isolation. As Medawar pointed out, the varieties of scientific experience pitched those devoted to the study of the natural world towards the making of greater and different mental connections, richer and denser than the intellectual connections of their intellectual forerunners.

In 1965 Mortimer Wheeler, the archaeologist and the then Secretary of the British Academy (he was both FBA and FRS), wrote to C. P. Snow inviting him to propose the toast to the British Academy at its annual dinner. As Wheeler explained, it was the function of the academy 'to represent the Humanities as the Royal Society represents the Sciences.' As he explained further, the academy was 'founded at the beginning to the present century, largely on the representation of the Royal Society at a time when, for administrative purposes at any rate, it was thought desirable to separate the two cultures.'[68] For Wheeler to dismiss the separation of the British Academy from the Royal Society as a matter of simple administrative exigency was perhaps too to much of an oversimplification of their histories. Both the Royal Society and the British Academy promoted and protected subjects that were aspirational. That is, the subjects of both societies were always incomplete and never achieved, nor ever could achieve any kind of final realisation that would meet the ambitions of certainty.[69] Incompleteness of this sort produces both feelings of hope and fear and prevents consistency. As Richard Rorty has pointed out, the subjects of neither society were neither natural kinds nor unnatural kinds; they were heterogeneous kinds that are stabilised only in particular configurations during processes of symbolic meditation.[70] Rather than finding sharp or single boundaries between their subjects, as Charles Taylor indicated, fellows

---

[67] Hinshelwood, *The Vision of Nature*, pp.11–12, 20, 23, 28, 32–33.

[68] Mortimer Wheeler to C. P. Snow, 1 March 1965, University of Texas, Ransome Center, C. P. Snow Ms. 62/11.

[69] For one meditation on aspirationality see Stefan Collini, Donald Winch and John Burrow, *That Noble Society of Politics: A Study of Nineteenth-Century Intellectual History* (Cambridge: 1983), p.3.

[70] Richard Rorty, 'Science and Solidarity,' in J. Nelson, A. Megill and D. McCloskey (eds), *Language and Argument in Scholarship and Public Affairs* (Madison:1987), pp.38–52.

of both the Royal Society and the British Academy formed these subjects through social and professional procedures and practices as they responded to collaborative and competitive situations.[71] Robert Oppenheimer, in his Reith Lectures of 1953, described the house of learning as 'so vast that there is not and need not be complete concurrence on what its chambers store and [where] those of neighboring mansions begin.'[72]

This is why members of the Royal Society's Council were nonplussed when they went to a conference at Weisbaden in 1892 to establish an International Association of Academies and discovered their continental colleagues expected them to form an association that would include, in the grand tradition of *Wissenchaft*, scholars of both the natural world and literary learning. They were no less nonplussed when they threw this question to the Royal Society generally and discovered they could reach no agreement about how to incorporate, in a common society, themselves and their literary brethren. Throwing up their hands, they left it to their literary colleagues themselves to form, 'from the standpoint of national prestige,' an association that would establish and defend the reputation of British literary scholarship.[73]

Left to themselves, people of literary learning decided who and what subjects would be included in the central temple of scholarship for learned letters in the twentieth century. As a survey of the presidents and members of its council in the first half of the twentieth century show, the British Academy was littered with men (and they were men until the middle of the twentieth century) marked by distinction. There were professors: Anthony Ashley Bevan, distinguished for his knowledge of Hebrew, of Old Testament literature, and Sanskrit; Bernard Bosanquet (though he resigned the chair of moral philosophy at St Andrew's University when he found lecturing incompatible with original work); Thomas William Rhys Davids, Professor of Comparative Religion at Manchester; Charles Harding Firth, Regius Professor of Modern History at Oxford; Francis Cornford. There were public figures who could also claim intellectual distinction: Balfour, Haldane, Courtney Ilbert, H. A. L. Fisher (who was both FRS and PBA). There were those who commanded attention because of their prominence in such societies as the British Museum: Maunde Thompson and Frederic Kenyon. They did not ignore a scattering of clergymen such as William Ralph Inge, Dean of St Paul's. But even at its foundation the British Academy was riven by feelings of corporate insecurity as its founders struggled with the question of who should belong. The Prothero papers in the Royal Historical Society archive at University College, London contain lists of names of prospective fellows culled from such volumes

---

[71] Charles Taylor, *Defining Science: The Rhetoric of Demarcation* (Madison: 1996), p.5 ff.
[72] J. Robert Oppenheimer, *Science and Common Understanding* (New York: 1966), p.84.
[73] [James Rivington, ed.] *The British Academy, 1902–2002: Some Historical Documents and Notes* (London: 2002), p.30.

of reference as 'Who's Who.' One list includes as those to be admitted: Alfred Lyall, Joseph Wright, Bradley, Bosanquet and Sidney Lee; but Andrew Lang and Sidney Colvin are stricken off. At a meeting of the general organisation committee on 19 November 1901 Janes Ward's name was added to the list and John Morley's was considered but not agreed to.

George Prothero, formerly professor of history at Edinburgh and later a successor to his brother, Lord Ernle, as editor of the *Quarterly Review*, felt the founding fellowship was too limited. While he favoured a 'high scientific standard,' he wished to avoid 'narrowness and pedantry.' The lists, he felt, were 'too professional, too specialist, on the whole too academic' to win general public acceptance. Mr Gladstone, had he been alive still, 'whatever may be the scientific value of his Homeric studies,' should surely have been on their list. John Seeley 'added little to the sum of positive historical knowledge' but an academy that would exclude him would have a poor chance of recognition. And what about the poets and the critics? Surely these would have to be counted among those who belonged to a society of 'letters?' How were those whom Stefan Collini called 'public moralists' to be fitted into whatever intellectual scheme the founders decided upon?[74] These belonged to a class of scholars Prothero felt had been ignored. Essayists and critics 'distinguished for knowledge and scientific method, and grasp of principle as well as literary power,' should not be excluded. 'Literary skill, the art of composition and exposition,' he argued, 'is of the highest importance in scientific work in those subjects we have agreed to recognize.' The academy, Prothero felt, should not 'sever itself too completely from those writers who have won a deserved reputation by mature and original reflection about facts rather than by industry and acuteness in the discovery of them.' Among those Prothero wished to admit on 'purely scientific grounds' were Frederick Furnivall, Alfred Lyall, Goldwin Smith and Edward Tylor. Among essayists and critics whom Prothero would admit were Canon Alfred Ainger, Sidney Colvin and Frederic Harrison.[75] When other founders rebuffed his more expansive plans, Prothero refused to become a charter fellow though he was elected shortly thereafter.[76]

Since fellows of the British Academy always recognised that election to their society should be based on candidates' intellectual achievements, and they realised that such were accomplished only late in their careers, they were, early on, plagued by fears that their society would be a geriatric one. John William Mackail, the classical scholar, literary critic and poet, pointed out in is presidential address in 1934 that there was a tendency of

---

[74]   Stefan Collini, *Public Moralists: Political Thought and Intellectual Life in Britain, 1850–1930* (Oxford: 1991).
[75]   Prothero Memorandum, 1901, Bodleian Library, Ms Bryce, 230, ff. 3–6.
[76]   Prothero Journal, 19 November 1901, 11 December 1901, King's College, Cambridge, GWP/1/7/1896–1902.

all academies to become 'encumber[ed] by Elder Statesmen.'[77] He quoted Prothero's memorandum of 1901, which argued for 'youthful and energetic' fellows. Mackail noted how in the elections to the academy in the period from 1931 to 1934 the average age of new fellows was over sixty; only 3 were under fifty, 9 were in their sixties and 7 were in their seventies. Preference might naturally be given to seniority, but this, Mackail argued, should be applied cautiously. It should not be forgotten, he observed, 'that election to the Academy is not only the conferment of honour, but the imposition of responsibility. Honors may be given too late: the call to more responsible duty is seldom made, can hardly be made, too early.'[78] David Ross, regarded as a moral realist, a non-naturalist and intuitionist, attempted to split the difference on the question of what age was desirable for election to the British Academy. In his presidential address in 1938 he pointed out how 'the claims of age against youth, and those of youth against age' frequently came up in discussions about prospective fellows.[79] Election to the fellowship, he noted, was regarded both 'as a recognition of services to learning already rendered [and] as an encouragement to further work.' He thought 'it best to make election depend simply on a certain standard of achievement, irrespective of whether it has taken few or many years to bring to pass.'[80]

The average age of new fellows in 1941, Sir John Clapham (who was sixty-eight at the time) noted, was 53.6, and two were still in their forties.[81]

[77] Mackail, John William (1859–1945): father, a Free Church minister in Scotland; ed. Ayr Academy, Edinburgh University, Balliol College, Oxford when Jowett was master; regarded as the most brilliant undergraduate of his time, first class in classical moderations (1879) and *literæ humaniores* (1881); he got the Hertford (1880), the Ireland (1880), the Craven (1882) and the Derby (1884) university scholarships; he got the Newdigate Prize (1881) for a poem on Thermopylæ; Fellow of Balliol (1882); he took a place in the education department of the Privy Council (1884–1919) of which he was appointed assistant secretary (1903) and played an important part in establishing a secondary education system; Professor of Poetry at Oxford (1906–1911); FBA (1914), PBA (1932–1936); OM (1935); though reticent about his beliefs, he was always suave, courteous and an interesting talker.

[78] J. W. Mackail, 'Presidential Address, 11 July 1934,' *Proceedings of the British Academy.* (1934): 19–20.

[79] Ross, William David (1877–1971): ed. Royal High School, Edinburgh, University of Edinburgh, Balliol College, Oxford; lectureship at Oriel College, Oxford, Fellow of Oriel (1902); joined the army (1915) and served in the Ministry of Munitions; White's Professor of Moral Philosophy (1923–1928); Provost of Oriel College (1929–1947); Vice-Chancellor of Oxford (1941–1944); Officer of the Order of the British Empire (1918); Knight Commander of the Order of the British Empire (1938).

[80] Sir David Ross, 'Presidential Address,' *Proceedings of the British Academy* (1938): 23.

[81] Clapham (Sir) John Harold (1873–1946): father, a jeweller and silversmith; mother, daughter of an accountant in Manchester; ed. Leys School in Cambridge (where he distinguished himself in games), King's College, Cambridge; first class in the Historical Tripos (1895); Professor of Economics, York College (soon to become the University of Leeds) in 1902; Fellow of King's College (1908–1946); first Professor of Economic History (1928–1938); Vice-Provost of King's (1933–1943); FBA (1928); knighted (1943); served on the Board of Trade in the First World War; a mountaineer and vice-president of the Alpine

Clapham welcomed this. Yet he feared the academy ran the danger of having a fellowship who having done their best work might not be 'disposed or perhaps able to take an active part' in the academy's affairs. Kenyon and Montague James, he noted, had been elected at about the age of forty. This he considered was necessarily rare but he hoped that electors would aim themselves towards the selection of new fellows who were about the age of fifty.[82] Clapham called for 'young blood' and appealed to the electors in the several sections of the academy to put forward candidates 'of appropriate immaturity.' The next year he reckoned the average age of new fellows to be 53.6. The mean age of two fellows put forward by the economics section was 'not quite 41,' which is what kept the average so low.[83] Clapham also expressed hope that the academy would elect women. When Beatrice Webb, the then sole female fellow of the academy, died in 1943 he was grateful that a woman replaced her and hoped that others would follow.[84]

The status and reputation of the British Academy rested in very large part on what George Prothero called 'those subjects which we have agreed to recognize.'[85] They thought long and hard about the scope of their studies and how to organise them. When James Bryce, as President of the British Academy in 1917, surveyed the work of the sciences of nature the vista was great. For students of the natural world the future prospect seemed infinite. 'The more they learn about nature the more they can foresee to be learnt. Every discovery opens a path to fresh discoveries.' Then he turned to their own studies. How do matters, he asked, 'stand with ourselves who have for our subject the thoughts and acts of man. Does a like vista of endless progress stretch before us?'[86] To some extent status anxiety and fear rested on their feelings of inferiority when compared to the Royal Society, which had – as has been shown – shunned them in the early going. Arthur Balfour, a founding fellow and later PBA, thought the British Academy, if it could achieve the position of the Royal Society, 'would be a great national advantage.' He wished to give it 'all due encouragement.' But as prime

---

club; supported the Liberal Party and Asquith's social reforms; his interest in economic history was always associated with his concern for contemporary issues but he regarded historical writing as a scientific activity detached from practical applications; robust in his *Quellenkritique,* his prose style has been called 'racy and vigorous,' if somewhat flawed in his later years by a tendency towards mannerism.

[82]   J. H. Clapham, 'Presidential Address, 9 July 1941,' *Proceedings of the British Academy,* 27 (1941): 20–21.

[83]   J. H. Clapham, 'Presidential Address, 15 July 1942,' *Proceedings of the British Academy,* 28 (1942): 15–16.

[84]   J. H. Clapham, 'Presidential Address, 14 July 1943,' *Proceedings of the British Academy.* 29 (1943): 16. Clapham strongly disapproved of the Webbs's book on the Soviet Union, but not because he disapproved of their support for the Soviet experiment ('the wind of appreciation must blow where it listeth'), but because they lacked the Russian language.

[85]   Prothero Memorandum, 1901, Bodleian Library Ms Bryce 230, f. 5.

[86]   James Bryce, 'The Next Thirty Years,' *Proceedings of the British Academy,* 8 (1917–1918): 4–5.

minister it was clear to him 'if we have any money to expend on Science and Learning, it is more required by such Institutions as the National Physical Laboratory rather than the Academy.'[87]

Feelings somehow persisted by scholars of literary learning that they were less intellectually gifted than fellows of the Royal Society. To which John Clapham, when President of the British Academy in 1945, protested: 'groups might be found within the Royal Society not superior in intellectual quality or achievement' to those in the British Academy. 'There may not be in the country from three to four times so many distinguished Naturalists as distinguished from Humanists.'[88] Wartime austerity and wartime distractions, of course, had taken a toll on intellectual life. Edgar Wind, acting on behalf of the Warburg Institute, approached the Rockefeller Foundation in New York with a scheme to assist the publication of books in Britain. Fritz Saxl went up to Oxford to fetch books to be published with these funds, but he came up trumps. David Ross, the provost of Oriel, knew of no manuscripts that were ready for publication. Saxl approached Maurice Powicke (Regius Professor of Modern History at Oxford from 1928 to 1947) and Vivian Galbraith (then Professor of History at Edinburgh and later Director of the Institute of Historical Research and Regius Professor of Modern History at Oxford from 1947) to get their suggestions for books to be published. Saxl lamented: 'It is heartbreaking that even the people who are not engaged on war are unproductive. There is no stimulus for them to work.'[89] And after the war Harold Idris Bell, in his addresses to the British Academy, raised the criticism that British contributions to learning compared unfavourably to those in other countries.[90] Some critics, Bell felt, regarded the 'main function of Fellows to write obituary

[87] Memorandum by the Prime Minister, [17 April] 1904, in Regard to the Question of a Grant to the British Academy, Balfour Papers, British Library, Add. Ms. 49856, f. 84.

[88] John Clapham, 'Presidential Address, 11 July 1945,' *Proceedings of the British Academy*, 31 (1945): 16.

[89] Fritz Saxl to Raymond Klibansky, 29 July 1941, Warburg Institute Archives, General Correspondence.

[90] Bell, Harold Idris (1879–1967): father, a chemist; ed. Nottingtham High School, Oriel College, Oxford, first class in classical moderations (1899) but barely missed a first in *literae humaniores* (1901); more important than his time at Oxford was his year at Hanover, Halle and Berlin where Wilamowitz-Moellendoft introduced him to the rigorous methods of scholarship; assistant in the manuscript department of the British Museum where he collaborated with Kenyon on Greek papyri (1903); deputy keeper (1927); keeper (1929–1944); honorary reader in papyrology, Oxford (1935); FBA (1932); OBE (1920); CB (1936); knighted (1946); President of the Society for the Promotion of Roman Studies (1937–1945); President of the International Association of Papryologists (1947–1955); President of the Classical Association (1955); found additional imaginative range in his fascination for Welsh poetry and literature services for which he was awarded the Cymmrodorion Medal (1946); President of the Cymmrodorion Society (1947); admitted to the Gorstedd as a druid (1949); a life-long supporter of the Labour Party; an agnostic for much of his life but after retirement from the British Museum in 1944 moved to Wales and played an important role as a member of the governing body of the Church of Wales; his training as

notices of one another.' He regarded the academy's publications as insufficient and 'unworthy of a body like ours'. In the short term he attributed this want to the shortness of government support for the academy. In the longer term he attributed it to lower intellectual standards in the twentieth century. There was a 'terrible coarsening and hardening of moral fibre' everywhere and '[s] lovely usages of all kinds are corrupting one of the noblest parts of our British inheritance, the English language.' The function of the academy he averred, 'whatever the idols of the market-place may be,' was to uphold 'through all social and political vicissitudes the austere ideal of excellence.'[91]

Between the wars the British Academy struggled to find ways to organise its work and create an environment of intellectual stimulus. But there was widespread disagreement about the designs and what designs and exemplars were to be followed. Bryce in his address to the British Academy in 1917 asserted that '[w]e seem to need a new science to govern [our] work.'[92] Mackail quoted Lord Reay's presidential address, which referred to history, philology and 'kindred subjects' as 'objects of scientific pursuit.'[93] As late as 1947 Harold Idris Bell, then president of the British Academy, referred to an era of 'disinterested science, of knowledge for its own sake.'[94] The recurring use of the concept of 'science' in these discussions may have been a defensive gesture to claim the kind of authority and intellectual legitimacy the Royal Society held, or it may be a memory of an earlier *Wissenschaft* in which philology and studies of the natural world remained entangled, sharing common questions and common styles of procedure.[95] Deep into the nineteenth century *Wissenschaft* and 'science' were treated as commensurable terms and it was only later that German *Kultur*, with its deeper spiritual connotations, began to be contrasted with what some Germans assumed to be a more shallow materialist view of British research.[96] But as has been shown above, the ballast of science itself began to shift in the twentieth century as a result of relativity theory and

---

an austere scholar, it was said, controlled but did not inhibit a mercurial temperament and a lively imagination.

91   H. I. Bell, 'Presidential Address, 16 July 1947,' *Proceedings of the British Academy*, 33 (1947): 25; H. I. Bell, 'Presidential Address, 14 July 1948,' *Proceedings of the British Academy*, 34 (1948): 17.

92   Bryce, 'The Next Thirty Years': 7.

93   J. W. Mackail 'Presidential Address,' July 12 1933, *Proceedings of the British Academy*, 1933: 20.

94   Sir H. I. Bell, 'Presidential Address, 16 July 1947,' *Proceedings of the British Academy*, 1947, 33 (1947): 26.

95   Lorraine Daston and Glenn W. Most, 'History of Science and History of Philologies,' *Isis*, 106 (2) (June 2015): 378–390.

96   Denise Phillips, 'Francis Bacon and the Germans: From When "Science" Meant "*Wissenschaft*,"' *History of Science*, 53 (4) (2015): 378–394. For Gilbert Murray's discussion of these distinctions see his 'German Scholarship,' *Quarterly Review*, 233 (443) (April 1915): 330–339.

quantum mechanics,[97] and as Medawar, Popper, Eddington and James Jeans began to take a more elastic view of research. Jeans observed in his *Mysterious Universe* (1930), the last chapter of which is called 'Into Deep Waters':

> Today there is a wide measure of agreement, which on the physical side of science approaches near unanimity, that the stream of knowledge is headed toward a non-mechanical reality; the universe begins to look like a great thought than like a great machine.[98]

Still, in the subjects for which the British Academy took responsibility positivism lingered as in the practices William Beveridge fostered at the London School of Economics. The reasons for this are not hard to find. As Noel Annan pointed out, they are to be found in the long tradition of Lockean individualism and in the long arguments over Darwinism, which had been fought out on all sides by positivist arguments, that is, on evidence verification and on hypothesis credibility.[99] In these contests for professional authority and legitimacy positivist arguments held great sway because they were so successful.[100] But even in the 'sciences' that the British Academy promoted and protected there was a softening. J. P. Bury, who had declared in his inaugural lecture that history is 'a Science, no less and no more,' relented somewhat. He thought he was never doing his duty unless he changed his views at least every two years. 'In vindicating the claims of history to be regarded as a science,' he later said, 'I never meant to suggest a proposition so indefensible as that the presentation of the results of historical research is not an art, requiring tact and skill in selection and arrangement which belongs to the literary faculty.'[101]

So, as the founders of the British Academy and their successors sought to establish their intellectual territory and map it in some comprehensible way, they worked within a constantly shifting sphere of aspirations and ambitions. They had to stake out and defend areas of intellectual activity whose boundaries were uncertain and shifting. One of their tasks, they thought, was to stabilise it. At the outset they thought they could contain their knowledge in four sections: history and archaeology; philology;philosophy; jurisprudence and economics. Even in the early days, however, the founders felt this simple scheme failed to capture the richness of their studies and they elaborated it into seven sections: history and archaeology; philology; legal and political science;

---

[97] Lorraine Daston, 'When Science Went Modern,' *Hedgehog Review*, 18 (3) (Fall 2016).
[98] James Jeans, *The Mysterious Universe*, p.148.
[99] Noel Annan, *The Curious Strength of Positivism in English Political Thought* (Oxford: 1959), pp.10–11.
[100] Frank M. Turner, 'The Victorian Conflict between Science and Religion: A Professional Dimension,' in *Contesting Cultural Authority: Essays in Victorian Intellectual Life* (Cambridge: 1993), pp.171–200.
[101] Quoted in J. P. Whitney, 'The Late Professor J. B. Bury,' *Cambridge Historical Journal*, 2 (1926–1928): 192, 195.

economics; philosophy (which was further divided into ethics, metaphysics and psychology); oriental studies; and biblical criticism.

In making these substantive classifications, they also identified the scholars they thought matched them. Here they identified the usual prospective suspects. Under history, had he lived, Acton, but also Bury (naturally), and York Powell, but also, strangely enough, Morley and Rosebery, Maunde Thompson, Courthope, Montague James and Colvin. They listed, sensibly enough, Jebb and Bywater and Frazer under philology, but also Arthur Evans and the traveller and geographer Henry Fanshawe Tozer. (In a later list Tozer is put under archaeology.) They listed Anson, Dicey Maitland and Pollock under legal and political science. Under economics, naturally enough, they listed Marshall and Edgeworth but also Cunningham, the vicar of Great St Mary's. Balfour and Caird were listed as philosophers, but also Leslie Stephen and Frederic Harrison. Under psychology only James Ward. Rhys Davids and Archibald Sayce were listed under oriental studies, but also Flinders Petrie the Egyptologist. They classified Joseph Armitage Robinson, Samuel Rolles Driver and William Sanday as biblical critics.[102] In 1933 these sections grew to nine.[103] In 1946 there were ten sections: ancient history; medieval and modern history; biblical and ecclesiastical studies; oriental studies; classical literature and philology; philosophy; jurisprudence; economic and social science; archaeology; and the history of art.[104] In 2015 there were eighteen sections.

These listings and grouping suggest both intellectual differentiation and, therefore, conceptual unsteadiness. This perhaps is unsurprising given the aspirational character of these studies as well as their tendency, as all intellectual studies have, to fissiparousness. Therefore, there was a continued effort to corral these studies and their students into more convenient and more accurate forms. In 1934, for example, the Council of the Academy asked the chairmen of the three existing sections having the term 'archaeology' in their titles to consider whether or not there should be a separate section in archaeology and the history of art. These chairmen then canvassed the members of their sections as to their placement in the various sections. Arthur Hamilton Smith, who had been Keeper of Greek and Roman Antiquities in the British Museum, did not feel he could be 'of much use' in the section to which he had been appointed originally and was happy to be a member of the new section. Stephen Herbert Langdon, Professor of Assyriology at the University of Oxford, was also happy to be included in the new section though his first interest was in philology, his second interest was in Semitic religion, and

---

102 See the Prothero Papers, Royal Historical Society Archive, University College, London. Minutes of the Meeting of the General Provision Committee at the British Musuem, 19 November 1901 (Sir Edward Maunde Thompson in the Chair), printed in Rivington (ed.), *The British Academy, 1902–2002*, pp.12–13.
103 Mackail, 'Presidential Address, 12 July 1933,': 20–21.
104 John Maynard Keynes Papers, King's College, Cambridge, JMK/BA/1/177–178.

archaeology was only his third interest. Percy Gardner did not think the new arrangement of sections was an improvement but he agreed to join the new section. Arthur Evans was much more enthusiastic about the formation of a section on archaeology and art history. Henry Chadwick, who would become Dean of Christ Church and Master of Peterhouse, did not regard his interests as primarily archaeological but he agreed to have himself put down as a member of the archeological section. In fact he did not regard the sectional arrangement of periods and cultures as particularly fortunate and hoped someday the academy 'will see a way to establish a Section which will embrace all sides' of the studies of history, philology and archaeology. Alexander Hamilton Thompson, Professor of Medieval History at Leeds, agreed to join the new section but he wished to remain attached to the section on medieval and modern history, to which he had been appointed. Robert Ranulph Marett also wished to remain attached to the sections on ancient history and philosophy, but he wished to join the new section because his duties as pro-vice chancellor at Oxford had brought him into close touch with the fine arts and because his 'private enthusiasms' also tended in that direction.[105]

The question of the relationship between archaeology and the history of art rose again in 1950. Andrew Gow, fellow of Trinity College, Cambridge and then a university lecturer in classics, and others, who claimed to represent art historians, urged that art history was 'sui generis' and ought to have a section unto itself. He thought it a grave mistake to merge the art historians into the section on medieval and modern history. The largest of the schools for which the academy is financially responsible to the Treasury was the British School in Rome, Gow argued, and it was 'largely the explicit representation of the History of Art amongst the Academy's Sections that had enlisted the authorities of the School on the side of the new scheme.'[106] Unanimously, the members of Section X asked the council to separate archaeology from the history of art. The two elements in the section had found it difficult in practice to concur in making recommendations for fellowships: 'The two sides apparently feeling that their respective techniques are so different that they cannot form a judgement about each other's candidates.'[107]

From time to time the question arose of finding a place for the creative arts in the academy. In 1917 Andrew Bradley, Professor of English Language and Literature at Glasgow, proposed that the academy should appoint, to a separate section, 'representatives of *Belles Lettres*.' Courtenay Ilbert, Clerk of

[105] Arthur Hamilton Smith to Kenyon, 11 November 1934, Landon to Kenyon, 9 November [1934]; Percy Gardner to Kenyon, 10 November 1934; Arthur Evans to Kenyon 9 November 1934; Henry Chadwick, 11 Nov[ember] 1934; A. Hamilton Thompson to Kenyon, 9 November 1934; Marett to Kenyon, 9 November 1934, BAA/SEC/2/3/12.

[106] Gow to the President of the British Academy, Minutes of the Advisory Committee, 12 July 1950, BAA/FEL/7/33.

[107] Mortimore Wheeler to Goronwy Edwards, 26 June 1950, BAA/FEL/7/33.

the House of Commons, opposed the proposal because it was 'outside the terms of reference' of the academy. 'Science and scientific study,' he said, 'are the only objects which the Academy is intended to promote':

> A literary genius, a creative artist, however eminent, is not, as such, qualified to become a member of the Academy. Admission to our portals is reserved for the humbler class of students.[108]

T. A. Stephenson, in the Department of Zoology at University College, Wales and a fellow of the Royal Society, brought up the question in a different way in 1955. He wrote to Sir Goronowy Edwards, FBA and Director of the Institute of Historical Research, asking if the academy could provide a small grant for a book Stephenson was writing called *Science Looks at Art*. The Royal Society had provided a small grant itself but it was only a small grant because the book 'lies outside the direct field in which the Society usually gives financial support.' Stephenson considered himself both a practising painter as well as a professional biologist. Because his book lay on the borderline between the subjects taken up by the British Academy and the Royal Society, he considered it appropriate for funding since it 'constructs a link between scientific and aesthetic aspects of painting' and it 'does its best to be impartial' and was independent of 'personal opinions and tastes.' It was, Stephenson contended, based upon 'many years of personal experiment into the subject of design.' Mortimer Wheeler, the Secretary of the British Academy at the time, was sympathetic in his response to Edwards; however, the 'subject is liable to fall between two stools' and could hardly expect to find its place on the academy's stool.[109]

The question arose again in 1957 when Roy MacGregor-Hastings, of the Poetry Society of Australia, wrote asking about the policies of the British Academy concerning *Belles Lettres* and wondering whether the academy 'might not be like the *Academie Française.*' Mortimer Wheeler responded by saying that 'the problem is one we have never formally undertaken,' but the section on literature and philology might be able to render a judgement. Wheeler thought the French analogy could not be pressed too closely. 'There is, after all,' he wrote, 'a considerably greater elasticity about the English language and its punctuation than there is about the French.'[110]

David Ross, in his time as president, had found these classifications of learning overly clumsy and inadequate. The human mind, he said, 'is not in fact so much sectionalized as is the constitution of the Academy.' A scholar's work, he noted, frequently ventured over the range of subjects

---

[108] C. P. Ilbert, 'The Proposal to Create a Literary Section,' 14 February 1917, BAA/SEC/1/48/5.
[109] T. A. Stephenson to Goronwy Edwards, 22 February 1955; and Mortimer Wheeler to Edwards, 14 March 1955, BAA, FEL/7/33.
[110] Wheeler to MacGregor-Hastings, 18 June 1957, BAA/SEC/3/3/26.

taken up by more than one section. Sometimes a scholar might be found whose branch of research failed to lie within the reach of any section. Cases such as this would be unlikely to be brought forward by any section for election, yet the general contribution of such a scholar might justify election to the British Academy. Ross proposed to the council, which brought it forward to be ventilated by the General Annual Meeting in 1939, that from time to time, but only very rarely, to put up for election a candidate who no section had sent up.[111] The next year the council brought forth the name of Sir Donald Tovey, the pianist and music critic who was also said to have strong philosophical leanings towards astronomy and higher mathematics.[112] Ross assured the fellowship that such an action should be employed sparingly to 'add to the strength of our body.'[113] Robin George Collingswood, who had been appointed to the sections on ancient history, philosophy, and archaeology and the history of art, vigorously protested. Candidates for election, he argued, were to be judged by 'experts in a subject on which they can speak with authority.' Since there were fellows of the British Academy who were expert in Tovey's range of intellectual interest, his nomination was 'more than distasteful. It might almost be called an affront to conscience':

> As a mere amateur in music, therefore, whose work and whose opinions are very likely mistaken, I have to say that I do not think Sir Donald Tovey is [a] suitable candidate. I do not think his musical compositions up to the standard which the Academy set before itself in electing composers as such. My acquaintance with them is very small; but I am familiar with his completing the *Kunst der Fuge*, which I do not think a successful essay in the style of Bach; nor have I spoken about it with anyone who thought otherwise. I do not think his books about music are of such a quality as to justify his election. Having made it my business for many years to study what is written about the fine arts, I am better acquainted with these than with his music; but I will not load this communication with detail.[114]

It is not possible to know the fate of his nomination because Tovey died on the very day his name was put before the British Academy's fellowship.

---

[111] Sir David Ross, 'Presidential Address, 12 July 1939,' *Proceedings of the British Academy*, 25 (1939): 25–26.
[112] Tovey, Donald (1875–1940): father, an Apostle at Cambridge and an Eton Beak; ed. firstly at the feet of Sir Walter Parrat, the organist at St George's Chapel, Windsor and then Sir Hubert Parry; went up to Balliol as the first holder of the Francis Nettleship scholarship in music (1894); BA (1898) with classical honours; doctor of music (1921); honorary fellow of Balliol (1934); toured the Continent where he attracted the attention of Joachim and Richter; Reid Professor of Music at Edinburgh (1914); knighted (1935); according to Joachim Tovey was the most learned man in music who ever lived.
[113] Sir David Ross, 'Presidential Address, 10 July 1940,' *Proceedings of the British Academy*, 26 (1940): 22.
[114] R. G. Collingwood to Kenyon, 5 April [1940?] BAA/SEC/2/3/12.

These sometimes tortured discussions of intellectual differentiations raised the issue of knowledge's unity. As Kenyon had observed as early as 1921, the British Academy existed to create a 'Fellowship of Learning.' Now, he felt relieved to say, the conflict between science and theology had dissipated. 'Science is no longer so sure that it knows everything, and Theology realizes that in its own sphere Science can be respected.' Learning's world, Kenyon argued, had arrived at a 'period of reconstruction.' Without specialisation knowledge could not progress, he recognised, but specialisation may 'too easily turn to rivalry,' which risked the breakup of the 'family of learning.'[115] This anxiety about specialisation took greater force in the 1930s when the promotion of learning was hitched to the resistance to fascism. Mackail, in 1933, hoped to enlarge the 'scope of our activities toward humanism in its widest sense.' The British Academy is not an academy of art or letters, he said, but an 'Academy of Learning.' Recognising the fascist threat, Mackail thought the British Academy could 'render a greater service to humanity' if it worked against all threats 'menacing the free development of the human intellect.'[116] The next year he called attention again to the general purposes of the academy, which were to 'maintain a standard of learning' at a time when they were being 'flooded with shallow culture' creating a 'prison of the mind' in countries that had been centres of humane learning.[117] He rose to the same theme in 1935. Maintaining a 'standard of learning' would make it possible to 'preserve the continuity of civilization.' Is civilization, he asked, 'specialization carried into apparent futility?' The task of this 'Academy of Humane learning is not to destroy nor create, but preserve.' Its task, he concluded, 'is to connect the continuity of learning with the continuity of life.'[118]

Specialisation was always in tension with the British Academy's interest in preserving the unity of the knowledge over which they had custody. They were continually concerned with what should be preserved, what should be excluded and what should be included. This had as much to do with the identity of the scholars of these studies as with the identity of the studies themselves. The study of religion is a case in point. From 1919 to 1934 biblical criticism was coupled with archaeology. From 1935 to 1993 it was liberated into a section of its own as 'biblical, theological and religious studies.' Mortimer Wheeler, when he was secretary of the British Academy, brought it under fire in 1959 when he pondered 'the shape of our Academy' and thought the section was an anachronism. 'The association of dog collars with research,' he wrote, 'is surely nothing like as close nowadays as it was a half-century and more ago.'

---

115 Kenyon, 'The Fellowship of Learning,': 4–6.
116 Mackail, 'Presidential Address, 12 July 1933': 23, 28.
117 Mackail, 'Presidential Address, 11 July 1934,': 23–24.
118 Mackail, 'Presidential Address, 10 July 1935,' *Proceedings of the British Academy* (1935): 25–27.

He proposed to 'redistribute our Reverend Professors' among other sections. He regarded ecclesiastical history as an integral part of history and theology, and considered 'in any abstract sense' could not be separated from history and philosophy and even anthropology.[119] Wheeler returned to this theme in 1964. Biblical, ecclesiastical history and theology, he wrote, 'is, heaven preserve me, an echo of another world, and there is not a single member of this reverend group who could not be put elsewhere.'[120] From 1994 to 1998 it was collared to 'African and Oriental Studies' but after 1999 it was liberated again into a section on theology and religious studies.

Then, of course, there was the emergence and legitimisation of new studies. Alfred Marshall, who had been a founding fellow, reminded Sir Israel Gollancz, the then secretary of the British Academy, in 1914 that when the academy had been established the Royal Society had let it be known that they would no longer take 'responsibility for sciences related to man' and such studies as economics should be taken up by the academy. Yet, in Marshall's view, the academy had not taken up the task fully and was 'conspicuously weak in the representation of recent & present economic facts & the scientific methods of dealing with them.'[121] Furthermore, from 1919 to 1965, these intellectual arrangements were complicated by the connection of political studies to economic studies as an aspect of 'social science.' Therefore, in 1965 Section IX on Economics and Social Science considered a letter from Raymond Firth, Professor of Anthropology at the LSE, which proposed the separation of economics and to create a new section containing sociology, social anthropology and demography to which social psychology and social geography would be added. In agreeing to Firth's proposal the section justified its position by pointing to its difficulties in electing 'representatives of an ever-widening range of social sciences.' They expressed their feelings that the representation of these sciences was smaller than their importance warranted. The new section, they believed, would take on, as 'an essential part of its business,' the exploration of the representation 'of the social sciences from fields about which as yet little is known within the Section.'[122]

On 29 June 1965 the council convened a special meeting of the section on economics and social science, who recommended the creation of two separate sections: 'Economics and Economic History' and 'Social and Political Studies.' As political studies have been shaping in Britain, they reasoned, it is 'more natural for them to be associated with the sociologists than with the economists.' At the same meeting the members of the section

[119] Mortimer Wheeler to Maurice Bowra, 28 December 1959, BAA/FEL/8/6.
[120] Mortimer Wheeler to Sir George Clark, 7 August 1964, BAA/SEC/3/3/19.
[121] Alfred Marshall to Israel Gollancz, 24 February [19]14, BA/SEC/1/43.
[122] Minutes of the Council Meeting, 26 May 1965, BAA/SEC/3/3/22.

gave thought to demographers, statisticians and geographers. For purposes of allocating them to sections, they argued, these 'border-line subjects' could not 'be rigorously classified.' They had to 'have regard to persons rather than to specialisms as conventionally labelled.' Most contemporary work in demography they argued is of interest to economists and, therefore, most demographers should be placed together with economists. Yet, some demographers might have more shared interest with sociologists and might be classed with them or with both. As with statisticians, similarly, if their interest is in 'pure theory,' the Royal Society was the place for them. If their interest was in the application of statistics they could be classed with the economists or the sociologists or, again, with both. Some geographers, depending on their interests, might find places with the economists and others with the section on social and political studies. The special meeting of the section in 1965 thought no further definition of the scope of each section was necessary. 'Indeed, we would urge that any attempt to list the subjects would lead to unnecessary problems in the allocation of persons.'[123]

These twistings and turnings illustrate the difficulties of finding fixed places for learning and the learned in knowledge's map. On one hand, these were expressions of the robustness of the British Academy's obligation to form and reform the unity of knowledge for which they had responsibility. On the other hand, they were expressions of disciplinary differentiation that had no, or little, logical trajectory. Yet further, they were expressions of the illusion that knowledge might be tamed and controlled and, therefore, acquire authority and legitimacy within some apparently reasonable and coherent system. These were struggles for expressing the unique intellectual identities of these studies as well as the unique identities of the scholars who studied them. They expressed the essential tension between the claims of the new against the old, the conventional against the innovative, the tight against the loose, and the claims of structure against charisma.

Throughout, the fellows and presidents of the British Academy were aware how little support it received from the government. Kenyon pointed out that after the war, and after the academy was twenty years into its history, how Britain was the only country having an academy that was ill-supported by its government. The five academies composing the *Institut de France* received £28,000 (at pre-war rates of exchange) from the state; the three academies of Belgium received about £11,000; the Academy of Berlin received over £16,000; the Academy of Vienna, £9,000; the Academy of Munich, £5,000. These were all signs of the ill-regard in which the British Academy was held in British governing circles. This was, Kenyon found, a humiliation not only to the British Academy but to the country. At international conferences

123 Minutes of the Council Meeting, 20 October 1965, BAA/SEC/3/3/18.

to promote intellectual work Kenyon had to confess 'we have no funds and cannot pay our due share for joint undertakings.' British scholars, as individuals, might 'hold their own with scholars of other countries' but the inadequacy of funding from the state meant Britain had 'a reputation abroad for being indifferent to intellectual culture.'[124] Such indifference fed the feeling, or fear, of what has been the 'denial thesis,' that Britain had no intellectuals.[125]

State assistance came only slowly. In 1924 the government began to award an annual grant to the British Academy of £2,000. Even this, though, as Sir David Ross observed in 1937, 'compar[ed] unfavorable with grants made by other countries less rich than ours to their national Academies.'[126] Reduced during the Second World War, it rose to £5,000 in 1950. In 1958 the Rockefeller Foundation gave a grant of £6,000 for the British Academy to assess the possibilities of financial support for research in the humanities and the social sciences. The report that ensued, based upon international comparisons, made a strong case for the pressing needs of scholarship in Britain. In 1962 Sir Maurice Bowra announced to the Annual General Meeting the provision of a government grant of £25,000 with the promise it would rise to £50,000.[127] Yet, throughout, there were persistent fears about the lack of public recognition of the academy's work. As Kenyon had argued in 1921, the academy:

> will justify its existence if it is recognized not as a society claiming titular superiority over other societies, but as existing to serve and assist both societies and individuals by the weight of competent and disinterested opinion.

'To justify this confidence,' Kenyon went on, 'it must be an active body and not merely a name.'[128] The British Academy, even with its meagre resources, with its government grant diminished to £1,000 during the Second World War, deployed its finances to assist the Warburg Institute (£100 in 1942 and again in 1943), the British Institute of Philosophy (£75), the Royal Asiatic Society (£200 in 1942 and again in 1943), and Raymond Klibansky's *Corpus Platonicum* (£270).[129] Of course, with state support came state controls and interference. When Mortimer Wheeler met with Treasury officials in 1962 he came away with their view that the social sciences were already 'catered for in

---

[124] Sir F. G. Kenyon, KCB, 'Presidential Address delivered at the Annual General Meeting,' 21 June 1920, *Proceedings of the British Academy* (1919–1920): 33–34.

[125] Stefan Collini, *Absent Minds: Intellectual in Britain* (Oxford 2006), *passim*.

[126] W. D. Ross, 'Presidential Address, 14 July 1937,' *Proceedings of the British Academy*, 23 (1937): 23.

[127] [Rivington, ed.], *The British Academy*, pp.21–22.

[128] Sir F. G. Kenyon, 'The Fellowship of Learning': 6–7.

[129] Annual Report, *Proceedings of the British Academy*, 29 (1943): 5–6.

other Government fashions' and that '[i]n the circumstances they want us to scrub out the social sciences' from the British Academy's appeal.[130]

As some were aware, the purposes and objectives of the British Academy were unknown to others even in the learned world. At a Royal Academy dinner Sir David Ross sat next to an eminent member of the Royal Academy who asked him 'Where is *your* Gallery?' Ross had to explain to the academician that the British Academy was not a rival to the Royal Academy 'in its distinguished sphere' but was distinguished in its own way since six members of the British Academy had been appointed to the Order of Merit.[131] The next year Ross called to the academy's attention the upcoming meeting of *Union Académique Internationale* in London. He invited fellows of the British Academy to dine with the delegates from abroad to gain greater national and international recognition:

> We are all modest people and perhaps our modesty has prevented the Academy from being as well-known as it should be; it may be hoped that a public dinner may do something to attract attention, and even some of the benefactions of which we could make much use for the furtherance of knowledge. The success of the dinner naturally depends on there being a large attendance of our own membership.[132]

Clapham noted how in time of war it would be less likely for the British Academy to provide useful advice to the government than the fellows of the Royal Society, but after the war he hoped that now 'we as a body have some suggestions to make or information to supply that would be useful to those who direct the state.'[133] Not only might this promote national recognition but the revival of traditions of sociability after the war might repair the ruptures within the academy that the war had caused. The academy, Clapham observed, was 'not quite so much of a *societas*, not so much of a fraternity' as he would have wished, but he left it to future presidents and councils 'to revive our modest social gatherings and do whatever else they may think proper to bind us together.'[134]

Henry Sidgwick advised the young G. M. Trevelyan to leave the university and go to London if he wished to do creative work.[135] Trevelyan did and wrote his three Garibaldi volumes. A more elderly Trevelyan, after he returned to Cambridge as Regius Professor of History, advised the young Steven Runciman to leave the university if he wished to do creative work.[136] Runciman did and wrote his three

---

130 Mortimer Wheeler to Maurice Bowra, 21 February 1962, BAA/FEL/8/6.
131 Ross, 'Presidential Address, 14 July 1937': 23.
132 Ross, 'Presidential Address, 14 July 1937': 23.
133 Clapham, 'Presidential Address, 9 July 1941': 21.
134 Sir John Clapham, 'Presidential Address, 11 July 1945', *Proceedings of the British Academy* 31 (1945): 13.
135 G. M. Trevelyan, *An Autobiography and Other Essays* (London: 1949), p.21.
136 Minoo Dinshaw, *Outlandish Knight: The Byzantine Life of Steve Runciman* (London: 2016), p.205.

volumes on the crusades. The Royal Society and the British Academy in London outside the universities were havens for intellectual legitimacy and authority in the twentieth century. Unlike continental academies and learned bodies they were, until deep into their histories, independent of the state and of private patronage. Such autonomy left them institutionally weak. Their officers and members depended upon the universities and such institutions as the British Museum for positions that might have provided opportunities for intellectual synergism had they not been tied in the universities to examination bureaucracies or, in such institutions as the British Museum, tied to bureaucratic routines there. Yet, autonomy from the state and patronage enabled the Royal Society and the British Academy greater independence in guiding problem articulation, theory generation and the very handling of the crude stuff of information.

These institutions of the great and the good were riven by the politics of method. The Royal Society and the British Academy in the twentieth century continued to be shackled by certain mental habits of their ancestors. The Huxleyian method of empirical inductivism – observation, experiment, comparison, classification – persisted. These mental habits, of course, had been tremendously and ruthlessly successful. They had become what Gilbert Murray called 'inherited conglomerates.' As he pointed out, these mental habits had 'no chance of being true or even sensible,' but no society could exist without them or even seek to correct them without 'social danger.' Yet, Murray warned, by submitting to them 'we are simply hugging our prison walls.'[137]

On the other hand, the fellows of the Royal Society and the British Academy were not entirely indifferent or impervious to efforts to modify or even violate the observation–verification orthodoxies of Huxleyanism. The Royal Society rejected the human and social sciences except in their more austere forms such as the study of demography. However, they admitted Karl Popper to its fellowship and Peter Medawar was among those who promoted Popper's philosophy of science and opposed rigid positivist inductivism. Eddington and Jeans pointed out the theoretical possibilities that quantum research opened, possibilities that violated strict positivism. Einstein once confided to Otto Stern: 'You know, once you start calculating you shit yourself before you know it.' He complained '[s]ince the mathematicians pounced on the relativity theory I no longer understand it myself.'[138] Positivism itself has never been monolithic nor beyond change nor has it been conceptually clear. One study confuses notions of objectivity (called 'objectivist' in this telling) with positivism. This is a reminder of the ways in which the forms, disciplinary locations and intellectual sources require investigation.[139] Baconianism and Francis Bacon himself

[137] Gilbert Murray, *Greek Studies* (Oxford: 1946), pp.66–67.
[138] Quoted in Petro G. Ferreira, *The Perfect Theory* (Boston/New York: 2014), p.12.
[139] George Steinmetz, 'Introduction,' George Steinmetz (ed.) *The Politics of Method in the Human Sciences: Positivism and Its Epistemological Others* (Durham/London: 2005),

had come to be criticised and dethroned in the nineteenth century.[140] Huxley himself recognised how 'the invention of hypotheses based on incomplete inductions, which [Bacon] specifically condemns, has proved itself to be a most efficient, indeed an indispensable, instrument of scientific progress.'[141] Even fellows of the British Academy such as William Beveridge, under certain circumstances, were prepared to entertain non-positivist intellectual positions. When the Nazi scourge lashed out in 1933 and the Frankfurt Institut für Sozialforschung was forced to flee, Beveridge, despite his own methodological preferences, was prepared to take on board the Frankfurt Institut's library with its strong collection of Marxist materials. The project failed due to the strong objections of Lionel Robbins and Mrs Jessy Mair, not on methodological grounds but because they feared an association with the Frankfurt Institut would damage the LSE's reputation for political independence.[142] Harold Laski thought the LSE would become a communist institution and found the Frankfurt Institut's combination of Marxism and Freudianism 'particularly repulsive.'[143] Some praise has been laid upon students of the human sciences such as Zygmunt Bauman, for whom empirical evidence meant little but for whom imagination and intellectual vision meant everything.[144]

Mental habits do not change easily, especially when encased in formal institutional arrangements, even in looser ones as in the Royal Society and the British Academy. So even in the twenty-first century Thomas Nagel has had to remind us that materialism is not dead, that 'science does not progress by tailoring the data to fit a prevailing theory,' and that '[t]o say that there is more to reality than physics can account for is not a piece of mysticism.'[145] As mathematician Roger Penrose has pointed out, those physicists who are 'familiar with the puzzling and mysterious ways matter *actually* behaves' take a 'less classically mechanistic view of the world.'[146]

So, it remains to consider other sites and intellectual niches where charisma can operate and yield the fruits that curiosity, originality and research can produce. Therefore, this study now turns away from the large and the grand, the universities and the great learned societies, to the small and the transient,

---

pp.30–33. Novick himself (*That Noble Dream: the 'Objectivity Question' and the American Historical Profession*, pp. 28–29) misunderstands the Rankean conception of objectivity when he regards von Rankean insistence on both 'accuracy' and 'intuition' as 'ambiguous.'
[140]   Richard Yeo, 'An Idol of the Marketplace: Baconianism in Nineteenth-Century Britain,' *History of Science*, 23 (3) (1985): 251–298; Phillips, 'Francis Bacon and the Germans: Stories From When "Science" Meant "*Wissenschaft*"': 378–394.
[141]   T. H. Huxley, 'The Progress of Science' (1887) in C. Bibby (ed.), *The Essence of T. H. Huxley* (London, 1967), p.42.
[142]   Harris, *William Beveridge*, pp.289–290.
[143]   Quoted in Dahrendorf, *LSE*, p.293.
[144]   Neil Gross, 'Social Science Without Data,' *New York Times* Sunday Review (12 February 2017): 8.
[145]   Thomas, Nagel, 'Is Consciousness an Illusion?' *New York Review of Books* (19 March 2017): 34.
[146]   Roger Penrose, *Shadows of the Mind*, p.50.

to other confraternities of 'acknowledged peers'[147]: the Bloomsbury group, Solly Zuckerman's Tots and Quots, Joseph Needham's Theoretical Biology Club, the Warburg Institute, those aiding the scholars fleeing from Nazi Germany, and the intellectuals, experts, specialists and the new intellectual aristocracy that formed those confraternities.

[147] Charles Rosenberg, 'Towards an Ecology of Knowledge,' p. 444.

Chapter 3

Interstitial Societies

Closed politics. The politics of small groups, where person acted upon person. You saw it in any place where people were in action, committees of sports clubs, cabinets, colleges, the White House, boards of companies, dramatic societies. You saw it perhaps at something like its purest (just because the society answered to no one but itself, lived like an island) in the college in my time. But it must be much the same in somewhat more prepotent groups, such as the Vatican or the Politburo.

C. P. Snow[1]

[F]or there is assuredly no more effectual method of clearing up one's own mind on any subject than by talking it over, so to speak with men of real power and grasp who have considered it from a totally different point of view.

T. H. Huxley[2]

Each of us knows the great freedom sensed almost as a miracle, that men banded together for some definite purpose experience from the power of their common effort ... Each of us knows how much he has been transcended by the group of which he has been or is a part; each of us has felt the solace of other men's knowledge to stay his own ignorance, or other men's wisdom to stay his folly, of other men's courage to answer his doubts or his weakness.

J. Robert Oppenheimer[3]

IN the twentieth century, one might have thought, those diffuse and diverse learned bodies, those relics of the nineteenth century, might have been swallowed up in the maw of Weber's iron cage of bureaucracy. As Weber famously put it:

[1]   C. P. Snow, *Last Things* (London: 1970), p 124.
[2]   Quoted in T. Whittaker, 'Review of *Science and Culture and Other Essays* by Thomas Henry Huxley (London: 1881)', *Academy*, 21 (25 February 1882): 141.
[3]   J. Robert Oppenheimer, *Atom or Void: Essays on Science and Community*, preface by Freeman Dyson (Princeton: 1989), p.70.

The face of our times is characterized by rationalization and intellectualization, and above all by the 'disenchantment of the world.'

But Weber saved himself from himself. He added:

Precisely the intimate and most sublime values have retreated from public life either into the transcendental realm of mystic life or in the brotherliness of direct and personal human relations.[4]

What we find, therefore, in even modest attempts to understand the twentieth-century world of learning, research and scholarship, is that small and informal cognitive social units, far from disappearing or being swallowed up, have thriven in a series of unsystematic systems with deeply riven asymmetrical symmetries at the peripheries and in the interstices of mental life.

Maynard Keynes's case is instructive. He hatched and disseminated the revolution in economics with which his name is associated within the diverse clubs and societies to which he belonged.[5] He founded the Political Economy Club (known as the Keynes Club) in Cambridge in 1909. Meeting in his rooms at King's College in term time, members read papers, other members in an order determined by lot commented, and then Keynes summarised the discussion. Some members – Dennis Robertson, Richard Braithwaite, Frank Ramsey, Austin Robinson – became future collaborators. At the time Keynes published his *Treatise on Money* (1930) a remarkable group of economists – Richard Kahn, Joan Robinson, Austin Robinson, Piero Sraffa, James Meade – began meeting in Keynes's rooms in King's and then in the Old Combination Room in Trinity College.[6] They came to be called 'the circus' and served as a body of critics whose views shaped the formation of the *General Theory of Employment, Interest, and Money* (1936).[7]

In London, the Political Economy Club, dating from 1821, elected Keynes as a member in 1912. He travelled weekly, on Wednesdays, to dine and engage in discussions with them. He and Oswald (Foxy) Falk founded the Tuesday Club as a dining club for officials, for men from the City and for financial journalists. They met in a private room in the Café Royal on a monthly basis to discuss monetary economics. Keynes became a member of the Other Club in 1927. Founded by Winston Churchill (because THE CLUB would not have him) the Other Club met on alternate Thursdays during the parliamentary session. More

4   Max Weber, 'Science as a Vocation,' in H. H. Gerth and C. Wright Mills (eds), *From Max Weber: Essays in Sociology* (London: 1947), p.155.
5   Richard Davenport-Hines, *Universal Man: The Seven Lives of John Maynard Keynes* (London: 2015), pp 133–137.
6   E. A. G. Robinson, 'John Maynard Keynes, 1883–1946,' *Economic Journal*, 57 (225) (March 1947): 39–40.
7   Peter Clarke, *The Keynesian Revolution in the Making, 1924–1936* (Oxford: 1991), pp.244–245; D. E. Moggeridge, *Maynard Keynes: An Economist's Biography* (London: 1992), pp.531–532.

diverse than other clubs to which Keynes belonged, its members consisted of old friends from the Apostles days (Edward Marsh and Desmond MacCarthy), Tory frontbenchers, and writers such as H. G. Wells, Arnold Bennett, and P. G. Wodehouse. Keynes, in groups such as these, worked out not only technical questions but also a longer view of the life of learning. They aided him in what Keynes called 'a long struggle of escape.' 'The difficulty,' he wrote, lies 'not in new ideas, but in escaping from the old ones, which ramify, for those of us brought up as most of us have been, into every corner of our minds.'[8]

Sociality in the history of cognition needed to be durable. There were always threats to it. As will be shown in this chapter, Cambridge University and the Rockefeller Foundation stymied the efforts of the Theoretical Biology Club to establish an institute for the integration of biology with mathematics, physics and chemistry because Joseph Needham and his lot proposed an institute that was organised laterally rather than hierarchically. It was a proposal that ran counter to the rigidity and control of bureaucratic procedures. Needham and his lot (and Solly Zuckerman, Keynes, Watson and Crick) spoke the language of learning that favoured ambiguity, uncertainty and was at home in social looseness. From the peripheries and in the interstices of mental life rose forms of knowledge that encouraged imagination, curiosity and originality. Rather than a knowledge of answers, it was a knowledge of questions. These people knew what they did not know. They had a knowledge of processes. Like all knowledge, twentieth-century knowledge (might we call it 'modern' knowledge?) was tacit and fragmented. Haunted by Nils Bohr's principle of complementarity and Werner Heisenberg's principle of uncertainty, even the physical world, Arthur Eddington could argue, was a world of shadows.[9] Twentieth-century knowledge, in this way, opened vast precincts of unexplored territory, which with some considerable fear and trembling we have only begun to understand. In the pages that follow I hope to raise some questions that might lead to such understanding.

Lives of learning expressed themselves in the hiving off of individuals into private groups – the Apostles, Bloomsbury, the circle around Logan Pearsall Smith in Chelsea, or Solly Zuckerman's Tots and Quots, Joseph Needham's Theoretical Biology Club, for example – that provided insulation and security for creative work. While Bloomsbury and the circle around Logan Pearsall Smith might not have engaged in what we might call research, they and other societies and clubs, such at the Kapitza Club and the V²V Club, were sites for creativity, curiosity, speculation and originality. The study of these attempts is an effort to create an ecology of knowledge that explores the relationship

---

[8] John Maynard Keynes, *The General Theory of Employment, Interest, and Money* (New York: 1936), p.viii.
[9] Eddington, *The Nature of the Physical World* (Cambridge: 1928), pp. xvii, 309.

between cognition and society in twentieth-century Britain.[10] It is exceptionally difficult to come to grips with small groups. Large groups are subject to statistical methods that make it possible to uncover general patterns. Small groups, on the other hand, defy such analysis and what we want to know about them is extremely elusive. Their elusiveness, in part, is a result of their exile and absence. What we wish to know is what Raymond Williams called the 'structure of feeling' that informs them.[11] Begging the question of whether feelings have a 'structure', it might be regarded as a matter of sensibilities.[12] Leonard Woolf quoted Henry Sidgwick in order to explain the nature of groups to which they belonged. Both were Apostles and Woolf was of Bloomsbury. Sidgwick had written about the spirit of such groups:

> I can only describe it as the spirit of the pursuit of truth with absolute devotion and unreserve by a group of intimate friends who were perfectly frank with each other, and indulged in any amount of humour, sarcasm and playful banter, and yet each respects the other, and when he discourses tries to learn from him and see what he sees. Absolute candour was the only duty that the tradition of the society enforced.[13]

Woolf, and for that matter Clive Bell, attempted to deny to Bloomsbury a kind of corporate identity. They were a group of friends both said. Yet, the social, political and cultural importance of such groups is so great that one yearns to capture their inner dynamics in some way.

Bloomsbury, therefore, serves as a trial test to examine the ways that knowledge was forged and framed in a group that rejoiced in being a coterie enjoying an oblique relationship to the institutions and people that were more central to the general British intellectual culture. Because their members denied to themselves corporate identity, it is difficult, even as important and as significant as they were, to find a point of purchase to examine their cultural formation and intellectual contribution. They represented two kinds of exile: geographical and cultural. Their geographical exile was marked by their flight from the tonier precincts of Kensington to the more bohemian regimes of Bloomsbury. Hyde Park Gate had been a 'good' address; Gordon Square – plebian, less expensive, lighter, and

---

[10]   Charles Rosenberg, 'Toward an Ecology of Knowledge: On Discipline, Context, and History', in Alexandra Oleson and John Voss (eds), *The Organization of Knowledge in Modern America, 1860–1920* pp.440–455.

[11]   Raymond Williams, 'The Bloomsbury Fraction', in John Higgins (ed.), *The Raymond Williams Reader* (Oxford: 2001), pp.229–248.

[12]   Daniel Wickberg, 'What is the History of Sensibilities?', *American Historical Review*, 112 (3) (June 2007): 661–684.

[13]   [A. S. and E. M. S.], *Henry Sidgwick: A Memoir* (London: 1906), p.34. Quoted by Leonard Woolf, *Sowing: An Autobiography of the Years 1880 to 1904* (New York and London: 1960), pp.129–130

free from the mental miseries of their earlier lives – was not.[14] This is the way Virginia Woolf described it:

> But it is the house I would ask you to imagine for a moment for, though Hyde Park Gate seems now so distant from Bloomsbury, its shadow falls across it.46 Gordon Square could never have meant what it did had not 22 Hyde Park Gate preceded it. It was a house of innumerably small oddly shaped rooms built to accommodate not one family but three. For beside the three Duckworths and the four Stephens there was also Thackeray's grand-daughter, a vacant-eyed girl who could hardly read, who would throw the scissors into the fire, who was tongue-tied and stammered and yet had to appear at the table with the rest of us … When I look back upon that house it seems to me so crowded with scenes of family life, grotesque, comic and tragic; with the violent emotions of youth, revolt, despair, intoxicating happiness, immense boredom, with parties of the famous and the full, with rages again, George and Gerald, with love scenes with Jack Hills; with passionate affection for my father alternating with passionate hatred of him, all tingling and vibrating in an atmosphere of recollection. The place seemed tangled and matted with emotion … When I returned from the illness which was not unnaturally the result of these emotions and complications, 22 Hyde Park Gate no longer existed … Vanessa had wound up Hyde Park Gate once and for all; she had burnt, she had sorted, she had torn up … And Vanessa – looking at a map of London how far apart they were – had decided that we should leave Kensington and start life afresh in Bloomsbury.[15]

When Vanessa married Clive Bell, Bloomsbury had two London addresses: Virginia and Adrian Stephen's address in Fitzroy Square, and Vanessa and Clive Bell's in Gordon Square. But Bloomsbury was not merely a metropolitan existence. It had country outposts: the Bell's at Charleston, and Keynes's Tilton, for example, both in Sussex. Geographically speaking, Bloomsbury was a moveable feast: London and the countryside as well as a more cosmopolitan one with holidays in Italy, Greece and France.

The exact membership of Bloomsbury is hard to settle on. Some would like to include E. M. Forster (who was a member of Bloomsbury's Memoir Club) or Lady Ottoline Morrell. Leon Edel rejects them because Forster's life was not 'intertwined' with the lives of the principals and Morrell was 'running a salon of her own.'[16] Leonard Woolf, who was more than Bloomsbury, took as his criterion the membership of Bloomsbury's Memoir Club and gives this list: Woolf himself, Virginia, Vanessa and Adrian Stephen, Clive Bell, Lytton Strachey, Maynard Keynes, Duncan Grant, Saxon Sydney Turner, Roger Fry, Desmond and Molly MacCarthy ('though they actually lived in Chelsea')[17]

---

14   Julian Bell, *Virginia Woolf: A Biography*, 2 vols (New York: 1972), I, pp.94–95.
15   Virginia Woolf, 'Old Bloomsbury,' in S. P. Rosenbaum (ed.), *A Bloomsbury Group Reader* (Oxford: 1993), pp.357–358.
16   Leon Edel, *Bloomsbury: A House of Lions* (Philadelphia/New York:1979), p.12.
17   Leonard Woolf, *Beginning Again: An Autobiography of the Years 1911 to 1918* (London/ New York: 1963), p.22.

and, because he read papers to the Memoir Club, E. M. Forster.[18] Clive Bell admits Henry Tertius James Norton and 'perhaps' Gerald Shove, but he has doubts about E. M. Forster and Desmond and Molly MacCarthy. 'Certainly Desmond and Molly MacCarthy and Morgan Forster were close and affectionate friends, but I doubt whether any of them had yet been branded with the fatal name.'[19] James Strachey, the brother of Lytton Strachey, claimed he never belonged to Bloomsbury because 'Bloomsbury almost completely lacked purely intellectual interests.'

> Bloomsbury had no real interests in intellectual things, or only a sham pretense of it; it was dominated by the visual arts & literature. Even music was almost absent. Science unheard of. I suppose this is why I personally felt remote from it.[20]

It may be a gift or a curse, perhaps both, that effort to name names, to give precise names to a group like Bloomsbury. It may be a penchant for positivists to try to establish with precision who belonged and who did not. It may be its very looseness that suggests Bloomsbury's capacity to admit new, or at least different, conceptions in literature, biography, economics and art.

If it is difficult to locate some of its members in Bloomsbury, it is even more difficult to find a location for Bloomsbury's members in some sort of definite social space. They had enough inherited incomes, or as Peter Stansky has said 'or acted as they did,' to tide them over until their work could produce enough for their earthly needs.[21] They were distinctly not 'upper class,' whatever that phrase might be taken to mean. As Jane Marcus has remarked about Virginia Woolf:

> Nothing in [*A Room of One's Own*] indicates that the speaker feels a natural alliance with the government ... [S]he refused all honours from a government she despised as a feminist, a socialist and a pacifist. You may well argue that her feminism was rudimentary, her socialism insufficiently revolutionary, or her radical pacifism (as it developed into *Three Guineas*) impossibly utopian. But to read into her articulate Outsider's political position the wish to be included, is a serious misreading of this and all her writing and the principles she struggled so hard to express.[22]

Both of the Woolfs refused appointments as Companions of Honour. But for Raymond Williams, Bloomsbury was 'an oppositional fraction of the English ruling class.'[23]

---

[18]   S. P. Rosenbaum (and James M. Haule), *The Bloomsbury Group Memoir Club* (London: 2014), p.178.

[19]   Clive Bell, *Old Friends* (London: 1956), pp.130–131.

[20]   James Strachey to Michael Holroyd (about July 1966), Holroyd Papers, British Library, Add. Ms. 81994, f. 83.

[21]   Peter Stansky, *On or About December 1910: Early Bloomsbury and its Intimate World* (Cambridge, Mass.: 1996), p.185.

[22]   Jane Marcus to the editor of the *Times Literary Supplement* (24 December 1993): 13.

[23]   Williams, 'The Bloomsbury Fraction': 236–237.

The movement of the Stephens from Kensington to Bloomsbury seemed to their old family friends and relations to move into a kind of Bohemian life. They had, as Leonard Woolf recognised, 'an intricate tangle of ancient roots and tendrils stretching far and wide through the upper middle classes, the county families, and the aristocracy.' Woolf himself felt set apart from them. He and his father's generation were of the professional middle classes but 'had only recently struggled up into it from the stratum of Jewish shopkeepers.' Of his new comrades Woolf felt:

> Socially they assumed things unconsciously which I could never assume consciously or unconsciously. They lived in a peculiar atmosphere of influence, manners, respectability, and it was so natural to them that they were unaware of it as mammals are unaware of the air and fish of the water in which they live.[24]

There were distinctions even within the same family. James Strachey felt aware of differences between the London and imperial Stracheys and their country cousins. He said: 'Richard [Lytton's and James's father] & John Strachey always despised & laughed at [the] Sutton Court (Edward Stracheys – particularly at the *Spectator* (& also the head of the family).'[25] As Lytton Strachey put it, the aristocratic tradition of the eighteenth century 'had reached a very advanced stage of decomposition.'

> My father and my mother belonged by birth to the old English world of country-house gentlefolk – a world of wealth and breeding, a world in which such things as footmen, silver, and wine were the necessary appurtenances of civilized life. But their own world was different: it was the middle-class professional world of the Victorians, in which the old forms still lingered, but debased and enfeebled.[26]

Bloomsbury's indistinct social position as Outsiders was by itself liberating. Their flight to Bloomsbury allowed them to flee into modernism, one feature of which was Bloomsbury's escape from dogma and dogmatism. It was a cultural rather than an academic coterie. From G. E. Moore they acquired an intellectual style. Instead of asking what their duty was they asked 'what is good,' the answer to which was aesthetic and cultural. As friends together they adopted and practised in their Thursday evening salons a particular conversational style that originated with Moore but which they developed into a way of life. They demanded honesty: each was expected to say exactly what their thoughts and especially their feelings were. Guided by Moore's manner they demanded precision, asking 'what exactly do you mean by that?'

24 Woolf, *Beginning Again*, pp.74–75.
25 James Strachey to Michael Holroyd (sometime about September 1964), Holroyd Papers, BL., Add. Ms. 81994, f.59.
26 Lytton Strachey, 'Lancaster Gate,' in S. P. Rosenbaum (ed.), *A Bloomsbury Group Reader* (Oxford: 1993), pp.351–352.

This manner gave them a sense of being somewhat apart and different from others.[27] What distinguished Bloomsbury as a 'group' and what made them modernists, therefore, was not a body of ideas or theories but rather a style in which they took pride and that annoyed others. As Virginia Woolf put it, 'they had no "manners" in the Hyde Park Gate sense.' It led her to announce that 'on or before December 1910 human character changed.' It was a way of life that they translated into certain mannerisms. Virginia Woolf described it in talking about Lytton Strachey:

> 'The Strache' was the essence of culture. In fact I think his culture a little alarmed Thoby [Stephen]. He had French pictures in his rooms. He had a passion for Pope. He was exotic, extreme in every way – Thoby described him – so long, so thin that his thigh was no thicker than Thoby's arm. Once he burst into Thoby's rooms, cried out, 'Do you hear the music of the Spheres?' and fell in a faint … He was a prodigy of wit. Even the tutors and the dons [at Cambridge] would come and listen to him. 'Whatever they [the examiners] give you, Strachey, Dr. [Henry] Jackson had said when Strachey was in for some examination, 'it won't be good enough.'[28]

This style and manner translated itself to the various forms of which might be called Bloomsbury's knowledge. To give it names: Keynesian economics, Strachey's memoirs, Roger Fry's and Clive Bell's post-impressionism.

Bloomsbury liked to pretend that its forms of knowledge represented a break from the past, which was not completely true. After a dinner in which Virginia Woolf, Maynard Keynes and T. S. Eliot discussed Eliot's book *After Strange Gods* Keynes remarked:

> I begin to see that our generation – yours and mine V[irginia] owed a great deal to our fathers' religion. And the young, like Julian [Bell (Woolf's nephew)] who are brought up without it, will never get much out of life. They're trivial; like dogs in their lusts. We had the best of both liberation and order. We destroyed Xty and yet had its benefits.[29]

Virginia Woolf and the others made a good deal of the ways they differed from their father's generations. There is the feeling of change in all of their writings. Strachey's modernist mockery in *Eminent Victorians* emerged by attacking his subjects 'in unexpected places,' in their 'obscure recesses.'[30] Thus Manning was 'supple and yielding.' It was necessary for him to be careful 'and Manning was careful indeed' (pp.13, 30). Nightingale could '[d]issect the concrete and distasteful fruits of actual life.' However, she 'was never at home

---

[27]   Williams, 'The Bloomsbury Faction': 233.
[28]   Woolf, 'Old Bloomsbury': 361, 363.
[29]   Virginia Woolf Diary, 19 April 1934, in Anne Olivier Bell (ed.), *The Diary of Virginia Woolf*, Volume 4 (London: 1983), p.208.
[30]   Lytton Strachey, *Eminent Victorians* (London: 1986), p.9. In the quotations that follow I use the pagination of this edition.

with a generalization.' 'Like most great men of action – perhaps like all – she was simply an empiricist' (p.155). Gordon was never confirmed but he took the sacrament every day. 'The Holy Bible was not his only solace.' Under the strong African sun 'he would drink nothing but pure water; and then … water that not so pure' (pp.191, 203). Dr Arnold conducted himself in a manner that 'denoted energy, earnestness and the best intentions' but 'his legs, perhaps, were shorter than they should have been' (p.165). F. A. Simpson accused Strachey of being morally flawed: 'In the last resort he did not care enough for the truth.' Strachey's portraits 'are not merely false but falsified.'[31] In prison Bertrand Russell burst out laughing when reading *Eminent Victorians*. Imprisonment, a warder had to point out, was no amusing matter.[32] Dennis Robertson, the Apostle and economist, thought Strachey might have been unfair to Cromer and Arnold, but 'the greatest personalities like Florence & Gordon (and Hartington) emerge from it greater rather than less.'[33] *Eminent Victorians* gave Goldsworthy Lowes Dickinson some 'consoling and profitable hours' during the horrors of war.[34]

Maynard Keynes could match these bundles of ironies. As a young man just arriving at King's College from Eton he looked about and found the college inefficient. He found a peacock roaming the garden tended by an ageing keeper. When the peacock and its keeper died neither were replaced, which Keynes regretted. He said '[y]ou cannot run a College without three or four gross abuses.' Keynes himself was a risk-taker. He was not some sort of clinical calculator though he knew precisely the number of mates necessary to keep a boar content (it was fourteen).[35] He admired Newton, but recognised him as a necromancer rather than as a scientist. He matched the ironies and the mockeries of *Eminent Victorians* in his *Economic Consequences of the Peace*, so much so that when he sent drafts of it to his mother she advised him to take a softer tone. Keynes called Georges Clemenceau 'the Tiger' and Lloyd George 'the Welsh witch.' Keynes wrote in a fragment he chose not to include in the *Economic Consequences*:

> Let the reader figure Mr. Lloyd George as a *femme fatale*. An old man of the world, a *femme fatale*, and a non-conformist clergyman – these are the characters in our drama. Even though the lady was very religious at times, the Fourteen

31 F. A. Simpson, 'Max Beerbohm on Lytton Strachey,' *Cambridge Review*, 4 (December 1943): 70. I am grateful to Dr Gordon Johnson for this reference.
32 Russell to Robin Mayor, 7 March 1918, Mayor Papers. These papers were in Lady Rothchild's keeping until her death and now they are in Trinity College.
33 Dennis Robertson to J. R. M. Butler, 17 August 1918, J. R. M. Butler Papers, Trinity College, Cambridge Ms. A1/114.
34 Goldsworthy Lowes Dickinson to Lytton Strachey, 24 May [1918], Strachey Papers, BL., Add. Ms. 60664, f. 146.
35 Noel Annan, 'Keynes and Bloomsbury,' in William Roger Lewis (ed.), *Still More Adventures with Britannia: Personalities, Politics and Culture in Britain* (London: 2003), p.113.

Commandments could hardly expect to emerge perfectly intact ... Lloyd George is rooted in nothing; he is void and without content; he lives and feeds on his immediate surroundings; he is an instrument and a player at the same time which plays on company and is played on by them too; he is a prism, as I have heard him described, which collects light and distorts it and is most brilliant if the light comes from many quarters at once; a vampire and a medium in one.[36]

It was a polemic and never an attempt at an actual history. In the *Economic Consequences* Keynes captured Wilson's hypocrisy, Lloyd George's venality and Clemenceau's cynicism. Lloyd George was a captive of the Conservative Party; Clemenceau was a captive of the France that had lost twice as many men in the war as had Britain. In a lecture, 'The Civil Service and Financial Control,' delivered to the Civil Service Association, Keynes characterised the Treasury as 'very clever' and 'very dry.' Its instruments, the Treasury Draft for example, deployed 'aesthetic methods' that enabled certain things to be done and 'made many things impossible.' Treasury control was like conventional morality. 'This frigid body,' he said, regulated against enthusiasm and 'overwhelming wickedness.' The Treasury 'came to possess attributes of institutions like a college or a City company, or the Church of England.'[37]

Bloomsbury was drawn to post-impressionism. Virginia Woolf declared that the age of Charles Furse and Singer Sargent was past and the age of Paul Cézanne, James Abbott McNeill Whistler and Augustus John had dawned. Keynes used his influence at the Treasury when he learned from Duncan Grant that paintings by Edgar Degas were up for auction. He got the Treasury to pay out £20,000 to buy the lot for the National Gallery. When the Keeper of the Gallery decided he had no time for Cézanne's *Apples*, Keynes bought it for himself. On leaving Versailles in disgust because of the peace treaty, Keynes fled to Charleston to stay with Vanessa Bell and Duncan Grant, with French paintings under his arm (which he thereupon deposited in a hedgerow for safe-keeping). The post-impressionist exhibition at Grafton Gallery, organised by Roger Fry and Desmond MacCarthy, contained paintings by Matisse and Picasso, thirty-six Gauguins and twenty-two Van Goghs.[38] Things French besotted Bloomsbury – its cuisine, its pottery, its wine and 'a certain way of looking at art.'[39] As Roger Fry wrote of Monet:

Gradually the objects he represented lost their consistency, everything was resolved into the flat mosaic of colour patches, which is, of course, more or

[36] John Maynard Keynes, 'Lloyd George: A Fragment,' in *The Collected Writings of John Maynard Keynes, Volume X: Essays in Biorgraphy* (Cambridge: 1972), pp.22, 24.

[37] J. M. Keynes, 'The Civil Service and Financial Control,' *The Collected Works of John Maynard Keyes, volume 16: Activities, 1914–1919, The Treasury and Versailles* (Cambridge: 1972), p.299.

[38] Stansky, *On or About December 1910*, pp.196–197.

[39] Mary Ann Caws and Sarah Bird Wright, *Bloomsbury and France: Art and Friends* (Oxford: 2000), p.9.

less accurate accounts of what the retina receives or what things would look like if our minds had never learned to interpret it as representing it as solid objects in space.[40]

They even married into France: Dorothy Strachey (Lytton Strachey's sister who also translated André Gide) married Simon Bussy, the painter.

Bloomsbury took on French intellectual life in other ways. Roger Fry, Julian Bell and the Stracheys (Lytton and his sisters Pippa, Pernel and Dorothy) attended Paul Desjardin's *Decades des Pontigny* in the 1920s. Modelled after gatherings described by Boccaccio in *Decameron* these were meetings of a cosmopolitan nature designed to discuss highly abstract questions. A literary *decade* in 1923 considered '*Le trésor poétique réservé ou de l'Intraduisible*.' Someone asked Strachey, who did not care for the quality of the discussions, to declare what concerned him most. 'Passion,' he responded. He was also asked to comment on confessional literature. He said '[l]es *confession ne sont pas dans mon genre*.'[41] Roger Fry thought the discussions were 'horribly metaphysical' and summarised one of his talks by stressing his empiricism, saying 'the scientific spirit had the last word and a great triumph over the abstractionists and metaphysicians.'[42]

If Bloomsbury had no settled doctrine or body of thought, it is fair to ask what their beliefs were and what kind of knowledge they developed. As to the first, they certainly strained and stressed over the question of beliefs. Keynes reminded Virginia Woolf that they had killed Christianity but they still owed something to their ancestors' religion. They were certainly not nihilists and their agnosticism owed something to religious feeling. Keynes seized on this theme in *My Early Beliefs*, his paper given to Bloomsbury's Memoir Club. In it he declared that he was still an immoralist, by which he meant he still followed the credo that G. E. Moore had set out in the *Principia Ethica*: that he put the pursuit of the good – states of mind, beauty and affection – above any duty he might feel towards the improvement of humankind. Keynes spoke of the 'habits of feeling, formed [at Cambridge] and still persist in a recognizable degree':

> It is those habits of feeling, influencing the majority of us, which make this Club a collectivity and separate us from the rest ... We accepted Moore's religion, so to speak, and discarded his morals. Indeed, in our opinion, one of the greatest advantages of his religion, was that it made morals unnecessary – meaning by 'religion' one's attitude toward oneself and the ultimate and by 'morals' one's attitude towards the outside world and the intermediate ... Nothing matters

40   Roger Fry, 'Impressionism,' in S. P. Rosenbaum (ed.), *A Bloomsbury Group Reader* (Oxford: 1993), p.261.
41   Caws and Wright, *Bloomsbury and France*, pp.293–294.
42   Roger Fry to Helen Anrep, 7 September 1925, in Denys Sutton (ed.), *The Letters of Roger Fry*, 2 vols (London: 1972), pp.579–580.

except states of mind, our own and other people's of course, but chiefly our own. These states of mind were not associated with action or achievement or with consequences. They consisted in timeless, passionate states of contemplation and communion largely unattached to 'before' or 'after' … The appropriate subjects of passionate contemplation and communion were a beloved person, beauty and truth, and one's prime objects in life were love, the creation and enjoyment of aesthetic experience and the pursuit of knowledge … Our religion closely followed the English puritan tradition of being chiefly concerned with the salvation of our own souls. The divine resided within a closed circle … [O]ur religion was altogether unworldly – with wealth, power, popularity or success it had no concern whatever, they were thoroughly despised.

Keynes composed these thoughts in 1938 and concluded that 'purer, sweeter air by far than Freud cum Marx' this religion 'remains nearer the truth than any other that I know.'[43]

The next year, in the shadow of the next war, E. M. Forster composed the essay 'What I Believe.' Though he said he lived in an age of faith – he meant fascism and Bolshevism – Forster confessed 'I do not believe in Belief.' Love, he declared, was 'the Beloved Republic':

I believe in aristocracy, though – if that is the right word, and if a democrat may use it. Not an aristocracy of power, based upon rank and influence, but an aristocracy of the sensitive, the considerate and the plucky. Its members are to be found in all nations and classes, and all through the ages, and there is a secret understanding between them when they meet. They represent the true human condition, the one permanent victory of our queer race over cruelty and chaos. Thousands of them perish in obscurity, a few are great names. They are sensitive for others as well as for themselves, they are considerate without being fussy, their pluck is not swankiness but the power to endure, and they can take a joke.

He hated 'Causes' and he distrusted 'Great men.' 'If I had to choose between betraying my country and betraying my friend,' he said, 'I hope I should have the guts to betray my country.' 'The Saviour of the future – if he ever comes – will not preach a new Gospel.' He will use what Forster considered his 'aristocracy' to 'make effective the good will and good temper which are already existing.'[44]

If not devoid of belief neither was Bloomsbury devoid of knowledge. Their knowledge was the sort of knowledge one would expect of people escaping from what they would regard as the *faux* respectability and conventionality of Kensington. It was the kind of knowledge one would expect of exiles, whether in Bloomsbury or France. Their exile was an escape into the freedom of imagination. Virginia Woolf and E. M. Forster expressed it in their novels. Vanessa Bell and Duncan Grant expressed it in their paintings. Keynes expressed it in

43 John Maynard Keynes, 'My Early Beliefs,' in *The Collected Writings of John Maynard Keynes, Volum X: Essays in Biography* (Cambridge: 1972), pp. 435–437, 442.
44 E. M. Forster, 'What I Believe,' in *Two Cheers for Democracy* (London: 1951), pp. 78, 82–83, 84.

his venture into probability. Speculation and iconoclasm marked their preoccupations with truth. And if these speculations led them to uncertainty it was an uncertainty marked with the traces of modernity. It would not be too much to say that Bloomsbury created modernity, or at least one strand of it. Though, as Noel Annan put it, they lived in squares and made love in triangles, their lives' work was irregular and asymmetrical. Unlike the Sitwells, who someone has called a part of the history of celebrity, Bloomsbury was a part of the history of cognition.

There was nothing soft or effeminate in this; it was a different form of masculinity, one of the pen, not the sword. It was not measured by physical strength or courage. It was a mental masculinity. Forster, commenting on *Die Walküre*, said '[t]he Valkyries are symbols not only of courage but of intelligence.' Forster's aristocracy was marked by imaginative courage. Their 'temple,' as he said, was 'the Holiness of the Heart's Affection' and their kingdom 'though they never possess it, is the wide-open world.'[45] Their beliefs were, as Keynes said, 'rational and scientific in character.' It was the 'application' of logic and rational analysis to the material presented as sense-data.[46]

Logan Pearsall Smith (Desmond MacCarthy's children called him 'Uncle Baldhead'[47]) gathered a group around him at 11 St Leonard's Terrace in Chelsea, a sort of rival Bloomsbury, for which 'words & phrases are the only things that matter.'[48] He and those around him, spurred on by the imperatives of the Second World War, wished to sustain England's literary culture by 'continuing to celebrate the richness of the national language, protecting its rules' and 'coining neologisms, parsing sentences, disputing grammar.'[49] James Lees-Milne described Smith as 'an old, frail man, of heavy, ungainly build. He may be a bore for he tells long stories "at" one, in a laborious, monotonous tone, laughing all the while and salivating a good deal.' Despite, or perhaps because of, his 'capacity for mockery and fun' he also had 'literary refinement.'[50] Smith, born to a Quaker's inheritance in Millville, New Jersey, was educated at the Penn Charter School, Haverford College and Harvard. He and his family settled in England and Smith went to Balliol College, Oxford. Though a favourite of Benjamin Jowett, Smith got but a second in *literae humaniores* (1891). In another breach with Balliol, Pearsall Smith was much influenced by Walter Pater. He became a British subject in 1913.

45 Forster, 'What I Believe': 82–83.
46 Keynes, 'My Early Beliefs': 436.
47 Hugh and Mirabel Cecil, *Clever Hearts: Desmond and Molly MacCarthy, A Biography* (London: 1990), p.218.
48 Quoted in Richard Davenport-Hines, 'Introduction,' Hugh Trevor-Roper, *The Wartime Journals* (London: 2012), p.13. See Logan Pearsall Smith, *The Forgotten Years* (Boston: 1939); Barbara Strachey, *Remarkable Relations: The Story of the Pearsall Smith Family* (London: 1981).
49 Davenport-Hines, 'Introduction,' Trevor-Roper, *The Wartime Journals*, p.18.
50 James Lees-Milne, *Ancestral Voices* (London: 1985), pp.166, 213.

Despite what is called occasional divergences from commendable conduct, he retained many of the Quaker virtues.

Those included in the St Leonard's Terrace set were Alys Russell, Pearsall Smith's sister (the first of Bertrand Russell's numerous wives), Robert Trevelyan (the brother of G. M. Trevelyan), Rose Macaulay, Desmond MacCarthy, Cyril Connolly, Robert Gathorne-Hardy, John and James Pope-Hennessy, Stuart Preston, Paul Sudley and Hugh Trevor-Roper. With their desire for verbal precision and their enthusiasm for neologisms, they were what was called 'walking dictionaries.' Trevor-Roper wrote to Smith 'words should be self-explanatory, & should not depend on the membership of an esoteric clique, or the knowledge of its elaborate anecdotes.'[51] Trevor-Roper was much taken by Pearsall Smith's brightness, liveliness and 'playful naughtiness.'[52] Pearsall Smith 'surpassed himself in monologue, and discouraged interruption by holding up his hand like a policeman halting traffic.' Trevor-Roper quoted Pearsall Smith as saying: 'I rather like singing for my supper; what grates on my ears is the song of other singers.'[53] Cyril Connolly, who had served Smith for some time as his literary assistant, called him a:

> Mandarin of the generation of the eighties, an admirer of Pater and Jowett and a friend of Henry James, he represents not a reaction against the new realism, but the old Adam, the precious original sinner, against whom the later realists took action.[54]

Pearsall Smith addressed himself to Trevor-Roper as 'your virginal octogenarian boyfriend – one moment flirtatious, the next coy.'[55] 'He was a wicked old man,' Trevor-Roper said, 'but I like wicked old men.'[56] Trevor-Roper wrote, or so he claimed, the *Last Days of Hitler* for Pearsall Smith. Smith had revived in him 'the desire (almost extinguished in my philistine years) to write elegant prose ... [H]is spirit guided my pen.'[57] Robert Trevelyan cut a different figure in the Chelsea coterie. For a long time he had kept a room on St Leonard's Terrace, staying there each week for a night or two. Max Beerbohm called Bob Trevy a 'Scholar Gypsy,' a bookman when he was out of doors and a woodsman in Pearsall Smith's library.[58] Desmond MacCarthy

[51] Quoted in Davenport-Hines, 'Introduction,' p.16
[52] Richard Davenport-Hines, 'Introduction,' Hugh Trevor-Roper, *Letters from Oxford to Bernard Barenson*, ed. Richard Davenport Hines (London: 2006), p.xiv.
[53] Quoted by Davenport-Hines, 'Introduction,' Trevor Roper, *The Wartime Journals*, p.5.
[54] Cyril Connolly, *Enemies of Promise*, rev. edn (New York: 1983), p.75.
[55] Quoted in Adam Sisman, *Hugh Trevor-Roper: The Biography* (London: 2010), p.98.
[56] Quoted by Davenport-Hines, 'Introduction,' Trevor-Roper, *The Wartime Journals*, p.14.
[57] Hugh Trevor Ropert to Blair Worden, 28 December 1984, in Richard Davenport-Hines and Adam Sisman (eds), *One Hundred Letters from Hugh Trevor-Roper* (Oxford: 2014), p.286.
[58] Davenport-Hines, 'Introduction,' Hugh Trevor-Roper, *The Wartime Journals*, p.17.

said of Trevelyan and his friends that, with their classical approach to literature they were 'beacons blazing out on a somber age.'[59]

Zuckerman's Tots and Quots, another of these coteries, also serves as a trial to test out the complex interactions between lives of learning and public life during the 1930s and 1940s. Zuckerman,[60] finding the two dining clubs to which he belonged 'dreary and at the same time quaint,' called into being one of his own in 1931. 'We'd only have ourselves to blame if it proved to be a bore,' he said.[61] At their second dinner Lancelot Hogben, who had just returned from South Africa where he encountered members of one tribe, the Hottentots, who were about to become extinct, proposed the name 'Quotenttots.' J. B. S. Haldane proposed to name themselves the Tots and Quots, an inverted abbreviation of Terence's tag 'Quot homines, tot sententiae' (so many men, so many opinions). So, first they were the Quottentons and then the Tots and Quots. Their first dinner was at Pagani's in Great Portland Street. Thereafter they dined in Soho restaurants, including one that had been the house on Dean Street in which Karl Marx had lived. Zuckerman's sociability was pronounced. He chose the menu and the wine and invited a principal quest who opened the discussion on any subject of his choice. One evening in 1940 H. G. Wells was the chief guest. The menu was *Hors-d'oeuvres Variés*, *Sauté de Boeuf Bourguignonne* and *Soufflé Vanille, sec Chocolate*. They discussed the reconstruction of the world after the war during an air raid. A bomb shook the building and plaster fell on the diners. H. G. Wells, regarding himself as a connoisseur, especially of red wine, which that evening was not the finest, spoke of 'Posthumous nourishment.' Glancing at the ceiling he observed 'at the last I could say I was drinking good old Empire.'[62] Other guests during the 1930s and 1940s were 'the Prof' (Lord Cherwell), Sir Archibald Clark Kerr, Herbert Morrison, Admiral Nimitz and J. B. Conant.

The members of Tots and Quots were largely men of science: Zuckerman himself, of course, Patrick Blackett, J. D. Bernal, Joseph Needham, Cyril Darlington, J. B. S. Haldane, J. Z. Young, Tom Harrison, Louis Rapkine and others, most of whom became FRS (several under the age of forty – Bernal, and Lancelot Hogben, for example). But there were also economists such as

---

[59] Quoted by Davenport-Hines, 'Introduction,' Trevor-Roper, *The Wartime Journals*, p.17.
[60] Zuckerman, Solly (1904–1993): born in South Africa; ed. South African College School, University of Cape Town, Yale, University College Medical School, London; began his career at the London Zoological Society, taught at Oxford, 1934–1945; a pioneer in the science of operations research during the Second World War; Professor of Anatomy, University of Birmingham; ended his teaching career at East Anglia University; chief scientific adviser to the government, 1964–1971; FRS, KCB (1956); OM (1961); raised to the peerage (1971).
[61] Solly Zuckerman, *From Apes to Warlords* [the autobiography (1904–1946) of Solly Zuckerman] (London: 1978), p.60.
[62] J. G. Crowther, *Fifty Years with Science* (London: 1970), p.222.

Roy Harrod; H. D. Dickinson; M. M. Postan, the economic historian; Kenneth Clark, then an arts administrator; and Sebastian Sprott, the psychologist and philosopher. There were also politicians among their lot: Herbert Samuel, Hugh Gaitskill, Richard Crossman. They sprang from all walks of life. C. H. Waddington's father had been a tea planter, John Cockcroft's had been in the weaving industry, Needham's had been a physician, Bernal's had been an Irish farmer. Bernal was saved from social obscurity by the fact that his mother, a very sophisticated woman, had been the daughter of a physician. Though in the 1930s some members had published their first books, they had not yet published their second or third. Nor had they been elected FRS in the 1930s, but in the end all the scientific members were – and most members of the Tots and Quots went on to distinguished careers.

In their politics most were men of the left, some strongly so. In general, Zuckerman considered them politically naive. Beatrice Webb called the intellectuals who went over to Moscow 'mild mannered desperados.'[63] Professionally united by common methods, yet they were a 'diverse group who aim[ed] at diverse political ends.'[64] Some called Blackett 'moderately red,' but in 1934 he gave a BBC radio lecture that others regarded as the 'reddest' lecture ever transmitted from Broadcasting House. Visitors to the Blacketts' house on Little St Mary's Lane in Cambridge on Sunday afternoons were treated to biscuits, lemonade, and films showing the glories of the Soviet Union.[65]

Joseph Needham was more than a little touched by Marxism. He called himself an 'equalitarian socialist' even before he read Marx and he never found dialectical materialism of much use in planning his research. Yet, in the 1930s he argued that '[c]ommunism provides the moral theology appropriate for our time.' He rejected classical materialism, 'the sharp distinction of the philosophers between the world of spirit and the world of matter':

> After all for the biologist there is no strict separation. In animal and human behavior there is a unity; the 'mental event' cannot really be separated from the 'physical neural event,' and it is profitless to try to do so. So in the coming into being of the world as a whole, we should envisage a unity ... Out of the original chaos a vast flowering of the new has originated, and that is all that can be said.[66]

What Needham found particularly valuable in the Marxist tradition was historical materialism: that it was not a succession of great men, nor racial or

---

[63]   Quoted in Neal Wood, *Communism and British Intellectuals* (New York: 1959), p.74; Margaret Cole (ed.), *Beatrice Webb's Diaries, 1924–1932* (London: 1956), p.14 (entry for 6 March 1924).

[64]   Zuckerman, *From Apes to Warlords*, p.394.

[65]   Mary Jo Nye, *Blackett: Physics, War, and Politics in the Twentieth Century* (Cambridge, Mass.: 2004), pp.1–2.

[66]   Joseph Needham, 'Thoughts of a Young Scientist on the Testament of an Elder One (John Scott Haldane) (1936),' in Joseph Needham, *Time: The Refreshing River Essays and Addresses, 1932–1942* (New York: 1943), pp.122–123.

genetic characteristics, nor chance, but rather the driving force in history was the 'relations of man with the productive processes in which he engages.'[67]

It was in J. D. Bernal that these thoughts found clearest expression. It was at the Second International Congress on the History of Science held in London – where N. I. Bukharin and other Soviet intellectuals argued that the history of science moved according to changes in society – that got Bernal thinking about ideas that would appear in his *Social Function of Science* (1939). It summarised Bernal's vision of the future: that, as C. P. Snow put it, 'we had the power, through the application of science, to take the animal miseries away from most of our fellow-men.'[68] Zuckerman had detailed discussions with Bernal and put forward thoughts about the ways in which research workers, rather than being passive advisers to practitioners, could play a dynamic role in the organisation of science. Bernal, showing his gratitude to the Tots and Quots, inscribed in Zuckerman's copy of the book:

> To Solly
> Quot honines, tot sententiae
> D

Zuckerman said: '[t]here must have been a bit of the flavor of our old Tots and Quots discussions in some of what he wrote.'[69]

The history of the Tots and Quots fell into two periods: the 1930s, until Zuckerman went off to the United States to teach; and the period of the Second World War. In its first period members sought to establish the nature and importance of science. As Zuckerman put it, they discussed 'the general significance of science to society and the conscious role science might play in social development.' Their abiding anxiety was what they considered the disorganisation of science. Roy Harrod, pointing to the 'muddled' condition of economic policy, showed that the scientists were not alone in this.[70] Hyman Levy opened one meeting in 1932 to a consideration of the economic implications of science. On another occasion they discussed the popularisation of science. At one point they discussed the question of 'How scientific was social science?' This roused Tom Harrison, the founder of Mass Observation, who regarded the social sciences as truly scientific. Harrod, perhaps more nomothetic than others, responded by observing that the 'general laws' that governed science had not yet been revealed to social scientists and in particular to economists. Max Planck, he reminded them, had once contemplated a career in the social sciences but abandoned the

---

67 Gregory Blue, 'Joseph Needham, Heterodox Marxism and the Social Background to Chinese Science,' *Science and Society*, 62 (2) (Summer 1998): 195–217, esp. 199, 200, 202.
68 C. P. Snow, 'J. D. Bernal: A Personal Portrait,' in Maurice Goldsmith and Alan Mackay (eds), *The Science of Science: Society in the Technological Age* (London: 1964), p.26.
69 Zuckerman, *From Apes to Warlords*, pp.395–396.
70 Crowther, *Fifty Years With Science*, p.212.

thought in favour of an 'easier' career in physics.[71] Zuckerman captured the tone of their discussions in the early days:

> There was nothing evangelistic about our meetings. If any of the club's members felt that way, they kept the sentiment to themselves. Nor was there a sign of C P Snow's 'two cultures.' We were not isolated scientists or economists. So far as I was concerned it was exciting to be with men like Hogben, with his acute mind which challenged everything; with Bernal, with his encyclopaedic knowledge; with Haldane, with his absolute, some would say arrogant assurance; and Roy Harrod, with his balanced intellectualism. But why mention only these four? All members had something to impart, and all, or nearly all, had one thing in common – they were totally free in spirit and speech, and were seemingly bound to no dogma.

Every discussion, Zuckerman observed, 'provoked a clash of opinion, and the greater the measure of disagreement, the more stimulating the meeting.' Not all were pleased by the club's proceedings. G. P. (Gip) Wells, H. G. Wells's eldest son and a member of the zoology department at University College, London, resigned after the first dinner. He had hoped that the enterprise would be nothing but fun and he feared they would become monastic and serious. 'We may have not been monastic,' Zuckerman said, 'but we certainly were serious.' Each dinner, Zuckerman said, added to his education. He became increasingly aware 'of the many sides there were to the simplest issue, and of the different attitudes from which each was viewed.'[72]

The war dominated the second phase of the club's existence and its discussions were considerations of the role science might play in the war effort. In 1938, as war loomed, Bernal and Zuckerman prepared a paper on mobilisation for war. Julian Huxley wrote a paper on the organisation of research in Britain and stressed the importance of executive authority and government coordination in planning.[73] Bernal's *Social Function of Science* was not the only book to emerge from the discussions of the club. What Zuckerman considered the 'crowning achievement' of the second phase of the club's history was their publication in 1940 of *Science in War*. Allen Lane, the publisher of Penguin Books and a guest at the dinner where the idea for the book was hatched, agreed to publish it if a typescript could be produced within a fortnight. Zuckerman and Bernal drafted an outline and then feverishly telephoned their colleagues to get their agreement. C. D. Darlington, E. J. (Bobby) Carter, Hugh Sinclair, Frank Yates, Louis Rapkine and J. G. Crowther contributed.[74] Zuckerman and Crowther corrected the proof in the laboratories of the Zoological Society:

---

[71] Zuckerman, *From Apes to Warlords*, pp.403–404.
[72] Zuckerman, *From Apes to Warlords* pp.393–395, 404.
[73] Crowther, *Fifty Years with Science*, p.212.
[74] Zuckerman, *From Apes to Warlords*, pp.111–112.

[Zuckerman] was in his shirt-sleeves, and he worked on the proofs with an energy and speed which I have never seen equaled. This extremely determined, quick, strong worker was the obverse of the sociable scientist who had previously been familiar to many of us. We now saw the tough hand beneath the charming manner.[75]

The authors gathered for a final inspection of the book in Crowther's flat on Russell Square on 23 June 1940. Julian Huxley, who reviewed the book in *Nature*, called it a 'tract for the times.' 'The world in which we live,' he argued, 'is a technological world, and that success in it therefore depends primarily on the utilization of scientific knowledge.' Tradition might be valuable but it becomes dangerous when it threatens technical efficiency. 'Means must be found for short-circuiting the present devious and dampening routes between science and the problems to be solved.' Doing one's duty 'in a conscientious and blind way is not what the situation demands, Thought, ordered and organized, thought directed to speedy decisions, is the first requirement.'[76] The book had a strong impact on science policy in the war, but it made only enough money to pay for some club dinners.[77]

During the war and afterwards, members of the Tots and Quots were preoccupied with international scholarly cooperation. Following the fall of France they, particularly Crowther and Cockcroft, were eager to find places for French scientists who fled before the Nazis could capture them.[78] After the war they held a dinner, to which Joliot-Curie came, to discuss the organisation of science and the re-establishment of the Anglo-French Society of Science. In November 1940 they met at Christ's College, Cambridge with guests from the American Embassy and their discussion concerned Anglo-American scientific cooperation.[79] Once the United States entered the war their discussions turned to plans for post-war cooperation. Roy Harrod was careful to avoid political provocations in these discussions. Hitherto planning was organised around national considerations but now, Harrod argued, it should be an international undertaking in order to stabilise international economics. He drew out James Conant on this point asking how Americans might come to see 'that investing in under-developed countries was a duty, not a privilege.'[80] John Winant, the American ambassador, began attending their dinners, bringing with him American professors of economics who had become temporary wartime civil servants, and representatives of the Rockefeller Foundation. Once the Nazis invaded the Soviet Union the Tots and Quots brought in the Soviet ambassador, Ivan Maisky, as their chief guest and their discussions turned to Anglo-Soviet scientific cooperation. The

75   Crowther, *Fifty Years with Science*, p.213.
76   [J. S. H.], 'Science in War' [a review of *Science in War* (London: Penguin, 1940)], *Nature*, 146 (27 July 1940): 112–113.
77   Zuckerman, *From Apes to Warlords*, pp.398–399.
78   Crowther, *Fifty Years with Science*, p.218.
79   Zuckerman, *From Apes to Warlords*, p.400.
80   Zuckerman, *From Apes to Warlords*, p.401.

British feared that the slowness in opening the western front might lead to the collapse of the Soviet Union. Maisky responded, 'with quiet but impressive force,' saying he had no fears of a Soviet collapse but wondered what price would have to be paid for a Russian victory.[81]

Tots and Quots's thrust into discussions of wartime policy may have been a worthwhile patriotic gesture but, as is shown in the case of American physicists and the Manhattan Project, it brought their discussions of science as an activity in itself to a halt. As always in cases of application, application acts as a distorting, distracting force, and it draws out feelings and sentiments that cut across the grain of curiosity and creativity. Applied science might have helped war work but it did not help 'science.' To a certain extent the war meant an end to the Tots and Quots. To some extent the war politicised science. As Zuckerman put it, 'the club ceased to exist because its members had become less tolerant of each other's political opinions.'[82] Joseph Needham, for all his political activism, was always modest in his claims for the role of scientists in politics:

> There has been much talk (and not uncommonly, in the editorials of *Nature*), about the importance of giving the scientist more say in government. The value of this is not to be denied. But when it is carried further, as in the views of the 'technocrats,' and when it is suggested that scientists should themselves be the rulers of society, the suggestion reveals its superficiality.[83]

There is also a cognitive question of some larger importance. Extra-scientific science – applications that merely pluck the low-hanging fruit – is less intellectually demanding than pure research and scholarship. G. H. Hardy regarded war work as essentially second-rate and dull. Praiseworthy and public spirited such activity might be, but such pursuits, according to Hardy, 'were not worthy of a first-rate man with proper ambitions.'[84] In wartime, patriotism trumps scholarship.

Bloomsbury and Logan Pearsall Smith's group in Chelsea represent the ways in which literature and the creative arts were shunted off from the university and the more formidable associations such as the Royal Society and British Academy and cornered into less formal coteries. Some scientists, as the case of the Tots and Quots shows, could find solidarity in the Theoretical Biology Club. Joseph Needham, then lecturer in biochemistry at Cambridge,[85]

---

81 Zuckerman, *From Apes to Warlords*, pp.402–403.
82 Zuckerman, *From Apes to Warlords*, p.370.
83 Joseph Needham, 'Pure Science and the Idea of the Holy (1942),' in Joseph Needham, *Time: The Refreshing River Essays and Addresses, 1932–1942* (New York: 1943), p.117.
84 Quoted in Gary Werskey, *The Invisible College* (London: 1978), p.23.
85 Needham, Joseph Terence Montgomery (1900–1995): father, a physician; mother, a composer of music; ed. Oudle School; Gonville and Caius College, Cambridge, BA (1921), MA (1925), DPhil (1925); fellow of Caius; worked in Gowland Hopkins's laboratory in the Department of Biochemistry at Cambridge, specialising in embryology and morphogenesis;

and Joseph Henry Woodger (they called him Socrates), then reader in biology at the Middlesex Hospital Medical School, founded the Theoretical Biology Club in 1932.[86] The historian of the club regards it as a 'scientific Bloomsbury,' and though not concerned with aesthetics in any principal way, it was an 'arena for both novel individual expressions and concerted action on behalf of shared avant-garde ideals.'[87] Karl Popper called it 'one of the most interesting study groups in the field of the philosophy of science.'[88] In general, the Theoretical Biology Club sought two objectives. First, they sought to redefine the boundaries of intellectual disciplines. Second, they sought to distribute intellectual authority along lateral rather than hierarchical lines.

There was a pre-history to the history of the Theoretical Biology Club. Needham made arrangements for Woodger to meet Wittgenstein in Cambridge. 'I would get you up here for a week-end,' Needham wrote. Wittgenstein 'is here for year lecturing at King's. He is a most remarkable person; even more so than his book, I think.'[89] Woodger responded:

> I would certainly welcome any opportunity of hearing Wittgenstein again. I spoke to him at Nottingham last summer. I quite agree that he is a very remarkable man. I should say he is one of the greatest geniuses in logic we have yet had. I hope he will not meet the same fate as his contemporaries and fellow geniuses – [?] and [Frank] Ramsey.[90]

Woodger published his *Biological Principles* in 1929.[91] Needham published his *Chemical Embryology* in three volumes in 1931. They each reviewed each other's books, leading to an extensive correspondence between them touching on the intellectual problems that would preoccupy the Theoretical Biology

---

learned Chinese studying with Shen Shih-Chang and Gustav Haloun; under direction of the Royal Society served as director of the Sino-British Co-operation Office in Chongqing (1942–1946); the first head of the Natural Sciences Section of UNESCO in Paris from the time of his return from China until 1948; resumed his fellowship at Gonville and Caius College and devoted himself to the history of Chinese science; elected Master of Gonville and Caius College (1966); FRS (1941); FBA (1971); CH (1992).

86 Woodger, Joseph Henry (1894–1981): ed. University College, London (1911–1922) except for the war years when he was mentioned in dispatches; after the war, took up the Derby Research Scholarship to which he had been appointed before he enlisted, honours in zoology and comparative anatomy; reader at the University of London Middlesex Hospital Medical School (1922–1947); professor (1947–1959).

87 Pnina G. Abir-Am, 'The Biotheoretical Gathering, Trans-Disciplinary Authority and the Incipient Legitimation of Molecular Biology in the 1930s: New Perspectives on the Historical Sociology of Science,' *History of Science*, 25 (1) (March 1987): 1; see also Erik L. Peters, *The Life Organic: The Theoretical Biology Club and the Roots of Epigenetics* (Pitttsburg: 2016).

88 Karl Popper, 'Obituary of Joseph Henry Woodger,' *British Journal for the Philosophy of Science*, 32 (3) (September 1981): 327.

89 Needham to Woodger, 3 April 1930, CUL., Needham Ms., M97.

90 Woodger to Needham, 2 June 1930, CUL., Needham Ms., M97.

91 Daniel J. Nicholson and Richard Gawne, 'Rethinking Woodger's Legacy in the Philosophy of Biology,' *Journal of the History of Biology*, 47 (2014): 243–292.

Club. Their disagreements, indeed, were the basis for the formation of the Theoretical Biology Club. Woodger wrote to Needham:

> I was disappointed in your review of my book in *Mind* because you seem to have misunderstood my intentions to a greater extent than I should have expected. How appallingly difficult it is for human beings to communicate with each other. A book is published in the hope of removing a few misunderstandings, and the only result is the production of a whole crop of fresh ones! … [W]e start out knowing what the author means to say better than the poor wretch himself, and if he does not say it we jolly well see to it that he does when we come to write up our review!!! What a hopeless mess the world is in. What Shelley said in 'The Defense of Poetry' seems to have been fulfilled in detail.[92]

That two intellectuals are interested in identifying and resolving biological questions and, at the same time, discussing Wittgenstein, Ramsey and Shelley is a remarkable instance of the ways disciplinary lines continued to be imbricated in the 1930s. Such imbrications point to the ways societies and groups such as the Theoretical Biological Club might tidy up the mental 'mess' to which Woodger referred. Woodger insisted there was nothing personal in his disagreements with Needham. 'All that matters,' he wrote, 'is that any obstacles to the free and clear development of biological science should be swept away.'[93]

Needham and Woodger met at Oxford in the spring of 1932 and then Woodger met with C. H. Waddington[94] (they called him Wad) and together they proposed a 'biotheoretical gathering' at Woodger's home on Epsom Downs in the summer. It was to be a spartan affair. Woodger had little money. His wife agreed 'to put up Waddington and his wife and baby.' In which case Needham and his wife, Dorothy, 'would have a choice between camping in the garden (in your own tent) or having a room in the Downs Hotel.'[95] They also wished to invite Desmond Bernal, who had the most acute mind Needham knew in Cambridge (they called him Sage),[96] but

---

92 Woodger to Needham, 2 June 1930, CUL., Needham Ms., M97.
93 Woodger to Needham, 1 August 1930, CUL., Needham Ms., M97.
94 Waddington, Conrad Hal (1905–1975): father, a tea planter in India; ed. Clifton and Sidney Sussex, Cambridge; Natural Sciences Tripos, first in Part II in Geology (1926); awarded the Arnold Gerstenberg Studentship at Cambridge University (1928) whose purpose it was to promote the study of moral philosophy and metaphysics among men and women students of natural science; fellow of Christ's College (1928–1942) and lecturer in zoology; during the war he was engaged in operations research and was scientific adviser to the Commander in Chief of Coastal Command (1944–1945); Professor of Animal Genetics, University of Edinburgh (1947 until retirement); FRS; CBE; before going up to university he studied chemistry with E. J. Holmyard who introduced him to the Alexandrian Gnostics and Arabic alchemists from which he came to an appreciation of interconnected systems and that prepared him for the philosophy of Alfred North Whitehead.
95 Woodger to Needham, 30 April 1932, CUL., Needham Ms., M98.
96 Needham to Woodger, 5 August 1932, CUL., Needham Ms. M98.

Bernal would either have to sleep in the Needhams's tent or take a room in the Downs Hotel himself.[97] Woodger proposed that they gather on a Monday afternoon and depart on the following Friday evening or Saturday. In the morning they would read the paper for that day and begin discussions (10.00am–1.00pm). Then lunch. From 2.30 to 4.30pm walking or other forms of recreation. They would continue their discussion from 5.30 to 7.30pm and then have supper.[98] So, during the daytime they would discuss scholarly matters around a blackboard in the sitting room; they would have 'politico-socio-economic' discussions over dinner; they would bathe by moonlight. Needham described their first gathering as the most interesting meeting he had ever attended. Dorothy Needham described it as a 'memorable time.' In their discussions they preserved complete freedom of individual expression, proposing interpretations that might stimulate each other's interests.

Woodger and Needham were particular about the size of the group. They favoured smallness. As Woodger put it, the smaller and the less formal 'the more business is likely to get done.'[99] They sought for both 'homogeneity and diversity of interests.'[100] They imagined that the size of the club would be five members and they were reluctant to go larger because they fretted about the spirit of the club. 'Any cooperative effort,' Woodger wrote, 'is likely to involve some sacrifice of personal wishes. Will everyone in the group or be added to it appreciate this and cheerfully play his (or her) part when the time comes.' They had three embryologists, one of whom was a biochemist, and they wondered how a potential member fit into this arrangement.[101] It became a small but elastic group, which eventually included: Needham, Woodger, Waddington, Bernal, Needham's wife Dorothy Moyle Needham, Woodger's wife Eden Woodger, Dorothy Crowfoot Hodgkin, Dorothy Wrinch, Max Black, Lancelot Law Whyte, Karl Popper and B. P. Wiesner (whom Popper had known from their Vienna days).[102] A new generation, led now by Lancelot Whyte and Peter Medawar, guided the club.[103] They met once at Magdalen College, Oxford and there is a photograph of them there: Peter Medawar, Francis Huxley, Hans Motz, J. Z. Young, Avrion Mitchison.[104]

Embryology was the subject of their discussions and, following Alfred North Whitehead, they opposed mechanistic and reductionist method. They proposed to take biology beyond mere morphology and make it an

97 Woodger to Needham, 23 May 1932, CUL., Needham Ms., M98.
98 Woodger to Needham, 23 May 1932, CUL., Needham Ms., M98.
99 Woodger to Needham, 30 April 1932, CUL., Needham Ms., M98.
100 Woodger to Needham, 23 May 1932, CUL., Needham Ms., M98.
101 Woodger to Needham, 29 September 1932, CUL., Needham Ms., M98.
102 There are two lists of members in the Needham Mss, J244.
103 Popper, 'Obituary of Joseph Henry Woodger': 330.
104 For the post-war generation see Peter Medawar, *Memoir of a Thinking Radish: An Autobiography* (Oxford/New York: 1988), p.85.

experimental science by taking on board chemistry, physics and mathematics. In his *Sceptical Biologist* (1929) Needham observed: '[O]n my walks abroad the allotments I have often seen a mass of ruins, already partly covered over with historical vegetation and commentatorial sheep.' He was unhappy with the scientific 'tool-shed now on the market':

> Ruins are ruins, and make the scientific method with its dependence on the inductive process, its constant employment of statistics, its suppression of the individual, its inevitable tendency to analyse, its rejection of all entitities which cannot be numerically expressed and in a word, its formidable subjectivity, into what we might call god's Own Method, is now more than ever a hopeless task.

Naturalism 'possesses no windows and so shuts out the view' and neo-vitalism 'has a leaky roof and so lets in the rain.' His answer: 'build your own tool-shed.' He thought, when dealing with difficult to define, tenuous questions, that it might be useful to consider thoughts drawn from literature, such as from Strindberg's *Master Olaf*. He was not prepared to plunge into mysticism, but mystic activity might be more important than its results:

> It may well be possible that it is in our periods of spiritual activity that we come as close as we can to reality, that unmovable something which lies, we are sure, behind the changing show of facts on which our minds feed, and the stimuli which release the play of our feelings.[105]

He was, after all, a High Anglican who worshipped at Ely, in Caius chapel, served as a lay-preacher at Thaxsted, and regarded himself as an 'honorary Taoist.' He wished for biology to be more than morphological classification. It must concern itself with molecules and atoms, chemistry and physics.

The intellectual concerns of the Theoretical Biology Club went far beyond technical questions. Needham, being Joseph Needham, had given thought to this before. For him, the distinction between speculative work and empirical work was 'singularly blind' because to appreciate the implications of one's method one had to be both a 'scientific worker' and a student of philosophy. This, he thought, was especially true for the biochemist:

> His central problem, the Nature of Life, is partly a philosophical one. And in his case this is much more than it is for other biological sciences; for zoology deals only with the forms of animals, botany with those of plants. In physiology and biochemistry, however, we approach life in its most intimate aspect; as we pass from distribution to form, and from form to function, we become progressively less able to neglect philosophical considerations.[106]

[105] Joseph Needham, *The Sceptical Biologist* (London: 1929), pp.13, 15–16, 23, 33, 35.
[106] Joseph Needham, 'The Philosophical Basis of Biochemistry,' *Monist*, 25 (1) (January 1925): 27–28.

In his review of Woodger's *Biological Principles* he spoke of the 'tantalizing mysterious processes of living things,' the study of which defies 'our present methods, logical as well as technical.'[107]

Needham developed these ideas in his relations with the members of the Theoretical Biology Club. His book *Order and Life* (1938) is dedicated to them.[108] Organisation and order were the club's central preoccupations. Needham and Waddington had been to Germany where the research of Hans Spemann had opened the 'borderline field of biochemistry and experimental embryology by his discovery of the primary inductor or "organizer," the morphogenetic hormone that stimulates the neural tube and vertebrae' in the amphibian and avian embryo.[109] This discovery encouraged Needham and Waddington to try to identify the molecules that act as morphogenetic hormones.[110] This was more than an experimental or technical matter. *Entwicklungsmechanik* was a an instrumental method, not a description, for understanding development in keeping with the procedures that characterised physiology and chemistry. It had substantial results, however, for the 'organizer phenomena' by revealing the processes whereby forms and patterns emerge from its simple beginnings in a fertilised egg.[111]

Needham used a quotation from Sir Thomas Browne's *The Garden of Cyrus* (1658) on the title page of *Order and Life*:

> All things began in Order, so shall they
> End, and so shall they begin again; according
> To the Ordainer of Order, and the mysticall
> Mathematics of the City of Heaven.

Needham realised the difficulty of these problems. 'The fusion of the two great realms of morphology and biochemistry,' he wrote, 'or, if we take the more all-inclusive term, biophysics, still remains.' He cited Woodger's *Biological Principles* to assert:

---

[107] Joseph Needham, 'Review of *Biological Principles: A Critical Study* by J. H. Woodger,' *Mind*, new series, 39 (154) (April 1930): 222.

[108] See the dedication page of Joseph Needham, *Order and Life* (New Haven 1936). 'To J. H. W., C. H. W., M. B., B. P. W., D. W., J. D. B., D. M. N., E. W.'

[109] Waddington to June Toulmin, 9 April 1965, CUL., Needham Ms., M89.

[110] Henry Holorenshaw [Joseph Needham], 'The Making of an Honorary Taoist,' in Mikuláš Teich and Robert Young (eds), *Changing Perspectives in the History of Science: Essays in Honor of Joseph Needham* (London: 1973): 7.

[111] Erik Peterson, 'The Conquest of Vitalism or the Eclipse of Organicism?: The 1930s Cambridge Organizer Project and the Social Network of Mid-Twentieth-Century Biology,' *British Journal for the History of Science*, 47 (2) (June 2014): 282–304, esp. 287–294. For a consideration of the long-term significance of such findings see Scott F. Gilbert and Sahotra Sarkar, 'Embracing Complexity: Organicism for the 21st Century,' *Developmental Dynamics*, 219 (2000): 1–9.

[F]orm is simply a short time-slice of a single spatio-temporal entity. We have enlarged our concept of structure so as to include and recognise that in the living organism there is no spatial structure with an activity as something over against it, but that the concrete organism is a spatio-temporal structure and that spatio-temporal structure is the activity itself.

Organisation exists in living life; it is 'not something mystical and unamenable to scientific attack, but rather the basic problem confronting the biologist.'[112]

Needham himself, writing under his *nom de plume* as Henry Holorenshaw, described his position as a 'middle way.' He traced this impulse to his parents. From his father, a former teacher of histology at the University of Aberdeen and latterly a Harley Street specialist, he derived 'the scientific mind.' From his mother, 'a gifted, though feckless,' musician, and composer, he gained 'a certain largeness of spirit generosity in action and initiative.' His parents did not get on and Needham described his childhood as a 'battle field' in which he found himself 'ferrying between two pieces of land separated by an arm of the sea.' He, therefore, set his mind in a 'posture of permanent bridge-building, searching always as it were for a union of things separated.' He sought to bridge the gulf between science and religion, between religion and socialism, between East and West in his great history of Chinese science, and between biochemistry and morphology. Seeking the organising principle that produced differentiation in organic life, Needham found 'something which was neither mechanical materialism nor spiritual vitalism.'[113]

Woodger, while claiming he would not 'want to dominate the show,' put forward a specific programme for the Theoretical Biology Club. They should examine, he proposed: 'the bearing of modern work in logic on *Theorienbildung* in natural science'; 'the relation between chemical concepts and biological ones'; 'the relation between "descriptive" and "experimental" branches of biology'; 'the mutual relations of taxonomy, embryology, and "phylogeny"'; 'the analysis of current notions in embryology, "determination," "potency," "segregation," etc.'[114] Dorothy Wrinch detected the different emphases in Woodger's and Needham's approaches. 'Socrates is said to hold that biology must remain for ever [sic] in two irreconcilable divisions, morphology and physiology.' Yet, Needham would argue that the 'morphologist is behaving as an artist searching for an aesthetic appreciation of significant form rather than "a scientific investigator."'[115]

---

[112] Needham, *Order and Life*, pp.6, 7.
[113] Henry Holorenshaw [Joseph Needham], 'The Making of an Honorary Taoist': 2–3, 7, 10.
[114] Woodger to Needham, 30 April 1932, CUL., Needham Ms., M98.
[115] D. Wrinch, 'Geometry in the Service of Biology,' nd but 1933, CUL., Bernal Mss., Add. 8287/160.

Wrinch also put her pen to the subject of the Theoretical Biology Club's purposes and direction.[116] A mathematician and student of Bertrand Russell, she acted as his unpaid assistant and secretary when he was sent to gaol for his anti-war activities. When Russell left for China she was charged with seeing Wittgenstein's *Tractatus* through to publication. Though she published twenty papers on pure and applied mathematics and sixteen on the philosophy of science, she failed to find a career as a mathematician, but Oxford marked her distinction by making her the first woman DSc. As a theoretical biologist, though, and through her association with Woodger, Bernal, Hodgkin and Needham, she brought mathematics to bear and sought to deduce the structure of proteins by the use of mathematical principles. Her concepts went beyond the structure of proteins and she laid out the problem of theoretical science, which is what commended her to the Theoretical Biology Club. As she had written:

> The question for theoretical science is to find all sets of postulates which are capable of giving, as logical consequences of themselves, certain definite sets of facts. The number of facts which for all practical purposes may be looked upon as established is tremendously large, and the vast multitude of them have been collected by means of inductions into comprehensive general propositions ... The task of theoretical science is then to investigate all the possible sets of postulates which when logically developed will give these facts as consequences.

Such findings, she held, 'can have no finality.' Certain postulates, it may be concluded, might 'cover the known facts admirably ... but we can never assert that they *alone* will cover them. There may be unnumbered others which will also explain them.' No theory can be final or permanent. Postulates must be judged by their logical consequences. If certain of them provide the conclusions investigators require they may be regarded as satisfactory. 'But there may be many other sets of them of which this is equally true.' No considerable progress can be made without logical insight. 'Logic alone can suggest the fundamental ideas which an understanding of structure requires.' Knowledge of logical construction, Wrinch argued, 'provides an entrancing field of intellectual activity, and just at the present time circumstances are particularly propitious.'[117]

---

[116] Wrinch, Dorothy Maud (1894–1976): born in Rosaria, Argentina; father, an engineer; ed. Surbiton High School and Girton College, Cambridge where she graduated as a wrangler (1916); stayed on for a fourth year to read the Moral Sciences Tripos and study symbolic logic with Bertrand Russell; lecturer in mathematics at University College, London (1918); returned to Girton as a research fellow (1920); married John William Nicholson, a fellow of Balliol and a mathematical physicist, and for the next sixteen years she held a number of temporary appointments, never secure in the university world; divorced Nicholson on his decline into insanity; moved to the United States (1939) where she married Otto Glaser, a biologist, and held appointments at Amherst College, Mount Holyoke College and Smith College.

[117] Dorothy Wrinch, 'The Relations of Science and Philosophy,' *Journal of Philosophical Studies*, 2 (6) (April 1927): 156, 157, 158, 163, 164, 165.

The members of the Theoretical Biology Club were by no means settled either professionally or socially, Joseph Needham admitted. He himself came from a family that was neither rich nor poor.[118] To gain a point of purchase and security in the university, Needham, Bernal, Waddington and Wrinch were eager to establish an Institute of Physico-Chemical Morphology at Cambridge. The Rockefeller Foundation had decided to work wholeheartedly to fund projects in biology where officers such as Warren Weaver believed 'physics and chemistry were ripe for a fruitful union with biology.'[119] At first these members of the Theoretical Biology Club thought the project would be limited to embryology but under Wrinch's urging, and here she cited the Rockefeller Foundation's policy, they broadened their proposal to broach all of morphology so that it might 'take its place on a level with the physical sciences.'[120]

Needham took Wrinch's ideas on board and proposed such an institute to the Rockefeller Foundation. Giving full credit to Wrinch for her insights and organisational proposals, the broadening of the proposal, he argued, would have the positive advantage of including 'the study of such phenomena as mitosis itself, apart from its implications in metazoan growth, by cytological and physic-chemical methods.' He sketched out an organisational structure for the institute consisting of six research units each led by a *Wissenshafliche Mitabeiter* (he apologised for using clumsy untranslatable terms). These were to be the units and their leaders: Chemical Embryology Morphology (Needham); Causal or Experimental Morphology (Waddington); Chrystal Physics of Substances of Biological Importance (Bernal), Dorothy Crowfoot (later Hodgkin) was to be his *Chef de Travaux*; Cytology and Histology (Wrinch); Theoretical Biology (Woodger).[121] This institute, they proposed, was to be governed by a council, organised laterally rather than hierarchically.

They were thwarted and the project came to nothing. The plans and proposals of charismatic individuals were crushed in the maws of two bureaucracies. The Rockefeller Foundation, ever sensitive to reporting procedures and administrative responsiveness, wished for tighter university control. W. E. Tisdale, the officer of the Rockefeller Foundation with whom Needham and his colleagues dealt, warned them that, while '*pourparlers* concerning grants undertaken with people like yourself and Dr Waddington, who are directly concerned with the problems involved, the Foundation, for reasons of expediency much prefers to have formal dealings with those in responsible charge of the institutions concerned.' He urged Needham to have such

---

[118] [Holorenshaw], 'The Making of an Honorary Taoist': 2.
[119] W. E. Tisdale to Needham, 28 January 1935, CUL., Needham Ms., B22. See Warren Weaver, *Scene of Change: A Lifetime in American Science* (New York: 1970), pp.58–75, esp. 69.
[120] Wrinch to Needham, 23 February 1935, CUL., Needham Ms., B22.
[121] Needham to Tisdale, 27 February 1935, CUL., Needham Ms., B22.

as Gowland Hopkins put forward the formal proposal.[122] Needham duly put the idea for bridging 'the gap between physio-chemical concepts and technique on one hand and morphological questions on the other' before the Vice-Chancellor and the Council of the Senate. This was not to be conventional descriptive embryology but rather 'embryology studied with the most powerful experimental methods of explanation and *Entwicklungsmechanik*, in the closest conjuction with bio-chemistry and biophysics.'[123] The university officers were leery of the workings of the Theoretical Biology Club. Needham's and Woodger's positions, since both held readerships, were relatively secure. But not Waddington's who, though he wished to pursue research in embryology, had been trained as a geologist. Bernal's interest in crystallography did not square with Rutherford's interests in particle physics. Nor did Bernal's unconventional outlook, bizarre lifestyle ('who can trust a man with hair like that,' some said) and his promotion of communist ideas make him attractive to Rutherford.[124] As Needham concluded sadly:

> [T]he work in Cambridge on the chemical aspects [of the] organizer phenomenon is menaced with complete stoppage. This is particularly distressing, since the Cambridge group were the first in the field, and the subject of the *morphogenetic stimuli* operating during embryonic development is the most interesting and alive part of chemical embryology to-day.[125]

So, Waddington continued his fellowship at Christ's College and as a lecturer in zoology until the war intervened, after which he went off to his professorship at the University of Edinburgh. Bernal went off to Birkbeck College, London. Dorothy Crowfoot Hodgkin stayed at Oxford. Dorothy Wrinch went off to the United States. The Needhams went to China.

The societies and associations sketched out above – Bloomsbury, Pearsall Smith's coterie in Chelsea, the Tots and Quots, the Theoretical Biology Club – are only examples of the ways in which universities and other powerful institutions, such as the Royal Society and the British Academy, were limited in capturing and incorporating novelty and innovation within formal structures of learning. Formal structures may provide legitimacy and resources for research and intellectual differentiation, but their rules and regulations that are necessary for intellectual robustness are often at odds with alternative lives of learning. Bloomsbury, Pearsall Smith's coterie, the Tots and Quots,

122 W. E. Tisdale to Needham, 28 January 1935, CUL., Needham Ms., B22.
123 Joseph Needham, 'Memorandum to the Vice-Chancellor and the Council of the Senate on the Question of the Extension of the Biological Laboratory,' Long Vacation, 1936, CUL., Needham Ms., B25.
124 Abir-Am, 'The Biotheoretical Gathering': 18–22, 63–64 n. 68.
125 Joseph Needham, 'An Account of the Negotiations Regarding Financial Aid to Technical Assistance, etc. for Studies on the Borderline Between Biochemistry and Embryology, 1933–1938,' 12 July 1938, CUL., Needham Ms., E114.

and the Theoretical Biology Club represent mental sites for those alternative concepts and intellectual procedures. Such societies have the opportunity to escape from what is conventional and acceptable. In them it is possible for the charismatic to contest the bureaucratic. In them it is possible (even necessary) to develop different forms of address and thought. In them it is possible to acquire and tolerate the unique and the unusual.

Francis Crick wrote to Desmond Bernal after Bernal had congratulated him for winning the Nobel Prize. 'I have always thought of you,' Crick wrote, 'as our scientific "grandfather," fortunately perennially young. But for your work and encouragement in the early days none of us would have dared to venture into these fields.'[126] Seven years later Crick wrote to Bernal again in a further meditation on the ways, years earlier, that escaping from the conventional could prove intellectually fruitful later:

> In this lab [the Laboratory of Molecular Biology, Hills Road] we have always regarded you as the scientific father of our subject. If it was not for your imagination in thinking about what seemed to be impossibly difficult problems, and the encouragement you gave to Max [Perutz] and Dorothy [Hodgkin] and the others, people like myself would not have had the opportunity to work in molecular biology, and would have been too timid to tackle the really interesting questions. I shall always remember the stimulation you gave us when you came to the visit the Cavendish when I was still a research student and particularly appreciate your support when I was having to, at that early stage, saying unkind things about protein crystallography. It is wonderful to see how the subject has developed since then, both on the structural side and on the biochemical side, but without the early work of people like yourself it would never have got off the ground.[127]

But if they are expressions of escape, these sites are also expressions of exile.

However, in sites of mental exile creative individuals are caught in the tightness of isolation. They lack legitimacy and have to acquire different forms of intellectual authority. Their virtues are also their vices and sites of exile can become claustrophobic and defensive, peculiar and even weird. These sites, or niches, however, hold open opportunities for conceptions that are unattractive and unacceptable. Located in the nooks, crannies, crevices and interstices of intellectual and social life, sites of escape and exile, by their very social looseness, make it possible for forms of what has been called network effects, emergent and diverse intellectual connections and associations. In them different forms of identity can emerge. In the nineteenth century they had been public moralists, gentlemen, and men of letters, people with vocations. In the twentieth century they had careers. For a development of this point see

---

[126] Francis Crick [writing from The Double Helix, 19 Portugal Place, Cambridge] to Desmond Bernal, 1 November 1962, CUL., Bernal Ms., Add. 8287/J24.
[127] Francis Crick to Desmond Bernal, 20 January 1969, CUL., Bernal Ms., Add. 8287/J24.

Chapter 5. They were experts and specialists and, sometimes, technicians who, in doing their scholarship, in hiving themselves off into sites of exile, could form different kinds of knowledge.

Knowledge is often tacit, a form of cult-like knowledge only known and accepted by those who come to share commensurable assumptions and values. 'Articulate systems which foster and satisfy an intellectual passion,' Michael Polanyi has argued, 'can survive only with the support of a society which respects the values affirmed by these passions.'[128] It is a kind of knowledge dealing with the deep processes of cognition. It exposes the tensions between conceptuality and evidence-based procedures. Such knowledge is mixed with the combining power of the relationship between what people think and the groups and institutions to which they belong. Stimulated by individual curiosity, the groups and institutions to which they belong, through their correcting power, provide their own legitimacy and authority. Because knowledge is never pure, the presence of impurity provides openings for creative opportunities that might not have existed had it been pure.[129] Tacit knowledge does not consist in coherent entities. It may be original and objective, but it is never final or certain. The tacit knowledge of interstitial associations is aspirational and preserves the hope of verification along with ambiguity, paradox and irony.

---

[128] Michael Polanyi, *Personal Knowledge: Towards a Post-Critical Philosophy* (Chicago: University of Chicago Press, 1958), p.203; *idem.*, *The Tacit Dimension* (Chicago/London: University of Chicago Press, 1966 [2009]).
[129] Steven Shapin, *Never Pure: Historical Studies of Science as if It Was Produced by People with Bodies, Situated in Time, Space, Culture, and Society, and Struggling for Credibility and Authority* (Baltimore: The Johns Hopkins University Press, 2010).

Chapter 4

Exile and Escape: Transporting Knowledge

> The composition of this book [his *General Theory* (1936)] has
> been for the author a long struggle of escape ... a struggle of
> escape from habitual modes of thought and expression ... The
> difficulty lies, not in the new ideas, but in escaping from the
> old ones, which ramify, for those brought up as most of us have
> been, into every corner of our minds.
>
> John Maynard Keynes[1]

INTERSTITIAL societies treated escape and exile as imaginative, mental journeys because knowledge is Promethean, many-sided and changing; it is not fixed in geographical spaces. It is a moveable feast. But it has neither will nor volition; it has to be moved. Knowledge moves in cognitive social units. Such movement has sometimes been treated as something fraught. Movingly, Edward Said put it this way:

> Exile is strangely compelling to think about but terrible to experience. It is the
> unhealable rift forced between a human being and a native place, between the
> self and the true home: its essential sadness can never be surmounted. And
> while it is true that literature and history can contain heroic, romantic, glorious,
> even triumphant episodes in an exile's life, these are no more than efforts to
> overcome the crippling sorrow of estrangement. The achievements of exile are
> permanently undermined by the loss of something left behind forever.[2]

So the gladness of escape into exile is coupled with sadness. It can be a misfortune and an opportunity, a reason for unhappiness and also a 'source of painful encouragement.' As Leszek Kolakowski has argued, in exile Marx, Freud and Einstein became 'world-conquerors':

> It was only by, as it were, exiling themselves from their collective exile that they
> became exiles in the modern sense. However hard they might have tried, they
> failed (at least most of them) to lose entirely their identity of old and to be

---

[1]   John Maynard Keynes, *General Theory of Employment, Interest and Money* (New York: 1936), p.viii.
[2]   Edward Said, *Reflections on Exile and Other Essays* (Cambridge, Mass.: 2000), p.173.

unreservedly assimilated, they were looked upon as alien bodies by the indigenous tribes and it was probably this uncertain status, the lack of a well-defined identity, which enabled them to see more than those who were satisfied with their inherited and natural sense of belonging.[3]

Geographical exile and escape, if one takes advantage of them, can have important intellectual consequences. They may make it possible to escape from long-held convictions and theories. Exercises in exile, the taking of refuge, can be an escape from the self and, therefore, assist in the formation of objectivity. Exile and escape eases intellectual boundary crossings and makes disciplinary maintenance and defence more difficult. It discourages conceptual essentialism. Exile and escape facilitates intellectual differentiation and complexity.

In his preface to the *Treatise on Money* (1930) Keynes said 'there is a good deal in this book which represents the process of getting rid of the ideas I used to have and of finding my way to those I now have.'[4] Still, escape into mental exile is neither direct nor easy. It is a thought with which Freud would sympathise. As Freud observed, our neuroses arise not from our ignorance but from our resistance to overcoming our ignorance. The neurosis of exile requires the development of forms of sociality noted in the cases found in Chapter 3: Bloomsbury, the Theoretical Biological Club, the Tots and Quots. When Keynes went into the exile that produced the *General Theory* he did not go into it alone. He took with him, as he noted himself, R. F. Kahn, Austin Robinson, Joan Robinson, Ralph Hawtrey and Roy Harrod.[5] The loneliness of exile found consolation in friendship.

Knowledge, as Richard Rorty has put it, is 'pictures, rather than propositions, metaphors rather than statements which determine most of our philosophical convictions.'[6] This is why the relations between knowledge and politics, between learning and the public world, are tense, strained and discomforting. The criticism of extreme positivism can be pushed too far into a criticism of objectivity and the legitimacy and authority of knowledge itself. Some of the reasons for exile can be put down to the awkward roles learned people themselves play in society. They are bearers of models and standards. They present those 'symbols to be appreciated' that 'guide, and form the expressive life of society.'[7] Consequently, learned people can become targets of resentment and subjected to reverse forms of snobbery, contempt and condescension.

3   Leszek Kolakowski, 'In Praise of Exile,' *Times Literary Supplement* (11 October 1985): 1123–1124.
4   Quoted in Peter Clarke, 'The Politics of Keynesian Economics, 1914–1931,' in Michael Bentley and John Stevenson (eds), *High and Low Politics in Modern Britain: Ten Studies* (Oxford: 1983): p.156.
5   Keynes, *The General Theory of Employment*, p.viii.
6   Richard Rorty, *Philosophy and the Mirror of Nature* (Oxford: 1980), p.12.
7   Edward Shils, *The Intellectuals and the Powers and Other Essays* (Chicago: 1972), p.5 ff.

Exile need not be physical; it can be mental and one can be a stranger at home, as in the case of Bloomsbury, the Tots and Quots, and the Theoretical Biology Club. Or, exile can take the form of escape into cosmopolitanism and the creation of loyalties beyond those to the state, the nation or the family. It can be insidious by creating false binaries reducing knowledge to 'this' and 'that,' but forgetting the 'other.' Exile and escape can take the form of denying the law of the excluded middle. It can take the form of the betrayal of the clerks, as in the case of the ninety-four German scholars who in 1914 shackled themselves to the state and defended Prussian militarism, betraying international learning. It can take the form of committing the compositional or ecological fallacies. One form of exile, as the standing authority on British intellectuals has said, is denial. He has put to exhaustive and exhausting analysis the thought that, somehow, the British are peculiar because they do not have those foreign (French) beings called intellectuals. 'Denial,' he has pointed out is a 'cunning feral beast, endlessly resourceful in protecting its willful nescience.'[8]

Sometimes the notion of exile has been put to work in the thought that there are certain important questions needing investigation, which have to be put to individuals or groups somewhat aside from established institutions. Lord Rees, the Astronomer Royal, past president of the Royal Society, and former master of Trinity College, has celebrated the resurrection of the Longitude Act of 1714 because of the need to 'channel more brainpower into innovation, to jump-start new technologies and to enthuse [sic] young people.'[9] One United States general, in his effort to combat ISIS ('We have not defeated the idea. We do not even understand the idea,' he said) shunted aside intelligence experts in the state and defence departments and convened a body of outsiders to consider how the Islamic State might be confronted.[10] This may all be the reciprocal of university reform. Even as universities became more receptive to research and scholarship, and more robust in their practice thereof, curiosity, creativity and originality were pushed outside to groups whose mental flexibility made them sites of intellectual innovation.

Exile and escape may be what Rowan Williams has called the proclamation of a moment of 'sovereign emancipation':

> Our intellectual life as human beings is properly a matter of constant wonder. That we are able to go on reconfiguring our world, learning not only new answers but radically new questions, that we are repeatedly pushed by our own enquiry beyond what our existing language can say, that we are continually – and

8   Stefan Collini, *Absent Minds: Intellectuals in Britain* (Oxford: 2006), *passim*; the quote is at p.502.
9   Martin Rees, 'A Longitude Prize for the Twenty-First Century,' *Nature* (509) (22 May 2014): 401.
10   Eric Schmitt, 'The Battle to Defang ISIS, U.S. Targets its Psychology,' *New York Times* (29 December 2014): A1, A6.

practically continuously – moving in and out of the deepest bewilderment in order that we may expose ourselves to a more comprehensive truth.

Research raises 'questions that are meant to generate new levels of puzzlement and enticing inconclusiveness, not to close down investigation, or consolidate a given position of power.' When serious, research 'changes the questioner.'[11] When Clifford Geertz came to the School of Social Science at the Institute for Advanced Study he argued that the purpose of the school was not to close questions but to open them, or, as he put it, to engage in 'the loosening up of things, not their solidification.' As Geertz went on to remark, the distinctions between 'thinking' and 'doing,' between 'pure' and 'applied' are often difficult to make, but his school was 'clearly on the "thinking" – writing, discussing, criticizing – "pure" side.'[12]

Exile, as Chapter 3 has shown, can express itself in the hiving off of individuals into private groups – the Apostles, Bloomsbury, the circle around Logan Pearsall Smith in Chelsea, Joseph Needham's and Joseph Woodger's Theoretical Biology Club, Solly Zuckerman's Tots and Quots – which provided insulation and security for creative work. Their exile did not end there. The children of Leslie Stephen moved from Kensington to their exile in Bloomsbury, but Bloomsbury also had outposts at Rodmell and Tilton in Sussex, and in France, Italy, Spain and Greece. Pearsall Smith was a Quaker born the in the United States. Needham and Waddington had been to Germany where they were captivated by the search for the organiser concept, and Needham had been, and was captivated by, China. Zuckerman was born in South Africa and had taught in the United States. Born in a trilingual family, George Steiner escaped with them to the United States where he was educated at Chicago and Harvard before going to Oxford. Britain, as he said, was his chosen land and he finally settled in Churchill College, Cambridge. But he never got a university teaching post at Cambridge. British literary culture was tightly parochial. T. S. Eliot, William Empson and F. R. Leavis wrote about British (that is to say English) figures. George Steiner wrote about the German-speaking figures of European modernism: Celan, Nietzsche, Gadamer and Husserl.[13] Exile and absence were many things to many people and one wants a fuller ecology of knowledge to explore in even greater detail the relationships between politics, society and cognition in twentieth-century Britain.[14]

[11] Lord Williams of Oystermouth, Sermon Before the University, King's College Chapel, 17 May 2015.

[12] Clifford Geertz, 'School Building: A Retrospective Preface,' in Joan Wallach Scott (ed.), *Schools of Thought: Twenty-Five Years of Interpretive Social Science* (Princeton: 2001), p.4.

[13] George Steiner with Larue Adler, *A Long Saturday: Conversations* (Chicago: 2017).

[14] Charles Rosenberg, 'Toward an Ecology of Knowledge: On Discipline, Context, and

That is what this chapter seeks to capture in its discussion of the Society for the Protection of Science and Learning, and the Warburg Institute.

The Society for the Protection of Science and Learning, originally called the Academic Assistance Council, facilitated the great diaspora of scholars and scientists from Germany and Austria in the 1930s. The society came into existence in the following way. In March 1933 William Beveridge was in a Viennese café with Lionel Robbins and Ludwig von Mises, the Austrian economist. Beveridge wrote:

> As we talked of things in general, an evening paper was brought in giving the names of a dozen leading professors in German universities who were being dismissed by the new Nazi regime on racial or political grounds. As Mises read out the names to our growing indignation, Robbins and I decided that we would take action in the London School of Economics to help scholars in our subjects who should come under Hitler's ban.

Beveridge saw at first hand the consequences of political terror while on a train to Frankfurt on his way back to London. A German professor in the carriage with him fell into a state of panic when he observed a small boy whom he took to be a Nazi agent charged with observing him before turning him over to the Nazi authorities. Beveridge found the experience 'mind-and-spirit destroying.'[15] Robbins, who was not always sympathetic to Beveridge's impulses, thought Beveridge's support for their German colleagues was Beveridge's finest hour. 'Slumped in a chair, with his great head characteristically cupped in his fists, thinking aloud, he then and there outlined with basic plan for what became the famous Academic Assistance Council – later the Society for the Protection of Science and Learning.'[16]

Back at the London School of Economics Beveridge consulted his colleagues and created there an Academic Freedom Committee that included Beveridge, Robbins, Eileen Power and Charles Webster. This committee reported to the LSE's Professorial Council, which took two important steps. First, they decided to invite scholars with international reputations to come to the school to engage in graduate instruction. Second, they recommended that members of the staff should contribute a percentage of their annual incomes (1 per cent from lecturers, 2 per cent from readers, 3 per cent from professors) to an assistance fund. In this way they collected in the next three years the sum of £2,850 to assist distinguished as well as promising displaced

---

History,' in Alexandra Oleson and John Voss (eds), *The Organization of Knowledge in Modern America, 1860–1920* (Baltimore: 1979): 440–455.
15   Lord Beveridge, *A Defense of Free Learning* (London: 1959), p.1. Beveridge also records this incident in his autobiography: *Power and Influence* (London: 1953), p.235.
16   Lionel Robbins, *Autobiography of an Economist* (London: 1971), p.144.

scholars. In this way the LSE became an important outpost for the giving of aid to the victims of German persecution.[17]

At the same time Beveridge opened a second front. On a weekend in April he journeyed up to Cambridge to stay with George and Janet Trevelyan at Garden Corner House. There he discussed the formation of a Society for the Protection of Science and Learning with Trevelyan and Frederick Gowland Hopkins, Professor of Biochemistry and President of the Royal Society. Hopkins got rooms for the society in Burlington House. They persuaded Ernest Rutherford, the Cavendish Professor, to become President of the Society. Beveridge and C. S. Gibson, Professor of Chemistry at Guy's Hospital, became its Honorary Secretaries. They formed a council, of which F. G. Kenyon and A. V. Hill were vice-presidents and included members of all branches of learning: W. H. Bragg, H. A. L. Fisher, A. E. Housman, Maynard Keynes, J. W. Mackail, Gilbert Murray, C. S. Sherrington and J. J. Thomson.

They got Walter Adams to surrender his pensionable lectureship at University College, London to become its full-time secretary, at the same salary but without pension benefits. Adams was young, steady and without political affiliations. 'British by birth, descent and education' (which seems to have been important), he had a firm grasp of the refugee problem, and was 'consumed with zeal for the relief of human suffering for which he has rare fire and eloquence.' In 1936 the authorities considered him as an appropriate candidate to lead the League of Nations office for refugees.[18] Even later he became Director of the London School of Economics. Esther Simpson, educated at the University of Leeds with accomplished musical and linguistic gifts, and who had travelled widely on the Continent, was another appointment. She served as secretary to Adams and was instrumental in the effective management of the society's affairs, dealing with correspondence and travelling personally to other societies such as the Polish Research Centre to assist refugees from Central and Eastern Europe.[19]

The society sought to raise a fund for displaced scholars. They put themselves in communication with the various universities in Britain and abroad, and served as a clearing house for information about academic positions. The society's function, as Beveridge put it, was to serve as a 'labour

[17] Dahrendorf, *LSE*, pp.287–288.
[18] Dr Charles Singer to Ernest Rutherford, 13 January 1936, Rutherford to Singer, 16 January 1936, CUL, Rutherford Ms.Add. S70/S71.
[19] See R. M. Cooper, *Refugee Scholars: Conversations with Tess Simpson* (Leeds: 1992). Katharina Scherke, 'Esther Simpson *und die Aktivitäten der* SPSL (Society for the Protection of Science and Learning) *im Zusammenhang mit der Emigration deutschspra-chiger Wissenshaftler zwichen 1933–1945*,' in J. M. Ritchie (ed.), *German Speaking Exiles in Great Britain* (Amsterdam/New York: 2001): pp.121–130. See, for example, Esther Simpson to Needham, 27 February 1940, 11 March 1940, and 3 April 1940, CUL. Needham Mss/J239.

exchange.'[20] Funds were always short, and such as they were able to raise among themselves soon ran out. In February 1935 Rutherford wrote to Lord Halifax saying that the society's funds would be exhausted by July and asked the Foreign Secretary, in his capacity as Chancellor of Oxford, to join other university chancellors by adding his signature to an appeal to raise new funds 'to help scholars and scientific men who have been displaced from their posts in Germany.' Cautious always, Rutherford said 'I think you will see that the letter is entirely non-political and in no way commits the University of which you are the Chancellor.'[21] The Council of the Society also contacted the Rockefeller Foundation and the Carnegie Corporation of the British Empire to gain funding for their efforts. In the period up to 1945 the Rockefeller Foundation spent $1,410,778 to aid 303 individual scholars. The society supported 561 scholars, 364 from Germany, 95 from Austria and 102 from other European countries. After the war only 45 returned to Germany, 17 returned to Austria and 56 returned to other European countries.[22] Robbins paid Beveridge full credit: through him 'hundreds of *émigrés* even now living in the English-speaking world owe the preservation of their careers and in some cases, probably their lives.'[23] It was a massive displacement and transfer of European learning.

A. V. Hill addressed the Nazi crisis in his Huxley Memorial Lecture in Birmingham on 16 November 1933. 'Science and learning,' he declared, 'are superior to and above the State.' Under normal conditions learning and science enjoyed immunity from interference because 'its method of thought' and 'its direct appeal by experiment to universal Nature' did not depend on the 'interests of any limited group.' Under normal conditions, if intellectual progress is to be made, learning 'must insist on keeping its traditional position of independence' and 'it must refuse to be meddled with, or be dominated by, divinity, morals, or rhetoric.' Under normal conditions learning required international cooperation:

> Germany, however, has lately rendered such intellectual co-operation impossible by offending the first and most fundamental rule that of providing freedom of thought and research. It seemed impossible, in a great and highly civilised country, that reasons of race, creed, or opinion, and more than the colour of a man's hair, could lead to the drastic elimination of a large number of the most prominent men of science and scholarship, many of them men of the highest standards, good citizens, good human beings. Freedom itself is at stake.

[20] Beveridge, *A Defense of Free Learning*, p.7 n.1, 105.
[21] Rutherford to the Rt Hon. Viscount Halifax, 11 February 1935, Rutherford Ms., CUL, Add. 7653/H93.
[22] Norman Bentwich, *The Rescue and Achievement of Refugee Scholars: The Story of Displaced Scholars and Scientists* (The Hague: 1953), pp.13–14, 105.
[23] Quoted in Dahrendorf, *LSE*, p.287.

Hill pointed to the thousands of lawyers, doctors and teachers who had been prevented from following their professions, to the thousands of scholars and scientific workers who had been dismissed, and to 100,000 who had been sent to concentration camps. 'It is difficult to believe in progress, at least in decency and common sense,' Hill concluded, 'when this can happen almost in a night in a previously civilised State.'[24]

J. Stark, writing from the *Physicalisch-Technisch Reichanstalt*, Berlin-Charlottenburg, responded. The National-Socialist government, he asserted, had brought in no measure directed against the freedom of scientific teaching and research. In fact, he asserted, the government 'wish to restore this freedom of research wherever it has been restricted by preceding governments.' Any measures affecting Jewish scholars were due only 'to curtail the unjustifiably great influence exercised by the Jews.' There were 10,000 not 100,000 people in concentration camps, and they were there 'not because of their desire for freedom of thought and speech, but because they have been guilty' of high treason or of actions directed against the community.'[25] Hill retorted: 'Men of high standing do not, without cause, beg their colleagues in foreign countries for help.' Whether scholars have been 'dismissed,' 'retired,' 'given leave' or merely been prevented from entering libraries or laboratories were trifling quibbles. The result was the same: 'it is not consistent with "the freedom of scientific teaching" and research which the German Government' is claiming to restore.[26]

Three years later Hill, Gowland Hopkins and Frederick Kenyon wrote to the *Universities Review* protesting against an account of the German universities written by Dr Köster, an official of the Anglo-German Academic Bureau, who had given a favourable view of the universities under Nazi rule. Hill, Hopkins and Kenyon pointed out that the Nazi regime had altered the constitution of the German universities. The rector of the university, unlike the vice-chancellors of Oxford and Cambridge, had become a permanent official. The title 'Rector' of Heidelberg had been changed to '*Führer*.' Under the leadership principal, the Senate of the faculties was no longer elected by their members but nominated by the *Führer*. Of the 7,000 faculty members in the twenty-three German universities, 1,300 had been dismissed or forced to retire. Knowledge itself was made to serve nationalistic ends. No one spoke of *Deutsch Physic*, *Deutsch Mathematic* and *Deutsch Himmelskunde*. Those who had not been dismissed but refused to persist in academic careers 'under a system which every lover of liberty must loathe' withdrew into private life. 'A German university,' Hill, Hopkins and Kenyon concluded, 'is as to one part

---

[24] A. V. Hill, 'International Status and Obligations in Science,' *Nature*, 132 (23 December 1933): 952–954.
[25] *Nature*, 133 (24 February 1934): 290
[26] *Nature*, 133 (24 February 1934): 290.

a regiment preparing for war, as to the other an intellectual concentration camp.'[27] Joseph Needham thought it impossible for biologists to do original research under conditions imposed by the Nazi regime. The Nazi government was antagonistic to non-military science, he pointed out. The halting of financial support, the absence of collaborators and students, and political terror created an atmosphere that prevented the 'calm of mind which scientific research needs for its successful prosecution.'[28]

Britain served as a staging ground for sending forth refugee scholars elsewhere. As Hanna Holborn Gray, herself the daughter of a German scholar fleeing Germany in 1933, said, British immigration policies limited stays there to a year.[29] Joseph Needham wrote to Edgar Adrian to see if there was a place for Dr Juret Konorski and his wife, Dr Liljana Lubinska, in Adrian's laboratory. Konorski had been a favourite pupil of Pavlov in the Soviet Union, but he and his wife returned to Poland where they were then trapped in the bombardment of Warsaw. Needham wished to get them to Brussels and thence to England. He applied on their behalf to the Society for the Protection of Science and Learning, and he and his wife were prepared to put them up. 'Would it not be a good thing,' he asked Adrian, 'to have more people in Cambridge who have specialised on conditioned reflexes?'[30] Adrian consulted with A. V. Hill about getting a grant to support Konorski and Lubinska from the Society for the Protection of Science and Learning. But Hill pointed out that the society's funds were limited and a grant could only be obtained for a very limited time. On the whole, Adrian thought, it was better for Konorski and Lubinska to find places of refuge in a neutral country. 'Coming here,' he said, 'rather sounds like coming out of the frying pan into the fire.' As to his own laboratory, Adrian could offer them only a small room that would be wanted as soon as other research projects got under way. 'There would be no chance of their doing any electro-physiological research for all the rooms are turned into air raid shelters.'[31] Needham applied for a place for them with W. Horsley Gantt at the Pavlovian Laboratory at the Phipps Clinic of the Johns Hopkins School of Medicine, and T. E. Boyd at the Loyola School of Medicine in Chicago. Though interested in their work, Boyd did not know Konorski and Lubinska. As Boyd pointed out, many European refugees were already in Chicago, permanent appointments were difficult to find and he could only consult professional people in the Polish community there about raising funds for their temporary maintenance.[32]

[27]   A. V. Hill, F. Gowland Hopkins, F. G. Kenyon, 'German Universities,' *Universities Review*, 8 (2) (April 1936): 102–105.
[28]   Joseph Needham to the chairman of the Aliens Tribunal, Country Hall, Cambridge, 10 May 1939, CUL., Needham Ms. M/31.
[29]   Hanna Holborn Gray to the editor of the *London Review of Books* (17 August 2017): 4–5.
[30]   Needham to Adrian, 22 December 1939, CUL. Needham Ms/M236.
[31]   Adrian to Needham, 8 January [19]40, CUL. Needham Ms/ J237.
[32]   Gantt to Needham, 12 January 1940 and T. E. Boyd to Needham, 15 January 1940,

Because of its character as a collegiate university and its commitment to tutorial rather than professorial teaching, Oxford University was ill-suited to serve as a final destination for large numbers of refugee scholars. The fourth report of the Society for the Protection of Science and Learning in 1938 pointed out that Oxford was giving aid and succor to twenty-seven exiles. (Cambridge had supported twenty-five and the combined colleges of London University, perhaps because of the proximity of the Warburg Institute, fifty-nine.) Oxford's colleges, richer than the university itself, though, provided support and sometimes posts for those fleeing the Nazi regime. St John's, Magdalen, Merton, Christ Church, Oriel, Lincoln, Queen's, Balliol, Lady Margaret Hall, and Somerville provided relief for but one exile each (All Souls provided for four). Other colleges, pleading penury, provided minor sums. Wadham, despite the vehement opposition to Nazism of its newly minted warden, Maurice Bowra, contributed nothing.[33] Bowra, however, became a very warm friend of Ernst Kantorowicz, the medievalist, in 1934 welcoming him to Oxford and visiting him in Germany.[34] Unlike some other refugee scholars, who found it difficult to shuck off the habits of German professorialism, Kantorowicz and others – Eduard Fraenkel and Nicolai Rubinstein also come to mind – made himself fully at home in the tutorial style of Oxford's common rooms. Raymond Klibansky, who had found a place for himself at Oriel College, spoke of Kantorowicz's cosmopolitanism and of his knowledge of English history. A colleague at New College spoke of Kantorowicz's ability to take part 'fully in the general conversation in Senior Common room' and of his popularity in the social life of the college. So it was also with other Oxford historians such as H. A. L. Fisher, Austen Lane Poole and T. S. R. Boase.[35] These and other examples reveal the ways in which personal contacts and rather casual meetings, rather than formal institutions, guided and shaped the reception of exiled scholars in Britain.[36]

Louis Rapkine (1904–1948) also moved within the orbit of the Society for the Protection of Science and Learning. He was born into a Russian-Jewish family in Minsk where his father was a tailor. The family migrated to Paris in 1911 and thence to Montreal where his father found employment in a factory and Rapkine began medical studies at McGill University. Finding himself attracted to biochemistry and experimental biology he returned to France and became associated with a group of international scholars, such as

---

CUL, Needham Ms/ J237.

[33] Laurence Brockliss, 'Welcoming and Supporting Refugee Scholars: The Role of Oxford's Colleges,' in Sally Crawford, Katharina Ulmschneider and Jaś Elsner (eds), *Ark of Civilization: Refugee Scholars and Oxford University, 1930–1945* (Oxford: 2017): pp.66–67.

[34] Leslie Mitchell, *Maurice Bowra: A Life* (Oxford: 2009), pp.105–106, 213–214.

[35] Robert E. Lerner, *Ernst Kantorowicz: A Life* (Princeton/Oxford: 2017), pp.174–175.

[36] See Crawford, Ulmschneider and Elsner (eds), *Ark of Civilization: Refugee Scholars and Oxford University, 1930–1945*: pp. 7–8, 19, 139, 229.

Joseph and Dorothy Needham, who spent summers at the marine biology station at Roscoff in Britanny. Thus, though he had not studied at Cambridge, he made intellectual connections with those associated with Gowland Hopkins's Biochemical Laboratory. Working in the borderland between biochemistry and experimental cytology and embryology he gained distinction by applying the techniques of micro-dissection to the study of spicule-formation in the larvae of echinoderms and the sulphuric acid cells of ascidians, gaining thereby grants from the Rockefeller Foundation and the Caisse de Recherches Scientifiques. By 1939 Gowland Hopkins could point the fundamental importance of Rapkine's contribution to the study of cell-division.

The Nazi crisis intervened and Rapkine, in 1934, established the Comité d'Accueil des Savants Étrangers to assist and find work for scientists and other scholars fleeing Germany, Austria and other German-controlled lands. The French government sent Rapkine to Britain. When France fell, Rapkine worked first in London to gain support for refugee intellectuals from the Royal Society and then in New York to get assistance from the Rockefeller Foundation. While in London he formed the Society for Visiting Scientists, a club designed to put refugee scientists in contact with British colleagues. His work assisted some thirty scientists, including the mathematician Jacques Hadamard and the physicist Jean Perrin, in finding positions in the United States. After the war he returned to France to continue his research in the Department of Chemical Cytology, which had been created for him at the Institut Pasteur.

Ever interested in the international claims of science and learning, Rapkine got Rockefeller funds to organise a series of symposia at the Centre National de la Researche Scientifique. The year after his death Sir Robert Robinson, PRS, chaired a meeting consisting of British and French colleagues to establish a fund in Rapkine's memory to assist young biologists and biochemists. Its committee included Edgar Adrian, Desmond Bernal, John Cockcroft, Julian Huxley, C. H. Waddington, Solly Zuckerman, Patrick Blackett, A. V. Hill, Dorothy and Joseph Needham, and Esther Simpson. Those who knew Rapkine intimately spoke of his high moral courage and his 'strangely piercing look' that 'made them feel responsive to their own best conscience.'[37] Esther Simpson remembered him:

> [He] was an extraordinary man. He was very practical, and at the same time he was a saint; he was fundamentally good, and had a very keen sense of humour. He was an utterly cultured person; you could talk to him about the theatre, about literature, about art, about music; he knew a lot about the dance and just anything.[38]

[37] 'Rapkine Memorial Fund, 1951,' CUL., Needham Ms/J/187.
[38] Cooper (ed.), *Refugee Scholars: Conversations with Tess Simpson*, p.87.

Knowing Rapkine in 1925, Joseph Needham said, 'was a real turning-point for my wife and myself.'[39] Simpson called him one of the heroes of her life.[40]

As Rapkine's career shows – born in Ukraine, moved to France and thence to Canada where he became a citizen, back to France, then to Britain and the United States and then back to France – these were wandering scholars. Max Born is another example. Born, deprived of his position as Director of the Physical Institute at the University of Göttingen, he held the Stokes Lectureship at Cambridge (where he took the MA degree and had dining rights at Gonville and Caius College), visited the Raman Institute at Bangalore for six months, was offered a chair at Moscow but took Tait Chair of Natural Philosophy at Edinburgh.[41] Einstein, who had been at Christ Church, Oxford went to the Institute for Advanced Study at Princeton. Erwin Schrödinger left a five-year post at Magdalen College, Oxford and went to the Institute for Advanced Study in Ireland. He was joined in Ireland by Walter Heitler. Hans Bethe had short-term appointments at Bristol and Manchester and then went to Cornell University. Fritz London left Oxford when his Imperial Chemical Industries financed fellowship ended and gained a post at Duke University. Robert Oppenheimer remarked on the contribution these refugees made to US scholarship:

> They all did an enormous amount, and the fact that they were all very good and yet wonderfully adaptable – in the sense that they genuinely came to this country not as a temporary and resented alternative but as something that could be lived with and enjoyed – made a great difference to American physics … They all, I think, were right to appreciate what was good in this country, coming from Europe in the thirties. They came with a good heart, very eager to do the physics they knew how to do, and very anxious to have companionship in that.

More than one hundred men and women, between 1933 and 1941, came from Europe to America to do physics.[42]

Perhaps the most dramatic transfer of knowledge occurred when the Warburg Library transported itself from Hamburg to London. In December 1933 two ships of the Hamburg line, the Jessica and the Hermia, sailed into the Thames estuary containing in their cargo the *Kulturwissenschaftlich*

39 Needham to Dr Gordon Wolsenholme, 13 June 1968, CUL, Needham Ms/J/193.
40 Cooper (ed.), *Refugee Scholars: Conversations with Tess Simpson*, p.85.
41 Born, Max (1882–1970): father an embryologist at the University of Breslau; ed. König Wilhelms Gymnasium, University of Breslau (where he studied Latin, Greek and German along with mathematics and physics), Cambridge University (where he attended the lectures of Thomson and Lamor); held chairs at the University of Berlin and Göttingen and the University of Edinburgh; naturalised (1939) the same year he was elected FRS; Nobel Prize (1954) for his statistical interpretations of the wave function.
42 Quoted in Charles Weiner, 'A New Site for the Seminar: The Refugees and American Physics in the Thirties,' in Donald Fleming and Bernard Bailyn (eds), *The Intellectual Migration: Europe and America, 1930–1960* (Cambridge, Mass.: 1969): pp.190–191; quote is at p.191.

Bibliothek, the private library of Aby Warburg. It was what has been called 'a remarkable, and possibly unique, instance of two-way cultural transmission.'[43] Roger Hinks, who was Assistant Keeper of Greek and Roman Antiquities at the British Museum, had been associated with the Warburg periodically for years.[44] In 1935 Fritz Saxl invited him to give a series of lectures in the summer of that year and Hinks chose myth and allegory in ancient art as his subject. In them Hicks captured the guiding ideas of the Warburg programme that Saxl brought to London:

> Allegory, as I see it is philosophical myth, and I shall try to show how the invention of logical thought by the Sophists had an influence of the structure of a symbolic form like art, whose character *ex hypothsi* must be mythogenic ... This sequence of investigation is not only convenient, but also historically reasonable: it indicates the movement of the mind from religion to philosophy, from daemonic to human, from the collective to the individual; but at the same time it shows how this movement is not one of superstition but of interpretation. If logic had completely superseded myth, allegory would not be necessary; it is precisely this metamythical phenomenon that proves how necessary the imaginative mode of thought is even in a society aware of rational mental processes. I shall also try to show that the concepts which allegory personifies are just those inexplicables, like time and space, public opinion, and moral qualities which can only be represented mythical [sic] and which physical science cannot ultimately explain, however much it may analyse them.[45]

Reflecting on these problems, Hinks pushed his thoughts further. 'Myth and logic are equally real,' he thought, 'because both represent the effort of the mind to interpret itself and its environment.' In fact, the 'direct incitement of mythical thinking is the miracle of life itself, impenetrable and inescapable in the centre of a concrete world of phenomena; and so long as the emphasis is on the knowing mind, the resulting reality is bound to be mythical.'[46] Having delivered the lectures 'more or less successfully in their verbal shape,' Saxl wished him to write them out so that they could be published in the 'Studies

---

43 Nicholas Mann, 'Two Way Traffic: The Warburg Institute as a Microcosm of Cultural Exchange between Britain and Europe,' in Basil Markesinis (ed.), *The British Contribution to the Europe of the Twenty-First Century* (Oxford: 2002): p.93. Mann had been Director of the Warburg Institute from 1990 to 2001.
44 Hinks, Roger (1903–1963): father, Arthur Hinks, CBE and FRS, had been secretary of the Royal Astronomical Society, Secretary of the Royal Geographical Society and Gresham Lecturer in Astronomy; ed. Westminster School where he was a King's Scholar, and Trinity College, Cambridge where he took a second class in the Classical Tripos; Assistant Keeper in the Department of Greek and Roman Antiquities at the British Museum (1926–1939) he was forced to resign in the scandal over the cleaning of the Parthenon Marbles; at the Warburg Institute (1939–1942); Second Secretary to the British Legation in Stockholm (1942–1945); joined the British Council (1945) and served as its representative in Rome (1945–1949), in Holland (1949–1954), Greece (1954–1957) and Paris (1959–1963).
45 Hinks Diary, 12 January 1935, Roger Hinks Papers, Box 1/2/ff.87–88, Department of Rare Books and Special Collections, Princeton University Library.
46 Hinks Diary, 27 January 1935, Hinks Papers, Box 1/2/ ff. 89.

of the Warburg Institute.' Hinks found this daunting, a task that, with the documentation required, could not be completed in fewer than three years. He found the lecture's 'scale and tone ... too fragile for such a gigantic project' yet he 'should be sorry not to preserve all this material in a permanent shape.'[47] He published his book in 1939.[48]

While fully appreciating the strictly intellectual purposes of the Warburg, Hinks found larger cultural values in it and regarded the institute as a 'unique instrument for the realization of human society.'[49] The collapse of liberalism and the emergence of what he called 'various forms of political irrationalism' carried with them a criticism of positivism and 'administered a salutary shock to the complacency of rationalist historiography' of the kind Einstein had brought to rational physical theory. If the scholar is honest, Hinks argued, human behaviour can no longer be explained 'as the product of a few grand, simple, intelligible and natural laws.' Plunged into disillusion and perplexity, 'it is only too clear that the intellect, unassisted by imagination, has failed to account for what has happened in the world':

> Hence the enormous value of an institution like the Warburg Library where the study of symbolic forms of culture introduces into the analysis of the historical mind something as nearly approaching the mutual control of experiment and hypothesis as the structural difference between natural science and mental science will permit.

Imagination, guided by reason, can give a plausible account of the experience and memory of human beings. As Hinks argued, epigraphy and archaeology stood in the relation to the science of culture as experiment did in natural science. Works of art and other material relics from the past, 'provided that we are in a position to interpret [them] correctly,' were self-explanatory and symbolic and 'necessarily give a true account of themselves' because 'they have no opportunity of saying one thing and meaning another as a literary document may.' Intellect might be the instrument for grasping the explicable, but imagination, for Hinks and for the Warburg in his telling of it, was the instrument for grasping the inexplicable, 'equally real and persistent,' leading 'an underground existence in our subconscious life.'[50] Hamburg, in the form of the Warburg coming to London, could guide a cultural rescue mission.

Hamburg, the home of the Warburg banking family, was an important commercial centre but with the establishment of Hamburg University it also became an important intellectual centre. As Peter Gay put it, Hamburg became a 'community of reason devoted to radical inquiry.' It was a community

47 Hinks Diary, 9 June 1935, Roger Hinks Papers, Box 1/2/ff. 99–100.
48 Roger Packman Hinks, *Myth and Allegory in Ancient Art* (London: 1939).
49 Hinks Diary, 13 February 1939, Roger Hinks Papers, Box 1/5, f. 7.
50 Hinks Diary, 1 January 1935, Hinks Papers, Box 1/2/ff/ 81–83, 87.

whose members, 'with their lack of piety, ruthless modernity, their search for reality through science,' were committed to the Weimar spirit.[51] There Aby Warburg installed his library. The library, according to family lore, emerged from a childhood agreement in which Aby Warburg forsook his birthright to the family inheritance and, in exchange, Max Warburg agreed to buy books for his brother for the rest of his Aby's life. Max Warburg is claimed to have said it was the largest blank cheque he ever signed. True or not, it is an example of the so-called Hamburg Model in which culture and commerce, in a distinctive civic setting, created the foundations for both Hamburg University and the Warburg.[52] The coming of the National Socialist regime dashed all that. The new regime prevented members of Warburg's staff from lecturing and students were advised not to use the library for their research. As Lord Lee of Farnham wrote to Max Warburg, 'it ceased to function as a living institution.' The Warburg family and the staff of the institute agreed to move the institute 'to a country in which the atmosphere was conducive to research and learning.'[53]

The cargo of the Jessica and Hermia contained 531 crates of some 60,000 books but also the physical apparatus of Warburg's library. The Hamburgarians first installed themselves at Thames House in Millbank. They moved to the Imperial Institute in South Kensington in 1939. During the war they exiled themselves further to Denham beyond Uxbridge at the end of the Piccadilly line in Buckinghamshire where they lived communally at 'The Lea.' The approach of the war enhanced feelings on the part of its supporters that the Warburg was at further risk. On 13 February 1939 Roger Hinks and Thomas Boase, the then director of the Courtauld Institute,[54] had lunch at the Reform Club and discussed schemes for the Warburg's protection. Hinks and Boase feared the Warburg would be regarded as a parasite in a foreign host and discussed some of the lingering internal difficulties the institute faced. Saxl, then the director of the institute, Hinks and Boase felt, suffered two defects. He had a pampered attitude to practical affairs because he had 'a rich man's toy,' and, Saxl had a 'neurosis about publicity.' Understandably, they felt, Saxl had 'a certain agoraphobia' common to all refugees who 'having been the subject

51 Peter Gay, *Weimar Culture: The Outsider as Insider* (New York/ Evanston: 1970), p.31.
52 Emily J. Levine, 'The Other Weimar: The Warburg Circle as Hamburg School,' *Journal of the History of Ideas*, 74 (2) (April 2013): 314.
53 Eric M. Warburg, 'The Transfer of the Warburg Institute to England in 1933' [October 1953], *University of London: The Warburg Institute Annual Report, 1952–1953*, pp.13, 15.
54 Boase, Thomas Sherrer Ross (1896–1974): ed. Rugby and Magdalen College, Oxford where he read modern history; fellow and tutor of Magdalen (1919–1921); fellow and tutor of Hertford College, Oxford (1922–1937); Director of the Courtauld Institute and Professor of the History of Art at London University (1937–1947); during the Second World War he worked in the Government Code and Cypher School at Bletchley Park and followed the RAF to Cairo (1939–1941); in charge of the British Council activities in the Middle East (1943–1945); President of Magdalen (1947–1968); Vice-Chancellor of Oxford (1956–1960); Slade Professor of Fine Arts at Oxford (1963–1964); FBA (1961).

of much public discussion they only ask to be allowed to mind their own business and lock themselves into their studies for the time being.' If, however, the Warburg tried to save itself by retiring into 'pure scholarship' they 'would deserve the fate which has overcome the intellectuals of Russia, Germany and Italy.' The price for 'this flight from reality would be annihilation.' Hinks and Boase, therefore, thought 'the gradual encirclement' of the Warburg, working through its association with the Courtauld and the emerging *Bulletin of the Warburg and Courtauld Institutes*, would have two effects. It would secure the Warburg. Also, by its assimilation into the university 'it would help to bring about the revival of the humanities, that rebirth of the responsible human personality, without which European civilization will perish.'[55]

The Warburg Institute became part of the School of Advanced Study of the University of London in 1944 when Lord Lee, acting on behalf of the Warburg and the Warburg family signed over a Trust Deed in which the university assumed financial responsibility for the maintenance of the institute, its members and its library. Thus the Warburg Institute would appear to have found safe haven. Until recently, that is, when the University of London went to court to break the Trust Deed and incorporate the institute's unique library into the university's library system. The court has frustrated the efforts of the university, at least temporarily, but as one scholar has remarked the university is trying to do what the Nazis could not do.[56] But in fact the transfer of the Warburg to London had from the beginning the feeling of impermanence. Lord Lee, in his letter to Max Warburg inviting the Warburg to London, spoke of 'lending' it for a period of three years.[57] At the end of the first three years of support Samuel Courtauld extended his support for a further seven years. However precariously, this cultural transfer included not only the physical materials of learning and the people who safeguarded them, but also a cluster of foreign concepts: *Kulturwissenschaft*. These concepts would transform British thought about culture from mere connoisseurship and collecting to the systematic study of humane letters.

Fritz Saxl, Raymond Klibansky, Edgar Wind and Gertrud Bing led the exodus from Hamburg. These were the intellectual children of Aby Warburg. Warburg described himself as 'a Hebrew by blood, a Hamburger at heart, Florentine in spirit.'[58] Warburg created his private library along unusual lines. His library, instead of being organised in some sort of traditional hierarchical, linear form was organised in such a way so that its materials were

---

[55] Hinks Diary, 13 February 1939, Roger Hinks Papers/1/5/ ff./6–7.
[56] Charles Hope, 'The Battle over the Warburg Institute,' *London Review of Books* (4 December 2014): 32–33. See also Rachael Donadio, 'Scholars Fear the Loss of Eden in London,' *New York Times* (11 October 2014): C1 and C6.
[57] Warburg, 'The Transfer of the Warburg Institute to England in 1933,' pp. 14–15.
[58] Anthony Grafton and Jeffrey Hamburger, 'The Warburg Institute,' *Common Knowledge*, 18 (1) (2012): 7.

arranged to reveal the connections among its subjects. He and researchers who followed him could use it to trace the interrelationships, continuous and discontinuous ones, among cultural concepts. His motto was 'Der liebe Gott stecktt in Detail,' but he was never an antiquarian. As William Heckscher pointed out, this amounted to the 'methodic[al] dismantling of borderlines.'[59] Warburg looked beyond scholarly accuracy to an approach that was heuristic and hermeneutic.[60] While Warburg had left behind him only fragments, Kenneth Clark thought he should have been a poet. According to Clark, Warburg had the gift of mimesis:

> He could 'get inside' a character, so that when he quoted from Savonarola, one seemed to hear the Frate's high compelling voice; and when he read from Poliziano there was all the daintiness and slight artificiality of the Medicean circle.[61]

Warburg's objective was to understand the consequences of antiquity for European intellectual life: Das Nachleben der Antike. His library was an instrument for creating cultural tools, as Ernst Gombrich put it, to 'hack a fresh path into the forest' of the protean problem of culture.[62] For the student of these matters, Warburg held, 'no "frontier police" should deter him from crossing [the] conventional borders of "academic fields."'[63] This was no abstract matter. To understand the 'survivals, the continuities, the transmigrations of culture itself' was to remind scholars that ideas persist and 'outlive the Ghetto and the concentration camp.'[64]

Both in word and in deed Saxl was very much the successor to Warburg. Educated in Vienna and Berlin, Saxl joined Warburg as librarian in 1913. Following a period of war service with the Austrian army he took a stronger role at the library, especially during those times when Warburg was indisposed in the Swiss sanatorium in Kreuzlinger. Saxl was a professor at the University of Hamburg from 1927 to 1933. After the death of Warburg in 1929 Saxl led the library into its exile in London. He became Professor of the Classical Tradition at the University of London (1945–1948). The rigors of Saxl's labours in establishing the Warburg Institute in its foreign setting may explain the relative meagreness of his publications. The spirit of the thing, however, may be caught in his contribution to the volume of essays that Klibansky and Ernst Gombrich published as Saturn and Melancholy:

---

59 William Heckscher, 'Petites Perceptions: An Account of Sortes Warburgian,' Journal of Medieval and Renaissance Studies, 4 (1) (1974): 101.
60 Grafton and Hamburger, 'The Warburg Institute': 8
61 Kenneth Clark, Another Part of the Wood: A Self-Portrait (London: 1974), pp.189–190.
62 Ernst Gombrich, 'In Search of Cultural History,' in Richard Woodfield (ed.), The Essential Gombrich (London: 1996): p.391.
63 Ernst Gombrich, Aby Warburg: An Intellectual Biography with a Memoir on the History of the Library by F. Saxl (Oxford: 1970 [1986]), p.323.
64 Harry Levin, Contexts of Criticism (Cambridge, Mass.: 1957), p.14.

Studies in the History of Natural Philosophy, Religion, and Art (1964), a very Warburgian project. The British Academy elected Saxl to its fellowship in 1944. According to the minutes of the British Academy's Council, he was qualified for more than one of its intellectual sections: Ancient History, Medieval and Modern History, Literature and Philology (Classical), Literature and Philology (Modern), Archaeology and the History of Art. He had, they noted, 'an extraordinarily wide knowledge of the history of art in all its bearings upon human civilization.'[65] They appointed him to its section devoted to archaeology and art history.

Raymond Klibansky was among the first to sense the danger to learning when the Nazis came to power. It was he who was among those who urged Saxl and members of the library to flee before it was too late. Born in Paris in 1905, he was educated at the University of Kiel, at the University of Hamburg, and the Ruprecht Karl University of Heidelberg where he received his PhD in 1928 as a student of Karl Jaspers.[66] In preparing his edition of Nicolas of Cusa and Meister Eckhart he realised the importance of Arabic and other Semitic scholars in the transmission of Platonic thought to the Middle Ages. It was a discovery that was unlikely to please his Nazi masters. He associated himself with the Warburg Library for the next decades. As Saxl put it, Klibansky wished to find 'a community where studies like [his] might go on undisturbed by political influence.' It was his idea that the Warburg Institute should serve abroad as a nucleus for studies in the history of civilisation in the same way as it had before in Germany.[67] Klibansky and his family fled first to Italy, then to Brussels, then to London and Oxford. In England he renewed his association with the Warburg Institute. At Oriel College, Oxford Klibansky began work on the edition of his *Corpus Platonicum Medii Aevi*. Klibansky was general editor of the project, supported by the Warburg Institute and the Medieval Academy of America, which was supervised by an editorial committee composed of David Ross, OBE, President of the British Academy and Provost of Oriel College; R. A. Nicholson, Emeritus Professor of Arabic at Cambridge; F. M. Powicke, Regius Professor of History at Oxford; and C. W. Previté-Orton, FBA and University Lecturer in History at Cambridge. Klibansky, with the assistance of Anthony Blunt, brought out his *Continuity of the Platonic Tradition during the Middle Ages* (1939), a thoroughly Warburgian book. There were also all sorts of the usual publishing problems, which were exacerbated by the looming war.

[65] Minutes of the Council Meeting, 17 May 1944, BAA/MB/7.
[66] Emily J. Levine, *Dreamland of Humanists: Warburg, Cassirer, Panofsky, and the Warburg School* (Chicago/ London: 2013), p.104.
[67] Fritz Saxl's Account to the Academic Assistance Council, 5 October 1934, 'The Move of the *Kulturwissenschaftlich Bibliotek Warburg* from Hamburg,' W[arburg] I[nstitute] A[rchives], G[eneral] C[orrespondence], Klibansky file, 1934.

Blunt consulted with Saxl and Gertrude Bing continuously.[68] Klibanksy, a naturalised British subject in 1938, served in the Second World War in the Political Warfare Executive, working on the invasion of Italy and then on the denazification programme in Germany. After the war he moved yet again, this time to Canada where he became Forthingham Professor of Logic and Metaphysics at McGill University. He returned to England and was a fellow of Wolfson College, Oxford from 1981 to 1995.

Edgar Wind (1900–1971) was another who quickly grasped the Nazi threat to learning and urged the Warburgians to flee to England. Born in Berlin, he was trained in mathematics and philosophy at the Gymnasium in Charlottenburg and at the universities of Freiburg, Berlin and Vienna. The first pupil of Edwin Panofsky, he earned his PhD at Hamburg. After two years in the United States at the University of North Carolina, Wind returned to England and attached himself to the Warburg Institute and founded, with Rudolph Wittkower and Anthony Blunt, the *Journal of the Warburg and Courtauld Institutes* (1937). He returned to the United States during the war, teaching at New York University, the University of Chicago and Smith College. Then he returned to England and was appointed the first professor of art history at Oxford. It was an appointment that would give great joy to Isaiah Berlin and Maurice Bowra, if only because it would pain T. S. R. Boase, Director of the Courtault Institute (1937–1947) and President of Magdalen (1947–1968). Bowra, behind Boase's back, referred to his 'cerebral thrombosis.' Bowra regarded Boase as an intellectual poseur who would follow any passing fashion. He mocked him with 'His topsail is trimming to all winds that blow,/Low the high and high to the low.' He could not believe Magdalen would elect a person 'of no public virtues and no private parts.'[69] Wind's appointment would also annoy Anthony Blunt who, according to Bowra, was a 'stuffed sausage.'[70]

Gertrud Bing (1892–1964) was raised among the commercial bourgeoisie of Hamburg but little is known of her early life. She took her PhD degree under Cassirer, writing on Lessing, at the University of Hamburg. Saxl appointed her in 1922 as assistant at the Warburg Library while Warburg was away recovering from mental illness. Bing's 'nun-like care'[71] assisted Warburg's return to health and she became his constant companion, travelling with him to Italy in 1927 and again from 1928 to 1929. She became vice-director of the institute from about 1929 to 1955 and director herself from 1955 to 1959. Bing undertook the heavy task of transferring the library to London. She and Saxl extended the range of the institute's research. Even more importantly, it was Bing who

68 Anthony Blunt to Raymond Klibansky, 27 June 1938, WIA, GC, Klibansky file, 1938.
69 Lerner, *Ernst Kantorowicz*, p.176.
70 See Isaiah Berlin to Edgar Wind, 15 March 1950, in Isaiah Berlin, *Enlightening: Letters, 1946–1960*, ed. Henry Hardy and Jennifer Holmes (London: 2009), pp.171–172; Mitchell, *Maurice Bowra: A Life*, pp.268, 160–161.
71 Clark, *Another Part of the Wood*, p.190.

re-created in London the mental environment of the Hamburg library.[72] Michael Baxandall recalls conversations with her, rather late in her life, in her home in Dulwich. These were not tutorials but were rather 'a sort of induction by-the-by, an informal indoctrination in a tradition.' She talked about books, people, music, about Warburg and Saxl 'in an unintense way about life generally.' Bing 'was communicating lore, tales, tips, a morale, and much of it was in the form of a moral placing of people.'[73] Hers was a somewhat subtle authority, a kind of authenticity that brought Hamburg to London.

Lord Lee of Fareham, C. S. Gibson of Guy's Hospital and a founding member of the Academic Assistance Council, W. G. Constable, Director of the Courtauld Institute, and Sir Denison Ross, Director of the School of Oriental and African Studies were among those in Britain who shepherded the Warburg to London. Arthur Hamilton Viscount Lee of Fareham, the son of a clergyman, was educated at Cheltenham College and the Royal Military Academy and enjoyed a successful military career including an important intelligence feat in China. Lee was appointed military attaché to the US army in Cuba during the Spanish-American war. He met Theodore Roosevelt and became an honorary Rough Rider. Establishing friendship with many Americans, he married Ruth Moore, the daughter of a prominent New York banker, and took her and her fortune back to Britain. Lee sat in the House of Commons as the Tory member for the Fareham division of Hampshire from 1900 to 1918, when he was elevated to the peerage. He made over Chequers, his country home, to the nation with its important collection of art, endowing it with £100,000 for its maintenance. Then he began a second collection, which ultimately he bequeathed to the Courtauld Institute of Art, the institution that owed much to his imagination and energy. But his energy, as Kenneth Clark pointed out, could be overbearing and tactless and Lee became 'the most detested figure in the museum world.'[74] But this very push and shove made it possible for Lee to devote his energy to the transfer of the Warburg from Hamburg to London.

William George Constable (1887–1976) ended his career as curator of the Boston Museum of Fine Arts but he began working in the Wallace Collection and at the National Gallery. Constable's father was the headmaster at Derby School where Constable himself was educated. He went up to St John's College, Cambridge where he took a first class in economics. He entered the Inner Temple and was called to the Bar in 1914. He served with the Sherwood Foresters during the war. Buried alive when a shell exploded near him, he suffered shell shock. Constable, while convalescing, revised his thesis

[72] Arnaldo Momigliano, *Essays on Ancient and Modern Judaism*, ed. S. Berti (London/ Chicago: 1987), pp.210–211; Levine, *Dreamland of Humanists*, pp.160–162.
[73] Michael Baxandall, 'Is Durability Itself Not Also A Moral Quality,' *Common Knowledge*, 18 (1) (2012): 24.
[74] Clark, *Another Part of the Wood*, pp.206, 178.

and St John's elected him to a fellowship (1919–1921). He then entered the Slade School and entered upon his career writing for the *New Statesman* and the *Saturday Review* and later became an arts administrator. Lord Lee lured him, in 1930, to the newly established Arts Historical Institute founded with Samuel Courtauld's fortune. Constable was keen about the Warburg because the Courtauld Institute's wealth was in its collections but it was stricken for research talent and funds. As Constable wrote to Saxl: 'I myself, as you know have no money whatever to help for research. In fact we have not got a penny to buy books next year.'[75] Certain of his views, Constable was no diplomat. Even when diplomacy was required his support for research and learning stood at odds with the founding grandees of the Courtauld who favoured connoisseurship.[76] When these grandees dismissed him a commentator observed in 1937:

> The study of art in England is neglected; the subject itself is despised. It needs much energy, great learning and a passionate conviction of the importance of the subject to establish its claims and extend its conquests.[77]

It was Constable's very support for research and scholarship that led him to throw his weight behind the moving of the Warburg from Hamburg to London.

Denison Ross, the son of a vicar, was educated at Marlborough and at University College, London. A master of continental and oriental languages, Ross gained his PhD from the University of Strasburg with a thesis on Shah Isma'il. First appointed Professor of Persian at University College, London in 1896, Curzon secured his appointment as Principal of the Calcutta Madrasha where he served from 1901 to 1911. He came to the British Museum as a special assistant for the Asian collections but the war brought an end to his studies there and he entered the postal censorship where he worked until 1916, when he was appointed Director of the School of Oriental Studies and Professor of Persian in the University of London. Because of these appointments and intellectual connections he was appointed CIE in 1912 and knighted in 1918. Ross visited Hamburg and Saxl described the occasion to Constable:

> Sir Denison Ross was here for the week end and we spent a very pleasant time together … hearing him tell of his travels and various studies … [T]he library seemed to please him; he showed much interest and appreciation of its character, and I believe really saw for himself what you so kindly told him beforehand.[78]

Ideally placed, therefore, Ross was suited to throwing his weight behind the transfer of the Warburg to London.[79]

75   Constable to Saxl, 3 August 1934, WIA, GC.
76   J. G. Links, 'W. G. Constable,' *Burlington Magazine*, 118 (878) (May 1976): 311.
77   *Burlington Magazine*, 71 (414) (September 1937): 108.
78   Saxl to Constable, 17 October 1933, WIA, GC.
79   See his posthumously published memoir, *Both Ends of the Candle* (London: 1943).

Kenneth Clark first heard of the impending cultural transfer at dinner in Oxford. Saxl telephoned to say that the time had come to bring Hamburg to England. Clark returned to the dinner table where Lord and Lady Lee were with the Clarks and described the wonders of the library (he had not been to the library but he had met Warburg in Italy) and the commitment of the scholars working there. Lee was convinced, and as a man of action acted.[80] He consulted some colleagues and drafted his formal letter to the Hamburg authorities, inviting the Warburg Library to London.[81] Felix Warburg, a son of Aby Warburg, wrote in response:

> I hear from my brother Max and my nephew Erich of the invitation you have extended for a three year period to the Warburg Institute and of the great personal interest which you take in this matter … May I seize this opportunity to thank you very sincerely for taking such an interest in this cause with which I myself and my family have been associated for so many years.[82]

C. S. Gibson's, W. G. Constable's and Ross's visits to the library opened the way to other opportunities.[83]

As a result of Ross's visit '[a] wealthy man [Samuel Courtauld] here wishes to remain anonymous,' but agreed to consider an amount of £3,000 a year for three years to allow the Warburg to continue its work in London.[84] Ross also reported that the Warburgs were prepared at the end of the three-year period to leave the library in London and to endow it permanently.[85] This international cultural diplomacy was not one-way. Edgar Wind, who by this time had been sacked from his Hamburg University position, went himself to London to urge the interest of the Warburg. He stayed with the Hon. Mrs Ernest Franklin, with whom he was distantly related, who introduced him to Gibson and Constable. At Oxford, at lunch at Corpus Christi College, he met Maurice Bowra, Sir Richard Livingstone and Professor E. F. Jacob whose devotion to the Warburg arose from their own lectures they had given there. He also met Kenneth Clark, then at the Ashmolean Museum, and Isaiah Berlin.[86] Lee held that it was only 'by means of personal conversations on the spot with me and my friends' that arrangements for this culture transfer could take place.[87]

---

80   Clark, *Another Part of the Wood*, pp.207–208.

81   Gertrud Bing, 'Fritz Saxl (1890–1948): A Memoir,' in D. J. Johnson (ed.), *Fritz Saxl, 1890–1948, A Volume of Memorials Essays from his Friends in England* (London: 1957), pp.22–23.

82   Felix Warburg to Viscount Lee of Fareham, 12 December 1933, WIA, GC.

83   Sir Denison Ross to Saxl, 8 October 1933, WIA, GC.

84   W. G. Constable to Saxl, 18 October 1933, WIA, GC.

85   W. G. Constable to Saxl (second letter) 18 October 1933, WIA, GC.

86   Hugh Lloyd-Jones, 'Historical Memoir of Edgar Wind,' in Edgar Wind, *The Eloquence of Symbols*, ed. Jaynie Anderson, rev. edn (Oxford: 1993), p.xix.

87   Lord Lee to Max Warburg, 27 November 1933, WIA, GC.

Once in England, as Bing pointed out, it would be an exaggeration to say that the Warburg was established, or even settled. Even the most ordinary living arrangements for its members were difficult. For years Ernest Gombrich and his friend Otto Kurz lived in adjoining rooms in a boarding house. The scholars from Hamburg were, after all, aliens and they had to have others vouchsafe their intellectual status and political neutrality. Lord Lee forwarded a note from Sir Ernest Holderness to Saxl, which he had to take to the Home Office. Saxl had to assure the authorities that first, the members of the staff were 'highly trained specialists' whose skills could not be found in England; second, their admission to England would not involve any charge on the country's public monies; and, third, that their work would be of a 'strictly literary character, and entirely free from any kind of political significance.'[88] To gain exemption from the rates under the Friendly Societies Act (1843) they had to provide a certificate from their barrister assuring the Valuer of the City of Westminster that their work was 'for the purposes of Science, Literature or the Fine Arts exclusively.'[89] Accordingly, Max Warburg wrote to Lord Lee:

> I beg to confirm that the Warburg Library serves merely for scientific purposes. It is maintained by voluntary annual contributions and has never distributed in any way a dividend or bonus.[90]

The authorities in the library at Hamburg and their friends in Britain prepared a public statement carefully:

> It is the idea that the importance and influence of the Warburg Library, which is known as highly specialized and unique centre for research into the influence of the Classic tradition upon European life and thought, would be greatly enhanced in an international sense by transferring it to London and bringing it, even temporarily, into contact with such departments of London University such as the Courtauld Institute of Art and the Historical Research Institute.[91]

Further, the Warburg scholars had to find positions with salaries. They patched together various schemes, working with the University of London, the Society for the Protection of Science and Learning, and the Rockefeller Foundation to provide for funds to sustain them, among which they prepared a Warburg budget. Saxl was to be paid £900, Bing £600, Wind £500 and Clibanky (sic) £100. Their idea was to have the staff of the institute 'planted out' to different branches of the university and have each of those branches apply independently to the Rockefeller Foundation.[92]

---

88 Lord Lee to Saxl, 11 November 1933, WIA, GC.
89 Louis Vaughan to Lord Lee, 16 November 1933, WIA, GC.
90 Max Warburg to Lord Lee, 18 November 1933, WIA, GC.
91 'Suggested Draft of a Press Communique,' 29 December 1933, WIA, GC.
92 Constable to Dr E. Deller at the University of London, 15 March 1934; Saxl to Constable, 16 March 1934, WIA, GC.

As their time ran out in Milbank and as they planned to move to South Kensington they needed those sympathetic to their cause in H. M. Office of Works to plead their case for structural alterations. One such was Frederick James Edward Raby. Thus their appeal:

> Mover of the Spheres – to us
> Almost God in Heaven;
> Listen with a gracious ear
> To the imploring voices,
> Clamouring from the wilderness
> To thee, scholar's patron![93]

Raby had been educated at Trinity College, Cambridge where he had been placed in the First Class in the Historical Tripos Parts I and II. He went to the H. M. Office of Works from 1911 to 1948. But he was also a scholar of Medieval Latin literature with marked intellectual credentials, so when he left the Office of Works he returned to Cambridge as a fellow of Jesus College (1941) and lecturer (1948–1955). He was appointed CB and was elected a fellow of the British Academy in 1941. The scholars of the Warburg Institute needed, at every turn, intellectual and political connections to integrate themselves into what was for them a foreign environment.

Integration of this kind was more than legal and institutional; it was mental. They had to trot out their wares to gain intellectual respectability. Into a culture of amateurism and connoisseurship they had to show the value of criticism. To this end they displayed their scholarship both in London and in other parts of Britain. They brought continental scholars to give important lectures, such as Niels Bohr on 'Some Humanistic Aspects of Natural Science,' and Johann Huizinga and Henri Focillon to give a series of lectures on 'The Cultural Function of Play.' The Warburg sent out its own scholars to demonstrate the power of *Kulturwissenschaft*. Cassirer gave lectures at All Souls College, Oxford, Klibansky lectured at Manchester, and Saxl and Wittkower lectured at the Courtauld Institute. Someone who heard Wind lecture at Smith College remarked:

> Those of us who claim to expertise ... felt that we were in a kind of never-never land, where rare viands grew on ordinary trees; the question was not that this fare was unusual, but whether the dish was better spiced with myrrh or frankincense. I know that I went home for vacation, filled with very heady doctrines, and proclaimed them as gospel to anybody who would listen. When my father suggested that they might be controversial, I scoffed of course, having been thoroughly entranced by Wind and his, may I say it, charisma.[94]

[93]   E. H. Gombrich, *The Warburg Institute and H M Office of Works – E. H. Gombrich in Memory of Frederic Raby* (Cambridge: 1984), np.
[94]   Quoted by Colin Eisler, '*Kunstgeschichte* American Style: A Study in Migration,' in Fleming and Bailyn (eds), *The Intellectual Migration: Europe and America, 1930–1950*: p.618.

In this way, and others, the Warburgians transmitted their interest in symbolism, the emblem and allegory into a foreign host.

Their lectures ranged widely. In 1939 a series of eighteen lectures given, along with others, by Frances Yates, Anthony Blunt, Rudolph Wittkower and Isaiah Berlin (replacing Wind) on 'Aspects of French Civilization' were devices to give the Warburg its momentum in England.[95] Saxl himself did not depend on his official and intellectual connections only. He threw himself personally into the cultivation of visitors. For him no inquiry was too trivial to command his attention. He always found something of interest to which he might respond. As Bing put it:

> [That][t]hey came and stayed was a tribute to the kind of inquiry which Saxl represented and to the way he put it forth; they felt that behind it there was an exact training and a strict adherence to evidence, while at the same time it opened another range of historically important facts and a more imaginative approach to the arts than that with which they had been familiar.[96]

Through these mental engagements, through lectures and personal connections, the Warburg scholars integrated themselves and the Warburg idea into a foreign land.

They could not isolate themselves into a closed coterie. *The Journal of the Warburg and Coutauld Institutes* was one avenue Saxl paved for gaining support for the institute and the work of its émigré scholars.[97] Founded by Wind and Rudolph Wittkower, it was intended to make *Kulturwissenschaft* understandable to the new environment in which it found itself. Therefore it served as a forum for bringing together philosophers and anthropologists to view art, religion, science and literature, and political life from their points of view. It was not designed to settle questions but rather its intention was aspirational and an attempt to capture the ongoing processes through which their studies worked.[98] A prospectus inviting authors' contributions stated the journal's central purpose: 'The formation and transmission of symbols will be the central theme.'[99] Jacques Maritain, who contributed the first article to the first issue, tried to capture the spirit of the thing. He wrote:

> No problems are more complex or more fundamental to the concerns of man and civilization than those regarding signs. The sign is relevant to the whole

---

95 Mann, 'Two-Way Traffic': 97–98.
96 Bing, 'Fritz Saxl (1890–1948)': 26.
97 See Elizabeth McGrath, 'Disseminating Warburganism: The Role of the Journal of the Warburg and Courtauld Institutes,' in Uwe Fleckner and Peter Mack (eds), *Vortäge Aus Dem Warburg-Haus: The Afterlife of the Kulturwissenschaftliche Biblioteck Warburg* (Berlin: 1997): pp.39–50.
98 Mann, 'Two Way Traffic': 99–100.
99 Quoted in McGrath, 'Disseminating Warburgianism': 41.

extent of knowledge and human life; it is a universal instrument in the world of human beings, like motion in the world of physical nature.[100]

Roger Hinks, on joining the enterprise, after losing his post at the British Museum, immediately resolved 'to rationalize the whole publishing side of the W I.' On his first day at his new post Anthony Blunt explained in detail the condition of all of the publications in the press. Hinks found this too haphazard and, he said, he was 'determined that no manuscript henceforth shall leave my room until Saxl is satisfied about the content and I am satisfied with the form.'[101]

The Warburgers had to draw others into their ambit. The Warburg scholars were attracted to Anthony Blunt. Blunt's conacts with them helped him to liberate himself from narrow Marxist treatments of scholarship. With his fluent abilities in French, German and Italian, he seemed a likely recruit. Further, he was comfortable with these foreign spirits. Though he had shaken off his narrow previous Marxist approach to culture, its stress upon the social and economic conditions necessary for the creative life was generally at one with the Warburg's commitment to the study of works of culture in its social environment. Blunt came to the Warburg in 1937 in what was a turning point in his life and career. Saxl went to Cambridge to hear Blunt lecture, and Blunt claimed he learnt more from Saxl in five minutes than from anyone else in an hour. John Pope-Hennessy said Saxl 'transformed Anthony Blunt from a jejune Marxist into one of the most accomplished art historians of his day.' The significance of their studies to civilisation and human nature convinced Blunt of the necessity of the Warburg's survival. Their form of study combined scholarly precision with deep emotional and imaginative power, requiring both an absolute commitment to accuracy as well as the deepest knowledge of art's place in its cultural environment.[102] This was a marked contrast to mere British connoisseurship.

The Warburg dearly desired to capture Erwin Panofsky. Educated in Berlin and Freiburg in art history and philology, Panofsky's career in Germany was at the universities of Berlin, Munich and Hamburg. Forced out by the Nazis in 1933 he went to the United States where he taught at New York University and Princeton. Panofsky's position was uncertain and though there were possibilities for him in the United States, the Warburg wished to lure him to England. Panofsky met with Constable and lectured at the Courtauld in January 1934, giving Constable and Saxl enough encouragement so that they explored the financial possibilities for

[100] Jacques Maritain 'Sign and Symbols,' *Journal of the Warburg Institute*, 1 (1937–1938): 1.
[101] Hinks Diary, 11 April 1939, Roger Hinks Papers/1/5/ff. 31–32.
[102] Amanda Carter, *Anthony Blunt: His Lives* (London: 2001), pp.209–210, 213; the quotation from Pope-Hennessy is on p.210.

getting him.[103] To get him for one year Constable and Saxl secured £250 from the Society for the Protection of Science and Learning, £250 from the Rockefeller Foundation and £150 from other sources. He was, it seemed to Constable, eager to work in Britain where he could deploy his considerable talents at the Warburg and the Courtauld institutes.[104] Panofsky was attractive to Saxl because of Panofsky's interest in hidden or disguised symbols in such works as the *Arnolfini Portrait* (1934). This was rather all in line with the Warburg's commitment to studying the inner ironies and contradictions contained in cultural artefacts rather than the superficial positivism of connoisseurs.

The Warburg also drew Jean Seznec (1905–1983) into its orbit. The son of school teachers, Seznec attended the Collège de Morlaix, the lycée at Rennes, and then went up to Paris to the Lycée Louis-le-Grand where Jean-Paul Sartre was his contemporary. In 1925 he went on to the Ecole Normale Supérieure where his contemporaries were Raymond Aron and, yet again, Sartre. There he took the *aggregation* in 1928 after which he went to Rome where he studied at the French Academy with Émile Mâle.[105] As Roger Hinks reported, Seznec became 'disgusted with Italy – or at all events with Fascism and with the destruction of cultivated life by the Axis. He has a fund of astonishing stories about the hatred of Germany which the political alliance has engendered in Italy.'[106] Aside from these political feelings, Seznec was attracted to the Warburgians and they to him because his work was a '*caractère hybride.*' He identified his own '*position indécise entre plusieurs disciplines.*'[107] He did not visit the Warburg in Hamburg but he established epistolary contact with Saxl in 1930 and, after the Warburg went to London, Seznec developed close relations with Saxl and the other Warburgians. His research appealed to them keenly. Seznec studied the ways the stories of the Olympian gods and the spirits of the field and spring persisted long after Christianity began to command western culture. He traced the ways in which these stories were transformed in late antiquity and embedded in medieval culture as astral divinities, in the magical and astrological systems of the time, and surviving in folk culture, taking on strange guises that emerged in the iconography of the Tuscan Renaissance. It was quite the line of research that appealed to the Warburg, and, working with Roger Hinks, Seznec published his findings with the Warburg as *La*

---

[103] Constable to Saxl, 2 January 1934, WIA, GC.
[104] Constable to Saxl, 23 January 1934, WIA, GC.
[105] A. H. T. Levi and Francis Haskell, 'Jean Joseph Seznec, 1905–1983,' *Proceedings of the British Academy*, 73 (1987): 643–656.
[106] Roger Hinks Diary, 5 August 1939, 1/5/f. 55.
[107] Elizabeth Sears, 'Seznec, Saxl and *La Survivance de dieux antiques,*' in Rembrandt Duits and François Quiviger (eds), *Images of the Pagan Gods: Papers of a Conference in Memory of Jean Seznec* (London/Turin: 2009): p.3.

Survivance des dieux antiques: Essai sur le role de la tradition mythologique dans l'uminisme de dans l'art de la Renaissance (1940).[108]

After the Second World War Saxl spurred Seznec into other lines of research, particularly the interpenetration of the histories of art and literature. Blunt persuaded him that the place to start was Diderot's *Salons* and Seznec's first volume of Diderot's salon criticism appeared in 1957 and the fourth in 1967.[109] After the Second World War Seznec went to Harvard with which he had a long association. Administrative duties there did not appeal to him and, at Maurice Bowra's goading and machinations, he accepted the Marshal Foch Chair of French Literature at Oxford with its fellowship at All Souls.[110] Honours came to him: *Officier de la Légion d'Honneur*, Member of the American Academy of Arts and Sciences, honorary degrees from Harvard and St Andrews, two *festschriften*, and election to the British Academy where he was appointed to Section 6, Medieval and Modern Literature and Philology, and Section 11, History of Art.

The Warburg scholars and their recruits in Britain transformed scholarship. Their chief gift was in their method: *Kulturwissenschaft*. But as Robert Klein put it, Aby Warburg created a discipline 'that, in contrast to many others, exists but has no name.'[111] Gertrud Bing told Roger Hinks over lunch that when people asked her what the Warburg method was she told them that the whole point of the Warburg was that it had no method. Hinks responded that if it had no method the Warburg had a mystique. Wind objected to this and in a letter to the *Times Literary Supplement* said it was a 'misjudged piety to obscure [Warburg's] original learning by fumes of incense.'[112] For Klibansky the concept of *Kulturwissenschaft* could not be separated from the idea of Aby Warburg's library itself:

> *Qu'sest que la Kulturwissenschaft? Pour répondre à cette question il faut, je crois, se retourner vers la bibliothèque qu' Aby Warburg avait fondée à Hambourg. C'est cette bibliothèque dont les nom exact est Kulturwissenschaflice Bibliothek Warburg, qui incarne le mieux le project intellectuale de cet hommede genie et nous permet de saisir sa personnalité.*[113]

Wind, in a lecture delivered at the Warburg Library in 1930, also pointed out the close connection between *Kulturwissenschaft* and the library's unique organisation. Instead of organising it in a static fashion as though its materials were

---

[108] See Roger Hinks Diary, 5 August 1939, Roger Hinks Papers 1/5/f. 55.

[109] Elizabeth Sears, 'Warburg Institute Archive, General Correspondence,' *Common Knowledge*, 18 (1) (2012): 47.

[110] Mitchell, *Maurice Bowra: A Life*, p.266.

[111] Robert Klein, *La form e et l'intelligible* (Paris: 1970), p.224; quoted by Giorgio Agamben, *Potentialities: Collected Essays in Philosophy* (Stanford: 1999), p.284.

[112] Quoted and cited in Elizabeth Sears, 'A Diarest's View: Roger Hinks and the Warburg Institute Twenty Five-Years after its Settling in London,' in Flekner and Mack (eds), *Vorträge aus dem Warburg-Haus*, pp.93–94, 213 n. 39.

[113] Raymond Klibansky, 'La Notion de Kulturwissenschaft,' *RACAR: Revue d'Art Canadienne/ Canadian Art Review*, 27 (1/2) (2000): 144.

passive, from the beginning Warburg wished to use the library as an intellectual instrument and exercise its dynamic and active properties. The library's strength 'lies precisely in the areas that are marginal; and since these are the areas that play a crucial part in the progress of any discipline, the library may fairly claim that its own growth is entirely in keeping with that of the particular field of study it seeks to advance.'[114] Warburg, according to Wind, used the concept of *Kulturwissenschaft* 'to tear down the barriers artificially set up between the various departments of historical research.' It was 'a precise method of interaction and correlation between those diverging scientific interests in the humanities which have shown a tendency to set up their subjects as "things in themselves."'[115] As Roger Hinks pointed out, Warburg protested against the dangers of over-specialisation that extreme positivism posed. The collection of information, though necessary, would be overwhelming unless it was guided by heuristic insights into the meaning and value of the subject as a whole. Unless the 'chaos of individual discoveries' was guided and coordinated, studies become meaningless. In this, his review of the first volume of *The Journal of the Warburg Institute*, which he took as the opportunity to assess the Warburg project, Hinks argued that the Warburg method showed:

> that nothing is meaningless, provided that we know how to unravel its secret, that the meaning of the past is not something outside ourselves, but the very fabric out of which our own minds are made.

For Warburg and his followers, Hinks argued, all human behaviour – religion, philosophy, science, art, statecraft – though seemingly autonomous, were 'equivalent symbolic forms of the same awareness' of human beings. Only by comparing them would it be possible to unlock the secrets of the human mind.[116]

Not only was this method alien and unusual, it also violated the expectation that change was linear and progressive; its method was distinctly anti-Whiggish. As Bing pointed out, the Warburg Institute was a 'foreign body' plunging itself into an unacknowledged field of study.[117] The British could hardly understand what they were doing. The Warburgers were aware of the difficulties they faced in introducing anything smacking of theoretical and continental speculation. A memorandum of 1934, 'Memo Regarding the Warburg Institute: How to get it Known in England', probably written by Saxl, stated: 'Missionary spirit arouses opposition ... Theories are abhorred

[114] Edgar Wind, 'Warburg's Concept of *Kulturwissenschaft* and its Meaning for Aesthetics,' reprinted in Edgar Wind, *The Eloquence of Symbols: Studies in Humanist Art* (Oxford: 1983), p.34.
[115] [Edgar Wind], *A Bibliography on the Survival of the Classics, First Volume, the Publications of 1931* ed. The Warburg Institute (London: 1934), p.v.
[116] Roger Hinks, 'The Warburg Institute,' *The Spectator* (9 September 1938): 412.
[117] Bing, 'Fritz Saxl (1890–1948)': 8–9.

by the English in general and the learned in particular.'[118] Kenneth Clark had a taste of British resistance. He went to a meeting at the Society of Antiquaries and concluded 'no public will swallow any chaff of German scholarship.' As he wrote to his mother, the meeting 'will do me for years. I would rather go to church.'[119] He gave two lectures at London University on Riegl and Wölfflin. There were only twenty people in a large hall, which included largely elderly women brought there by his wife Jane. Neither hearing nor understanding a word Clark said, his chairman, at the end, cast doubt on Riegl's seriousness as a writer. Clark wrote to Bernard Berenson: 'So ended the first effort to spread the gospel in Great Britain.'[120]

Since, like many concepts, the concept of *Kulturwissenschaft* defies literal translation it is rendered sometimes simply as intellectual history, the history of ideas, or the history of art.[121] But these renderings fail to capture the spirt of what the Warburg Institute actually did. The Warburg, in some ways, recaptured earlier intellectual styles. As Walter Benjamin, who had associated himself with the Warburg, put it in 1928: it 'increasingly takes down the dividing walls between disciplines, characteristic of the concept of the sciences in the last century.'[122] As outsiders, at the periphery of intellectual life, Warburg scholars could explore the inner lives of ideas and the ways cultural transmission was entangled in complex various social and intellectual formations. It led them to study not only the Apollonian tradition but the Dionysian tradition with its mystic, magical, esoteric and symbolic features. 'The student,' Wind pointed out, 'who seeks to understand how it came to pass that the Olympian gods were revived in the Renaissance as aesthetic ideals, must also understand how they came to survive in the Middle Ages as astronomical and magical demons.'[123] So Warburg and those who followed him took to the study of indeterminate and intermediate areas – religious cults festivals, magic and astrology in periods of change and conflict – deeply ambiguous regions that other scholars refused, or feared, to penetrate.[124] It was a scholarly revolution bringing a vitalising impulse to Britain and with it opportunities for different expressions of curiosity, serendipity, novelty and originality.

---

[118] Quoted by McGarth, 'Disseminating Warburgianism': 43.

[119] Quoted in James Stourton, *Kenneth Clark: Life, Art and Civilisation* (New York: 2016), p.75

[120] Clark to Berenson, 4 June 1931, in Robert Cummins (ed.), *My Dear BB: The Letters of Bernard Berenson and Kenneth Clark, 1925–1959* (New Haven/London: 2015), p.93.

[121] Dorothea McEwan, 'A Tale of One Institute and Two Cities: The Warburg Institute,' in Ian Wallace (ed.), *German-Speaking Exiles in Great Britain* (Amsterdam/New York: 1999): 25.

[122] Quoted by Michael Diers, 'Warburg and the Warburg Tradition,' *New German Critic*, 65 (Spring/Summer 1995): 60.

[123] [Wind], *A Bibliography on the Survival of the Classics*, p.vi.

[124] Edgar Wind, 'Warburg's Concept of *Kulturwissenschaft* and its Meaning for Aesthetics (1930),' in Donald Preziosi (ed.), *The Art of Art History: A Critical Anthology* (Oxford: 1998 [2009], pp.193–194.

The Warburgian fascination with symbols was important but, as Kenneth Clark warned, it was intellectually and even emotionally dangerous because *Kulturwissenschaft* was ironic. 'Symbols,' he wrote, 'are a dangerous branch of study as they lead easily to magic; and magic leads to the loss of reason.'[125] (How far Warburg's incarceration in Ludwig Biswanger's mental institution in Kreuzlingen from 1918 to 1924 – because of his fascination with symbols – can only be conjectured at.) What can be said, however, is that *Kulturwissenschaft* was ironic. It opened the thought that phenomena can be read in more than one way. If one's reading is light and Apollonian, another's can be darkly Dionysian. Neither relativistic or subjective, this is the concept of complementarity at work in the study of human cultures: the same phenomena are capable of more than one perception and hold more than one meaning and interpretation. Consequently *Kulturwissenschaft* sought to rediscover the past but in doing so it attacked the present, revealing what it is that we might not wish to know. It is dangerous to 'know thyself.' As Eliza Marian Butler, the Schröder Professor of German at the University of Cambridge who associated herself with the Warburg Institute, said, 'most of us would probably rather believe ourselves to be suffering the malignant persecutions of a merciless fate than realise that we are the slaves or the victims of our own subconscious minds.'[126]

The British support for the intellectual diaspora of the 1930s was generous and humane, but it was also threatening. This disapora had two effects. It transformed the demographic character of intellectual life. What Perry Anderson has called a 'phalanx of Continentals' penetrated what Noel Annan called the Edwardian-Victorian 'intellectual aristocracy.' Anderson listed those Europeans: Wittgenstein, Malinowski, Namier, Popper, Berlin, Gombrich, Eysenck, Melanie Klein, Deutscher.[127] Anderson must certainly be correct about this general point but his characterisation of the nature of this replacement is somewhat misjudged. His characterisation is coloured by ideas he set forth earlier and held for some time concerning the supine resistance of the British bourgeoisie to general ideas, to critical theory.[128] As Stefan Collini has put it: in seeking to explain aesthetic creations in terms of one special social circumstance 'one always risks hitting a paranoid note or seeming to understand this in terms of conspiracy theory writ large.'[129] There are other views that might moderate Anderson's rabid, narrow and

125 Clark, *Another Part of the Wood*, p.190.
126 E. M. Butler, 'Hoffmannsthal's [sic] "Elektra,": A Graeco-Freudian Myth,' *Journal of the Warburg Institute*, 2 (1938–1939): 174.
127 Perry Anderson, 'Components of the National Culture,' *New Left Review*, I/50 (July/ August 1968): *passim*.
128 Perry Anderson, 'Origins of the Present Crisis,' *New Left Review*, I/23 (January/ February 1964): *passim*.
129 Stefan Collini, *Common Reading: Critics, Historians, Publics* (Oxford: 2008), p.192.

excessively dogmatic views.[130] According to Anderson's interpretation, the continental diaspora was a 'white' migration, not a 'red' migration. That is to say, those who fled the Continent were those escaping from social turmoil and who sought refuge in Britain with its tradition of stability. There is evidence for this in the case of, say, Lewis Namier who came to have a deep sympathy for the British aristocracy, a rejection of political theorising as 'flapdoodle,' and a highly empirical (and archival) research on the history of parliament. But for Anderson to stress these aspects of Namier's writing underestimates Namier's deep and complicated interest in general ideas.[131] As Namier put it, because of our increased psychological awareness it is impossible to treat political ideas as 'the offspring of pure reason.' He went on: '[w]hat matters most is the underlying emotions, the music, to which ideas are a mere libretto.' Namier had been charged with 'taking the mind out of history,' to which he had a response. The human mind is important, but the 'mind does not work with the rationality that was once deemed its noblest attribute – which does not, however, mean that it necessarily works any worse … [T]he irrational is not necessarily unreasonable: it may only be that we cannot explain it, or that we misinterpret it, in terms of our conscious thought.'[132] Just as Anderson misunderstands Namier, so he also misunderstands Isaiah Berlin, with his multiple and conflicting concepts of liberties, or Wittgenstein, with his deep probing into the nature of language, and Freud, with his pursuit of the unconscious.

Though Namier did not get the recognition he thought he deserved, Berlin, Wittgenstein and Freud in their own ways got themselves absorbed into British learned life.[133] But others did not. Some refugees arrived destitute, having been deprived of their pensions and assets before they were allowed to leave Germany. Given the state of the economy in the 1930s, the universities were static and stagnant. The research imperative had not struck the universities with particular force and such positions as there were carried heavy teaching responsibilities, which worked to the disadvantage of those, such as Hans Baron, whose native tongues were not English. Given the limited opportunities in Britain there was a strong preference for restricting those to British scholars. Even at the Cavendish, as John Cockcroft recognised, not many refugees could be admitted.[134] Some attributed the difficulties of admitting refugees to

---

[130] See for example W. G. Runciman, *Very Different But Very Much the Same: The Evolution of English Society Since 1714* (Oxford: 2015).

[131] viz. Linda Colley, *Lewis Namier* (London: 1989), pp.21–46.

[132] Lewis Namier, 'Human Nature in Politics,' in *Personalities and Powers: Selected Essays* (New York/Evanston: 1965): pp.4–5.

[133] For Freud see John Forrester and Laura Cameron, *Freud in Cambridge* (Cambridge: 2017).

[134] Cockcroft, John Douglas (1887–1976): father, from a family of weavers; ed. Todmorden Secondary School; (during the First World War served on the western front with the

university positions to the lack of imagination of university administrators, of which there has always been considerable. Of course, there is always the problem of a latent anti-Semitism and resentment of foreigners. One of W. L. Bragg's correspondents wrote to him: 'we do not regard these Central Europeans as entirely reliable from the national point of view.'[135]

The fear was so great that when war came some were interned in Canada and Australia. F. G. Friedlander was one such. He had been educated in a British public school, had a brilliant career at Trinity College, Cambridge and was elected to his college's fellowship on the strength of his original scholarship in mathematics and mechanical science. When he was interned abroad A. V. Hill protested to *The Times*: there was an urgent need for people with his qualifications and though born abroad there was no suspicion of his loyalty and integrity. 'The action of [his] College seems more sensible than that of His Majesty's Government.'[136] Hill, as Independent MP for Cambridge, raised this case in the House of Commons on 3 December 1940. He began with a general point. Hitler's doctrine of racial superiority had to be opposed by 'something better and more credible.' In times of war 'moral factor counts as much as the material factor.' While it is difficult, Hill said, to establish with precision, the British conception of the world was 'inherent in the structure and customs of our society.' Then he raised the cases of Friedlander and others like him who had been interned. Hill protested against those who had said no stigma was attached to being interned:

> I know a man of some scientific distinction and the highest character who was interned until recently and then released. The friendliness and tolerance of his view of the whole business of internment are shown by an article of his which was published in the 'Spectator' of last week. I asked him recently what he was not allowed to do since he has been out. Here is the list: he may not possess or drive a motor car, he may not own or ride a bicycle, he may not have a radio, he may not be out after 10.30pm, he may not enter the laboratories or library when he might continue his work because of the secret work which is supposed to be going on in them. Personally, knowing him well, I should be glad to employ him, knowing his capacity and loyalty, in any work, however secret. He tells me, however, that he is still allowed to push the family pram, so that all is not lost.

Royal Field Artillery); Manchester Municipal College of Technology; St John's College, Cambridge where he sat the Mathematical Tripos and emerged as a wrangler (1924); took his PhD under Rutherford and served as an assistant to Peter Kapitza (1924); fellow of St John's College (1928) Supervisor in Physics (1931); Director of the Mond Laboratory (1935); FRS (1936); Jacksonian Professor of Natural Philosophy (1939); during the Second World War served as Assistant Director of Scientific Research in the Ministry of Supply; Director of the Atomic Energy Research at Harwell (1946); Knight Bachelor (1948); Nobel Prize for splitting the atom (1951); Knight Commander of the Order of the Bath (1953); OM (1956); first Master of Churchill College, Cambridge (1959).

135   Quoted in Paul H. Hoch, 'The Reception of Central European Refugee Physicists of the 1930s: U.S.S.R., U.K., U.S.A.,' *Annals of Science*, 40 (1983): 224.
136   Quoted in Bentwich, *The Rescue and Achievement of Refugee Scholars*, p.33.

Hill also told the tale of a biologist of considerable distinction at a British public school. Liked and respected by fellow masters and boys, yet he was interned. The school kept his position open for him but when he was released the authorities (not the school) told him he could not return. So he 'had to be maintained by charitable funds from the Society for the Protection of Science and Learning, instead of earning his living usefully.' These, Hill said, were instances of 'the failure to use brains, loyalty and skill freely available to our cause.' Had the Duke of Marlborough insisted 'that his troops should be of purest British descent Blenheim House would never have been built,' Hill said.[137]

Moritz Bonn, a somewhat atypical exile, had friendlier treatment. Born to a moderately wealthy Frankfurt family, he earned his PhD at Munich where his dissertation had been supervised by Lujo Brentano. Bonn cut a cosmopolitan figure (which alone might have made the National Socialists distrust him) and travelled widely developing deep social and political connections. He became close to Alfred Marshall in Cambridge, and translated Keynes's *Economic Consequences of the Peace* into German. After he was sacked as rector of the Berlin *Handelschochscule* in 1933 he received offers of appointment from universities in Manchester, California, Ohio, Princeton and the New School for Social Research, but he accepted Beveridge's offer to lecture at the LSE and became an adviser to the Society for the Protection of Science and Learning.[138] After the war 174 refugee scholars remained in Britain; 20 became fellows of the Royal Society; 6 became fellows of the British Academy; and 43 held chairs in British universities.[139]

The discussion of Namier above suggests a larger point: the intellectual diaspora of the 1930s brought with it foreign ideas that constituted an assault on British parish-pump positivism, linearity and literalness. Exile, after all, is a matter of 'dislocation, disorientation, and self-division,' which produce qualities that the post-modern mentality has come to admire and value: 'uncertainty, displacement, the fragmented identity.'[140] This intellectual diaspora, therefore, produced a sometimes threatening shift in Britain's mental life. Their assault on positivism was no assault on science, as the preceding paragraphs show, but rather an assault on reductionism. Freud, as Adam Phillips has pointed out, valued science as an imaginative and visionary act and as a 'figurative and fictive language.' '[I]t was to literature you had to go, as Freud knew from his youth, to find the unfinished, the possible, the ecstatic.'[141] To state the point in another way, their

---

[137] Hansard, Parliamentary Debates: 367, cols. 473–481, esp. 473–474, 477, 479.

[138] Patricia Clavin, 'A Wandering Scholar in Britain and the USA, 1933–1945: The Life and Work of Moritz Bonn,' in Anthony Grenville (ed.), *Refugees from the Third Reich in Britain* (Amsterdam/New York: 2002): pp.27–32 and Dahrendorf, *LSE*, pp.287–294.

[139] Bentwich, *The Rescue and Achievement of Refugee Scholars*, pp.13–14, 99–102.

[140] Eva Hoffman, quoted by Ian Buruma, 'The Cult of Exile,' *Prospect*, 61 (March 2001): 23.

[141] Adam Phillips, *Becoming Freud: The Making of a Psychoanalyst* (New Haven/

assault on positivism was through an enlarged heuristic and imaginative approach. There had long been efforts, one might almost call it a tradition within British intellectual life to blunt the Enlightenment's reductionist narrowness. One might name the names, or some of them: Coleridge, Arnold, McTaggart, Bosanquet.[142] The intellectual diaspora of the 1930s added a sharper impetus to these indigenous impulses. This was part of the 'sea change' of which H. Stuart Hughes has written.[143] The examples of Niels Bohr, Max Born, Edgar Adrian and Joseph Needham serve to illustrate the ways heuristic, interpretive and imaginative methods loosened the shackles of reductionist positivism.

As Max Born recalled, in his inaugural lecture, the Tait chair in Edinburgh 'bore the noble title of "Natural Philosophy."'[144] He declared 'the time of materialism is over.' He attacked positivism. Classical physics held that there is an objective world that could be investigated without disturbing it. Following Heisenberg, Born argued 'this assumption modern physics has shown to be wrong.' It was an assumption that in his mind raised a philosophical question: 'what do we mean by the expression "objective world."' For positivists every question is meaningless unless it can be subjected to an experimental test. This, Born said, has been productive in helping investigators 'to adopt a critical attitude toward traditional assumptions ... But I cannot agree with the application made by positivists to the general problem of reality.' The concepts of causality and determinism 'are not just wrong, but empty.' It may be possible to exclude references to other intellectual considerations in doing experimental work, but 'this does not hold for its philosophical interpretation':[145]

> The processes of life and mind need other conceptions for their description than the physico-chemical processes with which they are coupled ... If you want to study a specific biological or psychological process by the methods of physics and chemistry, you have to apply all kinds of physical apparatus which disturbs the process. The more you learn about atoms and molecules during the process, the less you are sure that the process is that you want to study. By the time you know everything about the atoms, the creature will be dead.[146]

In *The Restless Universe* Born observed: 'We have reached the end of our journey into the depth of matter. We have sought for firm ground and found none.' The deeper research penetrates 'the more restless the universe becomes,

London: 2014), p.106.
142 Sandra M. den Otter, *British Idealism and Social Explanation: A Study in Late Victorian Thought* (Oxford: 1996).
143 H. Stuart Hughes, *The Sea Change: The Migration of Social Thought, 1930–1965* (New York: 1975).
144 Max Born, *Physics in My Generation: A Selection of Papers* (London/New York: 1956), p.37.
145 Born, *Physics in My Time*, pp.40, 47, 49.
146 Born, *Physics in My Time*, p.52.

and the vaguer and cloudier.' Archimedes had claimed that if he had a place to stand he would move the world. Born asserted: 'There is no fixed place in the Universe: all is rushing about and vibrating in the wild dance.'[147]

Edgar Adrian noted how there are two approaches in all branches of the natural sciences. A strategist can 'devise a series of crucial experiments which will reveal the truth by some sort of Hegelian dialectic.' Then there is the empiricist 'who looks around to see what he can see.' New techniques of measurement, Adrian observed, show 'that there is so much going on in the nervous system that it is hard to resist the temptation to record anything that turns up.' Empiricism has the merit of revealing unexpected resemblances in the activities in different parts of the nervous system. But, 'it gives us facts rather than theories, and the facts may not mean very much.'[148]

It is more important in the formation of knowledge, Joseph Needham argued, to ask the right questions than to get the right answers. 'We prowl around and around' the 'the so-called psycho-physical problem' in a kind of innocent Arcadia. We fail 'to see what an absurd mixture of metaphysics and physiology it is.' Needham called for the deployment of imagination rather than reason or logic:

> [I]f we take an organism belonging to one of the higher levels (such as a rabbit or an archbishop), we are only too aware that we make progress in our understanding of it, not by confining our studies to one level in it, such as the psychological or the chemical, but by attacking its analysis at all levels, and by putting the results together in an imaginative synthesis.

He deplored the gulf between the 'morphological and biological investigators' and those who 'apply biochemical and biophysical methods.' He thought this gap might be bridged and knowledge might be advanced in the study of the 'relation between chemical substances and morphological form, in particular in the morphological hormones which we know largely by the name of Organizers.'[149] 'Relations' of all kinds are largely insusceptible to direct observation; they have to be grasped intuitively and imaginatively: heuristically and interpretatively.

Ian Beveridge, Needham's colleague, originally from Australia and now proceeding from the backwaters of the Department of Animal Pathology in Cambridge,[150] in a paper on 'Teaching the Art of Research' suggested

---

[147] Max Born, *The Restless Universe* (Mineola, NY/Dover: [1951] 2013).

[148] Edgar Adrian, *The Mechanism of Nervous Action: Electrical Studies of the Neurone* (London: 1932), p.93.

[149] Joseph Needham, 'New Advances in the Chemistry and Biology of Organized Growth,' *Proceedings of the Royal Society of Medicine*, 29 (1935–1936): 1577–1578.

[150] Beveridge, William Ian Beardmore (1908–2006): born in Australia; ed. University of Sydney, DVSc; awarded a Commonwealth Fellowship for study at the Rockefeller Institute at Princeton (1937); fellow of Jesus College, Cambridge (1948–2006): his research at Cambridge focused on pneumonia in pigs and influenza in horses; Professor of Animal Pathology; keenly interested in international affairs and worked with Martin Kaplan, the

other ways that the narrowness of positivism could be overcome. Beveridge argued that 'the scientific method' had been relegated to the philosophers who had made it sterile, a matter of logical procedures, when 'in fact it is a creative art.' He called for it to be clawed back by those who did research. If the study of research methods 'are treated realistically, as they would be by practicing scientists, there would be no danger of over-systematisation and dogmatism.' Because those doing research are continually faced with the problem of drawing conclusions based upon insufficient or incomplete evidence, 'personal judgement based on scientific taste' was required, and also style. Styles differed: some scholars were systematic, others were more speculative. But whether systematic or speculative, great people of research were also intuitive.

The concept of research, Beveridge argued, must be radically changed. While logical processes are valuable for the design, execution and assessment of experiments, 'intensely or frankly subjective' impulses, imagination and intuition, must also be deployed. Beveridge recalled the importance Pasteur attached to the 'prepared mind.' But the 'prepared mind,' he asserted, is not passive. It penetrates its materials and activates them. It interprets its materials by connecting the apparently trivial to other findings in order to call attention to the intellectual significance of research. Incentives to do research are complex and multiple, but its chief ones are curiosity and the joy of discovery. Discovery becomes more intriguing if it runs counter to current understandings. Not an end in itself, discovery is a tool and, by using it, entirely different fields of study may be opened. 'The really exciting thing about a discovery is not so much its intrinsic importance as its possible fruitfulness in leading to still more facts and theories.' Beveridge pointed to the importance of the psychology of research rather than its logic. For him intuition, that sudden flash or inspiration, often functioned unconsciously, and therefore, was unformulated in the mind of the investigator. In an age in which vast apparatuses were playing increasing roles, Beveridge held that the most important research tool was the human brain.[151] Beveridge illustrated and elaborated upon these ideas, giving examples from the history of science, in two books towards the end of his career: *The Art of Scientific Research* (1950) and *Seeds of Discovery* (1980).

The Warburg concept of *Kulturwissenschaft* and these other examples reveal the ways that the character of what might loosely be called the humanities and of even natural philosophy shifted and changed, subtly but importantly, blunting their nineteenth-century positivist and reductionist roots to become interpretive

---

chief of the Veterinarian Public Health Unit of the World Health Organization; chairman of the Veterinary Association (1957 Martin Kaplan, the chief of the Veterinarian Public Health Unit of the World Health Organization 1975) and presided over its congresses that were held every four years; author of *Influenza: The Last Great Plague* (London, 1977). [151] A copy of this typescript can be found in CUL., Needham Mss. M313. The letter attached to the typescript is dated 21 December 1950.

sciences as a result of the intellectual diaspora of the 1930s. These influences, often indirect and incomplete, worked themselves out as British scholars intermingled with their continental colleagues. The blunting of positivism was rarely direct. It was often insidious. As Forrester and Cameron have shown in their study of the dissemination of Freud's ideas, the work of émigré scholars was accomplished neither by a 'Great Man Model' nor by a 'bureaucratic transplant model.'[152] Rather, the work of continental scholars was accomplished through their personal interactions with their British colleagues. It was an elastic process of intellectual differentiation, which was always aspirational and, therefore, never complete. If not a new social and intellectual world, it was a different one marking a change from what Noel Annan once described as an 'intellectual aristocracy' to one he described as 'Our Age.' That is the subject to which this study now turns.

[152] Forrester and Cameron, *Freud in Cambridge*, p.2.

Chapter 5

The 'New Men':
'Intellectual Aristocracy' or 'Our Age'

Here lies the only member of the English middle classes who
did not think himself a gentleman.

A. E. Housman[1]

It is not financial assistance alone, however, which the nation
should provide for the investigator. This is not even the
most important stimulus that a nation can provide for him.
Recognition and proper standing in the body politic are his
due, and these should at last be forthcoming.

F. Gowland Hopkins[2]

An ounce of heredity is worth a pound of merit.

Olive Lloyd-Baker[3]

[S]cientific investigators are born not made, even by the magic
of the PhD.   Joseph Needham[4]

HOUSMAN's desire not to be known as a gentleman and Gowland
Hopkins's demand for recognition and proper respect raise the question
of the social standing of those people who in the twentieth century occupied
the cognitive niches and sites with which the present study is preoccupied.
Olive Lloyd-Baker's and Joseph Needham's remarks are reminders that even
deep into the twentieth century the very concept of merit was contested and

---

[1]   This is the epitaph Housman wished carved on his tombstone. Quoted in George
Watson, *Heresies and Heretics: Memories of the Twentieth Century* (London: 2013), p.127.
[2]   F. Gowland Hopkins, 'Medicine and Experimental Science,' in A. C. Seward (ed.),
Science and the Nation: Essays by Cambridge Graduates (New York: 1917 [1967]), p.255.
[3]   A remark, much treasured by John Betjeman, made by Olive Lloyd-Baker of Hardwicke
Court, Gloucestershire, a landowner and neighbour of Lees-Milne recorded in Lees-Milne's
diary, 2 June 1975. James Lees-Milne, *Through Wood and Dale: Diaries, 1975–1978* (London:
1988 [2007]), p.30.
[4]   Joseph Needham,, *The Sceptical Biologist: Ten Essays* (London: 1929), p.251.

the notion of hereditary talent still held its hold. An anxiety about status is reflected in a remark Cyril Hinshelwood, president of the Royal Society from 1955 to 1960, made to Isaiah Berlin: 'there is no quicker way of making a first-class institution third-class than by appointing second-class men.'[5] Even in 1968 the report of Lord Fulton's on scientists' place in the civil service struck a note of status anxiety:

> Many scientists ... get neither the full responsibilities and corresponding authority, nor the opportunities they might have. Too often they are organized in a separate hierarchy, while the policy and financial aspects of the work are reserved to a parallel group of 'generalist' administrators.

The historian who has studied these issues traces the discrepancy between the status of scientists and administrators in the civil service to the founding of the Department of Scientific and Industrial Research during the Great War.[6]

This chapter, therefore, is about the institutional and intellectual identities of British learned people from 1900 to 1950. It shows how far belonging and knowing were tied together and how far one's identity was tied to what one claims to know. It shows how far one's conception of oneself was connected to membership in various epistemic communities and how far these concep-tions of identity rested upon the recognition and respect such communities provided. Some notions of what an epistemic community is seem bleakly sterile. As one scholar has put it, an epistemic community 'is a network of professionals with recognised expertise and competence in a particular domain and an authoritative claim to policy relevant knowledge within that domain or issue-area.'[7] 'Professionals,' 'recognised expertise,' 'competence,' 'particular domain,' 'authoritative claims': such ways of putting it project a narrowly technical and impersonal mask that disguises the workings of the personal and the intimate in knowledge formation, articulation and organisation. To argue that knowledge formation and its articulation and organisation are personal and intimate is not to deny their objectivity. The purpose of what follows seeks to rescue people of learning from the conde-scension implied in sterile, bleak formulations.

Were the subjects of this chapter the 'New Men' of whom C. P. Snow wrote?[8] Noel Annan's 'The Intellectual Aristocracy,' originally written for G. M. Trevelyan's *festschrift* and reprinted in a later collection of essays, represents

5 Quoted in Isaiah Berlin to Hugh Trevor-Roper, 3 January 1984, in Isaiah Berlin, *Affirming: Letters, 1975–1997*, ed. Henry Hardy and Mark Pottle (London: 2015), p.227.
6 Eric Hutchinson, 'Scientists as an Inferior Class: The Early Years of the DSIR,' *Minerva*, 8 (3) (July 1970): 396–411. He quotes the report of the Fulton Commission at 396.
7 James K. Sebenius, 'Challenging Conventional Explanations of International Cooperation: Negotiation Analysis and the Case of Epistemic Communities,' *International Organization*, 46 (1) (Winter 1992): 323–365.
8 C. P. Snow, *The New Men* (Beeching Park: [1954] 2001).

what one might regard as a *terminus ad quem*,[9] a certain ending. His *Our Age* represents what might be regarded as a *terminus ad quo*,[10] a new beginning. The convention that the period from 1914 to 1919 marked a *satlezeit* in the history of knowledge is, properly, well known, which is why it is a convention. Maynard Keynes's *Economic Consequences of the Peace* (1919) and Lytton Strachey's *Eminent Victorians* (1919) are the established texts marking this transformation.[11] But Strachey lived on until 1932 and Keynes until 1946. And so it was for other ancients of days, relics of the Victorian–Edwardian ages: just to take some philosophers, Bertrand Russell (d.1970), G. E. Moore (d.1958), Ludwig Wittgenstein (d.1951) and Alfred North Whitehead (d.1947). G. M. Trevelyan (d.1962) went down from Cambridge in 1903 to take up a literary career but returned to become Regius Professor of History in 1927 and Master of Trinity College under the exigencies of war in 1940.[12] In this way the remnants of the intellectual aristocracy lingered on deep into the twentieth century. They became colleagues and associates of those of a different generation: just to take some scientists, Joseph Needham (b.1900), J. D. Bernal (b.1901) and Dorothy Hodgkin (b.1910). This intergenerational mingling was marked and telling and it is hard to know what was *terminus ad quo* and what was *terminus ad quem*, what was Alpha and what Omega. No society is fully homogeneous and fully integrated. The intellectual aristocracy was riven with internal divisions and contradictions. Our Age was also riven with internal divisions and contradictions, but different ones.

For example, when H. A. L. Fisher expressed his view of the shape of the British Academy's intellectual sections when he addressed his letter to 'My dear father-in-law', who was Sir Courtney Ilbert, an original fellow of the academy, the parliamentary draughtsman, the author of *The Government of India* (1898), and *Legislative Methods and Forms* (1901).[13] Fisher's daughter married, first F. W. Maitland and, second, Sir Francis Darwin. Her daughter, from her marriage to Maitland, married Gerald Shove. Fisher was no stranger

---

9   Noel Annan 'The Intellectual Aristocracy', in J. H. Plumb (ed.), *Studies in Social History* (London: 1955), pp.241–287; *idem., The Dons: Mentors, Eccentrics and Geniuses* (Chicago: 1999), pp.204–341.
10   Noel Annan, *Our Age: Portrait of a Generation* (London: 1990).
11   William C. Lubenow, 'Lytton Strachey's *Eminent Victorians*: The Rise and Fall of the Intellectual Aristocracy', in Miles Taylor and Michael Wolff (eds), *The Victorians After 1900: Histories, Representations, Revisions* (Manchester: 2004), pp.17–28.
12   Trinity's fellows wished to leave the mastership in abeyance until the war's end but John Colville believed the post was of more than academic importance and convinced Trevelyan to accept. John Colville left the threatening hint afloat that if Trevelyan refused the post would not be left vacant and would go to someone less attractive such as Viscount Cherwell. John Colville, *The Fringes of Power: 10 Downing Street Diaries, 1939–1955* (New York/London: 1955), pp.239–240, 250–251. See also David Cannadine, *G.M. Trevelyan, A Life in History* (London: 1992), p.20.
13   Fisher to Ilbert, 10 December 1914, BAA/SEC/1/43.

to Bloomsbury.[14] When he was president of the Board of Education in Lloyd George's government, he went to tea with Virginia Woolf on 15 October 1918 'obviously due to old family affection.' He had lost, Woolf noted, 'his lean intellectual look; his hollow cheeks are filled; his eyes with that pale frosty look which blue eyes get in age; his whole bearing very quiet, simple & when not speaking rather saddened & subdued.'[15] Fisher's connections were not unusual and his, like others, extended deep into the twentieth century.

Vita Sackville West and Harold Nicolson fretted about their generational connections. Both were aristocrats: he the service aristocracy (his father had been raised to the peerage as Baron Carnock for his services to diplomacy), she, of the Barons Sackville, the hereditary aristocracy (herself bearing long-held resentments because, being born a woman, she could not inherit Knole, the family palace in Kent). But whatever their family considerations both felt themselves to be aristocrats by virtue of their writings. He a biographer; she a writer about gardens and as a poet. Nicolson wrote:

> I have always been on the side of the under-dog, but I also believed in the principle of aristocracy. I have hated the rich and I have loved learning, scholarship, intelligence and the humanities. Suddenly I am faced with the fact that all these lovely things are supposed to be 'class privileges.' The snobbishness of the British people (that factor upon which the aristocratic principle relied and often exploited) has suddenly turned to venom. When I find that my whole class is being assailed, I feel part of them, a feeling I have never had before … I know that such a life, as lived by Vita and myself, is 'good' in a philosophical sense. We are humane, charitable, just and not vulgar. By God, we are not vulgar!

Walking through the frozen woods at Sissinghurst in 1940, with the war now well under way, Sackville West mused about the futilities of fighting a war for liberty and for the standards of civilisation and feared the war would destroy both liberty and civilisation. She wondered if she and Nicolson had not tied themselves too tightly to Edwardian values and had not been quick enough to move into the moods and values of the 1920s and 1930s.[16]

---

[14] Fisher, Herbert Albert Laurens (1865–1940): father, barrister, tutor and later private secretary to Albert Edward the Prince of Wales; ed. Winchester and New College, Oxford, first class in Classical Moderations (1886) and in *Literae Humaniories* (1888) and elected to a New College fellowship (1888); educated in ancient history but fearing there was nothing new to learn there he turned to modern history and studied at Göttingen and Paris where he was impressed by the technical accomplishments of the *Ecole des Chartes* and by the personalities of Taine and Renan; Vice-Chancellor of Sheffield University (1914); joined Lloyd George's government at the Board of Education (1916–1922) and sat as a Liberal for the Hallamshire division of Sheffield; held the seat for the Combined English Universities as a Liberal (1918–1926); Warden of New College, Oxford (1926); elected to the British Academy (1907); President of the British Academy (1928–1932); OM (1937).

[15] Anne Olivier Bell (ed), *The Diary of Virginia Woolf, Volume One, 1915–-1919* (New York/London: 1977), pp.202–203.

[16] Nicolson's diary for 13 January 1940 in Harold Nicolson, *The War Years, 1940–1945: Volume 11 of Diaries and Letters*, ed. Nigel Nicholson (New York: 1967), p.57.

The members of Our Age could certainly not be marked by greater specialisation than their forbearers. Learned people had always been specialists in some
way. The members of Federico Cesi's circle in the seventeenth century, though
bound together by what were defensive impulses of loyalty and shared values,
each had particular and peculiar intellectual interests.[17] The same might be said
of members of learned societies in the twentieth century, such as the Hardy
Club in Cambridge or the Theoretical Biology Club. What might be said is
that members of Annan's intellectual aristocracy were more intellectually and
socially dispersed and the members of Our Age were more intellectually and
socially concentrated. No one in either the intellectual aristocracy or in Our
Age could be like Thomas Young, of Emmanuel College, Cambridge, a man
'who knew everything.'[18]

The intellectual aristocracy occupied what Bourdieu called a habitus: those
preconscious, almost never directly observed structuring structures, consisting
of habits, practices and customs that produce certain cognitive dispositions.[19]
The intellectual aristocracy was the creature of late nineteenth-century college
life and extended patterns of intermarriage, families joined by blood as well as
brains. The Darwins's marriages connected them to the Jebb's, the Venns, the
Keyneses and the Cornfords. In addition to being dons and schoolmasters,
they ventured forth into the civil service and the empire. As Jowett (who by
virtue of his position as Master of Balliol placing his pupils thither) knew,
they used their positions as dons and schoolmasters 'to form good places for
ourselves out of the revenues of the Colleges.'[20] These families were descended
from the evangelical families of Clapham and consequently they were imbued
with a certain seriousness and a sense of public responsibility. While these later
generations drifted from their theological roots, some of them found moorings
elsewhere. Fitzjames Stephen's son, Herbert, for example, became a Roman
Catholic and Maynard Keynes became attracted to the values of G. E. Moore,
which though secular pieties were serious values nonetheless.

'Our Age' occupied a different habitus. Its members wove themselves into
different webs of social and mental connections. They could no longer be
Casaubons wittering away in country rectories quarrelling over their mythog-
raphies,[21] nor could they simply live off college livings, nor could they be literati

17   Lubenow, 'Only Connect': Learned Societies in Nineteenth-Century Britain, pp.20–24.
18   Andrew Robinson, The Last Man Who Knew Everything: Thomas Young, the
Anonymous Polymath Who Proved Newton Wrong, Explained How We See, Cured the Sick,
and Deciphered the Rosetta Stone, and Other Feats of Genius (New York: 2005).
19   For the concept of habitus see Pierre Bourdieu, 'Intellectual Field and Creative Project,'
Social Science Information, 8 (1969): 89–119 and 'The Genesis of the Concepts of Habitus
and of Field,' Sociocriticism, 2 (1985): 11–24. See also Fritz Ringer, Fields of Knowledge: French
Academic Culture in Comparative Perspective (Cambridge: 1992), pp.4–12.
20   Evelyn Abbot and Lewis Campbell, Life and Letters of Benjamin Jowett, 2 vols (London:
1897), II, pp.212–213.
21   See Colin Kidd, The World of Mr. Casaubon: Britain's Wars of Mythography,

writing for their daily bread. Our Age had a different style and tone. They were often salaried, connected to university faculties, and often funded (or seeking to be funded) by philanthropic foundations. Maurice Bowra, the leader of the Oxford Wits, coined the phrase 'Our Age' when someone asked him how old someone was. Noel Annan amplified this thought when he described those Bowra would have included within this habitus: poets, writers, artists and some politicians. Bowra 'would certainly have included animators – those who would liberate their contemporaries by their vitality, exuberance and spontaneity.'[22] All this was at some distance from the mental habits of Clapham Common and the intellectual aristocracy, and they felt some regret about this. As Annan confessed: 'Our Age played their times in a minor key. We were not original. We did not compose new themes and visions of life as our heroic predecessors before 1914 had done.'

The generations after 1914–1919 could not, and perhaps would not, detach themselves from their fathers and mothers. Joseph Needham paid careful attention to the family from which he sprang, his upbringing, and its effect on his mental conditioning. His father's library provided materials that helped Needham engage in what would be a life-long effort to unify differences and that freed him from what he called 'the bondage of conventional ideas.' In his father's library he found Schlegel's *History of Philosophy* (which he read at the age of ten), George Herbert's poetry, and Thomas Browne's *Religio Medici*. From them, he learned, 'words were a form of poetry, not to be dissected by the scientific scalpel or criticized by the methods of the linguistic philosopher.' There he also found Henry Rawlinson's treatise on the ancient Egyptians, 'which fixed so firmly in his mind at an early age that all the apparent absolutes of Christendom were not absolutes at all, but formulations of relative value, keyed to particular forms of one civilization only.'[23] From his father's library, then, Needham learned how to defy literalism, to bridge binaries, and to understand how intellectual problems could be resolved by paying close attention to the relations between differences rather than paying attention to the differences themselves.

So it is difficult to fit Needham into tight identity categories and to describe his fundamental loyalties. He was both FRS and FBA and as a fellow of the Royal Society sought to have the society take within its metes and bounds studies in the history and philosophy of science.[24] Needham gained the CH and, along with other foreign honours, was also appointed to the Order of

---

1700–1870 (Cambridge: 2016).

[22] And for what follows Annan, *Our Age*, pp.3–18.

[23] Joseph Needham [writing under his nom de plume as Henry Holorenshaw], 'The Making of an Honorary Taoist,' in Mikuláš and Robert Young (eds), *Changing Perspectives in the History of Science: Essays in Honour of Joseph Needham* (Dordrecht/Boston: 1973): pp.2, 5, 11 and for what follows *passim*.

[24] See Sir Howard Florey (President of the Royal Society) to Joseph Needham, 19

China's Brilliant Star. He was a fellow of Caius College, Cambridge, later its master, as well as Sir William Dunn, reader in the Cambridge Biochemical Laboratory. He, along with Joseph Woodger ('Socrates'), guided the investigations of the Theoretical Biology Club. He and his wife, Dorothy, were drawn to the village church in Thaxted where its charismatic vicar, Conrad Noel, formed an association noted for its Christian socialism, its musical tradition (Gustav Holst lived there and wrote much of the music for the church) and its liturgical beauty based upon medieval themes. He was a representative for the Association of Scientific Workers on the Cambridge Trades Council and tried to raise alerts about the dangers posed by the Spanish Civil War and the emergence of National Socialism in Germany. He was active in the Socialist League, a ginger group associated with the Labour Party. His marriage to Dorothy Moyl Needham lasted until her death, but in the 1930s he fell in love with Lu Gwei-Djen who had come from China to study with Dorothy Needham. It was Lu Gwei-Djen, whom he married after Dorothy's death, who stirred his interest in the history of Chinese technology and medicine, which preoccupied him in the last several decades of his life. As he wrote: 'The death of Gwei-Djen is such a terrible blow to me, for since 1937 I had her constant companionship and criticism. She was always the principal fact in my giving up scientific research and becoming a historian of Chinese science.'[25] Thoroughly enmeshed in the religious practices of his own country, he preached regularly at Thaxted and in Caius chapel, he sympathised thoroughly with the religious conceptions of the Confucians, the Buddhists and the Taoists. His loyalties and his social and intellectual affiliations were diffuse, dense and differentiated. Warned once by his father not to dissipate his energies, Needham found unifying impulses in these diverse relationships. Asked once whether he considered himself a scientist or a historian, Needham responded that he might be best regarded as an honorary Taoist.

Dorothy Crowfoot Hodgkin, Needham's colleague in the Theoretical Biology Club, was also attentive to her family and upbringing, finding in her attention to them certain clues to the work she would do in later life.[26] Hodgkin begins her recollections with her family life in Egypt. Her father, John Winter Crowfoot, had read classics at Brasenose College, Oxford after which a senior Hulme Scholarship took him to Greece, Cyprus and Asia Minor, where he intended to take up a career in archaeology. Finding such prospects meagre, after a period as a temporary lecturer in classics at Birmingham University he

December 1956 and Needham to Florey, 3 January 1957, Cambridge University Library, Needham Ms J224.

[25] Needham to Nathan Slavin (at the University of Pennsylvania], 24 May 1992, CUL., Needham Ms/M/435.

[26] For what follows see Dorothy Hodgkin, *Autobiographical Memoirs*, ed. Katherine Hodgkin, in Guy Dodson, Savaraj Ramaseshan et al., *The Collected Works of Dorothy Hodgkin*, 3 vols (Bangalore: 1994), III, pp.774–816.

took a position in Egypt and the Sudan in the Department of Education (1901) and became Assistant Director (1903–1908), and Director (1914). He was able to return to his archaeological interests in 1926 when he became Director of the British School of Archaeology in Jerusalem. Dorothy Crowfoot Hodgkin's visits to Egypt and the Sudan and her father's archaeological preoccupations in Palestine followed Hodgkin to Oxford and Cambridge just as her research interests followed her to the Sudan and the Middle East.

On an expedition with her father to Jerash, a city of the Decopolis, in Transjordan, Hodgkin (then of course Crowfoot) worked as what she called 'a beginner archaeologist.' In doing so she was fascinated by patterns, premonitions perhaps of a fascination with the patterns in crystals that she would later pursue in her studies with Desmond Bernal:

> I now began a lovely life. We would rise early and have breakfast together and then set out on our appointed errands, walking over the flower-filled hills to different sections of the work. Very early I settled down to make reproductions of two mosaic pavements. The first one was the floor of the chapel attached to St. Theodore. This was covered by a simple pattern of three twined bands surrounded by a border. The second was more complicated. The room it was found in was circular and described as a diaconal, probably a place where alms were distributed. It was attached to a church, the Propytea Church, some way from St. Theodore's, built across a road leading to the Temple of Artemis. This mosaic had an inscription giving its date as 564 A.D. and a quotation from the 68th psalm. The tesserae of both mosaics were made of coloured marble, about 1cm square. I drew in outline the patterns, reduced to 1/10th, which made each tessera 1mm square, and coloured small parts of each drawing for the record.

On returning to England, Hodgkin continued interests she had had in the Middle East. In Oxford she and the family stayed with Professor Griffiths and his wife, both Egyptologists. After she explained her interest in patterns, they told her of two important books on the subject. One, by Joan Evans, the sister of Evans of Knossos and later herself a president of the Society of Antiquaries, was a photographic study of French medieval decoration. The other was by Flinders Petrie, a record of his observations from his notebook. Hodgkin's father arranged to have a copy printed with interleaved pages so that she could record her finds alongside Flinders Petrie's. Even as she continued her studies at Somerville College, Hodgkin spent her Sundays with friends on archaeological expeditions. Her mother sent Hodgkin specimens of coloured tesserae from the walls of churches and asked her whether Hodgkin would analyse them with the gravimetric techniques she was using in her first-year chemistry studies. This involved silicate analysis and Hodgkin discovered that one of the tesserae was deep blue and contained cobalt. This, she said, 'should have been boring but I enjoyed it enormously.' In 1933 Hodgkin arrived in Cambridge to begin her studies with Bernal. She had been in Ravenna with her parents at the first International Congress of Christian Archaeology. 'Science and archaeology,' Hodgkin observed, 'are inextricably entangled.' So these, like examples from Needham's career, are illustrations of the ways that mental lives and also the lives of those in different intellectual generations connected with each other variously in complex and multiple affiliations and loyalties.

The concepts of an intellectual aristocracy and 'Our Age,' as loose and as flexible as they are, may be too tight to capture the range and density of twentieth-century feelings of institutional and intellectual belonging. As the examples of Needham and Hodgkin illustrate, identity is diffused, multiple, and a matter of various affiliations. The concepts of the gentleman and of character had perished and neither the intellectual aristocracy nor Our Age had ever taken aboard in a measurable way the German concepts of *Bildung* and *Beruf*, both alien, perhaps as bad as being an *intellectual.* Even in Germany concepts of *Beruf* and *Bildung* were losing their savour.[27] Franz Ernest Neumann's public utterances remained true to the concepts of *Wissenschaft* and, especially, *Bildung* with their understanding of the ways that systematic study drew out a scholar's natural talents, character and, therefore, vocation. In practice, however, Neumann prosecuted a programme of instruction (*Ausbildung*) in physics, which shaped technical skills more than it developed natural talents.[28]

Perhaps some traction concerning multiple intellectual identities and loyalties might be got from surveying those who became presidents of the Royal Society and the British Academy in the first part of the twentieth century. William Crookes (PRS from 1913 to 1916) had been elected FRS in 1863 but his father had been a tailor and businessman of north-country origin and Crookes himself had been educated at the Chippenham Grammar School and the Royal College of Chemistry, Hanover Square. He was appointed as an assistant at the Royal College of Chemistry in 1850 and became superintendent of the Radcliffe Observatory, Oxford in 1854. But Crookes had inherited sufficient money from his father to make him financially independent. Therefore, after his marriage in 1856 he passed his life in London carrying out independent work in his private laboratory at 7 Kensington Park Gardens, together with some journalism and some consulting. Though regarded as a doyen of his profession, Crookes's gifts were largely empirical rather than theoretical.

Joseph John Thomson, who succeeded Crookes, cut a very different figure. His father had been a publisher and bookseller and after education in a private day school young Thomson entered Owens College, Manchester, whose professorship included the likes of W. S. Jevons, Adolphus Ward

[27]   Fritz Ringer, *The Decline of the German Mandarins: The German Academic Community, 1890–1933* (Cambridge: 1969).
[28]   Kathryn M. Olesko, *Physics as a Calling: Discipline and Practice in the Königsberg Seminar for Physics* (Ithaca/London: 1991), pp.13–14.

and James Bryce. From thence he went thither at the age of fourteen to Trinity College, Cambridge where he finished as second wrangler and second Smith's prizeman. He became a fellow of Trinity in 1880 (with a dissertation on the transformation of energy), a mathematics lecturer at Trinity in 1882, a university lecturer in 1883, FRS in 1884, and Cavendish Professor of Experimental Physics in 1894. He was appointed Master of Trinity in 1918. This last appointment was a departure from tradition, but he was generous and hospitable, a member of the Family (a university dining society going back to the seventeenth century), and seriously religious, kneeling in private prayer every day. In his time as director he made the Cavendish Laboratory the greatest research school in experimental physics in his day.

Charles Scott Sherrington (PRS, 1920–1925), unlike the physicists Crookes and Thomson, was a neurophysiologist. Educated at Ipswich Grammar School, he went up to Gonville and Caius College, Cambridge where he took first class in both parts of the Natural Sciences Tripos (1881–1883). Completing his education at St Thomas's Hospital, London, he went to Germany from 1885 to 1886 for further studies. On returning, Caius College elected him to a fellowship. He became a lecturer in systematic physiology at St Thomas's and, in 1891, professor-superintendent at the Brown Animal Sanatory Institution, London. He moved to Liverpool as Holt Professor of Physiology in 1895 and in 1913 he was elected to the Waynflete chair of physiology with a fellowship at Magdalen College, Oxford. He found Oxford a 'trifle rigid' but he found in the home of Sir William Osler, a professor of medicine, a refreshing and stimulating refuge from what he thought an otherwise stifling intellectual world. Never a narrow-minded specialist, he began his book collection even before leaving Cambridge. He loved sailing, art, music and drama, and he skied in Switzerland. When, in 1913, British physiologists were invited to St Petersburg he dined privately with Pavlov. When entertained by the Tsar, the Tsar asked him for news of his cousin and Sherrington replied that he had not seen Edward VII recently. His Rede Lecture in 1933 was on the 'Brain and its Mechanism.' The relation between the mind and brain, he held, was not just unresolved but was devoid of any basis. He was elected to the Royal Society (1893) and appointed GBE (1922).

Ernest Rutherford (PRS, 1925–1930) brought the Royal Society presidency back to physics. Born in New Zealand and educated there, his father – variously a farmer, a wheelwright, a timber contractor, an engineer – concentrated on the large-scale production of flax. After studying at Nelson College and Canterbury College, Christ Church, encouraged by J. J. Thomson,[29] he went up to Trinity College, Cambridge. Because he was not elected to a fellowship there, he went over to Canada as Professor of Physics at McGill University (1898). Despite

---

[29]   J. J. Thomson [writing from 6 Scrope Terrace, Cambridge] to Rutherford, 24 September 1895, Rutherford Papers, CUL, Add .7653/T9.

J. J. Thomson's nomination, he failed to gain election to the Royal Society in 1902 (because, Thomson thought, no one on the council knew anything about 'modern developments in physics' and because Joseph Larmor, the new secretary of the Royal Society, was from Belfast and supported only his fellow towns-men).[30] Rutherford, however, was elected the next year. At McGill he advanced his career but he felt isolated:

> After the years in the Cavendish I feel myself rather out of things scientific, and greatly miss the opportunities of meeting men interested in Physics. Outside a small circle of the laboratory, it is seldom I meet anyone to hear what is being done elsewhere. I think this feeling of isolation is the great drawback to colonial appointments, for unless one is content to stagnate, one feels badly the want of scientific intercourse.[31]

Unlike Newton and Faraday, Rutherford needed intellectual comrades and so Thomson urged him to return to Britain and the University of Manchester. Thomson rather knew Rutherford would enjoy Manchester. Thomson had been born in Manchester and Thomson reminded him, that the 'weather is not nearly so bad as its reputation.' To work in the laboratory with Arthur Schuster, Thomson thought, would be good.[32] So Rutherford returned to Britain in 1907 where, as Langworthy Professor of Physics at Manchester, he discovered the nuclear structure of the atom.[33]

Rutherford seemed to be the natural successor to Thomson as Professor of Experimental Physics and Director of the Cavendish Laboratory. But the succession for both of them was not an easy one. Perhaps remembering Thomson's advice to him before going to Manchester, about having a clear working relationship with Arthur Schuster,[34] Rutherford, writing from the Savile Club, said:

> If I decided to stand & were elected to the post [as Director of the Cavendish], I feel that no advantages to the post would possibly compensate for any distur-bance of our long continued friendship or for any possible friction whether open or latent that might possibly arise if we did not have clear mutual understanding with regard to the Laboratory and research arrangements.[35]

Thomson responded by reminding Rutherford that the original arrangement had been to appoint Rutherford as director of the laboratory but to leave him,

---

30   J. J. Thomson to Rutherford, 1 May 1902, Rutherford Papers, CUL., Add. 7653/T18. Larmor had come up to St John's College, Cambridge where, in 1880, he was placed senior wrangler in the Mathematical Tripos. (J. J. Thomson was second wrangler that year.) Larmor was elected FRS (1892), one of its secretaries (1901–1912), Lucasian Professor of Mathematics (1903–1932), Unionist MP for the University (1911–1922).
31   Rutherford [writing from McGill University] to J. J. Thomson, 20 March 1902, Rutherford Papers, CUL, Add. 7653/T15.
32   J. J. Thomson to Rutherford, 18 December 1906, Rutherford Papers, CUL., Add.7653/T18.
33   J. J. Thomson to Rutherford, 15 November 1909, Rutherford Papers, CUL., Add. 7653/ T/32.
34   J. J. Thomson to Rutherford, 18 December 1906, Rutherford Papers, CUL., Add. 7653/T18.
35   Rutherford to Thomson, 7 March [1919], Rutherford Papers, CUL., Add. 7653/T43.

Thomson, as Cavendish Professor. But Thomson realised such an arrangement would not do and promised to leave Rutherford 'a perfectly free hand'.[36] And so Rutherford moved to Newnham Cottage on Queen's Road (where he lived until he died) and carried on at the Cavendish.

Patrick Blackett recalled his experiences as a young man working with Rutherford:

> It was a great event for a youth at the Cavendish, as I was in the early twenties, to be asked by Rutherford to count scintillations for an hour or two each evening. One went into the dark room, and waited half an hour in the dark chattering while one's eyes got dark adapted. While waiting Rutherford used to chat rather indiscreetly about his colleagues in Cambridge. Darkness seemed to encourage indiscretion! I wish I had a sound record of all Rutherford said in those hours of waiting in the dark.[37]

Blackett also recalled a remark Einstein had made about Rutherford: 'I concentrated on speculative theories, whereas Rutherford managed to reach profound conclusion on the basis of almost primitive reflection combined with relatively simple experiments'.[38] Desmond Bernal also recollected his years at the Cavendish with Rutherford. Rutherford's dictum was: 'Don't let me catch anyone talking about the Universe in my laboratory'.[39] Rutherford, therefore, was incapable of the kind of imaginative leaps managed by Arthur Eddington and James Jeans and he was unsympathetic to the speculative conjuring tricks conducted by the V²V Club in Cambridge.

Frederick Gowland Hopkins succeeded Rutherford at the Royal Society (1930–1935). As a biochemist Gowland Hopkins had very precarious beginnings. His family was engaged in the bookselling and jewellery trades, though his father was the first cousin of Gerard Manley Hopkins, the Jesuit poet. Gowland Hopkins was a Civilian, having been at the City of London School, but he worked in an insurance office for a time before being articled for three years at a consulting firm in the City. Gaining a small inheritance he studied chemistry in South Kensington with Sir Edward Frankland and then entered University College, London. After serving as an assistant to Sir Thomas Stevenson, the Home Office analyst and lecturer at Guy's Hospital, he entered Guy's as a medical student and gained his medical certification there in 1894. After serving at Guy's as an assistant in the department of physiology Sir Michael Foster invited Gowland Hopkins to Cambridge as a lecturer on chemical physiology (1898). He had to survive on tutorial work at Emmanuel

---

[36] Thomson to Rutherford, 10 March 1919, Rutherford Papers, CUL., Add. 7653/T44.
[37] P. M. S. Blackett, 'The Old Days of the Cavendish,' *Rivista del Nuovo Cimento*, 1 (*Numero Speciale*, 1969): xxxiv–xxxv.
[38] Quoted by Patrick Blackett in 'Rutherford,' *Notes and Records of the Royal Society of London*, 27 (1) (August 1972): 58.
[39] J. D. Bernal, *The Origin of Life* (London: 1967), p.x.

College, which was finally raised to a readership in 1902. A praelectorship at Trinity College, with no formal teaching responsibilities, allowed him to pursue his own research and he was elected to the Royal Society in 1905. By the beginning of the Great War, now as Professor of Biochemistry, he was able to develop a school of biochemistry. In 1920 the trustees of the Sir William Dunn estate provided funds for a chair in biochemistry, which Gowland Hopkins occupied until 1932. He was knighted in 1925.

Born in Cumberland, William Henry Bragg's father, after serving as an officer in the merchant navy, established himself as a farmer. Bragg was educated at King William's School, Isle of Man and then went up to Trinity College, Cambridge where he finished as Third Wrangler. He went to Australia where he took up a post at the University of Adelaide as Elder Professor of Physics and Mathematics (1886–1908). Settling himself in Australia at the university, he married and served on the Council of the South Australian School of Mines and Industries (1895–1908). Elected FRS (1907) he returned to Britain to hold the Cavendish Chair of Physics at the University of Leeds (1909) and thence to the Quaine professorship at University College, London (1915), in which year he won the Nobel Prize in physics with his son William Lawrence Bragg. Together they established the modern science of crystallography by showing how atoms are arranged in crystals in rocksalt and diamonds. From 1932 Bragg was the Fullerian Professor of Chemistry and Director of the Davy-Faraday Laboratory at the Royal Institution. There, though experimental work continued, he acted more as a guide to others through what were called 'genial lectures,' which made subtle and difficult questions clear. He paved the way for people like Desmond Bernal and Dorothy Hodgkin, who turned their attention to biological materials. He was appointed CBE (1917) and KBE (1920).

Henry Dale, a physiologist and pharmacologist, succeeded Bragg in the presidency of the Royal Society (1940–1945). From a family of limited means (his father was a manager in a manufacturing firm and his mother was the daughter of a furniture maker) Dale faced financial difficulties at each stage of his educational career. He attended the Leys School in Cambridge and Trinity College where he gained first classes in both parts of the Natural Sciences Tripos. Failing to gain a college fellowship he had to pursue a career by holding occasional demonstratorships and by private coaching. After four months at Frankfurt-am-Main he took a research post at the Wellcome Institute (1904–1914) and then became Director of the Department of Biochemistry and Pharmacology at the projected Institute of Medical Researches, which in 1920 became the National Institute for Medical Research at Hampstead. He became Director of the Institute (1928–1942) and then Director and Professor of Chemistry at the Royal Institution (1942–1946). He was elected to the Royal Society in 1914 and served as its secretary from 1925 to 1935. He was appointed CBE (1919), to a knighthood (1932), and the GBE (1943). During his presidency of the Royal Society the number of fellows to be elected each year rose from twenty to twenty-five and women were elected to the fellowship for the first time. All three of his children studied either physiology or medicine and his eldest daughter married Lord Todd, Professor of Organic Chemistry, Master of Christ's College, and President of the Royal Society (1975–1980).

Robert Robinson was president of the Royal Society from 1945 to 1950. The son of one of the inventors of cottonwood, he was educated at Chesterfield Grammar School and the University of Manchester. He was the first professor of pure and applied chemistry at the University of Sydney from 1912 and the Wayflete Professor of Chemistry at Oxford from 1930. Sceptical, he did not himself adopt measurement techniques using crystallographic methods, but he encouraged Dorothy Hodgkin and secured funds so that she could obtain the additional apparatus she required.[40] Elected to the Royal Society, he gained its Davy Medal (1930), its Royal Medal (1932) and its Copley Medal (1942) and was knighted in 1939. He was a strong chess player and claimed he married his second wife because she allowed him to teach her chess.[41]

Cyril Hinshelwood, like so many presidents of the Royal Society, came from a family of modest means. His father was a chartered accountant (though as a friend of Dickens he had literary connections). Hinshelwood had been to Westminster City School where he won a Brackenbury scholarship to Balliol. During the war, before going up to Oxford, he was a chemist in the explosives factory. There, he discovered a gift for research and became known as a 'boy wonder.' There, or so he claimed in his Nobel address, he discovered, in the testing of the stability of explosives, the importance of the dependence of energy and the environment of molecules for explaining chemical change. Following the war, Hinshelwood went up to Balliol and so distinguished himself he was appointed a research fellow. He became a tutorial fellow of Trinity College in 1921 and for the next twenty years conducted research in the cellars of Balliol and the outhouses of Trinity. In his lectures he was able to specify with clarity what was known and, especially, what was unknown. He encouraged his students to resist the temptation to attribute to current working propositions more authority than they apparently contained. He was fond of quoting Alice in Wonderland: 'Somehow I seem to fill my head with Ideas, but I don't know exactly what they are.'[42] He was elected to the Royal Society in 1929, knighted in 1948, and awarded the Nobel Prize in 1946 for his contribution to chemical kinetics. In addition to his presidency of the Royal Society, his presidency of the British Association for the Advancement

---

[40] L. W. B. Brockliss, *The University of Oxford: A History* (Oxford: 2016), p.508; J. B. Morrell, 'The Non-Medical Sciences, 1914–1939,' in Brian Harrison (ed.), *The History of the University of Oxford, Volume VIII: The Twentieth Century* (Oxford: 1994), p.151.

[41] Robert Robinson, *Memoir of a Minor Prophet: Seventy Years of Organic Chemistry* (Amsterdam: 1976).

[42] Cyril Hinshelwood, *Structure of Physical Chemistry* (Oxford: Clarendon Press, 1951).

of Society, and his presidency of the Chemical Society, Hinshelwood was also President of the Classical Association, a testimony to his broad learning, his elegance, and his love of beauty in all of its artistic forms. Holding the view that all forms of learning were unified, he retired to the same flat in Chelsea he had shared with his widowed mother since 1904, collecting Chinese porcelain, studying foreign languages (he spoke six and in 1939 he had been president of the Oxford branch of the Modern Language Association) and painting. In 1968 there was an exhibition of one hundred of his oil paintings at Goldsmiths Hall. In his Eddington Memorial Lecture (1961) Hinshelwood explored the mental worlds of the scientist and the artist and concluded that both consciousness and modern physics are both essentially symbolic.

In his Centenary Address to the Chemical Society (1947) Hinshelwood celebrated a society, not a discovery or a person, and reminded his audience that thoughts are the products of particular historical settings in which what is important is the relations of the 'people who [made the knowledge of chemistry] and are making it and the general condition of their lives.' The duty of the Royal Society, he remarked in his address to its Tercentenary (1950), was 'not to predict, nor to legislate but to maintain in the larger community the smaller one in which creative activity can flourish.' In his presidential address to the Royal Society (1957) Hinshelwood pointed out how the search for general principles that are aesthetically pleasing are often frustrated by nature's complexity. There is, he said, 'a conflict between imagination and [an] austere regard for truth,' which seem to pass through three phases:

> The first is that of gross-oversimplification, reflecting partly the need for practical working rules, and even more a too enthusiastic aspiration after form. In the second stage the symmetry of hypothetical systems is distorted and the neatness marred as recalcitrant facts increasingly rebel against conformity. In the third stage, *if and when this is attained*, a new order emerges, *more intricately contrived, less obvious, and with its parts more subtly interwoven, since it is nature's and not man's conception.*[43]

Thus Hinshelwood meditated on not only the workings of nature itself but also on the workings of investigators seeking to understand nature's workings. In his meditations he stressed the importance of techniques for discovering positive knowledge but also the power of imagination and intuition.

A number of the characteristics of the 'new men' who occupied the chair of the Royal Society stand out. First, there was their imperial experience. Rutherford came from New Zealand and went to Canada before returning to Manchester and Cambridge. Bragg and Robinson had careers in Australia before returning to the Royal Institution and Oxford. Second, if their social

---

[43] This and other quotations in this paragraph are taken from Harold Thompson, 'Cyril Norman Hinshelwood, 1897–1967, Elected FRS 1929,' *Biographical Memoirs of Fellows of the Royal Society, 1973*, volume 19 (London: 1973): 357–431, emphases added.

origins were not exactly humble, they rose to dominate their respective fields. William Crookes, J. J. Thomson, Charles Sherrington, Ernest Rutherford, Frederick Gowland Hopkins, William Henry Bragg, Henry Dale, Robert Robinson, Edgar Adrian, Cyril Hinshelwood and Patrick Blackett were appointed to the Order of Merit. J. J. Thomson, Sherrington, Rutherford, Gowland Hopkins, Bragg, Dale, Robinson, Adrian, Hinshelwood and Blackett got Nobel Prizes. Rutherford, Adrian and Blackett were raised to the peerage. C. P. Snow wrote to Blackett when Blackett was raised to the peerage: '[D]elighted but not surprised. Orthodoxy cannot catch up any further, can it?'[44] Blackett responded: 'you are quite right that orthodoxy has caught up with me, and I suppose for the last time.' Blackett's wife had said to him: 'Now you have nothing to achieve – except a funeral at Westminster Abbey.'[45] Not everyone was comfortable with such honours. A. V. Hill congratulated Blackett on his election to the presidency of the Royal Society but when Blackett was raised to the peerage, something he would have scorned in the 1930s, Hill wrote him a note (which he did not send): 'How are the mighty fallen. Yours sadly. A. V. H.'[46] Since their backgrounds were relatively modest, they had to earn their way in the world rather inherit it. In order to distinguish themselves from the aristocracy of the *ancien régime* Rutherford styled himself Baron Rutherford of Newton; Edgar Adrian styled himself Baron Adrian of Cambridge; Todd styled himself Baron Todd of Trumpington; Blackett styled himself Baron Blackett of Chelsea; and Frederick Lindemann was gazetted as Viscount Cherwell.

It is appropriate for comparative purposes to examine the careers of presidents of the British Academy. On the whole the presidents of the British Academy came from more socially and intellectually distinguished families than the presidents of the Royal Society. The exceptions to this generalisation are J. H. Clapham, whose father was a chemist and a silversmith and whose mother was the daughter of an accountant from Manchester; Idris Bell, whose father was a chemist from a family of yeoman farmers in the Midlands; and Charles Webster, whose father had been a shipping agent. On the other hand Frederic Kenyon's father had been a fellow of All Souls and Vinerian Professor of Law at Oxford. His mother was the daughter of Edward Hawkins, FRS, Keeper of Antiquities at the British Museum. Arthur Balfour's father belonged to the Scottish squirarchy who had scratched himself into a fortune as an Indian Civilian but whose mother was a Cecil, and Balfour's uncle, therefore, was Lord Salisbury. H. A. L. Fisher's father was a barrister, a student of

[44] C. P. Snow to Patrick Blackett, 21 November 1967, Ransom Center, University of Texas, C. P. Snow Mss., 58/17.

[45] Blackett to Snow, 1 December 1967, Ransom Center, University of Texas, C. P. Snow Mss., 58/17.

[46] 'Note in the A. V. Hill papers. Churchill College, Cambridge; A. V. Hill to the editor of the *Times*, 16 July 1974. Churchill College, Cambridge, AVHL, II/4/10.

Christ Church, and had been the Prince of Wales's tutor and later his private secretary. His mother's father served as a physician in the East India Company and was known as the leading English physician in Calcutta. John William Mackail's father had been a Free Church minister in Scotland.

Kenyon had been educated at Winchester and New College, Oxford where he took first classes in both classical moderations (1883) and *literae humaniores* (1886) and was elected a fellow of Magdalen (1888). Arthur Balfour had been educated at Eton and Trinity College, Cambridge where Henry Sidgwick became one brother-in-law and Lord Rayleigh, Cavendish Professor, became another. Like Kenyon, Fisher had been educated at Winchester and New College, where, like Kenyon again, he took first classes in classical moderation (1886) and *literae humaniores* (1888) and, after which, he was elected a fellow of New College. Mackail had been educated at Ayr Academy, Edinburgh University, and at Balliol during Jowett's time as master. Mackail was the most brilliant undergraduate of his time, taking a first class in both classical moderations (1879) and *literae humaniores* (1881) as well as an assortment of university scholarships: the Hertford (1880), the Ireland (1880), the Craven (1882), the Derby (1884) and the Newdigate (1881) for a poem on Thermopylæ. W. D. Ross had been educated at Edinburgh High School, Edinburgh University and Balliol College, Oxford. Clapham was educated as Leys School, Cambridge (where he distinguished himself as a games player) and King's College, Cambridge where he took a first class in the Historical Tripos (1895). Idris Bell was educated at Nottingham High School and Oriel College, Oxford where he was the Adam de Brome Scholar and placed in the first class in Classical Moderations (1899), narrowly missing a first class in *literae humaniores*. Charles Webster was educated at Merchant Taylors' School, Crosby and King's College, Cambridge. He was placed in the second class of part I of the History Tripos (1906), but in the first class of part II, winning the Whewell scholarship in international law (1907).

The presidents of the British Academy went on to distinguished careers, some at the British Museum such as Kenyon, who entered as an assistant in the department of manuscripts, cataloguing the collection of Greek Papyri (1889). He was promoted to assistant keeper of manuscripts (1898) and succeeded Sir Edward Maunde Thompson as the director of the British Musuem (1909–1930). Idris Bell, after a period of study at Hanover, Halle and Berlin, where he came to grips with the rigorous methods of Wilamowitz-Moellendorf, entered the manuscripts department of the British Museum where he worked with Kenyon on Greek papyri (1903). He became deputy keeper in 1927 and keeper in 1929.

Some had important university careers. W. D. Ross held a lectureship at Oriel College (1900) where he was elected a fellow (1902). He became White's Professor of Moral Philosophy (1923–1928) after which he was elected Provost of Oriel (1929–1947) and served as Oxford's Vice-Chancellor (1941–1944).

Clapham became Professor of Economics at Yorkshire College (soon to become the University of Leeds) and he was elected to a fellowship of King's College, Cambridge (1908) where he was the first professor of economic history (1928–1938) and Vice-Provost (1933–1943). After being elected to a fellowship at King's College with a dissertation on foreign policy (which dealt with the period 1814–1818), Charles Webster was appointed to the chair of modern history at the University of Liverpool (1914) at the age of twenty-eight. He was appointed to the chair of international relations at the University of Aberystwyth (1922) and then to the chair of international relations (the Stevenson Chair of International Relations) at the London School of Economics.

Other presidents had distinguished public careers. Arthur Balfour was Prime Minister and Foreign Secretary and much else besides. H. A. L. Fisher, after studying at Göttingen and Paris (where he was much impressed by the technical accomplishments of the École Nationale des Chartes and the humane scholarship of Taine and Renan), served on the Royal Commission on the public services of India (1912–1917) and then was elected Vice-Chancellor of the University of Sheffield. Then, however, he came to the attention of Lloyd George who appointed him to his government as President of the Board of Education (1916–1922). He was returned (unopposed) as the Liberal MP for the Hallam Division of Sheffield (1916) and sat as the national Liberal MP for the Combined English Universities (1918–1926), after which he returned to Oxford as Warden of New College. Mackail, instead of taking up a university career, took a place in the Education Department of the Privy Council (1884–1919), where as assistant secretary (from 1903) he played an important role in installing the system of secondary education under provisions of the act of 1902. Clapham served in the Board of Trade during the Great War and in his last years he chaired the so-called Clapham Committee on the organisation of social and economic research. He was always a supporter of the Liberal Party and social reforms of the Asquithian variety and, though he looked upon historical writing as a 'scientific' activity detached from practical purposes, his *Quellenkritk* was direct and acute (though in later years somewhat mannered) and never wholly divorced from an interest in contemporary social issues. In the Great War, Charles Webster, barred from active service because of short-sightedness, served in the intelligence section of the War Office (of which Harold Temperley was head) and then was seconded to the Foreign Office where he wrote his book on the Congress of Vienna (1919). After the war he worked eagerly for the League of Nations and after the Second World War served as a member of the British delegation at Dumbarton Oaks and as an adviser to the delegation in San Francisco. Committed always to the work of international bodies, Webster worked to strengthen them and their connection with each other and the Treasury. He was a delegate to the Union Academique Internationale for ten years.

As was the case with the presidents of the Royal Society, the presidents of the British Academy scored scores of public honours. Frederic Kenyon was elected to the British Academy in 1903, served as its president from 1917 to 1921, and served as its secretary from 1930 to 1949. He was also a fellow of the Society of Antiquaries and served as its president from 1934 to 1939. Kenyon was a fellow of Winchester College, his school, from 1904 and its warden from 1925 to 1930. He was appointed CB (1911), KCB (1912) and GBE (1918) and served as the usher of the purple rod for the latter order. Arthur Balfour was raised to the peerage and appointed to the Order of Merit. H. A. L. Fisher became Warden of New College, Oxford and was appointed to the Order of Merit. John William Mackail served as Professor of Poetry at Oxford and held the Order of Merit. W. D. Ross became Provost of Oriel College and was made an Officer of the Order of the British Empire (1918) and Knight Commander of the Order of the British Empire (1938). John Clapham was knighted in 1943 and, since he was a mountaineer, became Vice-President of the Alpine Club. Idris Bell was appointed OBE (1920), CB (1936) and knighted (1946). He was also President of the Society for the Promotion of Roman Studies (1937–1945), President of the International Association of Papyrologists (1947–1955), and President of the Classical Association (1955). Bell was also elected President of the Cymmrodorion Society and admitted to the Gorsedd as a druid. Charles Webster was appointed KCMG in 1946.

At the end of his essay on the intellectual aristocracy Noel Annan pondered the problem of persistence. He quoted Shakespeare: "'Where is Bohun, where's Mowbray? Nay which is more and most of all, where is Plantagenet? They are entombed in the urns and sepulchers of mortality.'" In Annan's view the intellectual aristocracy showed no signs of expiring.[47] The lives of Needham, Hodgkin and Hinshelwood suggest the importance of family feeling in the formation and consolidation of social and mental identity. The Darwin, Huxley and Haldane families illustrate the dynastic connections in the twentieth century in comparison to those Noel Annan celebrated in his discussion of Victorian and Edwardian intellectual aristocracy.

The Darwin family, following the death of the Great Man, dispersed themselves from Down House, several of them returning to Cambridge and taking up residence at Newnham Grange (very much later to be Darwin College), the Orchard and Wychfield. Gwen Raverat, the daughter of Sir George Howard Darwin, charmingly described the personalities of her uncles (among whom she included her father as a 'kind of specialized uncle anyhow') in *Period Piece*:

> Uncle William, Uncle George, Uncle Frank, Uncle Leonard, and Uncle Horace; a solid block of uncles, each more adorable that the other. There was a great

---

47 Annan, 'The Intellectual Aristocracy': 286.

family likeness among them; and when I was quite small, the chief difference among them, to my short-sighted eyes, was that three of them had short beards, and the other two only rudimentary whiskers. At a little distance I found it difficult to tell the three bearded ones apart – and they included my own father! For they all had the same kind of presence; the same flavor, and the same family voice – a warm, flexible, very moving voice; the same beautiful hands, and, of course, the same permanent chilly feet.[48]

They themselves did not seem to know why they had been given their particular baptismal names. Francis Darwin amused himself by thinking that his parents, lost in a moment of vagueness while standing at the font in the presence of the parish clerk, gave their children names that had no tradition in the family or for no particular reason of their own.[49] Given to nicknames, they called George 'Jingo' and Horace 'Pouter.' They conspired to cease calling Darwin 'Papa' and wished to call him 'F' instead. Darwin did not like this and said he would prefer to be called 'Dog.'[50]

William (1858–1914), the eldest son of Darwin, was educated at Rugby and, like his father at Christ's College, Cambridge. He was, according to Gwen Raverat, the most unselfconscious of the brothers, all of whom, she thought, were the most unselfconscious people who ever lived. 'He hardly knew that he had a self at all.'[51] He was admitted at Lincoln's Inn in 1861 but he and his father decided he was not suited for the Bar and after various fits and starts left Cambridge and with Sir John Lubbock's assistance became a director of Grant and Maddison's Union Bank in Southhampton. Then he returned to Cambridge briefly to sit the Tripos, complete his residency requirements, and took the BA (1862).[52] He was not disinterested in natural history and assisted his father's investigation of orchids and belonged to the geological and anthropological societies. In marrying Sara Sedgwick, the sister-in-law of Professor Charles Eliot Norton (of the other Cambridge), the friend of William and Henry James, he became a part of the American intellectual aristocracy. Retiring from the bank he moved to London, taking up his interests in art, literature ('fine fellow, old Homer'), architecture and music, picking out bits and pieces of Beethoven's symphonies on his pianoforte ('fine fellow, old Beet-oven').[53] According to myth and legend at his father's funeral in Westminster Abbey, feeling a draft on his bald pate, he took off his black gloves and balanced them on his head throughout the service. Bernard Darwin regarded William Darwin as the least intellectual of

---

48 Gwen Raverat, *Period Piece* (New York: 1952 [1976]), p.175.
49 Francis Darwin, *Springtime and Other Essays* (New York: 1920 [1967]), p.51.
50 Janet Browne, *Charles Darwin: The Power of Place*, volume II of a biography (Princeton/London: 2002), p.294.
51 Raverat, *Period Piece*, p.176.
52 Browne, *Charles Darwin: The Power of Place*, pp.188–189.
53 Raverat, *Period Piece*, pp.181–182.

the brothers, but he could rise to an occasion. He was called to give a speech at the Darwin centenary and he did so with 'complete simplicity and genuine feeling.' According to Bernard Darwin he 'played everyone else, including Mr. Balfour, who proposed the toast, off the stage.' Marlborough Pryor exclaimed, '[h]e's as good as any of them.'[54]

George Howard Darwin (1845–1912) was educated at Clapham grammar school where the Rev. Charles Priticard, FRS, later Savilian Professor of Astronomy at Oxford, was headmaster and whose school was favoured by families interested in natural history because its programme of studies included more mathematics and science than in the great public schools. Young Darwin was unsuccessful in the entrance examinations for St John's College, Cambridge in 1863 and for Trinity College in 1864 but he entered Trinity College in that latter year and read mathematics with E. J. Routh, the famous coach in the town. Consequently, while expected to do well in the Tripos, he surprised others, and himself, by becoming Second Wrangler, by taking the second Smith's Prize, and becoming a fellow of Trinity. His father wrote to him on hearing of his success in the Tripos:

> I always said from your early days that such energy, perseverance and talent as yours would be sure to succeed; but I never expected such brilliant success as this. Again and again I congratulate you. But you have made my hand tremble so I can hardly write. The telegraph came here at eleven. We have written to W[illiam] and the boys. God bless you my dear old fellow – may your life so continue.[55]

Still, George Darwin did not expect to find his life's work in mathematics and so he read for the Bar at Lincoln's Inn. Falling victim to the same digestive illnesses his father suffered, he sought treatment, but found no cures, at Malvern and Cannes.

Abandoning thoughts of the law, he returned to Cambridge and to his rooms in Trinity in 1873 and began composing curiously miscellaneous essays on such subjects as 'Cousin Marriage' and 'In Defense of Jevons.' George Darwin's interest in congenital disorders and the fears he shared with many of his time about human degeneration were quickened by his father's research in *Descent of Man*. His own speculations about the age of the earth stimulated his suspicions of Lord Kelvin's calculations on the same subject.[56] Two years later he came to grips more seriously and his paper on 'The Influence of Geological Changes on the Earth's Axis of Rotation' was read to the Royal Society in 1876 and was published in its *Philosophical Transactions* in 1877. He was proposed for the Royal Society in 1877 and was elected in 1879. When his Trinity fellowship expired he remained in Cambridge doing

---

54 Bernard Darwin, *The World Fred Made: An Autobiography* (London: 1955), pp.41–42.
55 Quoted in Browne, *Charles Darwin: The Power of Place*, pp.295–296.
56 Browne, *Charles Darwin: The Power of Place*, pp.435–436.

research on cosmogony. He was elected Plumian Professor of Astronomy in 1883 by the narrowest of votes (five to four). George Darwin's association with Lord Kelvin stimulated his interest in the history of the earth and of the solar system. He set out to put general conjectures to the test of precise calculations and he was led to conclude that the earth and the moon much have consisted of a single mass. This led his research to the point of considering how this single mass was broken up and his later papers concerning the solar system and the mass of stars always addressed these problems through a consideration of past history and development.

Thinking her father's generation was all strangely innocent, Gwen Raverat was stunned at a dinner party when Virginia Stephen (Woolf) made a slightly louche Bloomsbury joke and her father understood it.[57] George Darwin's life and personality suggest the eager impetuosity of someone always seeking new adventures. Not one for burning midnight oil, he reckoned he worked but three hours a day. His productiveness, probably, resulted from, at the outset, being able to set out his intellectual problems in their right order. He himself compared his methods to those of a burglar who, rather than picking the lock of a safe, blows its door off with dynamite. His daughter found him more alert, active and quicker in his moods than his brothers and he was extremely proud of his knowledge of languages and literatures. His successful presidency of the British Association for the Advancement of Science on its visit to South Africa resulted in his appointment to the Order of the Bath.[58] His daughter remembered his fondness for the romance of the Middle Ages and heraldry. Loving travel, he wished to know the history and language of every country to which he travelled. In addition to the ordinary European languages, he was fond of testing himself by learning unusual dialects: Provençal, Platt Deutsch and Icelandic. He enjoyed getting right the technical terms of games he played. Upon taking up archery, he spoke of the nock of the arrow and the bracer on the wrist.[59] One daughter, Margaret, married Geoffrey Keynes. His son Charles Galton Darwin married Katherine Pember, herself a mathematician, the daughter of the warden of All Souls and the granddaughter of Edward Henry Pember (1833–1911), the lawyer, brilliant conversationalist, and prominent member of the Dilettanti Society and THE CLUB.

Charles Galton Darwin (1887–1962), the son of George Darwin and grandson of Charles Darwin, was born (and died) at Newnham Grange. He was educated at Marlborough College and at Trinity College, Cambridge where he was placed fourth wrangler in part I of the unreformed Mathematical Tripos (1909) and in the first class of part II (1910). Going to Manchester

57   Raverat, *Period Piece*, p.187.
58   Raverat, *Period Piece*, pp.186–187.
59   Raverat, *Period Piece*, pp.184–185.

University as Schuster Lecturer in Mathematical Physics in 1910, he worked with Rutherford and was associated there from time to time with Niels Bohr. During the Great War he commanded a section of the Royal Engineer's unit organised to detect enemy guns by sound ranging. Late in 1917 he was reassigned to the Royal Flying Corps for work on aircraft noise. He became a fellow and lecturer at Christ's College, Cambridge (1919–1922) in which during the last year he was elected FRS and served as a visiting professor at the California Institute of Technology. He was elected the first Professor of Natural Philosophy at Edinburgh in 1924. From 1927 to 1929 he was at Niels Bohr's institute in Copenhagen. He became Master of Christ's College in 1936 in an election that was fictionalised in C. P. Snow's *The Masters*.[60] He became Director of the National Physics Laboratory in 1938 and promptly reorganised it for war work. During the war Darwin was seconded to Washington where he served as director of the British office established to improve scientific cooperation and acted as a liaison to the Manhattan Project. Knighted in 1942, on his return to Britain he became scientific adviser to the War Office. Reorganising the National Physics Laboratory again, now for peace work, he quickly grasped the potential for electronic computers and he created two new divisions, one in mathematics and another in electronics.

Darwin served as President of the Physical Society (1941–1944) and President of the Eugenics Society (1953–1959). J. J. Thomson's son, in his memoir of Darwin for the Royal Society, described him as an 'applied mathematician' rather than as a theoretical physicist because his ideas were derived from experiments and other scientists' work applying mathematics to these ideas rather than to formulating them himself. His chief contribution was to act as an interpreter of quantum mechanics to experimental physics. He had a gift for grasping the essentials of a question, which suited him for his work at the National Physics Laboratory and also for his war work, because of his broad range of intellectual understanding and his gift for seeing the essential ideas in a confusion of complicated calculations and competing experimental ideas.[61] He and his wife had one daughter who became a crystallographer, and four sons – an electronics engineer, a civil engineer, a Foreign Office lawyer and a zoologist.

Francis Darwin (1848–1925), Charles Darwin's third son and Charles Galton Darwin's uncle, made two signal services to intellectual life. First, he was his father's biographer and editor. Second, by turning away from mere description to the study of the fundamental nature of plants he helped invent vegetable physiology as a new subject. His research enlarged his subject by

---

60   Barry Supple, 'The Two World Wars,' in David Reynolds (ed.), *Christ's: A Cambridge College Over Five Centuries* (London: 2005), pp.148, 150, 151, 162.
61   George P. Thomson, 'Sir Charles Galton Darwin,' *Biographical Memoirs of Fellows of the Royal Society*, 9 (1963).

his investigations of plant movements, the localisation of their responses to stimulation by gravity, and the transpiration of water through the stomata of leaves. Like his brother, George, he was educated at Pritchard's Clapham grammar school. He matriculated at Trinity College, Cambridge taking first-class honours in the Natural Sciences Tripos in 1870. Henry Jackson, the Apostle later to become Regius Professor of Greek, Vice-Master of the college, FBA and OM, was the Trinity man whose kindness made the greatest impression on him:

> I have an image of him walking up and down his room in Neville's Court with a pipe in his mouth (which burned more fiercely than did the pipes of other men), and talking with a humour and enthusiasm which were a perpetual delight.

Mathematics, for which Darwin claimed he 'had no turn,' formed a large part of his studies and he regarded it as his great fortune to have James Stuart (another Apostle and later Professor of Mechanism and Applied Mechanics, Liberal MP, and Director of J. J. Colman Ltd), 'the only man, I imagine who ever made mathematics entertaining and amusing to an unmathematical pupil.'[62]

Going down from Cambridge, Francis Darwin studied medicine at St George's Hospital in London, living with his uncle Erasmus Darwin, known to his nephews and nieces as 'Uncle Ras.' There he produced a paper that served as the thesis for his MB degree, which he returned to Cambridge to take in 1875. However, having already been caught up in botanical studies, he never practised. Instead he went to Germany where he studied botany with Dr Julius von Sachs at Würzburg. Darwin found von Sachs kind and helpful, but their relationship ended when von Sachs resented some criticisms Darwin published, thinking them harmless, of von Sach's researches. Having gained the advantages of sharing in the work of German laboratories, Darwin returned to Down and acted as his father's secretary and assistant, living with his first wife in the village and after her death living with his small son, with his parents at Down House until his father died in 1882.

Francis Darwin moved to Cambridge and became a university lecturer in botany in 1884. He was elected to a fellowship by Christ's College in 1886 and was elected a reader in botany (1888–1904). From 1892 to 1895 he served as deputy to Professor Charles Cardale Babington (called 'Beetles' Babington because, in addition to being the secretary of the Ray Club for fifty-five years, he had founded the Entomological Society).[63] Darwin gave over his share of the stipend of the chair to the university to improve the facilities for teaching botany. Elected to the Royal Society in 1882, he served on its council from 1894 to 1895 and again from 1902 to 1908. Darwin served as its Foreign Secretary from 1903 to 1907. Like his brother George,

---

[62] Darwin, *Springtime*, pp.66–67.
[63] Lubenow, '*Only Connect': Learned Societies in Nineteenth-Century Britain*, pp.48–49.

Francis was president of the British Association for the advancement of Science (1908). Like his brothers, George and Horace, and like his nephew, he was knighted (1913). He married thrice. First, in 1874, he married Amy, daughter of Lawrence Ruck of Pantlludw, Machynlleth, North Wales who died giving birth to Bernard Richard Meirion Darwin. Second, he married Ellen Wordsworth, the daughter of John Crofts of Leeds, herself a fellow and lecturer in literature at Newnham College. Their daughter Frances, the poet, married Francis Cornford, the author of *Microcosmographia Academica* (1908), Laurence Professor of Ancient Philosophy (1931–1939) and FBA (1937). Their son, John Cornford, died in Spain during the civil war. Francis Darwin married, thirdly, Florence, the daughter of H. A. L. Fisher and the widow of Professor Frederic William Mainland.

Beyond botany, Francis Darwin was a person of wide interests and tastes. A lover of music, he played the flute, oboe, bassoon, recorder, and an instrument called the pipe-and-tabor, writing of them in his essay 'Old Instruments of Music.'[64] His light stylistic touch in essays such as these and in his poetry was something he passed on to his daughter, Frances, and his son, Bernard. His pithy and personal sayings were something his family rejoiced in repeating. On a social lie he was compelled to tell: 'I will do my best, but though I am willing, I am not a ready liar.' Of a dull book he felt compelled to read: 'I have tried to read it by repeated charges of the bayonet, but I have failed.' To a dull host who told him that if he left at that moment he would have to wait an hour at the station: 'I would rather wait *anywhere* but here.'[65]

Bernard Richard Meirion Darwin (1876–1961), the son of Francis Darwin's first marriage, was educated at Summerfields, Oxford, and Eton, where he was caught up in games, especially The Wall Game. A. C. Ainger was his classics master. The atmosphere Ainger created, Bernard Darwin found, was 'of well-bred, scholarly dignity' but 'not too prostrating.'[66] At Trinity College, Cambridge he was placed in third-class honours in part I (1896) and second-class honours in part II of the Law Tripos. He was called to the Bar at the Inner Temple (1903) but his heart was not in the law except for his fascination for murder trials with their contests between accuser and accused. So he never practised. At Cambridge, however, he played on the university golf team for three years and was its captain in 1897. So he found his life's work in the literary side of golf, turning out book after book on its various aspects and its various heroes. B. R. M. Darwin served in the Great War in the Royal Army Ordinance Corps as a lieutenant (acting major). He spent two years in Macedonia and for a time was the deputy assistant director of Ordinance Services for the 26th division and was mentioned in despatches. For many years he was the golf

---

64 Published in Darwin, *Springtime*, pp.99–114.
65 Raverat, *Period Piece*, pp.190–191.
66 Bernard Darwin, *The World that Fred Made*, p.126.

correspondent for *The Times* and *Country Life*. He married Elinor Mary, the daughter of William Thomas Monsell, and their son, Robin, became principal of the Royal College of Art (1948–1967) and was knighted in 1964.

Leonard Darwin (1850–1943), like two of his brothers, was educated at Clapham grammar school, with its large conservatory and fernery, in Pritchard's time. He came home from school one day and was reading a copy of *On the Origin of Species*. His father finding him thus wagered him, correctly, that he would not finish it.[67] He went to Woolwich, the training school for military engineers, because, he said, 'he was afraid of being afraid.' Possibly he considered the military a suitable life because he regarded himself less intelligent than his brothers. However, he came in second in the entrance examination, much pleasing his father. 'By Jove how well his perseverance and energy have been rewarded.' Somewhat amused his brother George wrote him: 'Bless your soul we're always second we are.'[68] He did not place much value in examinations. He and Kitchener were there at the same time and he exclaimed '[w]hy in one examination I came out on top and Kitchen was ploughed.'[69] His niece found him the least military person one could imagine. 'Even his moustache looked benevolent.'[70] During his twenty years in the Royal Engineers he travelled the world occupying himself with various technical jobs, observing eclipses, teaching chemistry and photography, and working on the topography of Africa. He saw action only but once. When he led a column down a lane and confronted an infuriated cow he called for a retreat.[71]

His time in the Royal Engineers provided Leonard Darwin with opportunities to apply his technical abilities. He became skilled as a photographer and in this capacity he was chosen to go to New Zealand to observe the Transit of Venus in 1874. He was sent to Singapore to determine the difference between the longitude there and Port Darwin. He became an instructor at Chatham, at the School of Military Engineering, in 1877. From 1883 to 1885 he was the instructor in chemistry at the Staff College at Camberley. Then he was appointed to the Intelligence Department at the War Office where he worked in the topographical and colonial sections. In 1886 he made another astronomical expedition, again in charge of photography, to observe the total eclipse of the sun in the West Indies. He published his report of the expedition's findings in the Royal Society's *Philosophical Transactions*.[72]

Leaving the military, Leonard Darwin began a public career serving on the London County Council as what he called a 'Moderate.' While he served on the council for only a short period of time the experience served him well

[67] Margaret Keynes, *Leonard Darwin, 1850–1943* (Cambridge: 1943), p.5.
[68] Quoted in Browne, *Charles Darwin: The Power of Place*, p.296.
[69] Raverat, *Period Piece*, p.195.
[70] Raverat, *Period Piece*, p.195.
[71] Raverat, *Period Piece*, p.196.
[72] Margaret Keynes, *Leonard Darwin*, pp.6–11.

and he published what he had learned in his book *Municipal Trade* (1903). He stood for Parliament as a Liberal Unionist candidate for the Lichfield division of Staffordshire in 1892, turning out the sitting Liberal member, Sir John Swinburne, 6th Bt, by a mere eleven votes. His mother, a very much more ardent anti-Gladstonian than he was, contributed mightily to election expenses and rallied his brothers to him. She wrote to them 'you will not have a brother elected to Parliament every day in the week ... I always feel how your father would have enjoyed it.'[73] He wrote to his mother to describe his first speech:

> The man before me came to a rather sudden end and I sprang to my feet with a horrible sensation in my stomach. However, after a few sentences I got calm and went on all right for some 30 or 40 minutes ... I got through all right, with one or two spasms of nervousness ... I think I was a little too argumentative to be effective, as what the House likes ... is a commonplace thought expressed in an epigram. Gladstone's voice was feeble, but his mind perfectly clear. Parts of his speech were excellent; but the part about the retention of the Irish members most unsatisfactory.

Leonard Darwin was not likely to have made a mark in politics, perhaps because of a tendency to see at least two sides of every question. As Maynard Keynes said of him, 'it was characteristic of Darwin that he was orthodox on one leg and unorthodox on the other ... [H]e combined that unsensational, conservative approach with the most alarming conclusions, which was a part of his Darwinian endowment, proving that in one case at least heredity was not less strong than environment.'[74] In the election of 1895 he was turned out by forty-four votes and when the election was declared void on petition he was defeated in the ensuing by-election by 528 votes.

Active in intellectual life, he went to the West Indies to observe the eclipse of the sun in 1896 and joined the Royal Geographical Society shortly thereafter. Darwin was president of the Geographical Section of the British Association for the Advancement of Science when it met in Liverpool. He assisted in the auditing of the Geographical Society's accounts and then became one of its secretaries. He was its president from 1908 to 1911 and two mountains were named after him, one Mount Leonard Darwin in New Guinea and the other in Antarctica.

Horace Darwin (1851–1929) was Charles Darwin's fifth son. Always sickly like his father and brothers, he was educated at Woodbridge School in Suffolk and Trinity College, Cambridge where he took the BA in 1874. He served an apprenticeship in the works of Easton and Anderson, engineers, of Erith, Kent where he designed and make a klinostat for measuring small

---

73 Quoted in Margaret Keynes, *Leonard Darwin*, p.17.
74 Quoted in Margaret Keynes, *Leonard Darwin*, pp.21, 22.

plants' rates of growth. Therefore, finding his life's work in the designing and manufacturing scientific instruments, he returned to Cambridge where his skills and instruments were very helpful to his brother, Francis, who would establish himself in a career as a university botanist as well as to the Natural Sciences School, which was growing and whose growth prompted the need for new laboratory instruments. The Cambridge Scientific Instruments Company was founded with Darwin as its chairman and chief shareholder. His brother, Leonard, said of Horace Darwin: 'Of all my brothers, Horace was the one whom I should have thought the least likely to make a success in life.' But his success as an engineer is undeniable. While some granted his technical abilities, they wondered if he could make a go of it in business. Yet here again he surprised them.[75] He became an associate member of the Institution of Civil Engineers in 1877 and a member of the Institution of Mechanical Engineers. Shortly after the Queen's Jubilee he became Mayor of Cambridge – using his term of service, and wearing his furred gown and gold chain, he did much to bring town and university together. He was elected FRS in 1903. Horace Darwin was a member of the Advisory Committee for Aeronautics that Asquith had formed (on R. B. Haldane's prompting) for dealing with such questions as navigating an aeroplane in clouds. During the war he was chairman of the inventions committee and was appointed KBE in 1918. He married the Hon. Emma Cecilia, the daughter of Thomas Henry Farrer, 1st Baron Farrer, the lawyer, a high-ranking civil servant and keen botanist. 'What a capital observer you are,' Charles Darwin wrote to Farrer. 'A first rate naturalist has been sacrificed, or partly sacrificed, to public life.'[76] The Darwins and the Farrers, as Gwen Reverat pointed out, were 'connected in rather complicated ways.'[77] The Horace Darwins had a son, Erasmus, who was killed at the Battle of Ypres, and two daughters.

The Darwins were deeply tied to the university world, which brought them into contact with all sorts and conditions of learned people. Francis, George and Horace belonged to the Ad Eundem Club and George also belonged to the Ambarum Club. Both clubs consisted of Cambridge and Oxford dons committed to university reform.[78] So a variety of people turned up at Darwin houses like Newnham Grange, the Orchard, and Wytchfield. Bernard Darwin (calling it 'A Foot in Each Camp') described an afternoon at his father's house:

[75] Raverat, *Period Piece*, p.203.
[76] Quoted in Browne, *Charles Darwin: The Power of Place*, p.296.
[77] Reverat, *Period Piece*, p.205.
[78] Bernard Darwin, *Pack Clouds Away* (London: 1941), p.64. For the Ad Eundem Club and the Ambarum Club see Lubenow, *'Only Connect': Learned Societies in Nineteenth-Century Britain*, pp.65–70.

The company at our house at Cambridge when I was young was by no means exclusively scientific; indeed the guests that I remember most clearly were in quite other lines of learning. I summon up a picture of tea on the lawn at my father's on some sunny afternoon in the May term, and the first visitor I see there is that beloved person, the late Mr J D Duff of Trinity. He certainly was not scientific for like another distinguished classic, Professor Jebb, he had had, so we were always told, a desperate struggle to defeat the mathematics in the little-go. In my picture he is reclining in a wicker chair, rather hot, pink and exhausted, for he has just walked by from Girton where he had been teaching.

Duff, a classic, had been doing what Bernard Darwin regarded as a remarkable thing: learning to read Russian so that he could read the great Russian writers in the original. So, Edmund Gosse turned up from London and Yorke Powell the historian, and 'another remarkable talker,' turned up from Oxford.[79]

Like the Darwin dynasty, the clan Haldane cut a wide swathe through British intellectual and public life from the Victorian–Edwardian years until the end of the twentieth century. Richard Burdon Haldane (1856–1928), a member of the prominent Scottish family, was educated at Edinburgh Academy and then Edinburgh University. There was some thought of him going on the Balliol but his parents, as formidable evangelicals, were suspicious of Oxford's Tractarian reputation and, taking the advice of Professor John Stuart Blackie, sent him to Göttingen instead. There he fell under the spell of R. H. Lotze and, through a reading of Berkeley, Fichte, Kant and Hegel, adopted the views of German idealism that dominated his thinking for the remainder of his life. So much so that, years later, when as a member of the Synthetic Society, some other members found it amusing to hear him express Hegelian views dressed in the garb of a privy councillor.[80] Returning to Edinburgh he took his degree with first-class honours in philosophy in 1876. There he became active in the Edinburgh Philosophical Society where, falling in with the views of Andrew Seth Pringle-Pattison and W. R. Sorley, he increasingly distanced himself from the views of his parents.

Haldane went to London to study law and, in 1879, was called to the Bar at Lincoln's Inn. For ten years he practised as a junior, taking silk in 1890, and carrying on work at the Bar until 1905. Moving in liberal (imperialist) circles he took part in the founding of the Eighty Club in 1880. He took his seat in the House of Commons in December 1885 as the Liberal member for East Lothian, which he held until 1911 when he was raised to the peerage as Viscount Haldane of Cloan. Admitted to the Privy Council in 1902, he was twice Lord Chancellor: in 1912–1915 and again in 1924 when, though by

---

79 Bernard Darwin, *Pack Clouds Away*, pp.62–64.
80 William C. Lubenow, 'Intimacy, Imagination and the Inner Dialectics of Knowledge Communities, The Synthetic Society: 1896–1908,' in Martin Daunton (ed.), *The Organization of Knowledge in Victorian Britain* (Oxford/New York: 2005), p.366; Lubenow. *'Only Connect': Learned Societies in Nineteenth-Century Britain*, p.191.

temper or tradition, he was not a member of the Labour Party and refused to join its organisations. In 1914, because of his education and his intellectual proclivities, he was accused of pro-German sympathies and he was not taken in when Asquith reconstituted his government. Yet, he continued to play an important public role and in 1917 he was chairman of the committee on the machinery of government, which recommended the formation of the Cabinet Office. Marrying the life of action with the life of the mind he always kept his hand in intellectual affairs. He gave the Gifford Lectures in 1902–1903, which were published in 1903 under the German idealistic title *The Pathway to Reality*. Here he deployed thinking typical of his philosophy. Namely, philosophy gave what science threatened to take away: faith in the reality of the spiritual world. He was elected to the Royal Society in 1906, to the British Academy in 1914, and was appointed to the Order of Merit in 1915.

Elizabeth Haldane (1852–1937) was Lord Haldane's sister and wrote the entry of him in the *Dictionary of National Biography*. Educated at home in a highly cultivated atmosphere, she shared her brothers' tutors and engaged with them in lively discussions on philosophy, politics and science. She went off to a private school at the age of fifteen where her abilities for languages, literature and mathematics were quickly recognised. On the death of her father in 1877 she spent a winter with her mother in Paris. Her daughterly attentions curtailed her intellectual activities while her mother lived, yet she was an intimate with the likes of Matthew Arnold. Like Lord Haldane, Elizabeth Haldane combined the *vita active* with the *vita contempliva*. A strong liberal all her life, she was a suffragist and, though opposing more militant methods, she worked for the freedom of women in education and the professions and made her name as a nursing administrator and social welfare worker. She was also her brother's sister in the sense that she dipped deep into German scholarship as the author of *Hegel's Philosophy of History* in three volumes (1892–1896) and *George Eliot and Her Times* (1927).

John Scott Haldane (1860–1936), who sought to establish an intellectual relationship between physiology and philosophy, was her other brother. Educated at the Edinburgh Academy and the University of Jena, he graduated in medicine at the University of Edinburgh in 1884. Then he went to University College, Dundee as a demonstrator in physiology before joining his uncle, Sir John Burdon-Sanderson, the Wayneflete Professor of Physiology at Oxford, as a demonstrator in 1887. He was elected to a fellowship at New College (1901) and became reader in physiology (1907–1913). Haldane investigated the composition of air in homes and schools and the suffocating gasses that collected in mines and, consequently got himself associated with people in the mining occupation. In 1911 he led an expedition to Pike's Peak to investigate the effects of low barometric pressure and the processes of acclimatisation at high altitudes.[81] He left his post as reader in physiology in 1913 and built a personal laboratory at Cherwell where he and his son and daughter did 'home experiments' on themselves. He found it difficult to leave the university laboratory where he had worked for twenty-five years, but his new laboratory allowed him to combine pure physiological research with what he found fascinating experiences with work connected with mines, factories and government departments.[82]

His daughter, Naomi Mitchison, attributed his interest in the politics of mining explosions and respiration to his being raised in a Free Church household when all of their neighbours were Episcopalians. This 'enforced a cutting off-from their own class and a kind of democracy.' From, the beginning he was 'out of place in a strict class system.' But for emotional reasons, she thought, 'politically he just got stuck.' He did not go so far as Naomi Mitchison, who married a Labour MP, or her brother, J. B. S. Haldane, might have wished. Her father, she said, 'was – like most people – a mixture, in streaks, sometimes he was maddeningly blind to something Jack [J. B. S. Haldane] or I wanted him to see; but then, when it came to practice he often did the right thing instinctively, as it were, and not according to anything he said.'[83]

Science guided his philosophy and philosophy guided his science. Chemistry and physics had their place in the study of life, and his career was devoted to finding ways to employ their methods to assist physiology. But, in his view, biology was autonomous with its own methods of interpretation, which were different from those of chemistry and physics. Biology demanded conceptions of the nature of life that were unnecessary in the study of the physical world. Haldane worked at a time in which interpretations were becoming more materialistic, so, as his Royal Society obituarist put it:

> To Haldane physiology implied the nature of the life of the organism, and he saw clearly that to understand this the organism must be studied as a living whole. His own work was to afford proof of the amazing delicacy with which the functions of the body are correlated during normal life, and this led him to the conclusion that the principle of organic regulation dominates the various activities that constitute life, and that from a physiological standpoint the phenomena of life, to use his own words 'express the maintenance of a coordinated whole which included within itself relations to the environment as well as the mutual relationships of details of internal structure and activity.'[84]

[81]   These studies, altering existing conceptions of respiration, formed the basis for his Stillman Memorial Lecture at Yale in 1916 and were published in *Respiration* (1922).
[82]   J. S. Haldane to A. V. Hill, 19 Nov[ember] [19]13. A. V. Hill Ms., Churchill College Cambridge, AVHL, I/29.
[83]   Naomi Mitchison to Joseph Needham, 17 [July 1936], Cambridge University Library, Needham Ms, H19.
[84]   G. C. Gould, 'John Scott Haldane, 1860–1936,' *Obituary Notices of Fellows of the Royal Society*, 2 (1936–1939): 115–139 at 116.

Physiology could only advance in as far as physics and chemistry advanced, but the study of life, as he pointed out to A. V. Hill, was something more than physics and chemistry. Chemists and physicists 'are simply leaving out of account what is characteristic of life, and are dealing only with snippets and fragments which can't be united in a consistent body of scientific knowledge.' The severance between biological and physical interpretations, he thought, was only apparent and, he hoped, it will be possible to extend biological ideas to the inorganic world.[85]

J. S. Haldane expressed his views on materialism in the Gifford Lectures he gave at Glasgow in 1927–1928. This series of lectures had been founded in the previous century to promote natural theology 'in its widest sense – the knowledge of God.' (That is to say, theology does not depend on revelation.) Haldane's lectures were published in *The Sciences and Philosophy* (1929), the *Philosophical Basis of Biology* (1931) and *The Philosophy of a Biologist* (1935). He sent A. V. Hill 'an all-round attack on the mechanical interpretation of the universe,' which he took to be 'only a piece of outworn scholasticism.' He regarded himself as a 'heretic' all his life. But he had lived, he thought, 'long enough to see the world gradually coming round to my heresies, or something very like them, and I am confident that I am right.'[86] Just before he died he wrote a paper for the World Congress of Faiths, which his daughter read out and on which Joseph Needham led the discussion.[87] Haldane had been elected FRS in 1897 and got the society's Royal Medal in 1916. A. V. Hill, not entirely wholeheartedly, put him forward for the Copley Medal but not everyone favoured the nomination. G. H. Hardy thought him too old and 'when a man has [?] discovered the universe is fundamentally spiritual and began giving the Gifford Lectures the case is hopeless.'[88] Yet, whatever he might have felt wanting in Haldane, Hill regarded him as a 'very great scientist who had great influence.' An 'appreciation of his philosophical outlook, and of its influence on his work, would probably be more welcome to him than any other tribute.' Hill thought Haldane would be 'remembered best for the fundamental value of his applications of science to problems not only of medicine, but of industrial and everyday life. These applications have shown no less skill and judgement and have been no less imbued with the scientific spirit, than his researches in pure physiology.'[89] The Royal Society conferred its Copley Medal on Haldane in 1935.

[85]   J. S. Haldane to A. V. Hill, 25 Oct[ober] [19]20, A. V. Hill, Ms., Churchill College, Cambridge, AVHL, I/3/29.
[86]   J. S. Haldane to A. V. Hill, 16 July [19]25, A. V. Hill Ms., Churchill College, Cambridge, AVHL, I/3/29.
[87]   Francis Younghusband to Joseph Needham, 8 June 1936, Cambridge University Library, Needham Ms. H19. Needham elaborated on his remarks on that occasion in 'Thoughts of a Young Scientist on the Testament of an Elder One (John Scott Haldane),' in *Time the Refreshing River* (Essays and Addresses, 1932–1942) (London: 1943), pp.121–140.
[88]   G. H. Hardy [writing from New College, Oxford] to A. V. Hill, nd but 1934, A. V. Hill Ms., Churchill College, Cambridge, AVHL, I/3/29.
[89]   Hill's comments are found in A. V. Hill Ms., Churchill College, Cambridge, AVHL, I/3/29.

John Burdon Sanderson Haldane (1892–1964) was J. S. Haldane's son. The elder Haldane did much to shape the younger Haldane's interest in science and J. B. S. Haldane and his sister (Naomi Mitchison) worked in their father's home laboratory, first at 11, Crick Road, North Oxford and later at Cherwell on the effects of poisoned gases. J. S. Haldane's friends from the Continent frequented the household. They included Nils Bohr, whom the children called the 'great wild boar.' Young Haldane could read English at the age of three and German at the age of five. J. B. S. Haldane was educated at the Oxford Preparatory School (then known as Lynam's) now known as the Dragon School. He won a scholarship to Eton. Arriving with a broken arm and an attitude of marked arrogance, consequently, he suffered more than a little bullying. His size served as a deterrent and the protection of his fagmasters, one whom was Julian Huxley, saved him from the worst of it. Though miserable, Haldane learned a lot of Latin poetry, became captain of the school, was elected to Pop, and enjoyed the power of the Pop cane.[90] He went up to New College, Oxford, where he was placed in the first class in both mathematical moderations (1912) and *literae humaniores* (1914).

Then the war intervened and Haldane served in the Black Watch, the family regiment. When his major was killed in an explosion, Haldane took over his work as a bomb officer in the trenches. His father's son, he combined his intellectual interests with their possible applications. As his father remarked to A. V. Hill: 'You will be glad to hear that he sent for a set of Mathematical tables a few days ago, so that Mathematics seems good even in a highland infantry battalion.'[91] His father asked for him to help in work countering gas attacks at Ypres.[92] Then going back to the trenches, he was wounded in 1915. He knew all the Black Watch songs, including the one about the behaviour of the regiment during the Peninsular Wars: 'Wha wisna there when the Prussian Guard brak through?'[93] Then he was sent to Mesopotamia where he was wounded again. Sent then to India, where he developed an affection for the country and its people, he lectured in a bombing school.

Elected to a fellowship at New College in 1919 Haldane lectured on physiology. Haldane then went to Cambridge in 1922 where, working under Gowland Hopkins, he was a reader in biochemistry. He sometimes horrified his colleagues as on those occasions he would place a bucket of urine on the Trinity High Table. He was stripped of his readership by the *Sex Viri* in 1925 when he was named as a correspondent in a divorce case, but he was restored to his position on appeal in 1926. The *Sex Viri* added a member to its body,

---

90   Naomi Mitchison, 'Beginnings,' in K. R. Dronamraju (ed.), *Haldane and Modern Biology* (Baltimore: 1968), pp.299–301.

91   J. S. Haldane to A. V. Hill, 12 April [19]15. A. V. Hill Ms., Churchill College, Cambridge, AVHL. I/3/29.

92   See Peterson, *The Life Organic*, pp.27–33.

93   Mitchison, 'Beginnings,': 305.

perhaps because of Haldane's translation of their name as the 'sex weary', and there has been no subsequent harassment of university officers because of their private lives. While in Cambridge, Haldane became the officer in charge of genetics research at the John Innes Horticultural Station (1927–1936) during which time he was also Fullerian Professor of Physiology at the Royal Institution (1930–1932). Elected FRS in 1932, he held the chair of genetics and biometry at University College, London (1933–1957) and from 1937 he was the first Weldon Professor of Biometry at University College.

From 1957 to 1962 Haldane was a member of the Biometry Research Unit at the Indian Statistical Institute at Calcutta and from 1962 until his death he was head of the Laboratory of Genetics and Biometry that had been established by the government of Orrisa at Bhubaneswar. He became interested in Hinduism, became a vegetarian, and he and his then wife, Helen Spurway (a former student), became citizens of India in 1961. He considered himself a citizen of the world but he treasured his citizenship of India because he regarded the country as the closest approximation of a free world. There, he thought people could riot, upset trams, and defy police authorities in a way that would have pleased Jefferson. Because of its diversity, India could be a model for a world organisation where, since one of the duties of a citizen was to be a nuisance to the government, he could be a nuisance to the government of India.

Though Haldane had no school or university training in science, he made major contributions by unifying Darwinian evolutionary theory with Mendelian genetics. He encouraged the development of human genetics by his own writings and, especially, through his discussions with colleagues. As René Wurmser, of the University of Paris, wrote of him:

> Science has now become a matter of collective effort, and not much is achieved in solitude. It is still true, however, that progress is due to the animating influence of a few individuals. Haldane was just only one of these few, a wonderful dispenser of ideas. His genius for expounding ideas [counted] for much in this role, and we in France very often benefitted from his lectures at the Sorbonne at the Institute Henri Poincaré, and at Roscoff. He had the rare quality of getting enthusiastic about other people's work and of liking to direct attention to it, often adding much from his own imagination.[94]

Haldane's strength, apparently, arose from his capacity to summarise complex systems in simple mathematics equations. His wide intellectual interests – cosmology, animal behaviour, the origins of life and (like his father) the physiology of diving – allowed him to grasp connections that others missed. Though less successful as an experimenter, he had a gift for

---

[94] René Wurmser, 'Haldane as I Knew Him,' in K. R. Dronamraju (ed.), *Haldane and Modern Biology* (Baltimore: 1968), p.315.

lucid and vivid expressions. Peter Medawar, a very clever person himself, called him 'the cleverest man I ever knew.'[95]

Haldane became a socialist as a student. Even at Eton, his friends included such as Richard Mitchison, later a Labour MP and life peer and later Haldane's brother-in-law. Until the 1930s his was a moderate and modest socialism more prone to attacking religious authority rather than social authority. His political nerves sharpened with the emergence of fascist authoritarianism. He supported the Second Spanish Republic and three times visited Spain during the civil war. He became chairman of the editorial board of the *Daily Worker* in 1940, a position he held until it was disbanded in 1950. He joined the Communist Party in 1942 but his allegiance loosened in the controversies over Lysenko's genetics. Though he continued to think there was something positive in Lysenko's science he became alarmed by some of Lysenko's – and Lysenko's supporters' – claims, which he found excessive. He never criticised the Soviet Union or the Communist Party and he said that Stalin was a great man and doing a good job. Some alleged he was a Soviet spy working for the GRU with the codename 'Intelligentsia.' But Haldane grew increasingly unsympathetic to Soviet policies and quietly resigned from the party, giving as his reason Stalin's meddling with science.

Naomi Mary Margaret Mitchison [née Haldane] (1897–1999) was J. S. Haldane's daughter and J. B. S. Haldane's sister, best known as an author of historical novels, many of them set in Scotland, travel books and autobiographies, and as a feminist campaigning for birth control and Scottish nationalism. Like her brother she was educated at the Dragon School (where she was the only girl) and at the Society of Oxford Home Students (later St Anne's College). Like her brother, she was wakened to socialist policies and in the 1930s went to Austria to smuggle out left-wing intellectuals. She was her father's daughter, and while a girl worked with her brother in their father's home laboratory doing experiments using guinea pigs in investigations of Mendelian genetics. When her brother went to war she took over carrying on their work. As she said:

> Early genetics was relatively unmathematical; we talked in terms of dominants and recessives. Chromosomes had not come into their own; the cell mechanism was still obscure; but guinea pigs were a mine of information: we had to arrange marriages, which sometimes went against the apparent inclinations of their partners, though I rather enjoyed exercising power over them. My interests went as far as sucking a teat to get the particular flavor of guinea pig milk.

---

[95]   Quoted by Stephen Jay Gould, *The Living Stones of Marrakech: Penultimate Reflections in Natural History* (Cambridge, Mass.: 2011), p.305.

Their joint paper in 1915 was the first demonstration of genetic linking in mammals, and was her first publication.[96]

Naomi Haldane married Gilbert Richard Mitchison, QC, MP. When he became a life peer she became Baroness Mitchison, but found the title abhorrent and never used it. The Mitchisons forged a home at Carradale House on the Mull of Kintyre, filled with an odd assortment of lively minds. James Watson dedicated his *Double Helix* to Naomi Mitchison. Watson, the best man at Avrion Mitchison's wedding, described a Christmas holiday at Carradale House:

> In the evenings there was no way to avoid intellectual games, which gave the greatest advantage to a large vocabulary. Every time my limpid contribution was read, I wanted to sink behind my chair rather than face the condescending stares of the Mitchison women. To my relief, the large number of house guests never permitted my turn to come often, and I made a point of sitting near the evening's box of chocolates, hoping that no one would notice that I never passed it. Much more agreeable were the hours playing 'Murder' in the dark twisting recesses of the upstairs floors. The most ruthless of the murder addicts was Av's [Avrion Mitchison's] sister Lois, then just back from teaching for a year in Karachi, and a firm proponent of the hypocrisy of Indian vegetable eaters.[97]

There the Mitchisons spawned a brood, several of whom rose to scientific eminence. Denis Mitchison (b.1919) who became a bacteriologist, was educated at the Dragon School and Trinity College, Cambridge where he was placed in the first class of the Natural Sciences Tripos. John Murdoch Mitchison (1922–2011), a pioneer in the study of cell biology, was educated at Winchester and Trinity College, Cambridge and became Professor of Zoology at Edinburgh University. Nicholas Avrion Mitchison (b.1928), a zoologist and immunologist, was educated at Leighton Park School, and Balliol College, to which he had secured a classical scholarship, and New College where his uncle, J. B. S. Haldane, had taught and where Peter Medawar was his research supervisor. Among his five children are Tim Mitchison and Hannah Mitchison, both cell biologists.

Then there are the Huxleys, the patriarch of which was Thomas Henry Huxley (1825–1895), Darwin's 'bulldog,' called simply 'man of science' in the *DNB*. He was elected FRS in 1851 on the strength of his 'On the Affinities of the Family of the Medusæ,' which he wrote on the voyage of the HMS *Rattlesnake* to survey the seas between Australia and the Great Barrier Reef. He returned to Britain and enjoyed a career promoting Darwin's theories, as a member of the X-Club, as a secretary of the Royal Society and as its president. However, in addition to his own research, he was a dominating figure in the

---

[96] Mitchison, 'Beginnings': 303.
[97] James Watson, *The Double Helix*, annotated and illustrated edition by Alexander Gann and Jan Witkowski (New York/London: 2012 [1968]), p.107.

drive to legitimate the teaching of research of the natural world against rival classical and theological traditions. His method, scientific empiricism – observation, experiment, comparison, classification – was an intellectual device and justification to push this legitimacy forward. It was not so much an epistemological matter, that is, a contest over the truths of science as opposed to the truths of theology, as it was a claim for the intellectual authority and autonomy of science itself. It would be too crude to describe this campaign for intellectual legitimacy as a contest between 'amateurs' and 'professionals.' It was larger than this narrowing binary would suggest. It was part of a programme to establish the place of scientific empiricism in the mental world of the late nineteenth century. It was part of a quest for status and standing. As the historian of this process puts it, it was a project to establish 'a new public image by formulating codes of ethics, strengthening professional organizations, and dispensing information to the general public.' Those working within these processes had to increase standards of competence, develop common social and mental bonds, and subject themselves to the judgement of their peers. To those outside these processes they had to project a reputation for independence and objectivity and establish their claim for a place in the social order. It was just as much a quest for power as it was a quest for truth.[98] T. H. Huxley's role in this made him – what his biographer calls – 'Evolution's High Priest.'[99]

Leonard Huxley (1860–1933), T. H. Huxley's son, was educated at University College, London, St Andrews University and Balliol College. He had got a classical exhibition to Balliol where he fell under Jowett's influence. He fell under other literary influences when he married Julia Arnold, the granddaughter of Dr Arnold, the headmaster of Rugby and the niece of Matthew Arnold. While he began his career as a classics master at Charterhouse, his wife, an imaginative and energetic person, founded a school of her own: Prior's Field, just beyond Charterhouse's perimeter. Gilbert Murray's daughter was a pupil there and so was Margorie her brother-in-law's (Henry's) daughter. The numbers at her school doubled in its first year and continued to grow, having more than eighty by 1913 and nearly a hundred at the outbreak of the Great War.[100] Huxley, after a period of competent-enough schoolmastering, but with few opportunities for promotion, joined the publishing firm of Smith Elder (later incorporated into John Murray) where he became assistant editor and later the editor of

98 Frank M. Turner, 'The Victorian Conflict Between Science and Religion: A Professional Dimension,' in his *Contesting Cultural Authority: Essays in Victorian Intellectual Life* (Cambridge: 1993), pp.171–200, at 176 and *passim*. For the general description and explanation of this professional programme see Harold Perkin, *The Rise of Professional Society: England Since 1880* (London/New York: 1989).
99 Adrian Desmond, *Huxley: From Devil's Disciple to Evolution's High Priest* (Reading, Mass.: 1994).
100 Ronald W. Clark, *The Huxleys* (New York/Toronto: 1968), pp.134 ff.

Cornhill Magazine. In the publishing world Leonard Huxley was able to carry on his father's work in the promotion of science as a secular vocation. By publishing his *Life and Letters of Thomas Henry Huxley,* two volumes (1900), his *Life and Letters of Sir Joseph Dalton Hooker, OM,* two volumes (1918) and his biography of Charles Darwin (1920) he used literary means, the engine of publishing, to champion and establish the authority and status of what Frank Turner has called the 'vigilant verification' of the empirical method.[101]

Leonard Huxley and Julia Arnold had three sons, Noel Trevenen (1889–1914) who died a suicide, Julian Huxley and Aldous Huxley. After the death of his wife Leonard Huxley married again, to Rosalind Bruce, and they had two further sons, David Bruce Huxley and Andrew Huxley OM and master of Trinity College, Cambridge. D. B. Huxley was a prominent QC who had an extensive career in Bermuda. His daughter, Angela Mary Bruce Huxley, married George Pember Darwin, the son of Sir Charles Galton Darwin, the physicist.

Julian Huxley (1887–1975) was the grandson of T. H. Huxley on one side and the great-grandson of Dr Thomas Arnold on the other. Matthew Arnold was his uncle. Deeply aware of this double inheritance Julian Huxley wrote:

> I was born with great advantages genetic and cultural – but there were disadvantages too. I inherited my Arnold grandfather's instability of temperament, as well as my Huxley grandfather's determination and dedication to scientific truth. These conflicting elements added to my own particular character, proved difficult to cope with and made me prone to so-called breakdowns. I was inwardly timid, but like getting my own way; unsure of myself, I was often afflicted by a sense of not living up to my parents' expectations. These certainly spurred me on to whatever success I may have achieved.[102]

Despite these psychological tensions, and perhaps because of them, Huxley kept tight to his generational connections. Educated at Eton, where he was a King's Scholar, he was uncertain whether his future lay in the civil service or as a writer, and he undertook the rigorous, if conventional, classical programme of studies.[103] Despite, perhaps because of his family's religious views, he was moved by his experience in Eton Chapel:

> In spite of all my intellectual hostility to orthodox Christian dogma, the chapel services gave me something valuable, and something which I obtained nowhere else in precisely the same way ... Indubitably what I received from the services in that beautiful Chapel of Henry VI was not merely beauty, but something

---

101 Turner, 'The Conflict Between Science and Religion: A Professional Dimension': 182.
102 Julian Huxley, *Memories* (London: 1950), p.vi.
103 For the various aspects of Julian Huxley's life and career see the various essays in C. Kenneth Waters and Albert Van Helden (eds), *Julian Huxley: Biologist and Statesman of Science* (Houston: 1992).

which might be called specifically religious ... It was none of the purely aesthetic emotions which were aroused, or not only they, but a special feeling. The mysteries which surround all the unknowns of existence were, however dimly contained in it, and the whole was predominantly flavoured with the sense of awe and reverence.[104]

Soon, he was attracted to the natural sciences and he won the biology prize four years running. At the age of sixteen, he had a choice of an extra subject and he chose zoology. The attractions of the classics never left him and he read Homer, Horace and Catullus for pleasure, sometimes composing poetry in Latin and Greek. He won the Brackenbury Scholarship in Science and went up to Balliol. There he won the Newdigate Prize for poetry and spent the £50 prize on a binocular microscope.[105]

Placed in the first class in the Natural Science Schools and winning the Naples Biological Scholarship he returned to New College as a don and as a demonstrator in the Department of Comparative Anatomy. There he mixed and mingled with his elders. Warden Spooner (when his hat blew off in Long Street Walk he remarked typically 'Please will no one pat my hiccup') still thrived. Huxley came to know Sligger Urquhart who provided a stabilising and civilising environment for young men in his college rooms and who invited Huxley to his chalet in the Alps. He had tea and supper with Gilbert Murray on Boar's Hill, coming into contact with what he came to consider the international intelligentsia. He called on the widow of John Tyndall, his grandfather's old colleague, at her home on the moors of Hindhead and she invited him to spend the summer at the chalet at Bel-Ap on the southern slopes of the Rhone Valley, which she and Tyndall had built.[106]

Huxley's career took a sharp turn in 1912 when he was invited to establish a department of biology at Rice Institute (which would become Rice University) in Houston, Texas. But once the war broke out he returned to Britain to serve as a second lieutenant in the Royal Army Service Corps. He was transferred to the General List and worked in the intelligence service, initially in Sussex and then in southern Italy. After the war he returned to Oxford to become senior demonstrator in the Department of Zoology. Huxley became Professor of Zoology at King's College, London in 1925 but he resigned his position (though keeping his hand in academic life as Fullerian Professor of Physiology at the Royal Institution) to work with H. G. Wells and his son on the *Science of Life*. From 1935 he was secretary of the Zoological Society of London, but his work with the Wellses committed him to a literary project rather like his grandfather's. To wit, to be an architect of the modern evolutionary synthesis.

---

104 Julian Huxley, *Religion Without Revelation* (New York: 1957), pp.72–73.
105 Ronald W. Clark, *The Huxleys* (New York/Toronto: 1968), p.145.
106 Julian Huxley, *Memories*, pp.63–65, 128, 135.

Julian Huxley attacked the problem at length in his book *Evolution: The Modern Synthesis* (1942). His interest in evolution lay in all of its aspects – embryology and genetics, and extended to what would become the field of cell biology. However his interests also extended to anthropology and ethnology. Carrying on the tradition of his father and grandfather, he had a generous and, it seems, a somewhat teleological conception of evolution. An example of the weight and thrust of his thought can be seen in his controversy over evolutionary fitness with Theodosius Dobzhansky. Dobzhansky held to a tight and precise notion of fitness. For Dobzhansky 'fitness' could be measured almost entirely by 'reproductive proficiency.'[107] For Huxley, '[t]his is simply not true.' As he expressed it pithily:

> [T]he idea that 'fitness' is to be defined solely in terms of the capacity to leave more descendants has been foisted onto general biology by students of population genetics, which happened to be one of the avant-garde subjects in contemporary biology. It contravenes the rules and decencies of scientific priority, as it bears no relation to what Darwin and the early Darwinians meant by fitness in phrases like 'the survival of the fittest.' For them 'fitness' signified all-round biological fitness, the ability to survive and reproduce in the competitive 'struggle for existence.'

For Huxley 'natural selection inevitably produces a basic trend or overall directional change during the process ... what Darwin loosely called "improvement."'[108] Holding, perhaps defensively, as he did to his grandfather's and father's conceptions he might have been caught in what Peter Stansky has called a time warp, and his confidence in evolutionary progress might have been more Victorian than a person of the twentieth century thinking through these issues.[109]

Nonetheless his writings on these subjects led to the award of its Darwin Medal by the Royal Society in 1956 and the award of the Darwin-Wallace Medal of the Linnaean Society in 1958. An internationalist all his life, Huxley travelled to the Soviet Union and was initially impressed by the notions there of central planning but he, like J. B. S. Haldane, found himself put off by Lysenko's neo-Lamackian criticism of genetics and by Stalin's high-handed political control of science. Huxley was the first General Director of the United Nations Educational, Scientific and Cultural Organisation in 1946, but his career there was cut off after two years, possibly because of his left-wing political views and his complex religious attitudes. Both he and his grandfather

---

[107] Theodosius Dobzhansky, *Mankind Evolving: The Evolution of the Human Species* (New Haven/London: 1962).

[108] Julian Huxley, 'Review of Theodosius Dobzhansky, *Mankind Evolving: The Evolution of the Human Species*,' *Perspectives in Biology and Medicine*, 6 (1) (Autumn 1962): 144–148, esp.145–146.

[109] Peter Stansky, 'Particulars in Huxley's Intellectual Climate,' in Waters and Van Helden (eds), *Julian Huxley: Biologist and Statesman of Science*, p.45.

had given the Romanes Lectures at Oxford in which they sought to articulate a relationship between evolution and ethics.

Aldous Huxley (1894–1963), called 'Ogie' – short for 'Ogre' – by his family, was the younger brother of Julian. Like his brother before him Aldous Huxley was educated at Eton and then Balliol College, Oxford where he took first-class honours in English literature. Disqualified for war service by temporary blindness, after going down from Oxford he worked at the Air Ministry ordering supplies. After the war he returned to Eton as a Beak where his pupils included Eric Blair (George Orwell) and Steven Runciman. Huxley, finding it difficult to maintain discipline in a room of unruly boys, never liked to be reminded of those days, but Runciman admired his eloquence and remembered how 'he taught us strange and rare words in a rather reflective way.'[110] He worked for a time in the chemical plant of Brunner and Mond, an experience that became important in forming his thinking about the dehumanising features of science, which he expressed in *Brave New World* (1932). He spent some of the war years working as a farm labourer at Garsington Manor, the home of Lady Ottoline Morrell, where he consorted with various Bloomsbury figures and where he met his first wife Maria Nys.

After working for a time in publishing with John Middleton Murray this Huxley and his family moved to southern California where he lived for the rest of his life. Increasingly impressed by the dangers of a materialistic world and its technological advances, Huxley's writings in the United States, such as *The Perennial Philosophy* (1945), increasingly stressed means for overcoming these dangers. These means encouraged criticisms that he was engaged in humbuggery by abandoning reason. Beginning in 1939 Huxley was attracted to Asian philosophy and associated himself with Swami Prabhavananda's Vedanta Society, contributing frequently to *Vedanta and the West*. He and his wife applied for US citizenship in 1953 but the atmosphere of the Cold War and the war in Korea prevented him from pledging himself to bear arms for the United States, claiming religious scruples (of which he had none). Unlike his brother, Julian, and his half-brother, Andrew, and, giving no reasons, he declined a knighthood when Harold Macmillan offered it to him. He and his first wife had one son, Matthew Huxley (1920–1965), who became a prominent anthropologist and epidemiologist. Diagnosed with cancer in 1960 Aldous Huxley continued his career as a novelist and gave lectures on 'human potentiality' at the San Francisco Medical Center of the University of California and at the Esalen Institute.

Andrew Huxley (1917–2012) was the half-brother of Julian Huxley and Aldous Huxley. Educated at University College School and then Westminster (where he was a King's Scholar), this Huxley won a scholarship and went up

110   Minoo Dinshaw, *Outlandish Knight: The Byzantine Life of Steven Runciman* (London: 2016), pp.39, 359.

to Trinity College, Cambridge in 1935. Originally intending to be an engineer, he read the Natural Sciences Tripos and then turned to physiology, taking the BA degree in 1938. Alan Hodgkin, who was interested in the transmission of electrical signals along nerve fibres, became Huxley's supervisor and, together, they worked on this problem at the Marine Biological Association laboratory at Plymouth.[III] Trinity elected Huxley to a research fellowship but the war intervened, during which, Huxley worked first at the British Anti-Aircraft Command on the radar control of gunnery but then he was seconded to the Admiralty where, on a team headed by Patrick Blackett, he applied himself to the study of naval gunnery.

After the war Huxley resumed his collaboration with Hodgkin and in 1952 they published a joint paper describing a computational model in biochemistry, which formed the basis for models used in neurobiology for the next four decades. Huxley was a Lalor Scholar at Woods Hole, in Massachusetts, in 1953. He gave the Herter Lectures at Johns Hopkins Medical School in 1959 and the Jesup Lectures at Columbia University in 1964. Editor of both the *Journal of Physiology* and the *Journal of Molecular Biology*, he was elected FRS in 1957, served on its council from 1960 to 1962, and won its Copley Medal in 1973. After holding posts at Cambridge, Huxley became head of the Department of Physiology at University College, London in 1960. He was awarded the Nobel Prize in 1963 and was appointed Royal Society Professor at University College, London in 1969.

Huxley became president of the Royal Society in 1980 and in his presidential address took up a defence of the Darwinian explanation of evolution, the same theme his grandfather had taken for his presidential address in 1860. He was knighted in 1974 and was appointed to the Order of Merit in 1983. He was appointed Master of Trinity College in 1984 where he was fond of reminding people that Trinity had had more Nobel laureates than the entire country of France. In 1947 Huxley married Jocelyn Pease, the daughter of Michael Pease, the geneticist, and his wife Helen Bowen Wedgwood, and so once again, by marriage, the Huxleys were joined to the vast Wedgwood-Darwin extended family network.

And so it went on. George Darwin's daughter, Margaret, married Geoffrey Keynes, the brother of Maynard Keynes. Their son, Richard Keynes, the physiologist, married Ann Adrian, the daughter of Edgar Adrian and the sister of Richard Adrian, the physiologist and Master of Pembroke College. Richard Adrian married Lucy Caroe, a historical geographer and a fellow of Newnham College, who, on her mother's side, was the granddaughter of Sir William Bragg. A. V. Hill married Margaret, the sister of Maynard Keynes and Geoffrey Kyenes, and their sons, David

---

[III] For this collaboration see Alan Hodgkin, *Chance and Design*, passim.

Hill and Maurice Hill, were respectively a fellow of Trinity and a physiologist and a fellow of King's and a geophysicist. Edgar Adrian, when once asked how these complicated kinship intertwinings occurred, explained simply that people married people they knew.

As inherently fascinating as these family relations are, one wonders about their intellectual significance. Noel Annan pondered this question, as in his untangling of the 'intellectual aristocracy' he was torn. On the one hand he regarded family connections as part of the 'poetry of history.'[112] On the other hand, Annan had a theoretical interest. Initially, he wished to write an essay showing how a new conception of society, one influenced by Durkheim, Weber and Franz Boas, affected the study of history vitally.[113] He was interested in studying history 'as a set of social facts & [functions?] which were explicable only in terms of each other' rather than from the point of the individual.[114] Yet, he was forced to confess he had been too preoccupied with setting out family connections and had not provided the analysis his subject required. In the end he concluded his effort was a 'very amateur affair.'[115] Annan returned to his earlier purposes in his Hobhouse Memorial Lecture. As he argued there, 'individuals are units in a group whose goals and norms of behaviour are built into the roles they are playing.'[116] This is a thought implicit in 'the intellectual aristocracy.'

So this trawl through the leadership of the Royal Society and the British Academy may run the risk of being too much caught up in the intimacies of social and kinship relations. Yet such detailed excursions allow a penetration into worlds of mind and manners that are often hidden beneath the surface superficialities of institutional studies. Much of the point of the present study has been to expose the relationships of concepts, people and institutions allowing one to escape from the mysteries of 'elites,' 'establishments' and their purported conspiracies. Annan's exploratory study allowed him to discover a group the members of which 'knew who was related to whom, and while they nearly always accepted anyone, whatever his origins, provided he had real intellectual merit, it always helped if you belonged to one of the families.'[117] So, one thing such studies reveal is the way solidarity can be formed through membership in groups and families.

112   Annan, 'The Intellectual Aristocracy': 243.
113   Noel Annan to J. H. Plumb, 24 December 1953, J. H. Plumb Papers in the possession of Mr William Noblett to whom I am grateful for making them available to me.
114   Annan to Plumb, 24 December 1953, Plumb Papers.
115   Noel Annan to David Cannadine, 4 December 1981, Annan Papers, King's College, Cambridge, NGA, 5/1/150.
116   Noel Annan, *The Curious Strength of Positivism in English Political Thought* (London: 1959), p.15.
117   Noel Annan to Gary Boyd Roberts, 7 July 1967, Annan Papers, King's College, Cambridge, NGA, 1/1/5.

They could not be like the fictional Edward Casaubon, who wished to uncover all the unities of knowledge; nor could they be like Thomas Young, fellow of Emmanuel College, the last man to know everything. Their identities shifted as they moved from one affiliation to another. These relations were lateral not hierarchical. If hierarchies confer power, lateral relations confer influence. If identity formation and social discipline were virtues of these connections, fragility and instability were other aspects of them. The mental health of the Huxleys is fairly well known. Thomas Henry Huxley was struck down by mental depression while on the HMS *Rattlesnake* in 1848 and again in 1871 and 1873 and his friend Hooker, from the X-Club, took him off to the Auvergne. In 1884, stricken again, he resigned as president of the Royal Society in mid-term. Of his grandsons, Trevenen committed suicide in 1914, Julian suffered several breakdowns, as did Aldous. The same point might be made about the Stephen family. James Fitzjames Stephen, the barrister, judge and author of *Liberty, Equality, Fraternity* (1873) had to be removed from the bench. His son, the brilliant James Kenneth Stephen, starved himself to death in an asylum. Virginia Woolf was his niece.

Another theme that sweeps through this flight of the social lives of people of learning is the shredding of the concept of 'two cultures.' Indeed, the blue plaque posted at 16 Bracknell Gardens, Hampstead commemorating Leonard Huxley and his sons Julian and Aldous denominates them as 'men of science and letters.' Indeed, some of the 'New Men' whose careers are discussed here belonged to both the Royal Society and the British Academy: Flinders Petrie, FRS (1902) and FBA (1904), R. B. Haldane, Arthur Balfour, Needham, Frazer, and H. A. L. Fisher. Now Fisher's fellowship in the Royal Society depended more on his political service in the education department but Gilbert Murray's memoir of Fisher was published in both the *Proceedings of the British Academy* and as a Royal Society obituary notice.[118]

J. J. Thomson, on retiring from the presidency and speaking for the council, as noted earlier, in fact, approached Arthur Balfour to become the next president of the Royal Society in 1920. Balfour, though he wished he could have done more 'in connection with our Scientific and Industrial Research,' declined. Despite his diverse intellectual interests, Balfour was no amateur. As he wrote to J. J. Thomson:

> Though I have always been deeply interested in matters scientific, and have been twice a member of the Council of the Royal Society, I have not the slightest pretention (need I say it?) to be counted as a man of science. I wish it were otherwise; but even if I could flatter myself that, with proper opportunities and training, I could have added something, however small, to our stock of scientific knowledge, the opportunities and training have both been wanting.

---

[118] Gilbert Murray's memoir of Fisher published in the *Obituary Notices of Fellows of the Royal Society*, vol. 3 (1939–1941) was the same essay he had published in the *Proceedings of the British Academy*).

The range of Balfour's intellectual and public interests is striking. At the moment Thomson offered the presidency of the Royal Society to him Balfour was president of the British Academy. He had Cabinet duties, League of Nations responsibilities, and, pursuing his intellectual interests, he was preparing his Gifford Lectures 'which involves more thinking and reading than I can find time for.'[119] No one would have found Balfour typical of anything, but the offer of the presidency of the Royal Society to him and the nature of his refusal is yet another example of how the nature of knowledge in the twentieth century cannot be captured or contained in the binary of 'two cultures.' The 'two cultures' controversy is, necessarily, a subject to which Chapter 6 must, likewise, touch on.

---

[119] Arthur Balfour to J. J. Thomson, 27 October 1920, Cambridge University Library, J. J. Thomson Ms. Add. 7654/B87.

Chapter 6

Tangled Loyalties

[W]e cannot yet assume that war will be impossible in the future, and that an army and a fleet are luxuries that we shall be able to do without. If our army or our fleet is to be effective, it must not be behind others in its equipment with the application of science to war.

J. J. Thomson[1]

Science and learning have for several centuries been regarded by all civilized communities as entitled by those who follow them a certain immunity from interference or persecution ... The reason is that its method of thought, its direct appeal by experiment to universal Nature, the new powers given to mankind in general by its application, so obviously do not depend upon the opinions or emotions, or interests of any limited group, that any civilised people will admit that it transcends the ordinary bonds of nationality.

A. V. Hill[2]

THIS book is not a history of knowledge – learning's content – it is a history of processes (some in their own way political) about the interactions and relations among learned people, their concepts and the institutions to which they belonged. Relations, processes: they cannot be observed directly. Yet, this study shrinks from that species of thought that regards itself as social constructivism or social determinism because it pays particular attention to agency and contingency. Politics and war are among the contingencies that are particularly important in shaping the relations and processes shaping knowledge in the twentieth century and so it is to those contingencies that this study now turns. Politics and war hardened the epistemological edges of

[1]   J. J. Thomson, 'Address of the President, Sir J. J. Thomson, OM, at the Anniversary Meeting,' *Proceedings of the Royal Society of London*, series A, volume XCV (July 1919): 250–257 at 253.
[2]   A. V. Hill, 'International Status and Obligations of Science,' *Nature*, 132 (23 December 1933): 952.

knowledge in twentieth-century Britain. They hardened those edges because the demands of politics and war reinforced latent stifling positivism in learned life. War and politics gave a kind of public legitimacy for which people of learning longed but, thereby, turning their learning in a more applied and utilitarian direction robbed them of intellectual autonomy and independence. The issues and incidents that this chapter discusses – patriotism and loyalty during the Great War; the encounter of British people of learning with Soviet scholars at the International Congress of the History of Science; the unwillingness to admit Charles Singer, the historian of science, to their fellowships by both the Royal Society and the British Academy; the reluctant admission of Karl Popper to the Royal Society; the Kapitza affair; the fostering (and controlling) of learning by philanthropic foundations – reveal a parochialism and localism of knowledge formation and organisation in the twentieth century.

J. J. Thomson, PRS, the Master of Trinity College, Cambridge, the late Director of the Cavendish Laboratory, at the end of the Great War hitched politics and war in the twentieth century to modern knowledge. How different this was from the time in the Napoleonic Wars when Humphrey Davy went to France and received the *Prix Napoléon*, which recognised the internationality of learning. According to some people, Davy knew, he should not accept such an honour, but he held that 'if two countries or governments are at war, the men of science are not.'[3] Even as late as 1933 Archibald Vivian Hill gave his Huxley Memorial Lecture as a protest against his Russian colleagues who had attended the International Congress on the History of Science in 1931 and who viewed science 'as the handmaiden of social and economic policy.' Hill said that 'in a certain sense, science and learning are superior to and above the State.' Hill held out hopes for knowledge's internationalism:

> The history of science since the War, has been largely of an effort to break down national barriers of mistrust or lack of understanding. It is quite certain that science cannot progress properly except by the fullest internationalism. Accepting freedom of thought and research is the first postulate, the second is that knowledge, however and wherever won, should be freely available for the use of all.[4]

Hill was a voice crying in the wilderness because in the twentieth century politics and war opened epistemological wounds. Loyalty was the issue at stake. What is sovereign? The state, the nation, the market, religious confessionalism or the Truth? If truth, what truth? Demands for political purity

---

[3]   Quoted by Richard Holmes in *The Age of Wonder: How the Romantic Generation Discovered the Beauty and Terror of Science* (London: 2008), p.353.
[4]   Hill, 'International Status and Obligations of Science': 952, 954.

weakened loyalty to those practices and procedures that constituted the intellectual environment out of which truth emerges.

The conception of intellectual sovereignty had its origins in the research environment of the German universities. Christian Matthias Theodor Mommsen, the great German historian of Rome, stated its imperial goals in his *Reden und Aufsätze*:

> We are certainly not modest, and we do not wish to be seen so. On the contrary, we want to continue in arts and science, state and church, in all living and striving, to reach for all that is highest, all at once, everywhere and absolutely.[5]

These were goals to which scores of American scholars, many of them the children of clergymen, swore obedience when they went to the German universities taking up the call of intellectual *Beruf* and then returned to the United States to establish beachheads of objectivity at Johns Hopkins University, the University of Chicago and the University of Michigan.[6] A scholar of British academics provides a list of fifty-five British intellectuals who had at least part of their educations in German universities. These include the historians John Acton, J. B. Bury, John Clapham, H. A. L. Fisher, James Bryce and R. W. Seton-Watson; the classicists Ingram Bywater, Lewis Farnell and Henry Nettleship; the philologists J. S. Blackie, A. S. Napier, John Peile and John Rhys; the philosophers Andrew Seth Pringle-Pattison, Henry Sidgwick, and J. C. Wilson; the anthropologist R. R. Marett; the psychologists W. H. R. Rivers and James Ward.[7] The German, especially the Prussian, example of scholarship, its research imperative, what has been called its *Wissenschaftideologie*, fired and fuelled the imaginations of the Anglophone world.[8]

Gilbert Murray formed a deep attachment to Ulrich von Wilamowitz-Moellendorff and their correspondence marked an early point in what has been called the Germanisation of British philological studies.[9] Murray, at the age of twenty-three, read Wilamowitz's edition of Euripides's *Herakles* and, as he wrote, 'I was overcome with admiration. Never had I seen such wide and exact

---

5   Quoted in Lorraine Daston, 'The Immortal Archive: Nineteenth-Century Science Imagines the Future,' in Lorraine Daston (ed.), *Science in the Archives* (Chicago/London: 2017), p.162.
6   Peter Novick, *That Noble Dream: The 'Objectivity Question' and the American Historical Profession* (Cambridge: 1988), pp.27–29. By placing the 'objectivity question' in scare quotes Novick reveals his unsettled and unstable feelings about the very concept of objectivity.
7   Stuart Wallace, *War and the Image of Germany: British Academics, 1914–1918* (Edinburgh: 1988), pp.227–228.
8   Turner, 'The Prussian Universities and the Concept of Research,' *Internationales Archiv für Sozialgeschichte de Deutchen Literatur*, 5 (1) (January 1980): 69–93, esp. 78; Charles E. McClelland, *Berlin, The Mother of All Research Universities, 1860–1918* (Langham/Boulder/New York/London: 2017), pp.1–46.
9   A. Bierl, William Calder III and R. L. Fowler, *The Prussian and the Poet: The Letters of Ulrich von Wilamowitz-Moellendorff to Gilbert Murray (1894–1930)* (Hildesheim: 1991), p.2.

learning inspired by such a lively and vigorous mind.'[10] He sent Wilamowitz a copy of Jane Harrison's *Themis* but the Great Man was not much interested in efforts to 'explain the adult man from the life of the embryo.' 'It does not interest me much how Hecuba's grandmother felt; nor Plato's for that matter,' he wrote. 'She was only an old woman and her faith was a hag's.'[11] Murray invited him to Oxford where he gave two lectures and then went on to Cambridge where Arthur Verrall's 'peculiar charm' impressed him.[12] Wilamowitz became interested in university life at Oxford. Walking with Murray he turned suddenly and asked: '*Was ist ein Spoonerismus?*'[13] Murray found in Wilamowitz 'the greatest and in many ways the most picturesque figure' in German scholarship, uniting in himself 'a strange and impressive combination of the haughty *virtus* of a Prussian noble in the Polish marches' with 'the warm imagination of a Slav.'[14]

Post-1914 antagonisms exaggerated national differences. Until the 1890s Germans formed the largest immigrant group coming to Britain from the Continent. By 1911 approximately 100,000 lived in Britain and there was considerable entanglement of ideas among individuals who could claim loyalty to both countries, or neither.[15] The Great War, however, ended a great period of intellectual cooperation and hopes for a cosmopolitan conception of knowledge. Only a few, such as Henry Sidgwick, the Knightbridge Professor of Moral Philosophy at Cambridge, and Henry Smith, the Oxford mathematician, had intimations of intellectual breaches at the time of the unification of Germany. Smith, blond and tall, wearing spectacles, was stopped by the French and accused of spying. He spoke French badly, he told them, but not with a German accent.[16] Sidgwick was pained when he visited Berlin in 1870 and found the German's 'wrathful' towards England and regarded England 'as a country of cowards,' which had 'made herself contemptable in the eyes of the civilised world.'[17] The breaking out of the war disturbed James Bryce greatly. He had been to Heidelberg and his admiration for German historical and legal scholarship was unstinting. Hegelianism, he recognised, was not a liberal variant but both, however, to his mind, were uplifting. But, as a jurist, treaties were treaties and the German invasion of Belgium was a breach that defied

[10] Gilbert Murray, 'Memories of Wilamowtiz', *Antike un Abendland*, 4 (December 1954): 9.

[11] Quoted in Bierl, Calder and Fowler, *The Prussian and the Poet*, p.4.

[12] Murray, 'Memories of Wilamowitz': 11.

[13] Quoted in Bierl, Calder and Fowler, *The Prussian and the Poet*, p.7.

[14] Gilbert Murray, 'Wilamowitz', *Classical Review*, 45 (5) (November 1931): 161.

[15] Jan Rüger, 'Revisiting the Anglo-German Antagonism', *Journal of Modern History*, 83 (3) (September 2011): 579–617, esp. 582–583.

[16] Henry Smith, *Biographical Sketches and Recollections (with Early Letters of Henry John Smith, MA, FRS* (London: 1894), p.27.

[17] Henry Sidgwick to Mrs Clough, 30 July and 2 August 1970, printed in A. S. and E. M. S., *Henry Sidgwick: A Memoir* (London: 1906), pp.234–235.

Bryce's emotional and intellectual commitments.[18] The war also disrupted H. A. L. Fisher's intellectual loyalties towards Germany. Then in the Cabinet as President of the Board of Education, he told Virginia Woolf how he had admired the Germans because he was educated and had friends there. '[B]ut I have lost my belief in them' because 'they have been taught to be brutal' and so 'the proportion of brutes is greater with them than with us.'[19]

The coming of the war disrupted social relations. After the war there was insufficient interest among the members of the Ambarum Society – the dining club of Oxford and Cambridge dons that met twice a year – for them to carry on. Sir Arthur Everett Shipley, the Master of Christ's College, the Cambridge secretary of the society, and one-time the university's vice-chancellor, declared tersely: 'The Ambarum was killed by the war.'[20] Some societies, such as the dining club of the Royal Astronomical Society, staggered on:

> [N]ever in any period was the value of the Club more clearly shown. Men wanted sympathy then, mutual encouragement and help; the Members drew near to each other and became a 'band of brothers.' Some were in the fighting line, and often when the toast to those absent ones was given, there came the shade of thought – 'Will they return? If so, how? Broken in health, maimed, blinded?' The Club rejoiced to see its Members climb the ladder of promotion and their good deeds recognized. It rejoiced still more when, timing their scanty leave to suit the meetings, they appeared at table fresh from the fight, and poured out their stories and their experiences.

On 13 November 1914 the club's toast was to 'Belgium, a great nation.' '[O]ur hearts were still hot within us at that country's heroic defense of the cause of humanity.'[21] The greatest of the dining societies, THE CLUB, persisted through the Second World War and beyond. As Maurice Hankey pointed out in his letter to A. V. Hill telling Hill of his election, 'In normal times THE CLUB is a Dining Club, but during the war it has become temporarily a Luncheon Club because many members of it, like myself, live out of town.' 'THE CLUB lunches at present at Brown's Hotel in Dover Street. The annual subscription is three guineas and the cost of any Luncheon at which a member is present is 5/-, which includes wine and cigars.' The members at the meeting at which Hill was elected included Cosmo Lang, Lord Crewe, G. M. Trevelyan,

---

[18]   Keith G. Robbins, 'Lord Bryce and the First World War,' *Historical Journal*, 10 (2) (1967): 255–278. For a more recent treatment of this subject see Sakiko Kaiga, 'The Use of Force to Prevent War? The Bryce Group's Proposals for the Avoidance of War, 1914–1915,' *Journal of British Studies*, 57 (2) (April 2018): 308–332.

[19]   Virginia Woolf Diary, 15 October 1918, in Anne Olivier Bell (ed.), *The Diary of Virginia Woolf, Volume One, 1915–1919* (New York/London: 1977), p.204.

[20]   A. E. Shipley to [?] Bartholomew, 2 October 1922, Cambridge University Library, Add. 4251/129.

[21]   F. J. M. Stratton (ed.), *Records of the Royal Astronomical Society Club, 1911–1924* (London: 1924), pp.xvi–xvii.

Kenneth Clark, Sir Eric Phipps, Lord Wigram (who had been the king's private secretary) and Lord Macmillan. When necessary, during the war, THE CLUB took a 'meatless menu.'[22]

With the Great War's coming, patriotism blinded even that staunch liberal Gilbert Murray. He fell back on some conventional clichés contrasting the German 'specialist professor' with the English 'scholar and gentleman.' 'We are always aiming at culture – in Arnold's sense,' he wrote. German scholars 'are aiming at research or achievement.' Admitting '[t]here is always Wilamowitz, of course,' Murray tried to rescue Wilamowitz by finding in him something of the qualities of the English gentleman scholar. But Murray's praise was for Frederic Kenyon's work on Egyptian papyri, for James Frazer's 'Pausanias,' for A. B. Cook's account of 'Zeus, the Indo-European Sky-God,' and for Arthur Evans's excavations at Knossus. For whom was Jane Harrison's work intended, he asked: 'For *Fachgenossen*?' 'No, because it is full of imaginative writing and *belle lettres*, and it gave translations, and even poetic translations of passages it cited from Greek authors.' Murray cited the books of Francis Cornford and A. E. Zimmern because they 'stand as much by their sense of beauty and their imaginative suggestiveness as by the particular conclusions which they try to prove.'[23]

Though unwillingly so, Murray, thereby, was complicit in driving a wedge between German and British scholars and, therefore, promoted the division of knowledge. That wedge had been sharpened by the publication at the outbreak of the war of the manifesto of ninety-three German scholars (*Aufrus an die Kulturwelt*) denying responsibility for violating Belgian neutrality and the burning of the library at Louvain. 'Believe us,' they wrote, 'believe that to the last we will fight as a civilized nation, to whom the legacy of a Goethe, a Beethoven and a Kant is no less sacred than hearth and home.'[24] Wilamowitz-Moellendorff, always a Prussianist, signed the manifesto though he had found an early draft of it 'undiplomatic.' He recognised though that it had been 'foolish and absurd' that he had done so without knowing the actual wording of the final text. Yet he remained largely unrepentant:

> [H]onest men of science, accustomed to serve truth, can and ought to serve both their fatherlands and peace by their patriotic temper, which can respect the patriotism of others, and their ungrudging co-operation for a common sacred cause. The song of the angels proclaimed peace on earth to 'men of His

[22] Maurice Hankey to A. V. Hill, 29 April 1942, Churchill College, Cambridge, A. V. Hill Papers, AVHL, H/3/1–2. See also Peter Hennessy, 'The Age of Baldwin and Beerbohm, 1914–1984,' in Charles Saumarez Smith, David Cannadine and Peter Hennessy, *New Annals of THE CLUB* (London: 2014), pp.104–123.

[23] Gilbert Murray, 'German Scholarship,' *Quarterly Review*, 223 (443) (April 19): 330–339, esp. 331, 336–338.

[24] Printed in George F. Nicolai, *The Biology of War* (New York, 1929), p.xiv.

good pleasure.' They are the true men of science, for to them the service of truth is the service of God.[25]

Frederic Kenyon, in his presidential address to the British Academy of 1920, recalled how the German manifesto 'disastrously poisoned all intercourse between German and English scholars.' He regarded it as 'a great crime against scholarship.'[26] Kenyon felt the war sharply for he had been an active member of the Territorial Army, having joined the Inns of Court Corps in 1899. He received a commission in 1906 and was promoted to captain in 1912. He served in France in 1914 and was promoted to lieutenant-colonel in 1917. Recalled to London at the behest of the trustees of the British Museum, from 1917 he served on the Imperial War Graves Commission and visited cemeteries in France and the Middle East.[27] It was not easy to repair these breaches. The Academic Committee of the Royal Society of Literature established a committee for the 'promotion of an Intellectual Entente *among the allied and friendly nations*' only.[28]

Yet hope lingered. As Lord Crewe and Henry Newbolt tried to remind their colleagues on the Academic Committee of the Royal Society of Literature, '[i]nternational good-will and understanding are to-day the greatest need of the civilized world.' Political alliances were not to be trusted. In an age of sectarianism religion divided rather than united. Commerce was competitive. Even science, for the most part was applied, and led to strife in war and industry. 'The arts alone remain as a common basis for friendship and it the art of literature which offers most opportunity for international intercourse.'[29] Frederic Kenyon, in his address to the British Academy in 1920, gave some ground:

> It is idle to suppose that we can ignore German scholarship in the future. We may have exalted it too much in the past; but it is childish to talk as if it had rendered no services to learning or as if it could be treated as negligible in the

[25] Ulrich von Wilamowitz-Moellendorff, *My Recollections, 1848–1914*, trans. G. C. Richards (London: 1930), pp.382–384.
[26] F. G. Kenyon, 'International Scholarship: Presidential Address, delivered at the Annual General Meeting, 21 July 1920,' *Proceedings of the British Academy, 1919–1920* (1920): 24–25, 27–28.
[27] There is considerable scholarly literature on these intellectual ruptures: Daniel J. Kelves, '"Into Hostile Political Camps": The Reorganization of International Science in World War I,' *Isis*, 62 (1) (Spring 1971): 47–60; A. G. Cock, 'Chauvinism and Internationalism in Science: The International Research Council, 1919–1929,' *Notes and Records of the Royal Society of London*, 37 (2) (March 1983): 249–288; Wolfgang J. Mommsen, 'German Artists, Writers and Intellectuals and the Meaning of War, 1914–1918,' in Jon Hoene (ed.), *State, Society and Mobilizaton in Europe during the First World War* (Cambridge: 1997).
[28] 'Objects of the Committee,' in the Henry Newbolt file, Cambridge University Library, Royal Society of Literature Archives. My emphasis.
[29] Lord Crewe and Henry Newbolt to the fellows of the Royal Society of Literatue, July 1920, Cambridge University Library, Royal Society of Literature Archives.

future. Science knows no distinction of allies or enemies ... The most we can do is to keep the door open, and trust to the healing influence of time. On our side we can avoid bitterness; on the other, we have a right to look for some evidence of the spirit which characterized German scholarship in the middle of the nineteenth century.[30]

Other threats, he warned, lurked. As Kenyon pointed out later, the fight between science and the classics has 'lost its bitterness.' 'The fight between Science and Theology had died down; Science is no longer sure it knows everything, and Theology realizes that in its own sphere Science must be respected.' The duty of the learned life, Kenyon argued, was to 'take advantage of this growth of greater toleration, and this sense of comradeship in the cause of knowledge against materialism, of high ideals against low.'[31]

Intellectual distinction did not protect people from suspicions of disloyalty, as the case of R. B. Haldane noted above shows. The career of Sir Arthur Schuster also illustrates the complicated turnings of political and intellectual loyalties. The Schuster family were Jewish converts to Christianity whose business in Frankfort-am-Main had connections with the British cotton trade going back into the nineteenth century. The elder Schuster, Francis Joseph Schuster (1823–1906), was a German nationalist but opposed prussianification and when Prussia annexed Frankfurt at the end of the Seven Weeks' War moved the family business to Manchester. The elder Schusters had four children: Paula, who married Sir Lawrence Jones, Bt; Ernest who specialised in international law and became a KC; Sir Felix Schuster, Bt, a banker and Liberal politician (whose granddaughter was Mary Warnock the philosopher); and Sir Franz Arthur Friedrich Schuster who became Professor of Physics at the University of Manchester and who married the niece of Sir Adolphus Ward, Professor of History, Principal of Owens College, Manchester and later Master of Peterhouse, Cambridge. By business, profession and marriage, therefore, the Schusters were deeply enmeshed in British life.

Sir Arthur Schuster (1851–1934) cut a cosmopolitan figure. He had been to school in Frankfurt and then in Geneva. Having tried his hand in the family business and discovering he had wider interests (he was a keen mountaineer and later in life a not uninteresting painter) he persuaded his father to allow him to study at Owens College, which became in his own time the University of Manchester. There he studied mathematics with Thomas Barker, physics with Balfour Stewart, and began research on the spectra of hydrogen and oxygen with Henry Roscoe. He maintained his intellectual connections in Germany and spent a year at Heidelberg studying with Gustav Kirchoff, gaining his PhD (1873). During the summer and autumn he was in Göttingen

[30] Kenyon, 'Presidential Address', delivered at the Annual General Meeting, 21 June, 1920: 27.
[31] F. G. Kenyon, 'The Fellowship of Learning: Presidential Address Delivered to the Annual General Meeting, July 6 1921,' Proceedings of the British Academy, 1921–1923: 6.

working with Wilhelm Weber and Eduard Reicke, and in Berlin working with Hermann von Helmholz. In 1875 the Royal Society sent him to Siam to observe the solar eclipse; he also participated in the solar eclipse expeditions to Colorado (1878), Egypt (1882) and the West Indies (1886). In 1874 Schuster attached himself to the Cavendish Laboratory (where he worked with James Clerk Maxwell and the Lord Rayleigh) and returned to Owens College as a demonstrator in physics, rising to become professor and helping to make Manchester a powerhouse for the study of spectroscopy, electrochemistry, optics and X-radiography. He was elected FRS in 1878 at the age of twenty-eight, received their Royal Medal (1893), their Rumsford medal (1926) and, their highest award, the Copley medal (1931). Schuster was president of the British Association for the Advancement of Science at their Manchester meeting in 1915. He was knighted 1920.[32]

Schuster served twice on the Council of the Royal Society and, eagerly taking up the society's work, he accepted the invitation to succeed Sir Joseph Larmor as Secretary in 1912. He served for seven years, moving from Manchester to an estate, Yeldall at Twyford, near Reading, Berkshire. These were difficult years. Because of their name and because they had been born abroad and because they had continental associations, despite their deep British connections, the Schuster family fell under suspicion during the war. Arthur Schuster's elder brother had been unwise enough to host a public dinner for the German community in London to mark the birthday of the Kaiser. Sir Felix Schuster had to issue a public statement testifying to the family's loyalty to Britain and that they all had sons fighting in the British army. In fact, on the day Arthur Schuster gave his presidential address to the British Association he learned his son had been wounded in battle.

Nonetheless, unpleasantness ensued. Schuster was alarmed when a notice in the press appeared saying that an 'apparatus,' which had been installed at Yeldall so that he could receive the Paris wireless signal, had been seized, 'with more or less veiled references to the purpose for which the apparatus was likely to have been erected.' The matter, 'on view of my position at the time, was serious, and it was with fear and trembling that I entered the Athenaeum a few days later and selected a solitary place in the coffee-room.' Schuster was comforted when on leaving, Lord Roberts, as a gesture of solidarity in the midst of large numbers of club members gathered in the Great Hall, assisted Schuster in the putting on of his coat.[33] 'A distinguished Fellow of the Royal Society' wrote to him 'suggesting that it would be in the interest of the Society if I retired from the Secretaryship.'[34] Schuster had the support of J. J. Thomson,

---

[32] G. C. Simpson, 'Sir Arthur Schuster, 1851–1934,' *Obituary Notices of the Fellows of the Royal Society*, I (1932–1935): 409–423.

[33] Arthur Schuster, *Biographical Fragments* (London: 1932), pp.259–260.

[34] Arthur Schuster to J. J. Thompson, 20 October [1917]. Cambridge University Library,

then president of the Royal Society, and gained a vote of confidence from the council. Grumbling, however, continued. Herbert Hall Turner, the Savilian Professor of Astronomy at Oxford, wrote to Schuster saying he 'could not shut my eyes to certain facts' and 'I feel compelled by some evil demon to shove them before your eyes too.' 'There is a considerable measure of discontent running through [the society's] system,' a vague yet 'a sensible and widespread discontent in the Society.' Turner wondered whether if 'it might be the best thing you could do for the Society to which you are devoted in so whole-souled a manner, as I know, to sacrifice your own predilections.'[35]

Schuster's internationalism may also have assisted in inflaming his colleagues' suspicions during the war. By education and temperament and by his love of travel (he commanded three European languages) he knew the leading figures in continental science. Schuster was at the founding meeting of the International Association of Academies at Wiesbaden and, in 1905, on the resignation of Sir Michael Foster, the Council of the Royal Society chose him to represent them on the Council of the International Association. Schuster endowed the Royal Society with £3,500, the investment income of which was to be used to pay the annual subscription of the society to the International Association and to subvent the expenses of delegates to attend its meetings. The war killed the International Association but after 1919 Schuster led the way for the formation of the International Research Council. Initially the Research Council's membership excluded representatives of the Central Powers, but Schuster, as the council's first secretary from 1919 to 1928, and trusted by German and French intellectuals, worked to end national misunderstandings and restrictions and make the council genuinely international.[36]

War and politics disrupted personal relations and the way towards reconciliation would be halting. In 1918 Frederick Kenyon, then president of the British Academy asked the Rev. Canon William Sanday, Lady Margaret Professor of Divinity at the University of Oxford and a founding fellow of the British Academy, to address the academy on the question of international intellectual cooperation after the war.[37] Sanday proceeded cautiously. He recognised the universal feeling that it was 'the worst war ever waged by Powers calling themselves civilized.' Because of unrestricted submarine warfare and the bombing of cities 'Germany must be regarded as a State with a stain upon its character which is not to be washed out in a day.' Sanday located the origins of

J. J. Thompson Ms. Add. 7654/ S20.

[35] Herbert Hall Turner [writing from the University Observatory, Oxford] to Schuster (copy), 7 December 1917, Cambridge University Library, J. J. Thomson Ms. Add. 7654/S26.

[36] Simpson, 'Sir Arthur Schuster, 1851–1934': 420–421.

[37] See James Rivington, with archival assistance from Karen Syrett, 'Canon Sanday on "International Scholarship after the War," May 1918,' *British Academy Review* (Summer 2018): 49–51.

German actions in its 'exaggerated doctrine of the autonomy of the State.' This led to a peculiar theory of war:

> Whereas among the Western nations W is regarded as an evil to be reduced within the narrowest limits possible, on the German view the incidental virtues called out by War are held to make it good to be cultivated for its own sake. Hence the whole nation has been systematically organized with a view to War – which it supposed to give what is called a 'biologically just decision.' In other words justice and an independent moral standard drops out ... Hence the conflict has not been confined to the belligerent armies.[38]

Because Prince Lichnowsky, who had been the German ambassador to the Court of St James at the outbreak of the war, had written a pamphlet criticising the conduct of his own government, Sanday thought he might be able to negotiate a 'real and not merely German peace'and foster an intellectual reconciliation among scholars. The moral conscience of the German people and in particular 'the learned classes, the thinking classes – the classes corresponding to those we represent ourselves' might be pricked by such as Ernst Troeltsch of Heidelberg, Adolf von Harnack of Berlin, and Friederich Loofs of Halle who might seize the opportunity to speak out, 'on behalf of the nation, to make amends that are due from it.'

> It is a great opportunity – the greatest that has ever fallen to a learned class of making itself felt on the course of history since history began. The learned class is the proper guardian of historical truth, the proper exponent of sound doctrine in politics and morals.

If Troeltsch, von Harnack, Loofs and other leaders of the 'learned class' provided such an example, Sanday opposed 'withdrawing privileges previously enjoyed by German scholars' or 'imposing special disabilities upon them.'[39]

In preparing his remarks Sanday consulted Edwyn Robert Bevan.[40] Having family money at his back Bevan could occupy himself as an independent scholar travelling to India after going down from New College and then spending time at the British School of Archaeology in Athens and attending to excavations in Egypt. During the Great War, after a short time in the Artists' Rifles, he went to the departments of propaganda and information and then to the political intelligence department of the Foreign Office and was appointed OBE (1920). Having thus served, Bevan thought a certain amount of stereotypical thinking about the German enemy might be valid but it was

38 William Sanday, 'International Scholarship After the War,' BAA/SEC/1/15/11/14.
39 Sanday, 'Inernational Scholarship After the War,' BAA/SEC/1/15/17, 27.
40 Bevan, Edwyn Robert (1870–1943): father, a banker; ed. Monkton Come School, New College, Oxford: first class in Classical Moderations (1890) and *Literae Humaniores* (1892); he gave the Gifford Lectures at Edinburgh in 1933 and 1934, published as *Symbolism and Belief* (1938); FBA (1942) and appointed to Section I (History and Archaeology).

also dangerous during wartime when '[o]ur thinking had been governed by the supreme end of destroying the enemy's military power':

> Then suddenly by the German collapse we were confronted with a wholly new situation. The problem was no longer how to defeat an enemy armed and formidable, but how to deal with a great European nation which had fallen in wide ruin and laid prostrate on this earth of ours. The new situation required a great change of mental processes on our part. For now it was just as important to take full account of any element of good there might be in the defeated nation as before it was important to keep the evil in mind.

The danger lay in passing 'almost without any feeling of transition, from a firm belief in the rightness of our cause to a pharisaical admiration of ourselves.' If the Germans wish to build up a new Germany 'animated by better ideals' they should have 'our interest and sympathy at every stage of the process.' If the doctrines of *Machtpolitik* were subscribed to by those most powerfully influenced in the state and even among educated people, it was also true, Bevan held, that there were always people who protested against those doctrines, especially by members of the Social Democratic Party and the members of the working classes. The shock of defeat, Bevan argued, led to the 'general desire to have done finally with the whole system of militarism and *Machtpolitik* which had led to disaster.' *Machtpolitik* had become a 'broken idol.' Instead of seeking to regain its material losses in the war, Bevan proposed help to 'restore to its place in the moral fellowship of the world a nation which had gone astray after false gods.'[41]

Sanday and Bevan (and Maynard Keynes for that matter) were isolated figures. Gollanancz consulted the Foreign Office concerning Sanday's paper, which regarded Sanday's effort as 'a fine and generous attempt to get over the situation by an appeal to the Germans themselves' but regarded its references to potential negotiations as 'entrench[ing] on pure questions of policy and politics' by leaving the 'impression that misunderstandings had been a much more considerable factor in the causation of the war than as a matter of fact they were.'[42] William Ramsay, Professor of Humanity at the University of Aberdeen and a founding fellow of the British Academy, opposed the publication of Sanday's paper because its 'mixture of politics and morality and religion' made it 'utterly apart from the business of an academy.'[43]

C. S. Sherrington, the Oxford physiologist who would become PRS and be appointed to the Order of Merit, recalled a conversation he had had with Troeltsch in Heidelberg in 1907. Troeltsch, to Sherrington's astonishment, said he regretted a war with Britain but he thought it would be necessary:

[41]   Edwyn Bevan, 'The Problem of the New Germany,' *Church Quarterly Review*, 88 (July 1919): 254, 255, 256, 258, 259, 263, 266, 268, 270.
[42]   [W. Headlam] from the Foreign Office to Gollancz, BAA/SEC/1/15/12.
[43]   William Ramsay to Kenyon, 17 May 1918 and 9 June, 1918. BAA/SEC/1/15/13a–b.

[I]n fulfilling her destiny [Germany] will forward the history of the world; they know that, and they know also that their Army and Navy are the weapons of blood and steel which can open the world and give them wealth and power as the competent directors of workmen who under their supervision would do more for the world than they would otherwise do.

Troeltsch concluded: England's king 'is non-entity whose chief interest is the race-course' and England 'as a political influence is becoming effete; her Governments exemplify that; they exhibit little insight into world politics to-day.'[44] Accordingly, Sherrington concluded, because such views persisted it was impossible to consider reconciliation. Kenyon also rejected Sanday's and Bevan's position because, while British scholars might assist in the process of the readmission of Germany to 'the fellowship of civilized nations,' they could only do so when German scholars 'renounced the crimes against civilization which Germany had committed.' Lord Reay, the first president of the British Academy, felt Sanday's optimistic proposals were premature. French learned circles would resent efforts at reconciliation and German savants would misinterpret it. 'We must make it clear to them,' Reay wrote, how 'all civilised races look with horror on the effects which their *Kultur* has had.' Lichnowski, Reay reported, was regarded as a traitor and '[f]airness, chivalry, truthfulness are impossible where iron discipline in the University as well as in the army, the church as well as in social and literary intercourse is considered essential for self protection and aggrandizement.'[45] Sanday himself thought his paper ought not be published. 'I am not a bit of a pacifist really,' he wrote, and 'quite agree that the only thing to be done is to go on fighting.'[46]

So, Sanday's gesture towards reconciliation lay dead in the water and his address has remained unpublished. The twistings and turnings of loyalties in the world of learning during the Great War illustrate the difficulties of squaring the demands of political life with those of mental life. Such conflicts would re-emerge in other twentieth-century episodes. One of such was the meeting of the International Conference on the History and Philosophy of Science in 1931 and another of such was the Kapitza affair. These episodes reveal yet again the dislocations within truth's sovereignty.

Charles Singer, who Joseph Needham regarded as the 'greatest living English historian of science of our time,' presided over the Second International Congress of the History of Science.[47] Singer's career and position in the intellectual world is of interest because, intellectually speaking, he was neither fish,

---

44 Quoted in Mark D. Chapman, *Theology at War and Peace: English Theology and Germany in the First World War* (London/New York: 2017), pp.113–114.
45 Reay, to [Kenyon?] 23 May 1918, BAA/SEC/1/15/14.
46 Sanday to Kenyon, 3 June 1918, BAA/SEC/1/15/16.
47 'Record of a Conversation on 21 May 1968 between Gary Weskey, Keith Roberts, and Harold Fruchtbaum and Joseph Needham on the "Science and Society Movement in the Thirties,"' Cambridge University Library, Needham Ms. A.701, p.14.

fowl, nor good red herring.[48] Walter Adams, later a force in the Society for the Protection of Science and Learning and as Director of the London School of Economics, regarded Singer, and the Second International Congress, as playing a significant role in the legitimisation of the history of science as a discipline:

A feature that emerged common to all these sessions was the demonstration that science itself had much to gain by becoming more historically self-conscious. Clearly it was desirable that students of the sciences should become aware that contemporary science is a single instant in a long process of 'becoming'; historical-mindedness provides a sense of proportion, almost of values, in the otherwise destructive rapidity of scientific developments to-day; an historical approach provides a basis for communication between scientists whose increasing specialization of studies threatens to make them mutually unintelligible; historical studies directly suggests new subjects and methods of experimental research; history would constantly remind the scientist to relate his own work to other departments of human endeavor.[49]

Such legitimisation was a long time in coming and one wonders if it was ever safe or secure.

In 1956 Sir Howard Florey, then president of the Royal Society and Professor Sir William Dunn, School of Pathology at Oxford, wrote to Needham saying that Singer was a candidate for election to the Royal Society, asking about Singer's 'scientific qualifications,' and asking whether 'he has influenced biological work by his historical writing.'[50] In response Needham, admitting he was not completely aware of the 'minutiae of Royal Society procedure[s]' for election and allowing that 'some among us' may feel that the history of science is an aspect of history rather than science and therefore properly belongs to the British Academy rather than the Royal Society. While such a view is tenable, Needham, who was FRS and would be elected FBA in 1971 (appointed to the sections dealing with Oriental and African Studies and Social and Political Studies), felt to act on such a view would be lamentable. The Royal Society he thought ought to find room for historians of science 'somehow' if their 'eminence reaches or passes a suitable level.' He went on to show how Singer's

48 Singer, Charles Joseph (1876–1960): father, a prominent classical and Hebrew scholar who became rabbi of the New West End Synagogue; ed. City of London School, University College London where he took a medical course, and Magdalen College, Oxford where he read zoology, and St Mary's Hospital, Paddington where he qualified in medicine and pathology; married Dorothea Cohen (1910), herself a scholar of the history of science and medicine, known for her catalogue of Greek, Latin and vernacular alchemical manuscripts in the British Isles; during the Great War served as a pathologist in the Royal Army Medical Corps rising to the rank of captain, seeing service in Salonica and Malta; after the war accepted a lectureship in the history of medicine at University College, London; president of the *Academie Internationale d'Histoire des Sciences*.
49 W[alter] Adams, 'The International Congress of the History of Science and Technology,' *History*, 16 (630) (October 1931): 202, 211–212.
50 Florey to Needham, 19 December 1956, Cambridge University Library, Needham Ms. J224.

research covered much wider ground than the history of biology. 'Singer's most massive contribution of this kind was not on the history of biology at all; it was "The Earliest Chemical Industry: Alum," an immense work with far-reaching implications in economic history, and forming a remarkable monument in the history of chemistry.'[51] In the event, Singer was elected to the fellowship of neither the Royal Society nor the British Academy. As late as 1972 Needham wrote: 'It is sad that there are so painfully few historians of science in either of the Academies.'[52]

The Second International Congress of Science and Technology marked an important encounter with the alien concepts of Soviet Marxist scholarship, which informed and altered British thinking about science in particular and knowledge in general. To these Walter Adams called attention. As he argued, the history of science 'might disclose to the scientist a hitherto unsuspected motivation for some of the processes of his studies.' By being conscious of them to the point where 'they could be analysed and defined,' they might increase the 'efficiency' of thinking.[53] What was especially impressive and important at the International Conference was, as Joseph Needham noted, 'the presence of a colossal Russian delegation.'[54] Their numbers surprised even the Russians. Originally there was to be but one Russian delegate to the Congress, but after eighteen months' strife between Russian intellectuals and the Soviet state Stalin broke the deadlock and he had Nicholai Bukharin lead a large group of politicians, administrators, scientists and historians to London.[55] Dramatically, they flew from Moscow. So rushed were they that an hour into the air they had to fly back to get Bukharin's address to the Congress, which he had forgotten to pack. Lancelot Hogben, Needham and other organisers of the Congress were faced with an aggressive group who, in effect, hijacked the Congress with long and detailed addresses.[56] Bukharin led the way and early on in his address said '[t]he crisis in modern physics – and equally in the whole of natural sciences, plus the so-called mental sciences (*Geisteswissenschaften*) has raised as an urgent problem, and with renewed violence, the fundamental questions of philosophy: the question of the *objective reality of the external world*, independent of the subject perceiving it, and the question of its *cognisablity* (or, alternatively, non-cognisabiltity).' Theory and practice, he argued,

---

51 Needham to Florey, 3 January 1957, Cambridge University Library, Needham Ms. J224.
52 Needham to Captain Stephen Roskill, RN, 18 January 1972, Cambridge University Library, Needham Ms. J. 15.
53 Adams, 'The International Congress': 212.
54 'Record of a Conversation on 21 May 1968' : Cambridge University Library, Needham Ms. A. 701, p.14.
55 For the Soviet background to this episode see Loren R. Graham, 'The Socio-Political Roots of Boris Hessen: Soviet Marxism and the History of Science,' *Social Studies of Science*, 15 (4) (November 1985): 707–710.
56 Gary Wersky, *The Visible College: A Collective Biography of British Scientists and Socialists of the 1930s* (London: 1988 [1978], pp.138 ff.

are social activities. If theory is examined these are not 'petrified systems.' If practice is examined these are not 'finished products.' Two forms of labour activity emerge: 'intellectual and physical labour.' Then he could conclude:

> [The] irrational current of life is the consequence of the anarchic character of the capitalist structure. The regularity in organized Socialist society is of a different type. It loses (if we are speaking of a process, it *begins to lose*) its elemental character: the future lies ahead as plan, an aim: causal connection is realized through social teleology: regularity shows itself not *post factum*, not unforeseen, incomprehensible, blind: it shows itself as 'recognised necessity' ('freedom is recognised necessity'), realized through *action organized on a social scale*.[57]

Bukharin's theoretical and dogmatic intervention might have been expected.

Not Boris Hessen's speech to the International Congress, however. His address was, as Needham argued, 'crude [and] plain blunt Cromwellian in style [but it was] a seminal document for everybody who lived through that time.'[58] The emergence of capitalism was, according to Hessen, the principal feature of Newton's age. Capitalism created deep fissions in English society and it also created new technological demands – for hydrostatics, for ballistics, for magnetism, for optics, for mechanics – which were peculiar to the time. Newton's work, Hessen argued, was the intellectual response to the social and political urges of the seventeenth century. He drew parallels between the English civil wars and the Russian revolution and pointed out that science is reconstructed in any era in which social relations are reconstructed. Scientific progress, Hessen believed, could not be achieved in a society that restricts technological advancement.[59] His views about quantum mechanics brought him to grief and the gulag when he returned home from London.

Such views, though striking, complicated intellectual and political loyalties for those attending the Congress. Dialectical materialism was almost unknown to but a few who had, like Lancelot Hogben, attempted to find ways, successfully or not, to fit it into the English conceptual world.[60] Desmond Bernal rather thought the appeal to Marxist dogma would fall upon English ears as too doctrinaire and ungentlemanly.[61] Needham himself had been brought to an interest in the seventeenth century and socialism earlier and much more informally – through Christianity, actually. As has been indicated earlier, he and his wife, Dorothy, had attached themselves to Conrad Noel's practices of

---

[57] N. Bukharin, 'Theory and Practice from the Standpoint of Dialectical Materialism,' in *Science at the Cross Roads: Papers Presented to the International Congress of the History of Science and Technology held in London from June 29 to July 3rd 1931 by the Delegates of the U.S.S.R.*, with a new foreword by Joseph Needham, and a new introduction by P. G. Werskey (London: 1971), pp.11, 13, 29.
[58] 'Record of a Conversation on 21 May 1968,' p. 15.
[59] Needham, 'New Introduction,' *Science at the Cross Roads*: p.xxi.
[60] Needham, *Time the Refreshing River*, pp.244–245, esp. note 1, p.245.
[61] Needham, 'New Introduction,' *Science at the Cross Roads*: p.xxi.

Christian socialism, 'an extremely thorough going Left variety' at Thaxted. He never thought socialism incompatible with Christianity though he thought Marxism had been 'unduly influenced by the materialism of mechanical materialists.' He was guided very much more by Rudolph Otto's 'Sense of the Holy': *das numinöse, das heilege*. The sense of the holy, he thought, 'was a form of experience itself, and I still believe this to be true,' Needham said in 1968.[62] Needham's Marxism, therefore, was of a peculiar sort. He published a book on the Levellers in the English Civil War, but under the name Henry Horolenshaw because he was hoping to be elected to the Royal Society and regarded his chances as hopeless if he became known as a writer of Marxist interpretations of seventeenth-century history.

Needham knew professional historians would disapprove of what he had to say. Still, once he realised it was possible to interpret the civil war as a bourgeois revolution 'everything fell into place.' '[W]hen I first understood things that way it made more sense than any other way of looking at it, and I think there must be fundamental truth in it.'[63] Yet, dialectical materialism was never for him of methodological importance in detailed research planning. It might, however, assist in general thinking and in expressing emergent evolution.[64] Because he regarded himself as an 'honorary Taoist' Needham regarded neither religion, nor science, nor philosophy as divisive impulses, but rather as unifying ones. As he put it, '[t]he union was of course not intellectual but existential, constructed within a single human being open by nature to all forms of experience.'[65] As to his own politics, Needham always associated himself with 'the progressive side of things' and shocked some of his elders by becoming one of the first presidents of the Association of Scientific Workers. However, he did not regard himself as 'in any way of the fiery left wing' – that he left to such as J. B. S. Haldane.[66]

While Needham and others were impressed by the International Congress on the History of Science in 1931 it is difficult to assess its general importance for twentieth-century British political and intellectual life. Those on the firm left – J. B. S. Haldane, Desmond Bernal – had had their political views quickened by the economic crisis of the 1920s. Needham's formative experiences had been in his father's library where he had read Schlegel's 'History of

---

62 'Conversation on 21 May 1968,' Cambridge University Library, Needham Ms. A. 701, pp.7–8.
63 'Conversation on 21 May 1968,' Cambridge University Library, Needham Ms. A. 701, p.11.
64 Gregory Blue, 'Joseph Needham, Heterodox Marxism, and the Social Background to Chinese Science,' *Science and Society*, 62 (2) (Summer 1998): 200.
65 Henry Holorenshaw. 'The Making of an Honorary Taoist,' in Mikuláš Teich and Robert Young (eds), *Changing Perspectives in the History of Science: Essays in Honour of Joseph Needham* (Dordrecht/Boston: 1973), p.20.
66 'Conversation on 21 May 1968,' Cambridge University Library, Needham Ms. A. 701, pp.12–13.

Philosophy.' Patrick Blackett had been convinced by Hessen's point about the ways practical economic problems lay in the background to Newton's scientific revolution. Blackett had been wearied by histories of science that treated scientists as 'if they lived so to speak in a vacuum.'[67] Blackett was certainly not hermetically sealed. He had served in the Royal Navy before coming up to Magdalene College and the Cavendish. He had even voted for the Tories in the Khaki Election of 1918. At Cambridge he had belonged to the Heretics – consisting of people such as Roger Fry, Bertrand and Dora Russell, and also the astronomer and pacifist Arthur Eddington and the physicist John Cockcroft – who discussed religion, art and philosophy. (Cockcroft said they were non-religious but still respectable; of the Ten Commandments, like the Tripos, only six need to be attempted.) Like Bernal and Zuckerman, Blackett firmly held that science should be used for the improvement of society and, consequently, he was impressed by the Soviet achievement. Consequently, despite his service in both wars and the fact that he was more of a Fabian and never a communist, Blackett was suspect and was only fully appreciated once Labour came to power after 1945. Perhaps it is safe to conclude that the gesture towards Marxism and the aggressive intervention of the Soviet delegates at the Second International Congress on the History of Science was that it leavened the loaf and opened intellectual life in such a way as to blunt and modify British positivism by the expression of continental ideas. It was a gesture towards intellectual internationalisation and cosmopolitanism of the sort the Great War ripped apart. If the International Congress was one such moment in twentieth-century British intellectual life, the Kapitza affair was another.

When Bukharin visited Cambridge on the occasion of the second International Congress of the History of Science and Technology, Pyotr Kapitza (1894–1984), who hardly ever resisted the opportunity to jest, introduced him to the staid and somewhat reserved fellowship of Trinity College's High Table as 'Comrade Bukharin.'[68] It was an illustration of the complex and entangled system of loyalties of which Kapitza was a part. Kapitza was born in Kronstadt, the son of a general in the Tsar's engineering corps, and received his early education there. He then studied at the Petrograd Technological Institute. Feeling his scientific ambitions in revolutionary Russia were limited, Kapitza gained a visa to study at the Cavendish Laboratory and arrived in Britain in 1921. Rutherford, initially, resisted admitting him, claiming the laboratory was overcrowded. Kapitza got himself admitted with a small joke. He asked Rutherford what accuracy he aimed at in his experiments. When Rutherford said about 3 per cent Kapitza could point out that since there

[67] Mary Jo Nye, *Blackett: Physics, War, and Politics in the Twentieth Century* (Cambridge, Massachusetts/London: 2004), p.30.
[68] J. W. Boag, P. E. Rubinin and D. Shoenberg (eds), *Kapitza in Cambridge and Moscow: Life and Letters of a Russian Physicist* (Amsterdam/Oxford: 1990), p.38.

were thirty people doing research in the laboratory one more could not matter since it fell within the experimental error. Rutherford, always susceptible to Kapitza's capacity for irreverent flattery, allowed him in after admonishing him that there would be no talk about communism in the laboratory. As indicated in Chapter 1, Kapitza became quite a presence in Cambridge by forming and leading the Kapitza Club.

Rutherford and Kapitza were quite different kinds of physicists. Rutherford belonged to an older generation who, after an earlier education in New Zealand came to the Cavendish in the first tranches of students who had already taken their first degrees. Rutherford belonged to an earlier generation of positivist, Huxleyite, physicists for whom large objects (elephants and archbishops, Needham said) could be studied using limited materials and methods, sealing wax and string, as Rutherford modestly put it. He would have no talk of the universe, he said, in his laboratory. Yet Rutherford was able to show that the atom was not a solid mass, like a billiard ball, but was actually largely empty space with an extremely small but dense nucleus at the centre and with electrons moving about within the atom's volume. It got him the Nobel Prize and prepared the way for later generations to explore nuclear structures.

Kapitza's generation, consequently, could turn in more speculative directions. Kapitza belonged to the more mathematically theoretical society in Cambridge called the V^2V Club. He and his generation could explore the mysterious small objects in the guts of the atom, which required large engines of science that only industry could build. Kaptiza was in that first generation of scholars at Cambridge to gain the PhD degree. Rutherford encouraged Kapitza to stand for the Clerk Maxwell Studentship, which he got and which was tenurable for three years. He was elected to the fellowship of Trinity College in 1925 and in his welcoming address J. J. Thomson, the Master, paid specific attention to the fact that Kapitza was the first Russian to be so elected. He was elected to the Royal Society in 1929.

Though different, Rutherford and Kapitza grew quite fond of each other. Kapitza called Rutherford 'The Crocodile' because, perhaps, the crocodile was Kapitza's favourite animal, but perhaps, because when coming to the Cavendish Kapitza found Rutherford quite formidable and named him after the fiercest animal he could think of. For his part Rutherford lavished his patronage on Kapitza. He obtained a grant from the government's Department of Scientific and Industrial Research to purchase equipment for a magnetic research laboratory of which Rutherford was director and Kapitza the assistant director below him. As Kapitza wrote to his mother:

> Rutherford is really exceptionally good to me. On one occasion he was not in a good mood and told me I must economize. I showed him that I was doing everything very cheaply and in the end he couldn't deny it and said: 'Yes, yes,

that's all true, but it is part of my duty to talk to you like this, Bear in mind that I am spending more on your experiments than on all the other work of the laboratory put together.' And, you know, that is true, for our equipment fairly runs off with his pennies. Although everything is going well at present, it is always easy to blunder in a new field, so great care is needed and I, my dear, am still very young and inexperienced.[69]

In 1930 Kapitza convinced Rutherford to build a new laboratory within the Cavendish, which would house high-field equipment and also cryogenic facilities to conduct research at much lower temperatures. Rutherford, backed by John Cockcroft, got the Royal Society to stump up £15,000 for the new building with funds from the bequest of Ludwig Mond the German-born but naturalised chemist-industrialist. At the same time the Royal Society appointed Kapitza to its Messel professorship and Kapitza became the Mond's director. Stanley Baldwin, as the university's chancellor, opened the Mond Laboratory in 1933 with its large engraving of a crocodile by the modernist sculptor Eric Gill carved in the brickwork of its entry gate.

Kapitza, therefore, by 1934, was well entrenched in British intellectual and social life. He went even so far as to wonder whether a corresponding member of the Academy of Sciences could become a British peer. According to C. P. Snow, who had attended the Kapitza Club, Kapitza 'had the touch of the inspired Russian clown' and the impertinence of a Dostoevskian comedian.'[70] He loved Russia and England. He loved working in the Cavendish Laboratory and he loved spending his holidays on horseback in the Caucasus. Though never a member of the Communist Party, he thoroughly agreed with Soviet scientific and industrial policy plans. As he wrote to Rutherford:

> I would only like that everyone concerned should know first of all, I am and always was in sympathy with the work of the Soviet Government on the reconstruction of Russia, on the principle of socialism and I am prepared to do scientific work here.[71]

In the summer of 1934 Kapitza and he wife, Anna, were on holiday in the Soviet Union and were informed that she could return to Cambridge to care for their children but that he could not leave the country. Kapitza was crushed. As he wrote to his wife:

> My life is so empty now. Sometimes I rage and want to tear my hair and scream. With my ideas, my apparatus, in my laboratory, others live and work. And here I sit all alone. What for? I want to scream and break the furniture, and sometimes I think I am beginning to go mad.[72]

---

[69] Kapitza to his mother, 22 October 1922, in Boag, Rubinin and Shoenberg (eds), *Kapitza in Cambridge and Moscow*, pp.158–159.
[70] C. P. Snow, *Variety of Men* (New York: 1966), p.17.
[71] Kapitza to Rutherford, about 14 May 1933, in Boag, Rubinin and Shoenberg (eds), *Kapitza in Cambridge and Moscow*, p.268.
[72] Kapitza to his wife, 13 April 1935, in Boag, Rubinin and Shoenberg (eds), *Kapitza in*

He called Cambridge '[t]he lost Paradise.' Rutherford's letters to him reminded Kapitza of his happy years in the Cavendish.[73] He despaired of returning any time soon. As he wrote to J. J. Thomson:

> I am very sorry I shall be unable to enjoy any more the College and the intercourse with all of my friends there. I miss it already very much and probably will miss it in the future no less. During my life in Cambridge the privilege which I enjoyed and valued most was no doubt my connection with the College. Coming as a stranger to Cambridge, I was indebted to the College not only for facilities for work, a home and friends, but also for intercourse with people which stimulated my work. Through the College I learned to like English people and will now always feel toward England like my second home country. I should very much like you to transfer to the Fellows of the College 'good bye' and tell them how deeply I appreciated my relations with them and the College.[74]

Thomson read out the letter to the college council and had copies sent to all the fellows of the college.

Throughout the early months of his sequestration Kapitza's comrades in Britain worked quietly for his return to Cambridge. Ivan Maisky, the Soviet ambassador to the Court of St James, however, set out his government's position. In the Soviet Union, government planned the distribution of labour including the distribution of 'scientific workers.' Normally it was possible for the government to manage its scientific institutions with the supply of scientists available to it and so Kapitza could work abroad. However, with the successful completion of the First Five Year Plan and the initiation of the Second Five Year Plan more Soviet scientists were needed. Therefore, Kapitza was 'offered highly responsible work' and could 'develop fully his abilities as a scientist and a citizen of his country.'[75] Rutherford, as the then president of Royal Society, and Gowland Hopkins, his successor, tried to ease Kapitza out of the Soviet Union quietly and diplomatically to sooth Soviet sensibilities. As Rutherford wrote to the *Times* on 29 April 1935, reports from the Soviet Union reveal Kapitza's health had been put at risk by 'anxiety and disappointment.' Men of originality and imagination, like him, Rutherford said, require 'an atmosphere of complete mental tranquility in which to do creative work':

> It is to be feared that while the Soviet Government has acted within its legal rights, and no doubt with the best intentions, there has been a lack of appreciation of the effects of its sudden action. We may hope that the Soviet Government, which has given so many proofs of its interest in the developments of science, will pursue

---

Cambridge and Moscow, p.235.
73 Kapitza to Rutherford, 26 February to 2 March 1936, in Boag, Rubinin and Shoenberg (eds), *Kapitza in Cambridge and Moscow*, p.279.
74 Kapitza to J. J. Thomson, 23 November 1935, in Boag, Rubinin and Shoenbert (eds), *Kapitza in Cambridge and Moscow*, p.275.
75 Maisky to Rutherford, 30 October 1934, in Lawrence Badash, *Kapitza, Rutherford, and the Kremlin* (Newhaven/London: Yale: 1985), pp.20–21.

a generous and long-sighted policy, and will see the way to meet the wishes of scientific men, not only of this country, but throughout the world, by enabling Kapitza to choose an environment in which he can most effectively utilize the special creative gifts with which he is endowed. It would be a tragedy if these gifts were rendered sterile by failure to grasp the psychological situation.[76]

Gowland Hopkins followed with a letter to the *Times* on 1 May 1935 pleading with the Soviet government to 'recognize the internationalism of science by allowing labours so well begun to continue where they can most rapidly progress.'[77]

Edgar Adrian, who was attending a physiological conference in the Soviet Union, and Paul Dirac, who was on a world tour, visited Kapitza and worked out arrangements that would enable Kapitza to continue his work in the Soviet Union. The Soviet government should pay out between £30,000 and £50,000 to compensate the university and the Royal Society for their support of Kapitza's work in the Cavendish. This sum was to be divided between Cambridge University and the Royal Society with no less than 12 per cent going to Trinity College. All of Kaptiza's apparatus, or duplicates, in the Mond Laboratory should be sent to the Soviet Union. Kapitza's assistants, while being guaranteed their positions and pension in Cambridge, should be seconded to the Soviet Union for three or four years to assist him in the reorganisation of his research. Kapitza wished to retain his Royal Society professorship and to obtain an equivalent professorship in the Soviet Union, in return for which he hoped to return to Britain and give a course of lectures there.[78] By November 1935 the complex negotiations between Rutherford, the university, the Royal Society and the Soviet authorities were completed, giving Kapitza almost everything he required (save the Royal Society professorship) to start his research anew in the Soviet Union. Kapitza was at last allowed to visit Britain in 1966 when he met for the final meeting of the Kapitza Club with David Shoenberg, John Cockcroft and Paul Dirac in the Senior Combination Room at Caius College.

The Great War, and the episodes surrounding the question of the loyalty of the Schuster family, the later Soviet intrusion into the sessions of the International Congress on the History of Science in 1931, and the Kapitza affair reveal some of the ways political and ideological elements affected knowledge's autonomy and sovereignty. Such elements also disrupted the concept of the internationality of knowledge of the sort Humphrey Davy enjoyed and A. V. Hill continued to hope for. The Great War, if nothing else, pulled people from mental life into other forms of public activity, some of them political, some of them military, and some of them into alternative forms of service.

[76] Rutherford to the *Times* printed as an appendix in Badash, *Kapitza, Rutherford, and the Kremlin*, p.120.
[77] Gowland Hopkins to the *Times* printed as an appendix in Badash, *Kapitza, Rutherford, and the Kremlin*, p.121.
[78] Report of Edgar Adrian to Rutherford, August 1935, in Boag, Rubinin and Shoenberg (eds), *Kapitza in Cambridge and Moscow*, pp.267–269.

To take Cambridge alone: J. H. Clapham was at the Board of Trade; Keynes was in the Treasury; Harold Temperley was a captain in the Fife and Forfar Yeomanry; James Butler served in the Scottish Horse; A. C. Pigou drove ambulances; D. H. Roberson was decorated for fighting in the Middle East; J. E. Littlewood was a lieutenant in the Royal Garrison Artillery; Donald Beves was chief instructor at the Central School of Drill; H. A. Holland was Deputy Assistant Adjutant-General in Haig's Headquarters; John Sheppard was Deputy Assistant Censor; F. E. Adcock was in Room 40 of naval intelligence. A few stayed behind in lonely isolation: Frazer and Housman at Trinity; Arthur Quiller-Couch at Jesus; E. J. Jepson, the Sanskritist, at St John's.[79] In the Second World War Asa Briggs and his wife were at Bletchley, as were Christopher Morris and his wife Helen. A similar list, no doubt, could be pulled up for Oxford.[80] The war not only distracted this long lot from learning it also shaped how they thought and felt in the interwar years, as the case of Keynes's *Economic Consequences of the Peace* shows.

It was with feelings of dread that the next war loomed. On 28 August 1939 Roger Hinks sat with friends in his father's garden and brooded not only on what the future might bring but also what they were losing from the past. They had been enthusiastic and sympathetic students of German culture and they had many German friends. It was difficult for them to conceive that shortly they would be called upon to engage in a total struggle to destroy what they had treasured. '[T]here is a distasteful flavor of unreality of the whole affair,' Hinks wrote. The moment required Hinks to consider what he would 'fight to the last gasp to defend.' He could not justify his actions by simply believing that he loved the Germans but hated only the Nazis. It would not be enough to destroy Nazi tyranny and militarism. '[T]he competitiveness and greed and exploitation of the imperial power must be destroyed also before the world can have peace.' Economic forms, Hinks thought, 'must necessarily be a mixed one – tended, no doubt toward socialization, but retaining the elasticity and flexibility of the individual system.'[81]

The brooding of Hinks and his friends expose a tension – the structures of 'socialisation' as over against the desire for the individual system's 'elasticity and flexibility' – which would affect the formation and organisation of knowledge in the twentieth century. In the nineteenth century the support and patronage of research and learning had been largely informal and personal as in the Duke of Devonshire's foundation of the Cavendish Laboratory and his establishment of the professorship of experimental physics, and as in the support for archaeological research by small private dining societies, such as the Dilettanti. In the twentieth century the support for research and learning

79 T. E. B. Howarth, *Cambridge Between Two Wars* (London: 1978), pp.26–27.
80 Christopher Hollis, *Oxford in the Twenties: Recollections of Five Friends* (London: 1976).
81 Princeton University Library, CO369, Hinks Diary 1/5/28/ff. 72, 78–79.

such as the Royal Society, the British Academy and the universities looked to government and philanthropic foundations. These interventions would both provide costs and benefits by the tensions created as those more rigid structures imposed themselves upon more elastic and flexible practices. These interventions, as one historian of twentieth-century patronage systems has put it, 'has meant a more complex social relationship with extramural sponsors, whose institutional values and agendas are not quite the same as the values and agendas of their clients.'[82] This has produced a number of consequences: resources flooded into communities of learning; epistemological edges became blurred when funds became available to support investigations into problems that no single discipline or department could claim to own; since some of these foundation patrons were Americans it served, to reinternationalise knowledge in a spirit that Davy and Hill might have wished.

Intellectual interests, even if cast into academic disciplines, are, after all, liminal boundary areas, mental trading zones, regions of exchange and negotiation. In this terrain multiple intellectual loyalties became entangled in the processes of the formation, organisation and reorganisation of knowledge. Positivism, Huxley's programme of observation, measurement, classification and comparison, was a defensive means, a series of mental procedures, to defend those intellectual actions and agents designed to fill the social space that had been left vacant when traditional *ancien régime* practices had to be evacuated. Positivism ('scientism','objectivism', the aping of the epistemologies of the natural sciences) was a highly successful series of mental procedures for creating the social identity of the 'expert' who became a public figure, what used to be called the 'man of affairs.'[83] It also produced, or reflected, a different form of intellectual legitimacy in which professionals derived their authority from the judgement of their peers on the basis of specialist criticism rather than from divine revelation or from force and coercion. As the historian of the professional society has put it, the twentieth century was not 'the century of the common man but of the uncommon and increasingly expert professional expert.'[84] The professional ideology, or idea, manifested itself in a way of life.[85] A colonial administrator in Lord Cromer's Sudan's Political Service described how self-reliance, the acceptance of responsibility, self-discipline and physical

[82] Robert E. Kohler, *Partners in Science: Foundations and Natural Scientists, 1900–1945* (Chicago/London: 1991), p.1.

[83] See Joel Isaac, 'Tangled Loops: Theory, History, and the Human Sciences in Modern America,' *Modern Intellectual History*, 6 (2) (2009): 397.

[84] Perkin, *The Rise of Professional Society: England Since 1880*, p.2.

[85] Burton J. Bledstein, *The Culture of Professionalism: The Middle Class and the Development of Higher Education in America* (New York: 1976). For a classic statement of the issue see Max Weber, 'Science as a Vocation,' in H. H. Gerth and C. Wright Mills (eds), *From Max Weber: Essays in Sociology*, pp.129–156. For a more recent statement of the issue see Steven Shapin, *The Scientific Life: A Moral History of a Late Modern Vocation* (Chicago/London: 2008), pp.1–46.

fitness were all aspects of his life and work.[86] Professionals marshalled these values and projected them, especially among those who were to promote what became the social, or human sciences, into linear programing, computational methodologies, rational choice theories, operations research, game theory, systems theory, and area studies.

However, since the professional ideology was a defence against the feelings of loneliness of living in a moral vacuum, it was also a fantasy. Positivism and the professional ideology were a projection of linearity, a Whig interpretation of history's search for progress and development. A moral vacuum cannot be filled by an illusion. Animated by defensiveness, in seeking legitimacy, authority and public recognition, these knowledge communities compromised and distorted research and inflicted an intellectual (and moral?) wound upon themselves. By entangling themselves with politics, government, philanthropy and war they threatened free inquiry, and the autonomy, integrity, independence and sovereignty of knowledge. They sought unity, universality and commensurability, and in attempting to become valuable they became vulnerable. This vulnerability, however, exposed different possibilities. Medawar's effort to get Popper elected to the Royal Society, Popper's confrontation with Wittgenstein in the Moral Sciences Club, Needham's search for the Organiser, the Kapitza affair, and the Warburg method (all of these continental interventions) all illustrate the necessity to qualify positivism's blunt force.

As Patrick Blackett concluded, 'an exact mathematical solution to any problem in physics is never required, but the object of the solution is to compare it with measured quantities and these can never be exact.' Intuitive judgement is valuable because the experimenter 'has a practical knowledge of the orders of magnitude of the various factors involved and so can judge immediately which have to be taken into account and which can be neglected.'[87] The recognition of the importance of intuition and imagination raised the possibility of introducing a hermeneutic element into studies that might be considered both *Naturwissenschaftem* and *Geisteswissenschaften*, what Dilthey had regarded as nomothetic and ideographic. Very much later Geertz called for an ethnography of knowledge that would be fuelled by an interpretative approach. That is, knowledge would have to be understood in terms of its informing environment, in terms of the activities that sustain it. Such an ethnography would produce incommensurabilities and this, in turn, Geertz realised, would raise intellectuals' *Grande Peur*: relativism.[88]

---

[86] Quoted in Perkin, *The Rise of Professional Society*, p.371.
[87] P. M. S. Blackett, 'The Craft of Experimental Physics,' in Harold Wright (ed.), *University Studies, Cambridge, 1933* (London: 1993), pp.89–90.
[88] Clifford Geertz, *Local Knowledge: Further Essays in Interpretive Anthropology* (New York: 1983), pp.147–166, esp. 152–153.

However, Karl Mannheim had anticipated this reservation. Mannheim (1893–1947), born in Hungary to Jewish assimilationist parents, took his PhD studying Kantian epistemology. He was displaced, geographically and mentally, several times. He fled Budapest after the fall of the revolutionary government there in 1919, went to Heidelberg, then Frankfurt, and found a place at the LSE in London. Early on he developed an interest in mysticism rather than physics and chemistry as a way of finding psychological orientation in the midst of the social and intellectual chaos after the Great War. He became convinced that the nomothetic and ideographic spheres could not meet and became committed to the view that cultural and historical approaches, rather than positivism, were more useful in facing the political and intellectual crises of the 1930s. He took this as a moral and political obligation.[89] Research, he held, was not an isolated act but occurs in an environment 'coloured by values and collective-unconscious, volitional impulses.' By bringing this mental environment into the 'area of conscious and explicit observation' a 'new type of objectivity' could be attained 'not through the exclusion of evaluations but through the critical awareness and control of them.'[90] In this way he offered a means of escaping the clutches of positivism's narrowness and, because there are criteria for finding correctness and incorrectness in intellectual disputes, and because it is possible to achieve decisions in factual disputes, he escaped the charge of being a relativist.[91]

At about the same time Sir James Jeans (1877–1946), the mathematician, theoretical physicist and astronomer, in a chapter called 'Into Deep Waters' of his book *The Mysterious Universe* (1930), rejected the notion of a universe planned by a biologist or engineer. '[F]rom the intrinsic evidence of his creation, the Great Architect of the Universe now appears to appear as a pure mathematician.' The terrestrial pure mathematician is not concerned with 'material substance, but with pure thought.' The terrestrial mathematician's creations 'are not only created by thought but consist of thought.'[92] Sir Roger Penrose (b.1931), the mathematical physicist, FRS and OM who had been the Rouse Ball Professor of Mathematics at Oxford, more recently wondered if the methods that had proved successful in understanding physical behaviour could address the question of human consciousness.[93] In his *Emperor's New Mind* (1989) and other writings, Penrose dismissed the notion that science is what can be put on a computer. He recognised that modern physical theory

[89]   David Kaiser, 'A Mannheim for All Seasons: Bloor, Merton, and the Roots of the Sociology of Scientific Knowledge,' *Science in Context*, 11 (1) (1998): 52–53.
[90]   Mannheim, *Ideology and Utopia: An Introduction to the Sociology of Knowledge*, p.5.
[91]   See David Bloor, 'Wittgenstein and Mannheim on the Sociology of Mathematics,' *Studies in the History and Philosophy of Mathematics*, 4 (2) (1973): 175–176, n. 9.
[92]   James Jeans, *The Mysterious Universe* (Cambridge: 1930), pp.134–135.
[93]   Roger Penrose, 'Science and the Mind,' in *Roger Penrose, Collected Works, Volume 6, 1997–2003* (Oxford: 2011), p.162.

is 'a bit strange' because it consists of two scales of phenomena that cannot be deduced from each other. 'I felt,' he wrote, 'that there must be something noncomputational going on in our thought processes.' 'I believed,' he went on, 'that you have to understand our thinking processes in terms of science in some way [but] it doesn't have to be a science that we understand now.'[94]

Such unsettled and unsteady epistemic impulses were fostered, in part, by the funding of philanthropic institutions. In this, US resources played an important role and penetrated global learning. In the first quarter of the twentieth century John D. Rockefeller's and Andrew Carnegie's families established seven foundations for advancing knowledge: the Rockefeller Institute (1901), the Carnegie Institution of Washington (1902), the General Education Board (1902), the Carnegie Corporation of New York (1911), the Rockefeller Foundation (1913), the Laura Spelman Rockefeller Memorial (1918) and the International Education Board (1923). These foundations penetrated the world of learning through means that were formal, impersonal and bureaucratic. Their functioning was rather in contrast to the more personal actions such as those of the Duke of Devonshire. (Though some of Andrew Carnegie's philanthropy was more personal as, for example, when he purchased Lord Acton's library and then lent it back to use in Acton's lifetime before he bequeathed it to John Morley, who sent it to its final resting place in the Cambridge University Library.[95]) Though less informal, the management of these philanthropic foundations was complicated as attested by the case of the estate of Sir William Dunn, Bt (1833–1912).

Dunn was born in Paisley but emigrated to South Africa where he accumulated a vast fortune valued at £1.3 million at his death. Dunn returned to London where he entered the world of banking and sat as a Liberal for Paisley from 1895 to 1906. His will commanded that half of his fortune should be used to found the Dunn Chair of New Testament Theology at Westminster College, Cambridge. The remainder was to be settled by the trustees of the Dunn Estate. Before the Great War they scattered its benefactions: £70,000 to fifty-two hospitals; £20,000 to institutions in Paisley; £6,500 to fifteen nursing homes; £20,000 to twenty-three orphanages; £105,000 to the Salvation Army. After the war the trustees made its benefactions in a more directed manner: £25,000 for a readership in pathology at Guy's Hospital; £103,000 for the Dunn Institute of Pathology at Oxford; and £210,000 for a professorship for Gowland Hopkins and the Dunn Institute of Biochemistry at Cambridge.[96] Walter Morley Fletcher guided this dispersal with his concept of patronage.[97]

---

94 Roger Penrose, 'Consciousness Involves Noncomputational Ingredients,' in *Roger Penrose, Collected Works, volume 5, 1990–1996* (Oxford: 2011), pp.595–598.
95 Roland Hill, *Lord Acton* (New Haven/London: 2000), pp.168, 288–289. 291–292.
96 Robert Kohler, 'Walter Fletcher, F. G. Hopkins, and the Dunn Institute of Biochemistry: A Case Study in the Patronage of Science,' *Isis*, 69 (3) (September 1978): 340.
97 Fletcher, Walter Morley (1873–1933): ed. Liverpool School; University College,

Fletcher's parents were Yorkshire Congregationalists and they seemed to have passed on to their son both a non-conformist independence and a sensitivity to art and culture.[98] After an early education in Liverpool and London he matriculated at Trinity College, Cambridge and entrenched himself in college and university life as an athletics 'blue' and as president of the Pitt Club. Placed in the first class of both parts I and II of the Natural Science Tripos, he was elected a fellow of his college and became a tutor, and senior demonstrator in Physiology. A. V. Hill was one of his pupils. Fletcher was deeply enmeshed in Cambridge life and even after going down to London to be Secretary of the Medical Research Council he remained a member of The Family, one of Cambridge's oldest dining societies. As he wrote to J. J. Thomson in 1932, 'I fully counted upon giving myself the pleasure of meeting the "Family" with you on Friday but I fell yesterday into the hands of my dentist,' who extracted a tooth and advised Fletcher to rest for a day or two.[99]

G. M. Trevelyan never regarded Fletcher as a narrow technician. Trevelyan claimed to have belonged to an 'intellectual set' (Trevelyan was an Apostle), which was by no means 'decadent,' but was 'intellectual in too narrow a way':[100]

[I]t was my occasional contacts with [Fletcher] in those undergraduate days that first gave me an idea how life might be enlarged into something more jolly, more all-embracing, in every sense more out-of-doors, but not for that less inspired and guided by intellect.

Fletcher and Trevelyan found that they shared a care for the 'best things in poetry, literature, [and] history.' Fletcher brought to cross-country walking the 'appreciation [of] the natural ardour of his spirit.' Trevelyan thought Fletcher combined the ideals of both Puritan and Cavalier. From his Puritan bedrock he took his seriousness for college, university and public affairs. From his Cavalier spirit he took his enjoyment of life. 'He was impatient

---

London; Trinity College, Cambridge, Athletics 'Blue' (1892), First Class in the Natural Science Tripos, Part I (1894), First Class in the Natural Science Tripos Part II (1895), MA (1898); MB (1900); MD (1908); ScD (1914); fellow of Trinity and Tutor 1897); Senior Demonstrator in Physiology (1903); Proctor (1904); Secretary of the Medical Research Council (later Committee) (1914); member of the Royal Commission on Universities of Oxford and Cambridge (1919–1922); FRS (1915); KBE (1918): CB (1929); Hon. Freeman, Society of Apothecaries.

98 [T. R. Elliot], 'Walter Morley Fletcher, 1873–1933,' *Obituary Notices of Fellows of the Royal Society*, 1 (1934): 153–163; Maisie Fletcher, *The Bright Countenance: A Personal Biography of Walter Morley Fletcher* (London: 1957).

99 Walter Fletcher to J. J. Thomson, 9 November 1932, Trinity College, Cambridge, J. J. Thomson Ms. C. 75/28-29. For The Family see Lubenow, *'Only Connect': Learned Societies in Nineteenth-Century Britain*, pp.43–44.

100 For Trevelyan's memories of Fletcher see *Memorial to the Late Sir Walter Morley Fletcher, KBE, MD, ScD, FRCP, FRS (1873–1933), Secretary to the Medical Research Committee and Council, 1914–1933* (Printed for the Memorial Fund by the University Press, Oxford, 1937), esp. pp.7–12.

of people who missed the opportunities of enjoying whatever was worth seeing, doing, reading, hearing.' Fletcher, Trevelyan thought, brought to these pleasures and interests 'the discipline and power of his mind.' His talk of prints, wine and antiquarianism (he was a constant companion of Monte James) was littered with 'accurate information.' Fletcher's favourite sport of deerstalking 'was a discipline and a science, with the poetry of great mountain spaces added.' Though he was president of the Pitt Club, whose principles of entry were hardly proletarian, Trevelyan thought Fletcher was 'essentially a Liberal in Mind.'

Trevelyan thought it was this cast of mind that Fletcher took to his work as Secretary of the Medical Research Council. The besetting sin of British government, Fletcher thought, was the separation of the life of learning from the world of political action. Fletcher believed, Trevelyan thought, 'every branch of statecraft required a full use of biological science' in order to raise the nation's health in body and mind. So he bent his energies in London to work with Fletcher Moulton (Lord Moulton of Bank), the first chairman of the Medical Research Council, Sir Robert Morant and Arthur Balfour, as Lord President of the Privy Council.[101] Fletcher sought to keep the work of the council 'scientific' and always 'in constant touch with the Royal Society and the best scientific minds.' He never regarded the council as merely a political or administrative department of the state. He thought its chairman should always sit in the House of Lords to keep a connection between learning and politics. This, he realised, would be difficult. As he wrote to Balfour:

> Our chief difficulty lies in the fact that very few peers have any scientific education, such, for instance, to enable them to know what research work is really like, or to know the difference between a scientific worker in medicine and a Harley Street physician or surgeon (British science is the only British activity left quite unrepresented in the House of Lords, except by the happy accident of Robin Strutt being there.)[102]

The political and intellectual environment in which Fletcher worked was, as Gowland Hopkins recognised, extremely complex. As Gowland Hopkins pointed out, Fletcher was at home in political, official, intellectual and social

---

[101] Walter Fletcher to Arthur Balfour, 1 November 1922, Balfour Papers, BL., Add. Ms 49753, f. 1. Balfour was typically modest. 'I have taken the profoundest interest in the work of your Board, but, alas, I cannot flatter myself that I have done much to further its successes. The truth is that my schemes in this connection were perpetually interfered with by my Missions abroad. Administrative work at home, however, severe, would not have been a complete bar to a sympathetic participation in your labours; but separation in space was fatal.' Balfour to Fletcher, 3 November 1922, Balfour Papers, BL., Add. Ms. 49753, f. 2.
[102] Walter Fletcher to Arthur Balfour, 24 November 1924, Balfour Papers, BL., Add. Ms 49753, f. 3. Strutt was the fourth Lord Rayleigh.

circles. In these 'he was welcome and from all or from most he gained sympathy for the objects he had at heart.'[103]

With his university connections (he was a member of the Asquith Commission on Oxford and Cambridge), his personal ties with Trinity College, his association with The Family, his wide intellectual interests, and from his perch in London, Fletcher could negotiate the complex and complicated relationships between intellectual and political life. Fletcher was alert to the ways traditional that social loyalties resisted intellectual penetration into public affairs:

> The families with the best resources, and so with the greatest responsibilities for leadership, and I speak here from former years of experience as a College don, have not in general thought it [as] even quite respectable for their sons to turn from the old traditional employments, namely family succession, the Church, the Army, or the Bar, – and to these has most recently been added the City or Commerce – to the new avenues of public [service] in science to be found, for instance, in medical or agricultural research. [Young men] are very sensitive to atmosphere and they are not easily drawn towards work if the best of the world as they know it appears to neither value it nor trust it. It is only one of our two ancient Universities – the two eyes of the English mind – is original research work, as such, the regular and normal avenue to recognition and promotion, – a circumstance bringing a clear partial wastage of a great heritance of prestige and endowment.

Lord Lister, he pointed out, was the only distinguished biologist who had been elevated to a peerage. In India, whose medical and agricultural problems to which Fletcher had become sensitive after travel there, the Viceroy's Council was composed of experts responsible for the military, the law, for commerce and finance but 'the only voice speaking for all the most primary natural needs of India has always been a man unversed altogether in the realities of scientific or the technicalities of natural knowledge.' Though he wished to harness the 'technicalities of natural knowledge' to public affairs, Fletcher, as Trevelyan's remarks attest, was no narrow positivist. The 'true worker in natural science,' he wrote, can be obedient to no knowledge 'however venerable' unless it is a truth 'that can be tested by the touchstone of an appeal to nature.' He cited the phrase from Horace (which the Royal Society shortened as its motto): *nullius additctus jurare in verba magistri*. Members of such a community 'must put in the first place not the material fruits that spring from it, but the service it does for our reverence of truth and for the beauty it portrays.'[104]

As previously noted, it was Fletcher's variously entangled loyalties that suited him to lead the Medical Research Council's patronage of biomedical research. Since he was a respected authority on biomedical policy the Dunn

---

[103] *Memorial to the Late Sir Walter Morley Fletcher*, pp.25–26.
[104] Walter Fletcher, *Medical Research: The Tree and the Fruit*, the Fifth Annual Norman Lockyer Lecture (London: 1929), pp.23–24. 27.

Trustees could rely on his advice from 1918 to 1920, precisely at the time after the ending of the war when the relations between various institutions and patrons were sorting out their relations. He was able to preserve the independence of biochemistry within the basic biomedical sciences rather than being shunted off into chemistry, agriculture or medicine. Because of his role as a panjandrum of biomedical science he could guide the funding of biochemists according to the criteria of basic biochemical science. Because of Fletcher's influence among the Dunn Estate Trustees, Hopkins and the Dunn Institute at Cambridge had an independent intellectual authority rather than being attached to a department of state such as the Department of Scientific and Industrial Research or the Ministry of Health.[105] It allowed Gowland Hopkins and the Dunn Institute to escape the narrow confines of existing disciplinary trammels and find a broader mental space to create a different intellectual field.

Learning's international engagement with philanthropic foundations can be illustrated by the benefactions of John D. Rockefeller's family. It established the International Education Board, which, guided by Wycliffe Rose, funded European scientific institutions and fellowships for European and American scholars. Such funds provided for the expansion of Niels Bohr's Institute for Theoretical Physics at the University of Copenhagen and for substantial sums for mathematics and theoretical physics at the universities of Göttingen, Leiden and Paris. As a consequence, many Europeans studied in the United States and as many Americans studied in Europe. Tellingly, many of the former were theoreticians and many of the latter were experimentalists.[106] This funding brought with it an important epistemic element: a complication of the latent positivism of British learning.

Fletcher's style led to a modest form of bureaucratic management. Others, however, such as Warren Weaver acting for the Rockefeller Foundation in the United States, invented a more formal social role that has been called the 'manager of science.' While this did not imply detailed supervision of intellectual investigation, it was an executive role having to do with the formulation of policy and oversight on a large scale. Managers of this sort selected projects according to preconceived plans, advanced schemes of investigation derived from those plans, and identified researchers to conduct them. They set priorities, identified weak points to be strengthened, and pointed to opportunities and directions for future growth. This was all a part of the projects of the Progressive Era, which sought to develop a vision of a 'well-managed society.'[107] Such a project did not quiet slumbering conflicts.

105 Kohler, 'Walter Fletcher, F. G. Hopkins, and the Dunn Institute of Biochemistry': 340, 352.
106 Stanley Cohen, 'The Scientific Establishment and the Transmission of Quantum Mechanics in the United States, 1919–1932,' *American Historical Review*, 76 (2) (April 1971): 448–450.
107 See Robert Kohler, 'The Management of Science: The Experience of Warren Weaver

Raymond Fosdick's concept of the advancement of knowledge, for example, was at odds with the stated objective of the Rockefeller Foundation's concern to apply knowledge for social improvement. Some wondered whether the university was a suitable place for the foundation's benefactions. As has been shown in Chapter 3, the Rockefeller Foundation was reluctant to support the proposed Institute for Mathematico-Physico-Chemical Morphology at Cambridge because they were sceptical of the capacity of the university to manage its government.[108] Yet, managers such as Warren Weaver advanced what has been called a 'reductionist programme,' that is schemes to apply physical and chemical approaches to biology or psychology. Weaver might not have adopted a whole-hogging view favouring a search for laws of living matter, but he believed biology was a body of studies whose potential was limited by inadequate methods and processes to acquire a knowledge of what he called 'vital processes.'[109]

While one might admire such efforts to use knowledge for human improvement, foundation management and bureaucratic decision-making had a narrowing effect on knowledge formation. As Raymond Fosdick, unabashedly, advised the officers of the Rockefeller Foundation:

> [W]e should avoid research for the sake of research without regard to its relevance. Moreover, there should be no exclusive interest in research as an end and aim. Indeed, we would strongly advocate a shift of emphasis not only of the dissemination of knowledge, but on the practical application of knowledge in fields where human need is great and opportunity is real. As a means of advancing knowledge, application can be as effective an instrument as research.[110]

The deployment of such knowledge could serve as a moral stabiliser. As one scholar has put it, such an approach could 'develop the scientific spirit' with high moral ideas and develop strength of character.[111] One effect of this view was the narrowing of research schemes to short-term projects that could achieve more immediate results at the expense of longer-term projects whose results might only be achieved much later, or never.

Consequently, critics of this approach for practical social applications regarded the life of research as a form of high culture whose charisma could not and should not be planned or managed. Simon Flexner, as Director, conducted the Rockefeller Institute as a centre of intellectual individualism.

---

and the Rockefeller Foundation Programme in Molecular Biology,' *Minerva*, 14 (3) (Autumn 1976): 279–306, esp. 279–280.
[108] See also Pnina Abir-Am, 'The Discourse of Physical Power and Biological Knowledge in the 1930s: A Reappraisal of the Rockefeller Foundation's Policy in Molecular Biology,' *Social Studies of Science*, 12 (3) (August 1982): 341–382.
[109] Kohler, 'The Management of Science': 287.
[110] Quoted in Kohler, 'The Management of Science': 293.
[111] Frank Ninkovich, 'The Rockefeller Foundation,' *Journal of American History*, 70 (4) (March 1984): 801.

Abraham Flexner, his brother, founded the Institute of Advanced Study. It was he who convinced Louis Bamberger and his sister, Caroline Bamberger Fuld, to deploy the large fortune they had gained from their sale of the Bamberger department store in Newark, to the Macys, into an institute devoted to unrestricted scholarship rather than, as they had planned, a medical school. As Abraham Flexner expressed it, the great discoveries, such as those of James Clerk Maxwell, were achieved by people who 'were driven not by the desire to be useful but by merely the desire to satisfy their curiosity.' 'The real enemy of the human race,' he went on to argue, is the person 'who tries to mold the human spirit so that it will not dare to spread its wings.'[112]

What emerged from competing aims – the desire for socially useful applications as against the concept of learning as an autonomous high culture – was a rich and complex system having at least two patterns. There was the development of a series of cooperative and complementary impulses across and between disciplines. It enabled the emergence of more specialised concepts and techniques within disciplines. As one scholar has observed, '[a] healthy academic ecosystem needs both strong disciplines and strong support for work that builds bridges among them.'[113] While rich, such a system was unstable as the established knowledge forms, sometimes, sentimentalised their 'Newtonism' and their claims of a more rigorous empiricism. Other, more aspirational forms of knowledge, tried to find their 'Newton' and were tempted to shuck off more qualitative and normative analytical forms by aping the methods of *Naturwissenschaften*.[114]

Because these forms of learning were conceived of as having both an intrinsic interest and having a public importance, concepts of accountability, including, very importantly, peer reviewing, increasingly emerged. The peer review served as a device for attempting to stabilise the entangled relationships that had emerged in the twentieth-century world of learning. Some scholars have traced the origins of the peer review back to the seventeenth century: the *Journal des Sçavans* in January 1665 and the *Philosophical Transactions* of the Royal Society under the direction of Henry Oldenburg, one of the two secretaries of the society, in March 1665. The *Philosophical Transactions* was conceived of as a device for the facilitation of communications among the *virtuousi*. It also was a means for protecting intellectual property rights and establishing the priority of discovery by recording the date the Royal Society received intellectual communications. By long tradition papers were

---

[112] Abraham Flexner, *The Usefulness of Useless Knowledge*, with a companion essay by Robbert Dijkgraaf (Princeton/London: 2017 [1939]), pp.56, 78.
[113] See, for example, Hunter Crowther-Heyck, 'Patrons of the Revolution: Ideals and Institutions in Postwar Behavioral Science,' *Isis*, 97 (3) (September 2006): 420–446, 422, 446.; *idem*, 'The Organizational Revolution and the Human Sciences,' *Isis*, 105 (2014): 1–31.
[114] Mark Solovey, *Shaky Foundations: The Politics–Patronage–Social Science Nexus in Cold War America* (New Brunswick/London: 2013), pp.4 ff.

communicated through a fellow who served as an insurer and sponsor to certify the quality of the submission. Increasing specialisation and increasing number of submissions complicated the process so severely that in 1967 the Council of the Royal Society authorised the appointment of twelve associate editors to the Secretaries to help manage the reviewing process.[115]

The process of peer refereeing proceeded neither uniformly nor linearly. For no little time the editors of journals, perhaps consulting trusted advisers, had acted on the basis of personal dictate in making decisions as to which submissions were worthy of publication. William Whewell, who had coined the neologism 'scientist', proposed that the Royal Society establish a commission to report on all papers submitted for publication. His proposal's object, modelled as it was on the example of the French Academy of Sciences, sought as much to acquire increased public visibility for the Royal Society as it was to protect the legitimacy of its decisions through the separation of dross from gold.[116] Yet through the nineteenth century, and into the twentieth, referee reports were considered optional and only in the later part of the latter century were they considered central to the legitimacy of intellectual life. The Watson-Crick communication to *Nature* on the structure of DNA was not even sent out for peer review and it was not until the 1960s that papers submitted to *Physical Review* were subject to scrutiny by external reviewers.[117] Even then the peer reviewing process varied greatly among intellectual disciplines. A study of the rejection rates of various scholarly journals in 1967 revealed average rejections ranged from 90 per cent to 20 per cent. The highest rejection rates were among historical journals (90 per cent), journals concerned with language of literature (86 per cent), philosophy journals (85 per cent), political science journals (84 per cent) and journals of sociology (78 per cent). The lowest rejection rates were in journals dealing with chemistry (31 per cent), the biological sciences (29 per cent), physics (24 per cent), geology (22 per cent) and linguistics (20 per cent).[118]

Such figures can be interpreted in more than one way. They might be said to reveal greater scholarly scrupulousness in history, literature, philosophy, political science and sociology as compared to chemistry, biology, physics and linguistics. Such an interpretation seems dubious. Rather, it might be said, having found their Newtons, there is probably greater agreement about what

[115] Harriet Zuckerman and Robert K. Merton, 'Patterns of Evaluation in Science: Institutionalization, Structure and Functions of the Referee System', *Minerva*, 9 (1) (January 1971): 68–69, 70; Peter Collins, *The Royal Society and the Promotion of Science Since 1960* (Cambridge: 2016), pp.251–252.

[116] Alex Csiszar. 'Peer Review: Troubled from the Start', *Nature* (19 April 2015); idem., *The Scientific Journal: Authorship and the Politics of Knowledge in the Nineteeth Century* (Chicago/London: 2018), pp.142–148.

[117] Melinda Baldwin, 'Scientific Autonomy, Public Accountability and the Rise of "Peer Review" in the Cold War United States', *Isis*, 109 (3) (2018): 538–558, esp. 542.

[118] Zuckerman and Merton, 'Patterns of Evaluation in Science: Functions of the Referee System': 76.

constituted proper scholarly criteria among chemists, biologists, physicists and linguists than among historians, scholars of literature, political scientists and sociologists who are still seeking their Newtons. There is another side to this. The greater looseness of what might be regarded as the proper scholarly criteria in history, philosophy, political science and sociology may open opportunities for greater charismatic creativity; the greater tightness of what might be regarded as proper scholarly criteria in chemistry, physics, biology and linguistics may open opportunities for greater certainty. However, there is some risk to this last possibility. It may introduce what one scholar has called 'commensuration bias' in which distinct epistemic qualities – accuracy, scope and fruitfulness, for example – are converted, perhaps unconsciously, or by institutional habit over multiple hierarchical levels, into a single metric. If novelty, for example, becomes considered as too lightly weighted, potentially transformative insights might be neglected or ignored. The practice of giving greater priority to some reviewing criteria in the aggregate as over against others can obstruct the very aims of research.[119] The claims for authority and legitimacy are transforming knowledges' territory as intellectual communities are enlarged and take on a global rather than a national character. The possibilities of open access create opportunities for wider dissemination of research work, to include reports that have not been reviewed by peers and might not have even been normally published at all. The fruits of these changes in peer-reviewing processes can only be guessed at.[120]

To conclude then, the incidents registered in this chapter – the disruptions of intellectual international sympathies during the Great War, the intervention of Soviet scholars at the meeting of the International Conference on the History and Philosophy of Science, the sequestration of Kapitza in the Soviet Union in the 1930s, the intervention of philanthropic funding of the sort managed by Walter Fletcher and representatives of the Rockefeller Foundation – illustrate the epistemological unsteadiness of knowledge's sovereignty. These entangled loyalties reveal the continued aspirational nature of the learned life. Intellectual processes and procedures were punctuated and disrupted requiring continual repair. Desmond Bernal for example, who had only been appointed to Birkbeck College in 1938, found his research programme lying in ruins when he returned from his wartime outpost in Princes Risborough in 1945. The college itself barely survived and Bernal had to reconstruct a scientific programme from almost nothing.[121]

---

[119] Carole J. Lee, 'Commensuration Bias in Peer Review,' *Philosophy of Science*, 82 (December 2015): 1275, 1277, 1280.

[120] For the thoughts of one convert and proponent of these changes see Harold Varmus, *The Art and Politics of Science* (New York/London: 2009), pp.242–269; idem., Harold Varmus, 'E-Biomed: A Proposal for Electronic Publication in the Biomedical Sciences,' (NIH preprint 04doc; Bethesda, MD: National Institutes of Health, 19 April 1999).

[121] Eric Hobsbawm, 'Bernal at Birkbeck,' in Brenda Swann and Francis Aprahaman (eds),

Often such reconstructions required individual rather than institutional action. Gilbert Murray sought to repair his and his British colleagues' relationship with Wilamowitz in the 1920s by acquiring British and US materials for the German scholar that he had been unable to obtain and by arranging other intellectual exchanges.[122] Conrad Waddington, aware of the ways that science and its technological expressions had become of elevated importance during the Second World War, feared knowledge might become 'unnecessarily narrow[ed]' and restricted. Both scientists and humanists should, he thought 'swallow their intellectual snobbery.' Specialists should be allowed to specialise as they pleased but they should 'realise the ways in which their specialised knowledge affects human affairs in general.'[123] He wrote to Bernal and to a wide scattering of scientists, artists, writers and historians, calling for the formation of a society that 'might be the focus for interest in the general contributions which science makes to the progress of civilization.' In addition to Bernal, Waddington addressed himself to the likes of Solly Zuckerman, Patrick Blackett and J. Z. Young but also Henry Moore, Ben Nicolson, Basil Willey, Geoffrey Faber, Cyril Connelly, C. E. Raven and C. P. Snow. Waddington's object was to have the society meet three or four times a year and have its members, from 'their different viewpoints,' address the ways in which 'an interest in natural history was involved in the development from the introverted mediaeval theological system to the extroverted Renaissance.'[124] It was a means to prevent the emergence of a cultural binary in which natural science opposed literature and letters, what famously would become called the 'two cultures.'

The 'two cultures' controversy marred the discussion of knowledge in the twentieth century because its nature was taken to be epistemological rather than, as it actually was, political and cultural.[125] It was sparked by C. P. Snow's famous Rede Lecture at Cambridge on 7 May 1959, in which he deplored vociferously the absence of the scientific life in British education and government. F. R. Leavis responded with even greater vociferousness in his equally famous Richmond Lecture at Downing College, Cambridge in 1962.[126] The 'two cultures' controversy was the expression of tangled and rival authorities

J. D. Bernal: A Life in Politics and Science (London/New York: 1999), pp.240–241.

[122] Murray to Wilamowitz, February 1923, quoted in Gilbert Murray, 'Memories of Wilamowitz,' Antike un Abenland, band 4 (1954): 13.

[123] C. H. Waddington, 'Humanists and Scientists: A Last Comment on C. P. Snow,' Encounter (January 1960): 72.

[124] Waddington to Bernal and others, 20 February 1946, Cambridge University Library, Bernal Mss., Add. 8287/235.

[125] David Egerton, Science, Technology, and the British Industrial 'Decline,' 1870–1970 (Cambridge: 1996), pp.7, 19, 68.

[126] C. P. Snow, The Two Cultures, with an Introduction by Stefan Collini (Cambridge: 1993 [1959]); F. R. Leavis, The Two Cultures? The Significance of C.P. Snow, with an Introduction by Stefan Collini (Cambridge: 2013).

struggling for legitimacy and recognition. From at least the third century of our era, it should be noted, there have been two scholarly practices: the search for what is general, that is overarching patterns (the nomothetic), and the identification of the unique and the particular (the ideographic). But these contrasting practices have been within what we would call the humanities rather than between what we would come to call science and the humanities. 'From a practice-based point of view,' one author concludes, 'the divide between the humanities and the sciences is nonexistent.'[127]

Two prominent scholars, not too little time ago, have sought to correct our conception of this problem by pointing out how in the early nineteenth century natural philosophers and scholarly literary people, while preoccupied with different matter, shared a common manner, approaches and methods. By paying attention to practices, rather than the content of their studies, philologists and astronomers, at the same time, can be shown to have participated in the forming of the very meaning of *Wissenschaft*. Both emphasised the importance of specialist methods developed in research seminars, founded by philologists but that natural philosophers soon joined in with, in the publication of their original research in specialised journals, in specialist learning in contrast to erudition, and in critical methods to separate wheat from chaff. More recently, scholars have directed our attention to the ways the history of science and the history of philologies have gained much from the joining of their forces by the widening of their vision, and by enlarging the range of their inquiries. In the future, collaboration among them might be even more fruitful.[128]

Far from being a clash of disciplines, the 'two cultures' became a clash of ideologies.[129] It was a contrast Aldous Huxley called between Snow's 'bland scientism' as over against the 'violent, and ill-mannered, the one-track literarism' of Leavis.[130] What had begun as a local Cambridge controversy spun itself out as a wider discussion of Britain's industrial and economic decline.[131] The material and social bases of these spurious contentions have been systematically scrutinised, statistically examined, and have been found wanting.[132]

[127] Rens Bod, 'Has There Ever Been a Divide? A *Longue Durée* Perspective,' *History of the Humanities*, 3 (Spring 2018): 15–26, quote is at 24.

[128] Lorraine Daston and Glenn W. Most, 'History of Science and History of Philologies,' *Isis*, 106 (2) (2015): 278–390, esp. 381, 389.

[129] Guy Ortolano, 'Human Science or Human Face? Social History and the "Two Cultures" Controversy,' *Journal of British Studies*, 43 (4) (October 2004): 484.

[130] Aldous Huxley, *Literature and Science* (New York: 1963), p.1.

[131] Correlli Barnett, *The Audit of War: The Illusion and Reality of Britain as a Great Nation* (London: 1986); Martin Wiener, *English Culture and the Decline of the Industrial Spirit, 1859–1980* (Cambridge: 1981).

[132] Lawrence and Jeanne C. Fawtier Stone, *An Open Society? England, 1540–1880* (Oxford: 1984); W. D. Rubenstein, *Elites and the Wealthy in Modern British History: Essays in Social and Economic History* (Sussex: 1987); idem., *Capital, Culture and Decline in Britain,*

Still, the argument has raged on.[133] As Noel Annan's *Our Age* shows, these questions have even been seized on autobiographically.[134]

To be sure, the controversy embraced local subjects: the founding of Churchill College, Cambridge, the founding of English social history, and the place of English studies in the Cambridge Tripos. However, as the scholar of this controversy has pointed out, '[t]he retreating British Empire emerged as the ultimate terrain where these arguments about the past present and future were joined.'[135] Snow himself, while he took and defended his position vehemently, as his career shows, belonged to both cultures. A 'man who mattered in his own time,'[136] as a young fellow of Christ's College Snow was a member of the Kapitza Club and read papers on the 'Nature of Viruses,' 'Extroverts and Introverts,' and 'The Novel (1922–1937)' to the Eranus Society at Cambridge.[137] As a mature man he wrote his string of novels *Strangers and Brothers* (and hoped to gain the Nobel Prize in Literature thereby). In the end Snow's concept of 'two cultures' has been dismissed as 'risible,' 'simple, indeed simplistic,' and 'laughingly wrong.' Leavis regarded Snow as 'an intellectual nullity.'[138] Kenneth Dover, as president of the British Academy, overheard Snow on a 'comparatively informal occasion,' refer to the humanities as an 'intellectual slum.'[139] Gorley Putt, one of the last survivors of a disappearing species, the bachelor don who made his college his home, was very much more generous to Snow. For Putt Snow, though given to 'headstrong gnomic statements,' was for undergraduates at Christ's a 'great emancipator.'[140]

Some have tried to calm the fuss. Harold Florey, as president of the Royal Society, addressed the British Academy in 1964. He welcomed the opportunity to address the academy because the day had long passed that 'scientists were chiefly associated in the minds of a few Academicians [as having] bad smells and dirty hands.' He wished to ripen the time when the British Academy and the

---

1750–1900 (London: 1991); David Edgerton, *The Rise and Fall of the British Nation: A Twentieth-Century History* (London: 2018) pp.115–119, 153–172.

[133] F. M. L. Thompson, *Gentrification and the Enterprise Culture: Britain, 1780–1980* (Oxford: 2001).

[134] Noel Annan, *Our Age: Portrait of a Generation*, pp.335–359.

[135] Guy Ortolano, *The Two Cultures Controversy: Science, Literature and Cultural Politics in Postwar Britain* (Cambridge: 2009), pp.101–139, 140–160, 161–193, quote is at 194.

[136] David Cannadine, 'The "Two Cultures," and the "Corridors of Power" Revisited,' in William Roger Louis, *Yet More Adventures with Britannia: Personalities, Politics, and Culture in Britain* (London: 2005), pp.101–118 at 113.

[137] Lubenow, *'Only Connect': Learned Societies in Nineteenth-Century Britain*, p.48.

[138] Edgerton, *The Rise and Fall of the British Nation*, pp.171, 394–396; idem., 'C. P. Snow as Anti-Historian of British Science: Revisiting the Technocratic Moment, 1959–1964,' *History of Science*, 43 (2005): 187–208; Guy Ortolano, 'The Literature and the Science of "Two Cultures" Historiography,' *Studies in History and Philosophy of Science*, 39 (2008): 143–150.

[139] Kenneth Dover, 'Presidential Address, 1981,' *Proceedings of the British Academy*, LXVII (1981): 81.

[140] S. Gorley Putt, 'Technique and Culture: Three Cambridge Portraits,' *Essays and Studies* (London: 1961): 18–19.

Royal Society, though separated by an 'accident of history,' might collaborate by upholding intellectual standards 'against the many pressures which lower them' because on these matters the society and the academy 'think as one.'[141] Mortimer Wheeler, as Secretary of the British Academy, regarded as 'archaic' the view that literary intellectuals occupied one pole of a binary and scientists occupied the other, 'separated by a gulf of incomprehension.' Such a view, he held, overlooked the increasing degree of intellectual exchange between them and ignored the ways many ideas and techniques used in the study of humankind were rooted in the disciplines called scientific. He regarded the separation of function of the two bodies as 'schizophrenic rather than rational.' The range of studies in both had extended themselves to such a degree that if there was 'no longer room for them all together in one old lady's shoe' the 'best that can be hoped for is that the pair of shoes may march comfortably.'[142] Kenneth Dover pointed out how there were at least three cultures not two. The third, in his view, consisted of those engaged in the creation of works of art, literature and music – those who are artistically creative. They, he thought, were engaged '[p]rofoundly, totally differ[ently] from the activity of posing and answering questions, whether in the sciences or in the humanities, about what is already there, attractive or not.'[143]

The 'two cultures' controversy, however, illustrates in an important way how the entangled loyalties in British intellectual life from 1900 to 1950 marked what was called a 'moral earthquake,' often undetected in the longsighted view historians sometimes take of the 'subterranean affinities and antipathies of the educated classes.'[144] The entangled loyalties among the British scientists and humanists (if we may now call them that) constituted, instituted and exposed the uncertainties and instabilities of their intellectual and social identities. The questioning of Arthur Schuster's patriotism during the Great War, the intervention of Soviet scholars at the Second International Congress of the History of Science, indeed the reluctance of the Royal Society and the British Academy to admit the likes of Charles Singer into their fellowships, the sequestering of Kapitza by the Soviets in the 1930s are all reminders of the failure of learned people to find recognition and status. Socially and intellectually they belonged nowhere. The collective nouns used to refer to them – 'professionals,' 'experts,' members of 'elites,' 'managers' of knowledge, 'intellectuals' – are all somehow inadequate to capture their intellectual and moral identities. Perhaps such is the lot of all creative people.

---

141 Royal Society Archives, Florey Ms. HF/1/13/4/1, 1 April 1964.
142 Mortimer Wheeler, *The British Academy, 1949–1968* (London: 1970), p.140.
143 Kenneth Dover, 'Presidential Address, 1981,': 77.82 at 81.
144 Ortolano, 'Human Science or Human Face?': 484, n. 7. Ortolano here is quoting Stefan Collini, *Public Moralists: Political Thought and Intellectual Life in Britain, 1850–1930* (Oxford: Clarendon Press, 1991), p.144, who was discussing the arguments between Matthew Arnold and T. H. Huxley over the relative places of the classics and natural history in British culture.

Conclusion

If we content ourselves with looking at the great permanent
problems of philosophy through the glasses of our present-day
western civilisation we are simply hugging our prison walls.

Gilbert Murray[1]

Think the unthinkable, but wear a dark suit when representing
the results.

Professor Sir Richard Ross[2]

Imagination is more important than knowledge. For knowledge
is limited, whereas imagination embraces the whole world,
stimulating progress, giving birth to evolution.

Einstein[3]

G ILBERT Murray, a great liberal all his life, articulated the problem of
knowledge's sovereignty in the twentieth century. He opposed 'hugging
the walls' of conventional thinking. He had been associated with Jane Harrison,
Francis Cornford and others who have been called the 'ritualists' who had introduced unconventional approaches to classical studies. He was also prominent
in promoting political projects such as the League of Nations.[4] In the 1940s

---

[1]   Gilbert Murray, *Greek Studies* (Oxford: 1946), p.67.
[2]   Ross, Professor Sir Claud Richard: the first Professor of Economics at the University of
East Anglia (1963–1968) who rose to be the university's vice-chancellor; Deputy Secretary
to Lord Rothschild of the Central Policy Review Staff (1971–1978); Vice-President of
the European Investment Bank (1978–1989); died 21 February 1996. The quotation is
in Kenneth Rose, *Elusive Rothschild: The Life of Victor, Third Baron* (London: 2003),
p.181. William Waldegrave, Ross's colleague in Lord Rothschild's 'Think Tank' called him
'charming, clever, and idle.' William Waldegrave, *A Different Kind of Weather: A Memoir*
(London: 2015), p.108. Because of his reflective cast of mind and his involvement with the
Treasury in dealing with macro-economic issues Ross became the Think Tank's 'resident
sage.' Tessa Blackstone and William Plowden, *Inside the Think Tank: Advising the Cabinet,
1971–1983* (London: 1988), p.29.
[3]   Quoted by Steven Shapin, 'Bare Bones,' *New York Review of Books* (8 March 2018): 25.
[4]   William C. Lubenow, 'The Cambridge Ritualists, 1876–1924: A Study of
Commensurability in the History of Scholarship,' *History of Universities*, 24 (1/2) (2009):

he feared people would creep 'back into their shells.' Anthropology, he argued, showed that what he rather awkwardly called 'inherited conglomerates' had 'practically no chance of being true or even sensible.' Yet, he recognised, no society could live without 'inherited conglomerates' or 'even submit to any drastic correction of them without social danger.'[5] The tension never ends between stabilising mental habits and what Clifford Geertz called escape from 'stoppered fly-bottles.'[6]

In Britain between 1900 and 1950 various societies formed, organised and also dissolved knowledge's sovereign legitimacy and authority. Their processes were both robust and charismatic but they were not mechanical classifications of mental materials. These processes recognised knowledge's instability and the difficulty of hedging it according to strict principles. The organisation of knowledge by learned people in learned societies consisted of a series of processes that were dynamic and complex. Organisations organise. Such is their heft and power. The most successful of these societies – the universities, the Royal Society and the British Academy, for example – found ways to renovate themselves as they adjusted their processes of organisation and dissolution. The University of London's capture of the Warburg Institute, to the institute's short-term advantage, is an example of such a renovation. It gave the Warburg reputation and, perhaps, the illusion, of permanence. Such an illusion, if that is what it is, might have advantages but also disadvantages. The clever and the charismatic, in societies that are often ephemeral – the Tots and Quots, the Theoretical Biology Club, the Society for the Protection of Science and Learning, for example – by appreciating the virtues of ambiguity, irony and paradox found ways to thwart stabilising mental habits and achieve traction and purchase for a time.

Whether in the robust societies, as in the cases of the universities, the Royal Society and the British Academy, or in the interstitial societies, such as the Warburg Institute, what is worth remarking upon is the durability of sociability and human relations in the history of cognition. The notion of cooperating and competitive communities is of no little interest. As one who wrote about Kuhn's concept of community says, 'community actually extends no further than this or that individual who represents it.'[7] Because these communities are loose clusters or coalitions of people with their theories

---

280–308. See also Christopher Stray (ed.), *Gilbert Murray Reassessed: Hellenism, Theater, and Intenational Politics* (Oxford: 2007).

5   Murray, *Greek Studies*, pp.66–67.

6   Clifford Geertz, *Available Light: Anthropological Reflections on Philosophical Topics* (Princeton: 2000), p.xi.

7   M. Norton Wise, 'A Smoker's Paradigm,' in Robert J. Richards and Lorraine Daston (eds), *Kuhn's Structure of Scientific Revolutions at Fifty: Reflections on a Science Classic* (Chicago/London: 2016), p.37. For Kuhn's own reconsideration of his concept of 'community' see his 1969 postscript to the *Structure of Scientific Revolutions*, esp. pp.176–181.

and evidence, their practices, commitments and beliefs, a particular kind of discourse develops. It was not a discourse in which information or even facts were of cardinal significance. Social and cognitive values were intermixed in breaking the shackles of what Weber called the 'iron cage.' Babel brought them into communion with each other as they discovered common problems; Babel threatened to drive them apart as they broke with communities to which they had already belonged and led them towards different forms of specialisation.[8] Geertz found guidance in Wittgenstein. As Geertz put it, 'the answers to our most general questions – why? how? what? wither? – to the degree they have answers, are to be found in the fine detail of lived life.'[9] These forms of knowledge and discourse ran counter to social tightness and the rigidity and control of bureaucratic life. These communities produced forms of knowledge and discourses that gave priority to ambiguity and social looseness. These were forms of knowledge and discourse about processes and practices; forms of knowledge and discourse that favored research and creativity. Thomas Kuhn himself, without falling into relativism or subjectivity, pointed to the relaxed nature of such communities. They are, he says, characterised by the '*relative* fullness of communication within the group,' the '*relative* unanimity of the group's judgment in professional matters,' and the '*similar* lessons' they have drawn from literature they have read.[10]

It would go too far to call these forms of knowledge and their discourses 'post-positivist.' Yet, these discourses defied the naive kind of narrow Huxleyite empiricism that has been called the 'orthodox epistemology,' which depends 'on neutral observational data which confirm or falsify theories.'[11] Positive knowledge itself, based upon concepts of objectivity, in its original utterances, as expressed by such as Leopold von Ranke, contained both the demand for accuracy and, at the same time, the deployment of intuition, imagination and interpretation.[12] This was not an ideological clash over the epistemic character of knowledge. It was not philosophical in any disciplinary or formal sense. The reconstitution of knowledge by these communities was cast in what Wittgenstein considered 'forms of life.' It was inspirational, and a matter of tone. These communities recognised that knowledge, or certain aspects of it, rested upon a priori categories. They conceived of the groups to which they belonged (as well as 'society' and the 'state') as having a genuine corporate

---

8   See, for example, Soraya de Chadarevian, *Designs for Life: Molecular Biology after World War II* (Cambridge: 202), pp.92–93.

9   Geertz, *Available Light*, p.xi.

10   Thomas Kuhn, 'Second Thoughts on Paradigms,' in *The Essential Tension: Selected Studies in Scientific Tradition and Change* (Chicago/London: 1977), p.296. Emphases in these quotations are mine.

11   Mary Hesse, 'Review of *The Structure of Scientific Revolutions*,' *Isis*, 54 (1963): 286.

12   See the quotations from von Ranke cited by Novick in *That Noble Dream: The 'Objectivity Question' and the American Historical Profession*, p.29.

identity and that the whole is greater than the sum of its parts. They regarded their objectives as the interpretation of meaning and purpose rather than the finding of causal explanations. They were more nomothetic than they were ideographic. These forms of knowledge, and the discourses in which they were expressed, constituted a reorientation of the way members of these knowledge communities conceived of what Weber called their 'vocation.' Such a reconstitution was important because it reshaped the members of these communities identities and loyalties. After the Second World War, and after he was given charge over Werner Heisenberg, Patrick Blackett wondered whether he was Heisenberg's host or warder.

Bohr's principle of complementarity, Heisenberg's uncertainty principle and Eddington's declaration of death's causality have led at least one writer to show how knowledge is 'never pure.'[13] Never pure, always personal, knowledge emerges in the coordinating power of the relationship between what people think, the concepts they use, and their intellectual practices they deploy in the groups to which they belonged. Learned people, stimulated by individual curiosity in the communities to which they belonged, created and invented intellectual legitimacy, authority and even authenticity. Consequently, England's knowledge map between 1900 and 1950 became a vast precinct of undiscovered territory that we, with some considerable fear and trembling, have only begun to explore. This book, one hopes, makes a tentative gesture towards such an exploration.

---

[13] Steven Shapin, *Never Pure: Historical Studies of Science as if It Was Produced by People with Bodies, Situated in Time, Space, Culture, and Society, and Struggling for Credibility and Authority* (Baltimore: 2010).

Bibliography

Unpublished sources

Noel Annan Papers, King's College, Cambridge
Arthur Balfour Papers, British Museum, London
Bernal Mss., Cambridge University Library
Patrick Blackett Papers, Royal Society, London
Brenner Papers, Cold Springs Harbor Laboratory Archives
British Academy Archives, London
James Bryce Manucripts, Bodleian Library, Oxford
J. R. M. Butler Papers, Trinity College, Cambridge
Goodeve Papers, Churchill College, Cambridge
Hardy Club Minute Book, Richard Keynes Papers, Churchill College, Cambridge
Archibald Vivian Hill Papers, Churchill College Cambridge
Roger Hinks Papers, Department of Rare Books and Special Collections, Princeton University Library
Holroyd Papers, British Library, London
Kapitza Club Minutes, Cockcroft Papers, Churchill College, Cambridge
John Maynard Keynes Papers, King's College, Cambridge
John Lennard-Jones Papers, Churchill College, Cambridge
Mayor Papers, Trinity College, Cambridge
Joseph Needham Mss., Cambridge University Library
J. H. Plumb Mss, held privately
Prothero Journal, King's College, Cambridge
Prothero Papers, Royal Historical Society Archive, University College, London
Royal Society of Literature Archives, Cambridge University Library
Rules of the V²V Club, Churchill College, Cambridge [WLTN/1/11]
Rutherford Mss, Cambridge University Library
C. P. Snow Mss., Harry Ransom Center, University of Texas
Strachey Papers, British Library, London
J. J. Thomson Mss., Cambridge University Library
J. J. Thomson Mss., Trinity College, Cambridge
Warburg Institute Archives, General Correspondence, London

Published primary sources

Abbot, Evelyn and Lew Campbell, *Life and Letters of Benjamin Jowett*, 2 vols (London, 1897)

Adams, W[alter], 'The International Congress of the History of Science and Technology,' *History*, 16 (630) (October 1931)

Adrian, Edgar, *The Mechanism of Nervous Action: Electrical Studies of the Neurone* (London, 1932)

Annan, Noel, *Our Age: Portrait of a Generation* (London, 1990)

'Annual Report,' *Proceedings of the British Academy*, 29 (1943)

Badash, Lawrence, *Kapitza, Rutherford, and the Kremlin* (New Haven, 1985)

Bell, Clive, *Old Friends* (London, 1956)

Bell, I. H., 'Presidential Address,' *Proceedings of the British Academy*, 33 (1947)

Bell, I. H., 'Presidential Address,' *Proceedings of the British Academy*, 34 (1948)

Berlin, Isaiah, *Affirming: Letters, 1975–1997*, ed. Henry Hardy and Mark Pottle (London, 2015)

Berlin, Isaiah, *Enlightening: Letters, 1946–1960*, ed. Henry Hardy and Jennifer Holmes (London, 2009)

Bernal, J. D., *The Origin of Life* (London, 1967)

Bevan, Edwyn, 'The Problem of the New Germany,' *Church Quarterly Review*, 88 (July 1919)

Beveridge, William, *A Defence of Free Learning* (London, 1959)

Beveridge, William, 'Economics as a Liberal Education,' *Economica*, 1 (1 January 1921)

Beveridge, William, *Power and Influence* (London, 1953)

Beveridge, William, 'The Place of the Social Sciences, in Human Knowledge,' *Politica*, 2 (9) (September 1937)

Bierl, A., William Calder III and R. L. Fowler (eds), *The Prussian and the Poet: The Letters of Ulrich von Wilamowitz-Moellendorff to Gilbert Murray (1894–1930)* (Hildesheim, 1991)

Bing, Gertrude, 'Fritz Saxl (1890–1948): A Memoir,' in D. J. Johnson (ed.), *Fritz Saxl, 1890–1948, A Volume of Memorial Essays from Friends in England* (London, 1957)

Blackett, Patrick, 'Old Days of the Cavendish,' *Rivista del Nuovo Cimento*, 1 (*Numero Speciale*) (1969)

Blackett, Patrick Lord, 'Rutherford,' *Notes and Records of the Royal Society of London*, 24 (1) (August 1972)

Blackett, Patrick, 'The Craft of Experimental Physics,' in Harold Wright (ed.), *University Studies: Cambridge, 1933* (London, 1933)

Blackstone, Tessa and William Plowden, *Inside the Think Tank: Advising the Cabinet, 1971–1983* (London, 1988)

Boag, J. W., P. E. Rubinin and D. Shoenberg (eds), *Kapitza in Cambridge and Moscow: Life and Letters of a Russian Physicist* (Amersterdam/Oxford, 1990)

Bohr, Niels, 'Natural Philosophy and Human Cultures,' *Nature*, 143 (18 February 1939)

Born, Max, *Physics in My Generation: A Selection of Papers* (London/New York, 1956)

Born, Max, *The Restless Universe* (Nineola, New York/Dover, 1951 [2013 edn])

Boydston, Jo Ann (ed.), *John Dewey, the Middle Works, Volume 4* (Carbondale, 1976)

Bryce, James, 'The Next Thirty Years', *Proceedings of the British Academy*, 8 (1917–1918)

Bukharin, N., 'Theory and Practice from the Standpoint of Dialectical Materialism', *Science at the Cross Roads: Papers Presented to the International Congress of the History of Science and Technology held in London from June 29 to July 3rd 1931, by the Delegates of the U.S.S.R*, with a new foreword by Joseph Needham, and a new introduction by P. G. Werskey (London, 1971)

Butler, E. M., 'Hoffmannstal's [sic] "Electra": A Graeco-Freudian Myth', *Journal of the Warburg Institute*, 2 (1938–1939)

Clark, Kenneth, *Another Part of the Wood: A Self-Portrait* (London, 1974)

Clapham, J. H., 'Presidential Address', *Proceedings of the British Academy*, 27 (1941)

Clapham, J. H., 'Presidential Address', *Proceedings of the British Academy*, 28 (1942)

Clapham, J. H., 'Presidential Address', *Proceedings of the British Academy*, 29 (1943)

Clapham, J. H., 'Presidential Address', *Proceedings of the British Academy*, 31 (1945)

Cole, Margaret (ed.), *Beatrice Webb's Diaries, 1924–1932* (London, 1956)

Colville, John, *The Fringes of Power: 10 Downing Street Diaries, 1939–1955* (New York, 1955)

Connolly, Cyril, *Enemies of Promise* (New York, rev. edn, 1983)

Cooper, R. M., *Refugee Scholars: Conversations with Tess Simpson* (Leeds, 1992)

Crick, Francis, 'Ruthless Research in a Cupboard', *New Scientist* (21 May 1987)

Crick, Francis, *What Mad Pursuit: A Personal View of Scientific Discovery* (New York, 1988)

Crowther, J. G., *Fifty Years with Science* (London, 1970)

Crowther, J. G., *The Cavendish Laboratory* (London, 1974)

Cumming, Robert (ed.), *My Dear BB: The Letters of Bernard Berenson and Kenneth Clark, 1925–1959* (New Haven/London, 2015)

Curson of Kedleston, Lord, *Principles and Methods of University Reform: Being a Letter Addressed to the University of Oxford* (Oxford, 1909)

Dale, Henry, 'Edgar Vincent, Viscount D'Aubernon, 1857–1942', *Obituary Notices of Fellows of the Royal Society*, 4 (11) (November 1943)

Dale, Henry, 'Frederick Gowland Hopkins, 1861–1947', *Obituary Notices of Fellows of the Royal Society*, 6 (1918–1949)

Darwin, Bernard, *Pack the Clouds Away* (London, 1941)

Darwin, Bernard, *The World Fred Made: An Autobiography* (London, 1955)

Darwin, Francis, *Springtime and Other Essays* (Freeport, New York, 1920 [1967 edn])

Davenport-Hines, Richard (ed.), *One Hundred Letters from Hugh Trevor-Roper* (Oxford, 2014)

Dirac, P. A. A., 'Pretty Mathematics', *International Journal of Theoretical Physics*, 21 (8/9) (1982)

Dobzhansky, Theodosius, *Mankind Evolving: The Evolution of the Human Species* (New York/London, 1962)

Douglas, G. C., 'John Scott Haldane, 1860–1936', *Obituary Notices of Fellows of the Royal Society*, 2 (1936–1939)

Dover, Kenneth, 'Presidential Address, 1981,' *Proceedings of the British Academy*, LXVII (1981)

Eddington, Arthur, *Science and the Unseen World* (London, 1920)

Eddington, Arthur, *The Cavendish Laboratory* (Cambridge, 1935)

Eddington, Arthur, *The Nature of the Natural World* (Cambridge, 1929)

'The Elect of Science,' *Economist* (16 June 1960)

[Elliott, T. R.], 'Walter Morley Fletcher, 1873–1933,' *Obituary Notices of Fellows of the Royal Society*, 1 (1934)

Farnell, Lewis, *An Oxonian Looks Back* (London, 1934)

Fletcher, Maisie, *The Bright Countenance: A Personal Biography of Walter Morley Fletcher* (London, 1957)

Fletcher, Walter, *Medical Research: The Tree and the Fruit, the Fifth Annual Norman Lockyer Lecture* (London, 1929)

Fleure, H. J., 'Alfred Cort Haddon, 1855–1940,' *Obituary Notices of Fellows of the Royal Society*, 3 (1939–1941)

Fleure, H. J., 'James George Frazer, 1854–1941,' *Obituary Notices of Fellows of the Royal Society*, 3 (1939–1941)

Flexner, Abraham, *The Usefulness of Useless Knowledge*, with a companion essay by Robbert Dijkgraaf (Princeton/London, 2017 [1939])

Forster, E. M., *Two Cheers for Democracy* (London, 1951)

Fry, Roger, 'Impressionism,' in S. P. Rosenbaum (ed.), *A Bloomsbury Group Reader* (Oxford, 1993)

Gardner, Percy, *Oxford at the Crossroads: A Criticism of the Course of Litterae Humaniores in the University* (London, 1903)

Gombrich Ernst, *Aby Warburg: An Intellectual Biography with a Memoir on the History of the Library by F. Saxl* (London, 1970 [1986 edn])

Gombrich, Ernst, 'In Search of Cultural History,' in Richard Woodfield (ed.), *The Essential Gombrich* (London, 1996)

Gombrich, E. H., *The Warburg Institute and H.M. Office of Works – E.H. Gombrich in Memory of Frederic Raby* (Cambridge, 1984)

Gorley Putt, S., 'Technique and Culture: Three Cambridge Portraits,' *Essays and Studies* (London, 1961)

Gould, G. C., 'John Scott Haldane, 1860–1936,' *Obituary Notices of Fellows of the Royal Society*, 2 (1936–1939)

Gray, Hanna Holborn, to the editor of the *London Review of Books* (17 April 2017)

Hardy, G. H., 'Mathematics,' *Oxford Magazine* (5 June 1930)

Hartley, Harold, 'The Contribution of College Laboratories,' *Chemistry in Britain*, 1 (1965)

Hill, A. V., 'International Status and Obligations in Science,' printed in *Nature*, 132 (23 December 1933)

Hill, A. V., F. Gowland Hopkins and F. G. Kenyon, 'German Universities,' *Universities Review*, 8 (2) (April 1936)

Hill, A. V., 'William Bate Hardy (1864–1933),' *Obituary Notices of the Fellows of the Royal Society*, 1 (1932–1935)

Hinks, Roger, 'The Warburg Institute,' *The Spectator* (9 September 1938)

Hinks, Roger Packman, *Myth and Allegory in Ancient Art* (London, 1939)

Hinshelwood, Cyril, *Structure of Physical Chemistry* (Oxford, 1951)

Hinshelwood, Cyril, *The Vision of Nature* (Cambridge, 1961)

History of the Cavendish Laboratory, 1870–1910 (London, 1910)

Hodgkin, Alan, *Chance and Design: Reminiscences of Science in War and Peace* (Cambridge, 1992)

Hodgkin, Dorothy, *Autobiographical Memoirs*, ed. Katherine Hodgkin, in Guy Dodso, Savaraj Ramaseshan et al., *The Collected Works of Dorothy Hodgkin*, 3 vols (Bangalore, 1994)

Hogben, Adrian and Anne Hogben (eds), *Lancelot Hogben, Scientific Humanist: An Unauthorized Autobiography* (Woodbridge, 1998)

Hogben, Lancelot, 'The Foundation of Social Biology', *Economica*, 31 (February 1931)

Hopkins, F. Gowland, 'Medicine and Experimental Science', in A. C. Seward (ed.), *Science and the Nation: Essays by Cambridge Graduates* (Freeport, 1917 [1967 edn])

Huxley, Aldous, *Literature and Science* (New York, 1963)

Huxley, Julian, *Memories* (London, 1950)

Huxley, Julian, *Religion without Revelation* (New York, 1957)

Huxley, Julian, 'Review of Theodosius Dobzhansky, *Mankind Evolving: The Evolution of the Human Species*', *Perspectives in Biology and Medicine*, 6 (1) (Autumn 1962)

Huxley, T. H., *Lay Sermons, Addresses and Reviews* (London, 1872)

Huxley, T. H., 'The Progress of Science' (1887) in C. Bibby, *The Essence of T. H. Huxley* (London, 1967)

Jeans, James, *The Mysterious Universe* (Cambridge, 1930)

[J. S. H.], 'Science in War', [a review of *Science in War* (London, 1940)] *Nature*, 146 (27 July 1940)

Kenyon, Frederic, 'Presidential Address', *Proceedings of the British Academy, 1919* (1919–1920)

Kenyon, Frederic, 'Presidential Address', *Proceedings of the British Academy, 1920* (1919–1920)

Kenyon, Frederic, 'Presidential Address' *Proceedings of the British Acaemy, 1921* (1921–1923)

Keynes, John Maynard Keynes, *A Treatise on Money*, in Donald Moggeridge (ed.), *The Collected Writings of John Maynard Keynes*, Volume 5 (London, 1971)

Keynes, John Maynard, 'Lloyd George: A Fragment', in *The Collected Writings of John Maynard Keynes, Volume 10: Essays in Biography* (Cambridge, 1972)

Keynes, John Maynard, 'My Early Beliefs', in *The Collected Writings of John Maynard Keynes: Volume 10: Essays in Biography* (Cambridge, 1972)

Keynes, John Maynard, 'The Civil Service and Treasury Control', in *The Collected Works of John Maynard Keynes, Volume 16: Activities, 1914–1919: The Treasury and Versailles* (Cambridge, 1972)

Keynes, John Maynard, *The General Theory of Employment, Interest, and Money* (New York, 1936)

Keynes, Margaret, *Leonard Darwin, 1850–1943* (Cambridge, 1943)

Klibansky, Raymond, '*La Notion de Kulturwissenschaft*', *RACAR: Revue d'Art Canadienne/ Canadian Art Review*, 27 (1/2) (2000)

Leavis, F. R., *The Two Cultures? The Significance of C. P. Snow*, with an introduction by Stefan Collini (Cambridge, 2013)

Lees-Milne, James, *Ancestral Voices* (London, 1985)

Lees-Milne, James, *Through Wood and Dale: Diaries, 1975–1978* (London, 1988 [2007])

Levi, A. H. T. and Francis Haskell, 'Jean Joseph Seznec, 1905–1983', *Proceedings of the British Academy*, 73 (1987)

Lloyd-Jones, Hugh, 'Historical Memoir of Edward Wind', in Edgar Wind, *The Eloquence of Symbols*, ed. Jaynie Anderson, rev. edn (Oxford, 1993)

Mackail, J. W., 'Presidential Address', *Proceedings of the British Academy* (1933)

Mackail, J. W., 'Presidential Address', *Proceedings of the British Academy* (1934)

Mackail, J. W., 'Presidential Address', *Proceedings of the British Academy* (1935)

Mannheim, Karl, *Ideology and Utopia: An Introduction to the Sociology of Knowledge*, trans. Louis Wirth and Edward Shils (New York, 1936)

Maritain, Jacques and Mary Morris, 'Sign and Symbol', *Journal of the Warburg Institute*, 1 (1937–1938)

Medawar, Peter, *Induction and Intuition in Scientific Thought* (London, 1969)

Medawar, Peter, *Memoirs of a Thinking Radish: An Autobiography* (Oxford/New York, 1988)

Medawar, Peter, 'Science and Literature: Perspectives in Biology and Medicine', *Encounter* (January 1969)

Medawar, Peter, *The Strange Case of the Spotted Mice and Other Classic Essays on Science* (Oxford/New York, 1996)

Memorial to the Late Walter Morley Fletcher, KBE, MD, ScD, FRCP, FRS (1873–1993), Secretary to the Medical Research Committee and Council, 1914–1933 (Oxford, 1937)

Mitchison, Naomi, 'Beginnings', in K. R. Dronamraju (ed.), *Haldane and Modern Biology* (Baltimore, 1968)

Moggeridge, Donald (ed.), *The Collected Writings of John Maynard Keynes, Volume 14: The General Theory and After, Defense and Development* (London, 1973)

Momigliano, Arnold, *Essays on Ancient and Modern Judaism*, ed. S. Berti (London/Chicago, 1987)

Moulton, John Fletcher Lord, 'Introduction', A. C. Seward, *Science and the Nation: Essay by Cambridge Graduates* (Freeport, 1917 [1967])

Murray, Gilbert, 'German Scholarship', *Quarterly Review*, 233 (443) (April 1915)

Murray, Gilbert, *Greek Studies* (Oxford, 1946)

Murray, Gilbert, 'Memoir of H. A. L. Fisher', *Obituary Notices of Fellows of the Royal Society*, 3 (1939–1941)

Murray, Gilbert, 'Memories of Wilamowitz', *Antike un Abenland*, 4 (December 1954)

Murray, Gilbert, 'Wilamowitz', *Classical Review*, 45 (November 1931)

Myres, J. J., 'Arthur John Evans, 1851–1941', *Obituary Notices of the Fellows of the Royal Society*, 3 (1851–1941)

Namier, Lewis, 'Human Nature in Politics', in *Personalities and Powers* (New York/Evanston, 1965)

Needham, Joseph, 'Sir Frederick Gowland Hopkins, OM, FRS (1861–1947), *Notes and Records of the Royal Society of London* 17 (2 December 1962)

Needham, Joseph, 'New Advances in the Chemistry and Biology of Organized Growth', *Proceedings of the Royal Society of Medicine*, 29 (1935–1936)

Needham, Joseph, *Order and Life* (New Haven, 1936)

Needham, Joseph, 'Review of *Biological Principle: A Critical Study* by J. I I. Woodger', *Mind*, new series, 39 (154) (April 1930)

Needham, Joseph [writing as Henry Holorenshaw], 'The Making of an Honorary Taoist', in Mikuláš Teich and Robert Young (eds), *Changing Perspectives in the History of Science: Essays in Honor of Joseph Needham* (London, 1973)

Needham, Joseph, 'The Philosophical Basis of Biochemistry', *Monist*, 25 (1) (January 1925)

Needham, Joseph, *The Sceptical Biologist* (London, 1929)

Needham, Joseph, *Time the Refreshing River*, essays and addresses (New York, 1932–1942)

Nicolai, George, *The Biology of War* (New York, 1929)

Nicolson, Harold, *The War Years, 1940–1945: Volume 11 of Diaries and Letters*, ed. Nigel Nicolson (New York, 1967)

Oppenheimer, J. Robert, *Atom or Void: Essays on Science and Community* (Princeton, 1989)

Penrose, Roger, 'Consciousness Involves Noncomputational Ingredients', in *Roger Penrose, Collected Works, Volume 5, 1990–1996* (Oxford, 2011)

Penrose, Roger, 'Science and the Mind', in *Roger Penrose, Collected Works, Volume 6, 1997–2003* (Oxford, 2011)

Perutz, Max, 'Forty Years Friendship with Dorothy', in G. G. Dodson, J. P. Glusker, S. Rameshan and K. Venkasesan (eds), *The Collected Works of Dorothy Crowfoot Hodgkin, Volume III: General Cyrstallography and Essays* (Bangalore, 1994).

Polanyi, Michael, *Personal Knowledge: Towards a Post-Critical Philosophy* (Chicago, 1958)

Polanyi, Michael, *The Tacit Dimension* (Chicago/London, 1966 [2009 edn])

Rameshan, and K Venkasesan (eds), *The Collected Works of Dorothy Crowfoot Hodgkin, Volume III: General Crystallography and Essays* (Bangalore, 1994)

Raverat, Gwen, *Period Piece* (New York, 1952 [1976 edn])

'Research Students, 1829–1929', *Cambridge University Reporter*, 59 (23 February 1928)

'Research Students, 1938–1939', *Cambridge University Reporter*, 69 (21 February 1939)

'Research Students, 1952–1953', *Cambridge University Reporter*, 83 (13 March 1953)

Robbins, Lionel, *Autobiography of an Economist* (London, 1971)

Robinson, E. A. G., 'John Maynard Keynes, 1883–1946', *Economic Journal*, 57 (225) (March 1947)

Robinson, Robert, *Memoirs of a Minor Prophet: Seventy Years of Organic Chemistry* (Amsterdam, 1976)

Ross, David, 'Presidential Address', *Proceedings of the British Academy*, 23 (1937)

Ross David, 'Presidential Address', *Proceedings of the British Academy*, 24 (1938)

Ross, David, 'Presidential Address', *Proceedings of the British Academy*, 25 (1939)

Ross, David, 'Presidential Address,' *Proceedings of the British Academy*, 26 (1940)

Ross, Denison, *Both Ends of the Candle* (London, 1943)

Russell, Bertrand, 'Journal [1902–1914],' in *Collected Papers of Bertrand Russell, Volume 12: Contemplations and Action, 1902–1914*, Richard Rempel, Andrew Brink and Margaret Moran (eds) (London, 1985)

Russell, Bertrand, *Portraits from Memory and Other Essays* (London, 1956)

[A. S. and E. M. S.], *Henry Sidgwick: A Memoir* (London, 1906)

Schuster, Arthur, *Biographical Fragments* (London, 1932)

Simpson, F. A., 'Max Beerbohm on Lytton Strachey,' *Cambridge Review*, 4 (December 1943)

Simpson, G. C., 'Sir Arthur Schuster, 1891–1934,' *Obituary Notices of the Fellows of the Royal Society*, 1 (1932–1935)

Smith, Henry, *Biographical Sketches and Recollections (with Early Letters) of Henry John Smith, MA, FRS* (London, 1894)

Snow, C. P., 'J. D. Bernal: A Personal Portrait,' in Maurice Goldsmith and Alan MacKay (eds), *The Science of Science: Science in the Technological Age* (London, 1964)

Snow, C. P., *Last Things* (London, 1970),

Snow, C. P., *The Two Cultures*, with an introduction by Stefan Collini (Cambridge, 1996)

Snow, C. P., *Varieties of Men* (New York, 1966)

Strachey, Lytton, *Eminent Victorians* (London, 1986 edn)

Strachey, Lytton, 'Lancaster Gate,' in S. P. Rosenbaum (ed.), *A Bloomsbury Group Reader* (Oxford, 1993)

Stratford, F. J. M. (ed.), *Records of the Royal Astronomical Club, 1911–1924* (London, 1924)

Sutton, Denys (ed.), *The Letters of Roger Fry*, 2 vols (London, 1972)

Thomson, George Paget, *J.J. Thomson and the Cavendish Laboratory of His Day* (London, 1964)

Thomson, George Paget, 'Sir Charles Galton Darwin,' *Biographical Memoirs of Fellows of the Royal Society*, 9 (1963)

Thompson, Harold, 'Cyril Norman, Hinschelwood, 1897–1967, Elected FRS 1929,' *Biographical Memoirs of Fellows of the Royal Society, 1973*, vol. 19 (London, 1973)

Thomson, J. J., 'Address of the President Sir J. J. Thomson, OM, at the Anniversary Meeting,' *Proceedings of the Royal Society of London*, series A, volume XCV (July 1919)

Thomson, John Joseph, *Recollections and Reflections* (New York, 1937)

Trevelyan, G. M., *An Autobiography and Other Essays* (London, 1949)

Waldegrave, William, *A Different Kind of Weather: A Memoir* (London, 2015)

Warburg, Eric, 'The Transfer of the Warburg Institute to England in 1933,' [October 1953], *University of London: The Warburg Institute Annual Report, 1952–1953*

Watson, James, *Genes, Girls and Gamow: After the Double Helix* (New York, 2002)

Watson, James, 'Minds that Live for Science,' *New Scientist* (21 May 1987)

Watson, James, *The Double Helix*, annotated and illustrated edition by Alexander Gann and Jan Witkowski (New York/London, 2012)

Wells, H. G., *The New Machiavelli* (London, 2015 edn)

Wheeler, Mortimer, *The British Academy, 1949–1968* (London, 1970)

Whitney, J. P., 'The Late Professor J. B. Bury', *Cambridge Historical Journal*, 2 (1926–1929)

Whittaker, T., 'Review of *Science and Culure and Other Essays* by Thomas Henry Huxley (London, Macmillan, 1881),' *Academy*, 21 (25 February 1882)

Wilamowitz-Moellendorff, Ulrich von, *My Recollections, 1848–1914*, trans. G. C. Richards (London, 1930)

[Wind, Edgar], *A Bibiliography on the Survival of the Classics, First Volume, the Publications of 1931*, ed. The Warburg Institute (London, 1934)

Wind, Edgar, 'Warburg's Concept of *Kulturwissenschaft* and its Meaning for Aesthetics', reprinted in Edgar Wind, *The Eloquence of Symbols: Studies in Humanist Art* (Oxford, 1983)

Woolf, Leonard, *Beginning Again: An Autobiography of the Years 1911–1918* (New York, 1963)

Woolf, Leonard, *Sowing: An Autobiography of the Years 1880–1904* (New York/ London, 1960)

Woolf, Virginia, *The Diary of Virginia Woolf, Volume 1, 1915–1919* , ed. Anne Olivier Bell (New York, 1977)

Woolf, Virginia, *The Diary of Virginia Woolf, Volume 4*, ed. Anne Olivier Bell (New York, 1983)

Woolf, Virginia, 'Old Bloomsbury', in S. P. Rosenbaum (ed.), *A Bloomsbury Group Reader* (Oxford, 1993)

Wrinch, Dorothy, 'The Relations of Science and Philosophy', *Journal of Philosophical Studies*, 2 (6) (April 1927)

Wurmser, René, 'Haldane as I Knew Him,' in K. R. Dronamraju (ed.), *Haldane and Modern Biology* (Baltimore, 1968)

Zuckerman, Solly, *From Apes to Warlords: An Autobiography (1904–1946)* (London, 1978)

Secondary sources

Books

Agamben, Giorgio, *Potentialities: Collected Essays in Philosophy* (Stanford, 1999)

Annan, Noel, 'Keynes and Bloomsbury', in William Roger Lewis (ed.), *Still More Adventures with Britannia: Personalities, Politics, and Culture in Britain* (London, 2003)

Annan, Noel, *The Curious Strength of Positivism in English Political Thought* (Oxford, 1959)

Annan, Noel, 'The Intellectual Aristocracy,' in J. H. Plumb (ed.), *Studies in Social History* (London, 1955)

Backhouse, Roger E. and Philippe Fontaine, *A Historiography of the Modern Social Sciences* (Cambridge, 2014)

Barnett, Correlli, *The Audit of War: The Illusion and Reality of Britain as a Great Nation* (London, 1986)

Bell, Julian, *Virginia Woolf: A Biography*, 2 vols (New York, 1972)

Bentwich, Norman, *The Rescue and Achievement of Refugee Scholars: The Story of Displaced Scholars and Scientists* (The Hague, 1953)

Bledstein, Burton J., *The Culture of Professionalism: The Middle Class and the Development of Higher Education in America* (New York, 1976)

Bloom, Harold, *The Anxiety of Influence: A Theory of Poetry* (New York, 1973)

Bockstaele, P., 'The Mathematical and the Exact Sciences,' in Walter Rüegg (ed.), *A History of the University in Europe, Volume III: Universities in the Nineteenth and Early Twentieth Centuries (1800–1945)* (Cambridge, 2004)

Brockliss, L. W. B., *The University of Oxford: A History* (Oxford, 2016)

Brockliss, Laurence, 'Welcoming and Supporting Refugee Scholars: The Role of Oxford's Colleges,' in Sally Crawford, Katharina Ulmschneider and Jaś Elsner (eds), *Ark of Civilization: Refugee Scholars and Oxford University, 1930–1945* (Oxford, 2017)

Brooke, Christopher, *A History of Gonville and Caius College* (Woodbridge, 1985)

Browne, Janet, *Charles Darwin: The Power of Place* (Princeton/London, 2002)

Butterfield, Herbert, *The Whig Interpretation of History* (Cambridge, 1931)

Cannadine, David, 'The "Two Cultures," and the "Corridors of Power" Revisited,' in William Roger Lewis (ed.), *Yet More Adventures with Britannia: Personalities, Politics, and Culture in Britain* (London, 2005)

Cannadine, David, *G. M. Trevelyan: A Life in History* (London, 1992)

Carter, Amanda, *Anthony Blunt: His Lives* (London, 2001)

Caws, Mary Ann and Sarah Bird Wright, *Bloomsbury and France: Art and Friends* (Oxford, 2000)

Cecil, Hugh and Mirabel Cecil, *Clever Hearts: Desmond and Molly MacCarthy, A Biography* (London, 1990)

Chapman, Mark D., *Theology at War and Peace: English Theology and Germany in the First World War* (London/New York, 2017)

Clark, Ronald W., *The Huxleys* (New York/Toronto, 1968)

Clarke, Peter, *The Keynesian Revolution in the Making, 1924–1936* (Oxford, 1991)

Clarke, Peter, 'The Politics of Keynsian Economics, 1914–1931,' in Michael Bentley (ed.), *High and Low Politics in Modern Britain: Ten Studies* (Oxford, 1983)

Clavin, Patricia, 'A Wandering Scholar in Britain and the U.S.A., 1933–1945: The Life and Work of Moritz Bonn,' in Anthony Frenville (ed.), *Refugees from the Third Reich in Britain* (Amsterdam/New York, 2002)

Colley, Linda, *Lewis Namier* (London, 1989)

Collini, Stefan, *Absent Minds: Intellectuals in Britain* (Oxford, 2006)

Collini, Stefan, *Common Reading: Critics, Historians, Publics* (Oxford, 2008)

Collini, Stefan, 'Introduction,' to C. P. Snow, *The Two Cultures* (Cambridge, 1959 [1963])

Collini, Stefan, *Public Moralists: Political Thought and Intellectual Life in Britain, 1850–1930* (Oxford, 1991)

Collini, Stefan, Donald Winch and John Burrow, *The Noble Science of Politics: A Study in Nineteenth-Century Intellectual History* (Cambridge, 1983)

Collins, Peter, *The Royal Society and the Promotion of Science Since 1960* (Cambridge, 2016)

Crawford, Sally, Katharina Ulmschneider and Jaś Elsner (eds), *Ark of Civilization: Refugee Scholars and Oxford University, 1930–1945* (Oxford, 2017)

Csiszar, Alex, *The Scientific Journal: Authorship and the Politics of Knowledge in the Nineteenth Century* (Chicago/London, 2018)

Dahrendorf, Ralf, *LSE: A History of the London School of Economics* (Oxford, 1995)

Dangerfield, George, *The Strange Death of Liberal England* (London, 1935)

Daston, Lorraine, 'The Immortal Archive: Nineteenth-Century Science Imagines the Future,' in Lorraine Daston. (ed.), *Science in the Archives* (Chicago/London, 2017)

Davenport-Hines, Richard, 'Introduction,' Hugh Trevor Roper, *Letters from Oxford to Bernard Berenson* (London, 2006)

Davenport-Hines, Richard, 'Introduction,' Hugh Trevor Roper, *Wartime Journals* (London, 2012)

Davenport-Hines, Richard, *Universal Man: The Seven Lives of John Maynard Keynes* (London, 2015)

de Chadarevian, Soraya, *Designs for Life: Molecular Biology after World War II* (Cambridge, 2002)

den Otter, Sandra M., *British Idealism and Social Action: A Study in Late Victorian Thought* (Oxford, 1996)

Desmond, Adrian, *Huxley: From Devil's Disciple to Evolutions's High Priest* (Reading, Mass., 1994)

Diggins, John Patrick, *Max Weber: Politics and the Spirit of Tragedy* (New York, 1996)

Dinshaw, Minoo, *Outlandish Knight: The Byzantine Life of Steven Runciman* (London, 2016)

Dry, Sarah, *The Newton Papers: The Strange and True Odyssey of Isaac Newton's Manuscripts* (Oxford, 2014)

Edel, Leon, *Bloomsbury: A House of Lions* (Philadelphia/New York, 1979)

Edgerton, David, *Science, Technology, and the British Industrial 'Decline,' 1870–1970* (Cambridge, 1996)

Edgerton, David, *The Rise and Fall of the British Nation, a Twentieth Century History* (London, 2018)

Eisler, Colin, '*Kunstgeschichte* American Style: A Study in Migration,' in Donald Fleming and Bernard Bailyn (eds), *The Intellectual Migration: Europe and America, 1930–1950* (Cambridge, Mass., 1969)

Farmelo, Graham, *The Strangest Man: The Hidden Life of Paul Dirac, Mystic of the Atom* (New York, 2009)

Ferreira, Petro G., *The Perfect Theory* (Boston/New York, 2014)

Forrester, John and Laura Cameron, *Freud in Cambridge* (Cambridge, 2017)

Fuller, Steve, 'Disciplinary Boundaries and the Rhetoric of the Social Sciences,' in Ellen Messer-Davidow, et al., *Knowledges: Historical and Critical Studies in Disciplinarity* (Charlottesville/London, 1993)

Furner, Mary, *Advocacy and Objectivity: A Crisis in the Professionalization of American Social Science, 1865–1905* (Lexington, 1975)

Gay, Peter, *Weimar Culture: The Outsider as Insider* (New York/Evanston, 1970)

Geertz, Clifford, *Available Light: Anthropological Reflections on Philosophical Topics* (Princeton, 2000)

Geertz, Clifford, *Local Knowledge: Further Essays in Interpretive Anthropology* (New York, 1983)

Geertz, Clifford, 'School Building: A Retrospective Preface,' in Joan Wallach Scott (ed.), *Schools of Thought: Twenty-Five Years of Interpretive Social Science* (Princeton, 2001)

Geertz, Clifford, *The Interpretation of Cultures: Selected Essays* (New York, 1973)

Gilman, Nils, *Mandarins of the Future: Modernization Theory in Cold War America* (Baltimore, 2005)

Gould, Stephen Jay, *The Lying Stones of Marrakech: Penultimate Reflections in Natural History* (Cambridge, Mass., 2011)

Green, E. H. H. and D. M. Tanner (eds), *The Strange Survival of Liberal England* (London, 2007)

Hall, Marie Boas, *All Scientists Now: The Royal Society in the Nineteenth Century* (Cambridge, 1984)

Halsey, A. H., 'Oxford and the British Universities,' in Brian Harrison (ed.), *The History of the University of Oxford, Volume 8: The Twentieth Century* (London, 1994)

Harris, Jose, *William Beveridge: A Biography* (Oxford, 1997)

Haskell, Thomas L., *The Emergence of Professional Social Science: The American Social Science Association and the Nineteenth-Century Crisis of Authority* (Urbana, 1977)

Hobsbawm, Eric, 'Bernal at Birkbeck,' in Brenda Swann and Francis Aprahamian (eds) *J. D. Bernal: A Life in Politics and Science* (London, 1999)

Hodges, Andrew, *Alan Turing: The Enigma* (New York, 1983)

Hollis, Christopher, *Oxford in the Twenties: Recollections of Five Friends* (London, 1976)

Holmes, Richard, *Age of Wonder: How the Romantic Generation Discovered the Beauty and Terror of Science* (London, 2008)

Howarth, T. E. B., *Cambridge Between Two Wars* (London, 1978)

Hughes, H. Stuart, *The Sea Change: The Migration of Social Thought, 1930–1950* (New York, 1975)

Isaac, Joel, *Working Knowledge: Making the Human Sciences from Parson to Kuhn* (Cambridge, Massachusetts/London, 2012)

Jeffrey, Alexander, Philip Smith and Matthew Norton (eds), *Interpreting Clifford Geertz: Investigation in the Social Sciences* (London/New York, 2011)

Kamminga, Harmke, 'Hopkins and Biochemistry,' in Joseph Needham and Ernest Baldwin (eds), *Cambridge Scientific Minds* (Cambridge, 2002)

Keynes, John Maynard, 'Newton the Man,' in Donald Moggridge and Elizabeth Johnson (eds), *The Collected Works of John Maynard Keynes, Vol. 10* (Cambridge, 1972)

Kidd, Colin, *The World of Mr. Casaubon: Britain's Wars of Mythography, 1700–1970* (Cambridge, 2016)

Kohler, Robert E., *Partners in Science: Foundaations and Natural Scientists, 1900–1945* (Chicago/London, 1992)

Kuhn, Thomas, *The Essential Tension: Selected Studies in Scientfic Tradition and Change* (Chicago/London, 1977)

Kuhn, Thomas, *The Structure of Scientific Revolutions* (Chicago, 1962)

Kuklick, Henrika, *The Savage Within: The Social History of British Anthropology, 1885–1945* (Cambridge, 1991)

Lakatos, Imre, *Mathematics, Science, Epistemology*, ed. John Worrell and Gregory Currie (Cambridge, 1980)

Latour, Bruno, *Pandora's Hope: Essays on the Reality of Science Studies* (Cambridge, MA, 1999)

Latour, Bruno, *We Have Never Been Modern*, trans. C. Porter (Cambridge, MA, 1993)

Lerner, Robert E., *Ernst Kantorowicz: A Life* (Princeton/Oxford, 2017)

Levin, Harry, *Contexts of Criticism* (Cambridge, Mass., 1975)

Levine, Emily J., *Dreamland of Humanists: Warburg Cassirer, Panofsky, and the Warburg School* (Chicago/London, 2013)

Lubenow, William C., 'Intimacy, Imagination and the Inner Dialectis of Knowledge Communities: The Synthetic Society, 1896–1908,' in Martin Daunton (ed.), *The Organization of Knowledge in Victorian Britain* (Oxford, 2005)

Lubenow, William C., 'Lytton Strachey's *Eminent Victorians*: The Rise and Fall of the Intellectual Aristocracy,' in Miles Taylor and Michael Wolff (eds), *The Victorians After 1900: Histories, Representations, Revisions* (Manchester, 2004)

Mandler, Peter and Susan Pedersen (eds), *After the Victorians: Private Conscience and Public Duty in Modern Britain* (London/New York, 1994)

Martin, Stanley, *The Order of Merit: One Hundred Years of Matchless Honour* (London, 2007)

McEwan, Dorothea, 'A Tale of One Institute and Two Cities: The Warburg Institute,' in Ian Wallace (ed.), *German-Speaking Exiles in Great Britain* (Amsterdam/New York, 1999)

McGarth, Elizabeth, 'Disseminating Warburgianism: The Role of the *Journal of the Warburg and Courtauld Institutes*,' in Uwe Fleckner and Peter Mack (eds), *Vorträge Aus Dem Warburg-Haus: The Afterlife of the Kulturwissenschaftliche Bibliothek Warburg* (Berlin, 1997)

Mehta, Ved, *Fly and the Fly-Bottle: Encounters with British Intellectuals* (London, 1963)

Mitchell, Leslie, *Maurice Bowra: A Life* (Oxford, 2009)

Moggeridge, D. F., *Maynard Keynes: An Economist's Biography* (London, 1992)

Mommsen, Wolfgang J., 'German Artists, Writers and Intellectuals and the Meaning of War, 1914–1918,' in Jon Hoene (ed.), *State, Society and Mobilizaation in Europe during the First World War* (Cambridge, 1997)

Morowitz, Harold J., *Energy Flow in Biology: Biological Organization as a Problem in Thermal Physics* (New York/London, 1968)

Morrell, J. B., 'The Non-Medical Sciences, 1914–1939,' in Brian Harrison (ed.), *The History of the University of Oxford, Volume VIII: The Twentieth Century* (Oxford, 1994)

Novick, Peter, *That Noble Dream: The 'Objectivity Question' and the American Historical Profession* (Cambridge, 1988)

Nye, Mary Jo, *Blackett: Physics, War, and Politics in the Twentieth Century* (Cambridge, MA, 2004)

Olesko, Katheryn M., *Physics as a Calling: Discipline and Practice in the Königsberg Seminar for Physics* (Ithaca, New York, 1991)

Oppenheimer, J. Robert, *Science and Common Understanding* (New York, 1966)

Ortolano, Guy, *The Two Cultures Controversey: Science, Literature and Cultural Politics in Postwar Britain* (Cambridge, 2009)

Penrose, Roger, *Shadows of the Mind: A Search for the Missing Science of Consciousness* (Oxford, 1994)

Perkin, Harold, *The Rise of Professional Society: England Since 1880* (London/New York, 1989)

Perutz, Max, *I Wish I Had Made You Angry Earlier: Essays on Science and Scientists* (Oxford, 1998)

Phillips, Adam, *Becoming Freud: The Making of a Psychoanalyst* (New Haven/London, 2014)

Pietsch, Tamson, *Empire of Scholars: Universities, Networks and the British Academic World, 1850–1939* (Manchester/New York, 2013)

Rabinow, Paul and William M. Sullivan, *Interpretative Social Science* (Berkeley/London, 1979)

Richards, Robert J. and Lorraine Daston (eds) *Kuhn's Structure of Scientific Revolutions at Fifty: Reflections on a Science Classic* (Chicago/London, 2016)

Ringer, Fritz, *Fields of Knowledge: French Academic Culture in Comparative Perspective* (Cambridge, 1992)

Ringer, Fritz, *The Decline of the German Mandarins: The German Academic Community, 1890–1933* (Cambridge, MA, 1969)

Ritchie, A. D., *Reflections on the Philosophy of Sir Arthur Eddington* (Cambridge, 1948)

[Rivington, James], *The Brtish Academy, 1902–2002; Some Historical Documents and Notes* (London, 2002)

Robinson, Andrew, *The Last Man Who Knew Everything: Thomas Young, the Anonymous Polymath Who Proved Newton Wrong, Explained How We See, Cured the Sick, and Deciphered the Rosetta Stone, and Other Feats of Genius* (New York, 2005)

Rorty, Richard, *Philosophy and the Mirror of Nature* (Oxford, 1980)

Rorty, Richard, 'Science and Solidarity,' in J. Nelson, A. Megll and D. McCloskey (eds), *Language and Argument in Scholarship and Public Affairs* (Madison, 1987)

Rose, Kenneth, *Elusive Rothschild: The Life of Victor, Third Baron* (London, 2003)

Rosenbaum, S. P. and James M. Haule, *The Bloomsbury Group Memoir Club* (London, 2014)

Rosenberg, Charles, 'Towards an Ecology of Knowledge: On Discipline, Context and History,' in Alexandra Oleson and John Voss (eds), *The Organization of Knowledge in Modern America* (Baltimore/London, 1976)

Ross, Dorothy, 'Changing Contours of the Social Science Disciplines,' in T. M. Porter and Dorothy Ross (eds), *The Cambridge History of Science, Volume 7: The Social Sciences* (Cambridge: 2003)

Ross, Dorothy, *The Origins of American Social Science* (Cambridge, 1991)

Rothblatt, Sheldon, *The Revolution of the Dons: Cambridge and Society in Victorian England* (Cambridge, [1968] 1981)

Rubinstein, W. D., *Capital, Culture and Decline in Britain, 1750–1900* (London, 1991)

Rubinstein, W. D., *Elites and the Wealthy in Modern British History: Essays in Social and Economic History* (Hassocks, Sussex, 1987)

Runciman, W. G., *Very Different But Very Much the Same: The Evolution of English Society Since 1714* (Oxford, 2015)

Said, Edward, *Reflections on Exile and Other Essays* (Cambridge, Mass., 2000)

Schaeper, Thomas J. and Kathless Schaeper, *Rhodes Scholars, Oxford and the Creation of an American Elite* (New York/Oxford, 1998)

Searle, G. R., *The Quest for National Efficiency: A Study in British Politics and Political Thought* (Berkley, 1971)

Shapin, Steven, *Never Pure: Historical Studies of Science as if It Was Produced by People with Bodies, Situated in Time, Space, Culture and Society and Struggling for Credibility and Authority* (Baltimore, 2010)

Shapin, Steven, *Scientific Life: A Moral History of a Late Modern Vocation* (Chicago/London, 2008)

Shils, Edward, *The Intellectuals and the Powers and Other Essays* (Chicago, 1972)

Simpson, Renate, *How the PhD Came to Britain: A Century of Struggle for Postgraduate Education* (Guildford, 1983)

Sisman, Adam, *Hugh Trevor-Roper: The Biography* (London, 2010)

Slaughter, Anne-Marie, *The Chess-Board and the Web: Strategies of Connection in a Networked World* (New York/London, 2017)

Soffer, Reba, *Ethics and Society in England: The Revolution in the Social Sciences, 1870–1914* (Berkeley, 1978)

Solovey, Mark, *Shaky Foundations: The Politics–Patronage–Social Science Nexus in Cold War America* (New Brunswick/London, 2013)

Stansky, Peter, *On or About December 1910: Early Bloomsbury and its Intimate World* (Cambridge, MA., 1996)

Stansky, Peter, 'Particulars in Huxley's Intellectual Climate,' in C. Waters and A. Van Helden (eds), *Julian Huxley: Biologist and Statesman of Science* (Houston, 1992)

Steiner, George and Laure Adler, *A Long Saturday: Conversations* (Chicago, 2001)

Steinmetz, George, *The Politics of Method in the Human Sciences: Positivism and its Epistemological Others* (Durham/London, 2005)

Stone, Lawrence and Jeanne C. Fawtier Stone, *An Open Society? England, 1540–1880* (Oxford, 1984)

Stourton, James, *Kenneth Clark: Life, Art and Civilization* (New York, 2016)

Stray, Christopher (ed.), *Gilbert Murray Reassessed: Helenism, Theater, and International Politics* (Oxford, 2007)

Supple, Barry, 'The Two World Wars,' in David Reynolds (ed.), *Christ's: A Cambridge College Over Five Centuries* (London, 2005)

Taylor, Charles, *Defining Science: The Rhetoric of Demarcation* (Madison, 1996)

Taylor, Charles, *Philosophy in the Human Sciences: Philosophical Papers, 2* (Cambridge, 1985)

Thompson, F. M. L., *Gentrification and the Enterprise Culture: Britain 1780–1980* (Oxford, 2001)

Turner, Frank M., 'The Victorian Conflict between Science and Religion: A

Professional Dimension,' in *Contesting Cultural Authority: Essays in Victorian Intellectural Life* (Cambridge, 1993)

Varmus, Harold, *The Art and Politics of Science* (New York/London, 2009)

Wallace, Stuart, *War and the Image of Germany: British Academics, 1914–1918* (Edinburgh, 1988)

Warwick, Andrew, *Masters of Theory: Cambridge and the Rise of Mathematical Physics* (Chicago, 2003)

Warwick, Andrew, 'The Worlds of Cambridge Physics,' in Richard Staley (ed.), *The Physics of Empire* (Cambridge, 1994)

Waters, C. Kenneth and Albert Van Helden (eds), *Julian Huxley: Biologist and Statesman of Science* (Houston, 1992)

Watson, George, *Heresies and Heretics: Memories of the Twentieth Century* (London, 2013)

Weaver, Warren, *Scene of Change: A Lifetime in American Science* (New York, 1970)

Weber, Max, 'Science as a Vocation,' in H. H. Gerth and C. Wright Mills (eds), *From Max Weber: Essays in Sociology* (New York/London, 1946)

Weinberg, Steven, *To Explain the World: The Discovery of Modern Science* (New York, 2015)

Weiner, Charles, 'A New Site for the Seminar: The Refugees and American Physics in the Thirties,' in Donald Fleming and Bernard Bailyn (eds), *The Intellectual Migration: Europe and America, 1930–1960* (Cambridge, Mass., 1969)

Werskey, Gary, *The Invisible College* (London, 1978)

Wiener, Martin, *English Culture and the Decline of the Industrial Spirit, 1859–1980* (Cambridge, 1981)

Williams, Raymond, 'The Bloomsbury Fraction,' in John Higgins (ed.), *The Raymond Williams Reader* (Oxford, 2001)

Wood, Neal, *Communism and British Intellectuals* (New York, 1959)

Wray, K. Brad, 'Kuhn's Social Epistemology and the Sociology of Science,' in William J. Devlin and Alisa Bekuvich (eds), *Kuhn's Structure of Scientific Revolutions Fifty Years On* (Cham: 2015)

Articles

Abir-Am, Pnina G., 'The Biotheoretical Gathering: Trans-Disciplinary Authority and the Incipient Legitimation of Molecular Biology in the 1930s: New Perspectives on the Historical Sociology of Science,' *History of Science*, 25 (1) (March 1987)

Abir-Am, Pnina, 'The Discourse of Physical Power and Biological Knowledge in the 1930s: A Reappraisal of the Rockefeller Foundation's Policy in Molecular Biology,' *Social Studies of Science*, 12 (3) (August 1982)

Anderson, Perry, 'Components of the National Culture,' *New Left Review*, I/50 (July/August 1968)

Anderson, Perry, 'Origins of the Present Crisis,' *New Left Review*, I/23 (January/Februry 1964)

Baldwin, Melinda, 'Scientific Autonomy, Public Accountability and the Rise of "Peer Review" in the Cold War United States,' *Isis*, 109 (3) (2018)

Baxandall, Michael, 'Is Durability Itself Not Also a Moral Quality', *Common Knowledge*, 18 (1) (2012)

Bleaney, B., A. H. Cooke, N. Kurti and K. W. H. Stevens, 'F. A. Lindemann, Viscount Cherwell (1888–1957)', *Physics Bulletin*, 7 (6) (1986)

Bloor, David, 'Wittgenstein and Mannheim on the Sociology of Mathematics', *Studies in the History and Philosophy of Mathematics*, 4 (2) (1973)

Blue, Gregory, 'Joseph Needham, Heterodox Marxism and the Social Backgrund of Chinese Science', *Science and Society*, 62 (2) (Summer 1998)

Bod, Rens, 'Has There Ever Been a Divide? A *Long Durée* Perspective', *History of the Humanities*, 3 (Spring 2018)

Bourdieu, Pierre, 'Intellectual Field and Creative Project', *Social Science Information*, 8 (1969)

Bourdieu, Pierre, 'The Genesis of the Concepts of *Habitus* and *Field*', *Sociocriticism*, 2 (1985)

Buruma, Ian, 'The Cult of Exile.' *Prospect*, 61 (March 2001)

Calver, Neil, 'Sir Peter Medawar: Science, Creativity and the Popularization of Karl Popper', *Notes and Records of the Royal Society of London*, 67 (2013)

Calver, Neil and Miles Parker, 'The Logic of Scientific Unity: Peter Medawar, the Royal Society and the Rothschild Controversy', *Notes and Records of the Royal Society of London*, 70 (1) (20 March 2016)

Cock, A. G., 'Chauvinism and Internationalism in Science: The International Research Council, 1919–1929,' *Notes and Records of the Royal Society of London*, 37 (2) (March 1983)

Cohen, Stanley, 'The Scientific Establishment and the Transmission of Quantum Mechanics in the United States, 1919–1932,' *American Historical Review*, 76 (2) (April 1971)

Crowther-Heyck, Hunter, 'Patrons of Revolution: Ideas and Institutions in Postwar Behavioral Science', *Isis*, 97 (3) (September 2006)

Crowther-Heyck, Hunter, 'The Organizational Revolution and the Human Sciences, *Isis*, 105 (2014)

Csiszar, Alex, 'Peer Review: Troubled from the Start', *Nature* (19 April 2015)

Daston, Lorraine, 'When Science Went Modern,,' *Hedgehog Review*, 18 (3) (Fall 2016)

Daston, Lorraine and Glenn W. Most, 'History of Science and History of Philologies,' *Isis*, 106 (2) (June 2015)

Diers, Michael, 'Warburg and the Warburg Tradition', *New German Critic*, 65 (Spring/ Summer 1995)

Dolton, Peter, 'Identifying Network Effects', *Economic Record*, 93 (Special Issue) (June 2017)

Donadio, Rachael, 'Scholars Fear the Loss of Eden in London,' *New York Times* (11 October 2014)

Edgerton, David, 'C. P. Snow as Anti-Historian of British Science: Revisiting the Technocratic Moment, 1959–1964,' *History of Science*, 43 (2005)

Ellis, George F. R., 'Does the Multiverse Really Exist?,' *Scientific American*, 392 (2) (August 2011)

Ellis, George and Joe Silk, 'Defend the Integrity of Physics,' *Nature*, 516 (10) (25 December 2015)

Gellner, Ernest, ' No School for Scandal: Dahrendorf's LSE and the Quest for the Science of Society,' *Times Literary Supplement* (26 May 1995)

Gilbert, Scott F. and Sahotra Sarkar, 'Embracing Complexity: Organicism for the 21st Century,' *Developmental Dynamics*, 219 (2000)

Grafton, Anthony and Jeffrey Hamburger, 'The Warburg Institute,' *Common Knowledge*, 18 (1) (2012)

Graham, Loren R., 'The Socio-Political Roots of Boris Hessen: Soviet Marxism and the History of Science,' *Social Studies of Science*, 15 (4) (November 1985)

Granovetter, Mark S., 'The Strength of Weak Ties,' *American Jounal of Sociology*, 78 (6) (May 1973)

Gross, Neil, 'Social Science Without Data,' *New York Times*, Sunday Review (12 February 2017)

Heckscher, William, 'Petites Perceptions: An Account of Sortes Warburgianae,' *Journal of Medieval and Renaissance Studies*, 4 (1) (1974)

Hennessy, Peter, 'The Age of Baldwin and Beerbohm,' in Charles Saumarez Smith, David Cannadine and Peter Hennessy (eds) *New Annals of THE CLUB* (London, 2014)

Hoch, Paul H. 'The Reception of Central European Refugee Physicists of the 1930s: U.S.S.R., U.K., U.S.A.,' *Annals of Science*, 40 (1983)

Hope, Charles, 'The Battle over the Warburg Institute,' *London Review of Books* (4 December 2014)

Hutchinson, Eric, 'Scientists as an Inferior Class: The Early Years of the DSIR,' *Minerva*, 8 (3) (July 1970)

Isaac, Joel, 'Tangled Loops: Theory History, and the Human Sciences in Modern America,' *Modern Intellectual History*, 6 (2) (2009)

Kaiga, Sakiko, 'The Use of Force to Prevent War? The Bryce Group's Proposals for the Avoidance of War, 1914–1915,' *Journal of British Studies*, 57 (2) (April 2018)

Kaiser, David, 'A Mannheim for All Seasons: Bloor, Merton, and the Roots of the Sociology of Scientific Knowledge,' *Science in Context*, 11 (1) (1998)

Kelves, Daniel J., '"Into Hostile Political Camps": The Reorganization of International Science in World War I,' *Isis*, 62 (1) (Spring, 1971)

Kim, Dong-Won, 'J. J. Thomson and the Emergence of the Cavendish School, 1885–1990,' *British Journal for the History of Science*, 28 (2) (June 1995)

Kitson Clark, George, 'A Hundred Years of the Teaching of History at Cambridge, 1873–1973,' *Historical Journal*, 26 (3) (1973)

Kohler, Robert, 'The Management of Science: The Experience of Warren Weaver and the Rockefeller Foundation Programme in Molecular Biology,' *Minerva*, 14 (3) (Autumn 1976)

Kohler, Robert, 'Walter Fletcher, F. G. Hopkins and the Dunn Institute of Biochemistry: A Case Study in the Patronage of Science,' *Isis*, 69 (3) (September 1978)

Kolakowski, Leszek, 'In Praise of Exile,' *Times Literary Supplement* (11 October 1985)

Laidler, Keith L., 'Chemical Kinetics and Oxford College Laboratories,' *Archive for the History of the Exact Sciences*, 38 (3) (1988)

Lee, Carole J., 'Commensuration Bias in Peer Review,' *Philosophy of Science*, 82 (December 2015)

Levine, Emily J., 'The Other Weimar: The Warburg Circle as Hamburg School,' *Journal of the History of Ideas*, 74 (2) (April 2013)

Lind, Michael, 'Let's Abolish Social Science: A Proposal for the New University,' *The Smart Set* (August 2015)

Links, J. G., 'W. G. Constable,' *Burlington Magazine* 71 (414) (September 1937)

Lubenow, William C., 'Mediating the "Chaos of Incident" and the "Cosmos of Sentiment": Liberalism in Britain, 1815–1914,' *Journal of British Studies*, 47 (3) (July 2008)

Lubenow, William C., 'The Cambridge Ritualists, 1876–1924: A Study of Commensurability in the History of Scholarship,' *History of Universities*, 24 (1/2) (2009)

MacLeod, Roy and Russell Moseley, 'The "Naturals" and Victorian Cambridge: Reflections on the Anatomy of an Elite, 1851–1914,' *Oxford Review of Education*, 6 (2) (1980)

Nagel, Thomas, 'Is Consciousness an Illusion,' *New York Review of Books*. (19 March 2017)

Naughton, John, 'Thomas Kuhn: The Man who Changed the Way the World Looked at Science,' *Observer* (13 August 2012)

Nicholson, Daniel J. and Richard Gawne, 'Rethinking Woodger's Legacy in the Philosophy of Biology,' *Journal of the History of Biology*, 47 (2014)

Ninkovich, Frank, 'The Rockefeller Foundation,' *Journal of American History*, 70 (4) (March 1984)

Ortolano, Guy, 'Human Science or Human Face? Social History and the "Two Cultures" Controversy,' *Journal of British Studies*, 43 (4) (October 2004)

Ortolano, Guy, 'The Literature and the Science of "Two Cultures" Historiography,' *Studies in the History and Philosophy of Sciencee*, 39 (2008)

Peterson, Erik, 'The Conquest of Vitalism or the Eclipse of Organicism?: The 1930s Cambridge Organizer Project and the Social Network of Mid-Twentieth-Century Biology,' *British Journal for the History of Science*, 47 (2) (June 2014)

Phillips, Denise, 'Francis Bacon and the Germans: Stories from When "Science" Meant "*Wissenschaft*,"' *History of Science*, 53 (4) (2015)

Popper, Karl, 'Obituary of Joseph Henry Woodger,' *British Journal for the Philosophy of Science*, 32 (3) (September 1981)

Rees, Martin, 'A Longitude Prize for the Twenty-First Century,' *Nature* (509) (22 May 2014)

Rees, Martin, 'Anniversary Address, 30 November 2009,' *Notes and Records of the Royal Society*, 64 (2010)

Rivington, James with archival assistance from Karen Syrett, 'Canon Sanday on "International Scholarship After the War," May 1918,' *British Academy Review* (Summer 2018)

Robbins, Keith G., 'Lord Bryce and the First World War,' *Historical Journal*, 10 (2) (1967)

Ross, Dorothy, 'Getting Over It? From the Social to the Human Sciences,' *Modern Intellectual History*, 11 (1) (2014)

Rowland, P. J., 'Student Participation in Science Teaching: The Early Years of he Oxford Junior Scientific Club,' *Oxford Review of Education*, 9 (3) (1983)

Rüger, Jan, 'Revisiting the Anglo-German Antagonism,' *Journal of Modern History*, 83 (3) (September 2011)

Sayes, Edwin, 'Actor-Network Theory and Methodology: Just What Does it Mean to Say that Nonhumans Have Agency?' *Social Studies of Science*, 44 (1) (February 2014)

Schaffer, Simon, 'The Eighteenth Brumaire of Bruno Latour,' *Studies in the History and Philosophy of Science Part A*, 22 (1) (1991)

Scherke, Katharina, 'Esther Simpson *und die Aktivitäten der SPSL* (Society for the Protection of Science and Learning) *im Zusammenhang mit der Emigration deutschsprachiger Wissenschaftler zwischen 1933–1945,'* in J. M. Ritchie (ed.), *German Speaking Exiles in Great Britain* (Amersterdam/New York, 2001)

Schmitt, Eric, 'The Battle to Defang ISIS; U.S. Targets its Physchology,' *New York Times* (29 December 2014)

Sears, Elizabeth, 'A Diarist's View: Roger Hinks and the Warburg Institute Twenty-Five Years after its Settling in London,' in Uwe Fleckner and Peter Mack (eds) *Vortäge Aus Dem Warburg-Haus: The Afterlife of the Kulturwissneschaftliche Biblioteck Warburg* (Berlin, 1997)

Sears, Elizabeth, 'Seznec, Saxl and *La Survivance de dieux antiques*,' in Rembrandt Duits and François Quiviger (eds), *Images of Pagan Gods: Papers of a Conference in Memory of Jean Seznec* (London/Turin, 2009)

Sears, Elizabeth, 'Warburg Institute Archive, General Correspondence,' *Common Knowledge*, 18 (1) (2012)

Sebenius, James K., 'Challenging Conventional Explanations of International Cooperation: Negotiation Analysis and the Case of Epistemic Communities,' *International Organization*, 46 (1) (Winter 1992)

Sviedrys, Romualdas, 'The Rise of Physics Laboratories in Britain,' *Historical Studies in the Physical Sciences*, 7 (1976).

Sviedrys, Romualdas and Arnold Thackray, 'The Rise of Physical Science at Victorian Cambridge with Commentary and with Reply,' *Historical Studies in the Physical Sciences*, 2 (1970)

Turner, R. Steven, 'The Prussian Universities and the Concept of Research,' *Internationales Archiv für sozialgeschichte der deutschen Literatur*, 6 (1) (January 1980)

Varmus, Harold, 'E-Biomed: A Proposal for Electronic Publication in the Biomedical Sciences,' (NIH Preprint 04doc, Bethesda, MD, 19 April 1999)

Waddington, C. H., 'Humanists and Scientists: A Last Commentary on C. P. Snow,' *Encounter* (January 1960)

Wickberg, Daniel, 'What is the History of Sensibilities?,' *American Historical Review*, 112 (3) (June 2007)

Williams, Rowan, Lord Williams of Oystermouth, 'Sermon Before the University,' King's College Chapel (17 May 2015)

Wolchover, Natalie, 'A Fight for the Soul of Science,' *Quanta Magazine* (August 2015)

Yeo, Richard, 'An Idol of the Marketplace: Baconianism in Nineteenth-Century Britain, *History of Science*, 223 (3) (1985)

Zuckerman, Harriet and Robert K. Merton, 'Patterns of Evaluation in Science: Institutionalization, Structure and Function of the Referee System,' *Minerva*, 9 (1) (January 1971)

Index

References appearing in **bold** indicate short biographies of the persons thus referenced.